A Social History of Europe, 1945–2000

A SOCIAL HISTORY OF EUROPE, 1945–2000

Recovery and Transformation
after Two World Wars

By
Hartmut Kaelble

Translated By
Liesel Tarquini

Berghahn Books
New York • Oxford

Published in 2013 by
Berghahn Books
www.berghahnbooks.com

English-language edition
©2013 Berghahn Books

German-language edition
©2007 Verlag C.H. Beck oHG, München
Sozialgeschichte Europas
By Hartmut Kaelble

Library of Congress Cataloging-in-Publication Data

Kaelble, Hartmut.
[Sozialgeschichte Europas. English]
A social history of Europe, 1945–2000: recovery and transformation after two World
    Wars / by Hartmut Kaelble; translated by Liesel Tarquini. — 1st ed.
        p. cm.
    Includes bibliographical references and index.
    ISBN 978-1-84545-643-6 (hbk: alk. paper) — ISBN 978-0-85745-377-8 (pbk: alk.
paper) — ISBN 978-0-85745-237-5 (institutional ebook) —
ISBN 978-0-85745-518-5 (retail ebook)
    1. Europe—Social conditions—20th century. 2. Europe—Social conditions—21st
century. I. Title.
HN374.K3413 2011
306.094'09045—dc23
                                                                            2011025036

British Library Cataloguing in Publication Data

A catalogue record for this book is available from the British Library

Printed in the United States on acid-free paper.

ISBN 978-1-84545-643-6 (hardback)
ISBN 978-0-85745-377-8 (paperback)
ISBN 978-0-85745-237-5 (institutional ebook)
ISBN 978-0-85745-518-5 (retail ebook)

For Brigitte, Hendrik, Laure, and Martin

CONTENTS

FIGURES AND TABLES

Figures

Tables

ACKNOWLEDGMENTS

This book has incorporated many suggestions. I have presented individual chapters in Aachen, Berlin, Bochum, Bologna, Bonn, Bruges, Budapest, Florence, Göttingen, Paris, Prato, Kobe, Copenhagen, Leipzig, Nantes, Osaka, Peking, Potsdam, Prague, Salamanca, Tokyo, Warsaw, and Yokohama, and learned quite a bit from the discussions that took place when doing so. I tested many theses out in my lectures and seminars at Humboldt University and profited immensely from students' reactions. The discussion at the collaborative research center "Changing Representations of Social Orders" at Humboldt University and the lectures at the Berlin College for Comparative European History were exceptionally inspirational in the making of this book. I would like to thank the German Research Foundation for a half-year sabbatical from teaching and the president of the Social Science Research Center Berlin (WZB), Jürgen Kocka, for the invitation for what turned out to be a very stimulating one-year guest professorship. I thank Michael Werner from CIERA and the French Department of Education for the Gay Lussac Humboldt Prize, which allowed undisturbed and focused work stays in Paris. My thanks to Dagmar Lissat, Jan Lipsius, Christian Methfessel, and Michael Schmiedel for proofreading the manuscript, and Claudia Althaus for her excellent editing. I am very grateful to the Beck-Verlag and to Marion Berghahn from Berghahn Books for the inclusion of this book in their program.

INTRODUCTION

Europe as Part of a Multiple Modernity

What is expected of a book about the social history of Europe in the second half of the twentieth century? It could focus on a Europe in decline, a Europe that still dominated the world in the first half of the twentieth century and that as a result also implicated numerous countries in the Second World War. Having completely lost its place of supremacy as a result of both world wars, it became one of the quiet corners of the world in the second half of the twentieth century, retreating within itself to a large extent. It attracted large numbers of tourists to its ruins and lovingly tended antiquities, but it was not regarded as a model, let alone an ideal, for any country outside of Europe. This history of Europe took place primarily between the First World War—the seminal catastrophe of the twentieth century—and the 1970s.

A Europe in the midst of a comeback could also be expected. After a crisis that threatened its very survival—the European civil war between 1914 and 1945—this newborn Europe in the second half of the twentieth century surprisingly experienced a stable inner framework of peace and a new economic and political blossoming, at least until the 1970s.

Finally, a history of Europe that is one, among multiple, civilizations can also be explored. Like every great world civilization, Europe has traveled its own path to modernity. This book, on the social history of Europe in the second half of the twentieth century, is primarily written from this third perspective. It took two centuries for Europe's place in the world to become as clearly a part of a multiple modernity as it was in the second half of the twentieth century: a place with a growing worldwide exchange of ideas, people, goods, and services, the development of a global public, and the emergence of global political players. But while Europe's decline and comeback will indeed be consistently addressed here, these will not be the key questions.

Key Questions

This book examines three strands of a central thread in every chapter. As in every history book, historical change takes center stage. The book traces how European society changed during the second half of the twentieth century: how much of what every mid-century European was familiar with disappeared, and how much of what today is taken for granted was introduced, in the second half of the twentieth century. But the account here is not of a single transformation, nor does it divide the second half of the twentieth century into a before and after. In many areas of European society, several transformations followed one on top of another in the second half of the twentieth century. What appeared to be extremely modern around 1970 was often long consigned to history by the 1990s. Change will not be covered in the same way in each chapter. In some chapters each of the four eras of the second half of the twentieth century is examined separately: the immediate postwar period, the period of prosperity in the 1950s and 1960s, the economically difficult period of the 1970s and 1980s, and the period after the upheaval of 1989–91. In other chapters, in contrast, only a single, continuous transformation process will be discussed.

Furthermore, this volume will also examine whether European society was marked by divergence or convergence: it will trace differences not only between individual nations or groups of nations, but also between the poor periphery and the wealthy center, and between Eastern and Western Europe. These divergences will be contrasted with convergences, which admittedly never include all European countries but rather a majority of them at best. Such convergence refers not only to similarities, but also to increasing interweaving, more intense mutual experiences, and experience-saturated mutual images. Interweaving consists not only of international trade and foreign capital investments, but also of various social interweavings such as job-, education-, and age-related migration, business travel and tourism, international marriage, the emergence of immigrant minority groups and hybrids thereof, and completely international cultures within European businesses and in European scholarship as well as in European politics in Brussels. These social integrations also include the changed spheres of experience for Europeans and the changes in attitude toward each other. This aspect of integration is quickly conceived of, but not always easily implemented. More the stepchild of social-historical research, as a rule it is tracked through binational projects; multinational interdependencies have almost always escaped attention. These integrations and transfers are not covered in a single chapter, but rather always examined together with divergences and convergences.

Lastly, this book will also cover, to the extent that it is reasonable and possible, social characteristics of Europe—in particular in comparison with similar modern societies outside of Europe. This is not a return to the perceptions of European superiority that shaped debates about the "character" of Europe for centuries. Completely to the contrary, Europe's societal features often include stress, backwardness, and the dark pages of European history. Furthermore, it is also rarely about the European path of the "longue durée," as perhaps followed by Shmuel Eisenstadt or Michael Mitterauer (Eisenstadt 2003; Mitterauer 2003). The period of time covered here is too short for this. Many European traits were short-term, lingered a couple of decades, and then vanished again. Ultimately, they often came about through integrations or conflicts with non-European societies. To wish to explain European particularities through European constellations alone would not fully coincide with reality (cf. Kaelble 2005).

What Is Social History?

Social history does not have a clear profile today. Since its revival in the 1960s and 1970s, it has differentiated into many specialized areas whose common denominator is still identifiable only with difficulty. Furthermore, social history has been conceptualized in quite different ways over the past decades. What is expected of it is therefore also varies quite a bit.

Social history is usually seen today in the narrowest sense as a history of social classes, social strata, or estates. For many, differentiating history by social classes is the proper sociohistorical approach to the nineteenth and twentieth centuries. This book does not limit itself to this narrow perspective, as social history was never de facto confined to so narrow a class history—not even during its heyday in the 1960s and 1970s. Other topics, such as family, the welfare state, and mentalities, also played important roles from the very beginning. Moreover, social classes and social milieus that did in fact shape European history in the nineteenth and early twentieth centuries lost their influential power in the second half of the twentieth century. The end of the twentieth century can be spoken of in terms of a society shaped by the middle classes, but rarely with regard to a class-based society.

Meanwhile, many hold that social history's central concern should be the effects of lasting, compulsory social structures within politics and culture that were modifiable only with difficulty. In this view, the differentiation between the basis of social structures and political and cultural superstructures is the basic concept of social history. Constellations, constraints, and terms are at the center of social history, not scope of action, players, and decisions. This book does not adhere to this concept, for every historian should examine the scope of action, even when he or she does not wish to disregard constellations and constraints. It is difficult to understand why one historical subdiscipline should solely specialize in constraints and another limit itself exclusively to the scope of action.

Lastly, social history can also be understood as the common denominator of manifold specializations of this subdiscipline, that is, the sum of all themes that are dealt with at the few European social history forums, at the biennial European Social History Conference, and in social history journals and reference books on social history. This provides no easily grasped formula, however. Social history cannot be well defined by the themes with which social historians are engaged. If there is a common thread in social history research at all, it passes through three major topics: first, the history of societal circumstances and lifestyle, including the spheres of family, work, consumption, values, and religiosity as well as urban and rural life; second, a variety of social inequalities and hierarchies that are not limited to social classes and milieus but also involve inequality between the sexes, locals and immigrants, and generations, as well as inequalities in material standing, income, wealth, education, and life expectancy; and third, the connections, interdependencies, and differences between society and state, social movements and conflicts, media and the political public, the welfare state, educational policy, city planning, and health care policy. This book follows this broad understanding of social history.

Social history in the fullest sense comprises not only the history of structures and institutions but also the history of social meanings, social symbols, rites, and myths. The borders between social history in this sense and cultural or political history cannot be sharply drawn. Some chapters of this book would also fit in a cultural or political history of Europe.

Differences from Other Syntheses

No presentation of European social history since 1945 has focused on the aims discussed above. This book overlaps with four types of syntheses, but only in part. An array of good German-, French-, and English-language overviews have covered the social history of *Western* Europe, with varying geographical scopes (van Dijk 1994; Sutcliffe 1996; Guedj and Sirot 1997; Hradil and Immerfall 1997; Bussière et al., 1998; Marseille 1998; Saly et al. 1998; Schulze 1998; Crouch 1999). They leave out the eastern part of Europe, however, and in part also do not cover the last quarter of the twentieth century or the entire breadth of sociohistorical topics. Additionally, there are several good overviews of the *economic and social* history of Europe in the twentieth century; however, most of these appeared in the 1980s and thus could not cover the last quarter of the twentieth century (Cipolla 1972; Ambrosius and Hubbard 1986; Fischer 1987). Furthermore, in the recent past a few good overviews of the *general* history of twentieth-century Europe that also deal with social history have been published. They cannot go into society as broadly and extensively as this book (Duignan and Gann 1992; Gaillard and Rowley 1998; Mazower 1999; Ahrweiler and Aymard 2000; Schmale 2000; Fulbrock 2001; Berstein and Milza 2002; Altrichter and Bernecker 2004; James 2004; Judt 2005).

Lastly, a few world history overviews go into Europe and its social history as well. They can only ever narrowly cover Europe (Hobsbawm 1995; *Histoire du monde* 1996; Bairoch 1997; Fernandez-Armesto 1998; *Histoire universelle* 1998; Brockhaus 1999; Nouchi 2000; Reynolds 2000; Stearns et al. 2001; Crossley et al. 2004). The intelligent and very worthwhile overview by the Swedish sociologist Göran Therborn (Therborn 1995) is closest to this book and diverges from it in primarily two directions: it addresses not just differences within Europe but also similarities between European societies, and it elaborates more on the individual eras of social history since 1945.

The Spatial Definition of Europe

The debate about Europe's borders has intensified among historians since the upheaval of 1989–91. The intra-European east-west border has disappeared, shifting attention to blurred boundaries, primarily in Europe's east and southeast. Decisions regarding the expansion of the European Union have also newly reintroduced the problem of Europe's boundaries. Historians and social scientists essentially discussed three options: a narrower Latinity that encompasses only Western and East Central Europe, advocated, for example, by Henri Mendras (1997); a broader Europe that, however, excludes the great and middle powers of Russia, Turkey, and the Caucasus, which have their own cultural and political relationships pointing outside of Europe—that is, the Europe that most handbooks choose; and the vast Europe of the Council of Europe and the Bologna Process, which includes Russia, the entire Caucasus, and Turkey.

This book is based on a pragmatic definition of Europe. It will cover Europe as a whole, including Eastern, East Central, and Southeastern Europe, and will attempt to transcend the overconcentration on the western part of Europe, to the extent that the state of research allows.

At the same time, the book will address two decidedly controversial geographical constraints. The USSR and Russia are not completely incorporated, as this region's stronger contribution to the European and Atlantic region after 1989–91 cannot negate the historical fact that before then, the USSR was only ever a half-European power, alongside also being a half-Asian and a global power, and also viewed itself as something special. The USSR and Russia can therefore not be indiscriminately included in Europe. With the inclusion of the USSR and Russia, Europe would look fundamentally different in many social fields, such as birthrate, family, standard of living, social conflict, and inequalities as well as state intervention. Yet because fully excluding Russia and the USSR is also problematic, I have to the best of my ability as a non-expert, comparatively included the USSR and Russia in this overview in such a manner that not just the region's differences but also its similarities with Europe remain identifiable.

Turkey, the second point of contention with regard to the spatial definition of Europe, is also not simply included in Europe in what follows. In the decades since 1945, Turkey has certainly belonged to the Western European and US military security zone and, like many Middle Eastern and African countries, oriented itself to the European model concerning both modernization policies and anti-modernization movements. In the second half of the twentieth century, however, it was not a part of European culture and society. To this day Turkey distinctly differs from Europe with regard to its social structures and values, more so even than Russia. It would be artificial to throw Turkey in with Europe simply because it would like to align itself more with Europe in the coming decades in order to be able to enter into the European Union. Turkey will therefore be included in this book wherever possible, but it will not be simply added on to Europe.

Time Frame

Various chronological arrangements can apply to a social history of Europe in the twentieth century. Three different approaches are currently under discussion or practiced among historians. The first, which ultimately attempts to stick to a division into centuries, begins with a long nineteenth century spanning from the French Revolution to the First World War and then often, though not always, continues with a short twentieth century from the First World War to the upheaval of 1989–91. Twentieth-century history is written as a history of often extremely violent competition between democracy, fascism, and communism and the political division of Europe. In this approach, the First World War and then the collapse of the Soviet empire are the central upheavals of the twentieth century (Hobsbawm 1995).

A second approach divides the twentieth century more distinctly, viewing the Second World War as the central political, as well as economic, upheaval. In this approach, the period of excessive violence and decline seems more of a consequence of the age of nationalism that roughly began in the mid eighteenth century or even with the Napoleonic wars and first ended with the Second World War. Thereafter began a new period of internationality and a new European framework for peace, a period of weaker nation-states, the new position of the United States as a world power, and the final decline of the European colonial empires, but also a new era of European economic recovery and, until 1989–91, of the ideological and economic division of Europe (Therborn 1995).

The third approach, which considers the 1960s and 1970s as the central European and global upheaval of the century, sees this period as ushering in a real implementation of internationality, the weakening of the traditional nation-states, and new social and cultural, postmaterialistic values—a new world order no longer determined by the West, and a new globalization (Maier 2000).

There is no ideal solution to the question of chronological approach. Choosing an approach depends on the respective work's basic research questions. For this book, choosing the end of the Second World War as a date of departure seemed most practical for two pragmatic reasons.

One, a new epoch for Europe began with the end of the Second World War. A new international political and economic system came into being, a system in which Europe was no longer the center of the world. Democracy began its triumphal procession after the deep crisis of the 1930s and 1940s. An inner process of rapprochement among European societies began after a long period of divergences. New relationships between Europe and non-European societies emerged through Europe's fundamental change from an emigration to an immigration society. In comparison with non-European societies, social particularities of Europe can be recognized in the global implementation of the modern consumer society and the new familial, work, and social security models, as well as in the general change in values. For the first time supranational European institutions were established and joined by ever more European countries, which also impacted the social history of Europe. Like most upheavals in history, this one occurred gradually—not suddenly in 1945—and was moreover also a process full of continuities. Yet it occurred distinctly enough to support a synthesis, which certainly also takes continuities into account, with the end of the Second World War.

Furthermore, the other significant convulsions of the twentieth century—the First World War, the radical change in the 1960s and 1970s, and the upheaval of 1989–91—were not so far-reaching that the upheaval of the Second World War would fall into their shadows. Nor do they weigh heavier with regard to social change, the international system, the development of democracy, the relationships of European societies with each other, Europe's relationships with other civilizations and major societies, or the origin of emergence of European social particularities.

Organization

This book outlines the most important social fields at a glance from 1945 through to the present. The chapters are arranged in three broadly defined sections, which have already been mentioned.

The first section covers changes to the *Basic Social Constellations*, which are seen by Europeans as the most significant pillars of their private lives: family, work, consumption, value change, and religiosity.

The following section presents *Social Inequalities and Hierarchies*. It first examines the elites, intellectuals, and various social milieus such as the middle class, working class, farmers, and petty bourgeoisie; then focuses on inequality of income, wealth, and opportunities for social mobility; and finally turns to migration and the emergence of immigrant milieus due to Europe's transformation from a continent of emigration to one of immigration. Inequality between the sexes will be covered in the respective chapters and in particular in the chapters on family, labor, and education. Inequality in health care will be broached only briefly in the chapter on the standard of living, as this topic is currently very difficult to deal with at the European level.

In the third and final section of the book, the relationships and tensions between *Society and State* are covered. This begins with the influence of society on policy-making, that is, with chapters on social movements and conflicts, and on media and the public. After this, the effect of policies on society will be explored in chapters on the welfare state, cities and urban planning, and education.

References

Altrichter H. and W.L. Bernecker. *Geschichte Europas im 20. Jahrhundert*. Stuttgart 2004.
Ambrosius G. and W.H. Hubbard. *A Social and Economic History of 20th Century Europe*. Cambridge 1989.
Ahrweiler, H. and M. Aymard, eds. *Les Européens*. Paris 2000.
Bairoch P. *Economics and World History: Myths and Paradoxes*. Chicago 1993.
Berstein S. and P. Milza. *Histoire de l'Europe contemporaine: De l'héritage du XIX siècle à l'Europe d'aujourd'hui*. Paris 2002.
Brockhaus, F.A. ed. *Die Weltgeschichte*. 6 vols. Leipzig and Mannheim 1999; also: *Welt- und Kulturgeschichte. Epochen, Fakten, Hintergründe*. 20 vols. Hamburg 2006.
Bussière E. et al. *Industrialisation et sociétés en Europe occidentale 1880–1970*. Paris 1998.
Cipolla C., ed. *Fontana Economic History of Europe*. 5 vols. London 1972ff.
Crossley P.K., L.H. Lees, and L.W. Servos. *Global Society: The World Since 1900*. Boston 2004.
Crouch C. *Social Change in Western Europe*. Oxford 1999.
Duignan P. and L.H. Gann. *The Rebirth of the West: The Americanization of the Democratic World 1945–1958*. Cambridge, MA, 1992.
Van Dijk H. *De moderninsering van Europa: twee eeuwen maatschappij-ge-schiedenis*. Utrecht 1994.
Eisenstadt S.N. *Comparative Civilizations and Multiple Modernities*. 2 vols. Leiden 2003.
Fernandez-Armesto F. *Millenium: A History of the Last Thousand Years*. New York 1995.
Fischer W., ed. *Handbuch der europäischen Wirtschaft- und Sozialgeschichte*, vol. 6: *Europäische Wirtschaft- und Sozialgeschichte vom Ersten Weltkrieg bis zur Gegenwart*. Stuttgart 1987.
Fulbrock M., ed. *Oxford History of Europe since 1945*. Oxford 2001.
Gaillard J.-M. and A. Rowley. *Histoire du continent européen de1850 à la fin du Xxe siècle*. Paris 1998.
Guedj F. and S. Sirot, eds. *Histoire sociale de l'Europe: Industrialisation et société en Europe occidentale 1880–1970*. Paris 1997.
Histoire du Monde. 5 vols. Paris 1996.
Histoire Universelle. 3 vols. Paris 1998.
Hobsbawm E.J. *Age of Extremes: The Short Twentieth Century, 1914–1991*. London 1994.
Hradil S. and S. Immerfall, eds. *Die westeuropäischen Gesellschaften im Vergleich*. Opladen 1997.
James H. *Europe Reborn: A History 1914–2000*. Harlow 2003.
Judt T. *Postwar: A History of Europe since 1945*. New York 2005.
Kaelble H. "Eine europäische Gesellschaft?" In *Europawissenschaft*, ed. G.F. Schuppert, I. Pernice, and U. Haltern. Baden-Baden 2005, 299–330.
Maier C.S. "Consigning the 20th Century to History: Alternative Narratives for the Modern Era." *American Historical Review* 105 (2000): 807–831.
Marseille J., ed. *Industrialisation de l'Europe occidentale, 1880–1970*. Paris 1998.
Mazower M. *Dark Continent: Europe's Twentieth Century*. New York 1999.
Mendras H. *L'Europe des européens: Sociologie de l'Europe occidentale*. Paris 1997.
Mitterauer M. *Warum Europa? Mittelalterliche Grundlagen eines Sonderwegs*. Munich 2003.
Nouchi M. *Le 20e siècle: Tournants, temps, tendances*. Paris 2000.
Reynolds D. *One World Divisible: A Global History since 1945*. New York 2000.
Saly P. et al. *Industrialisation et sociétés: Europe occidentale 1880–1970*. Paris 1998.
Schmale W. *Geschichte Europas*. Vienna 2000.
Schulze M.-S., ed. *Western Europe: Economic and Social Change since 1945*. Harlow 1998.

Sutcliffe A. *An Economic and Social History of Western Europe since 1945*. London 1996.
Stearns P. et al., eds. *European Social History from 1350 to 2000*. 6 vols. Detroit 2001.
Therborn G. *European Modernity and Beyond: The Trajectory of European Societies 1945–2000*. London 1995.

Part I

Basic Social Constellations

Chapter 1

FAMILY

The history of the family has become an extremely topical issue. In most European countries, declining birthrates, decrease in lifelong marriages, emergence of new types of family units, and the aging family unit are subjects of heated discussion. Of these discussions, the most disputed prognoses concern the effects on the social welfare system, schools, and the workforce as well as societal values and norms. These debates are, as a rule, national. Indeed, the "European family," and how it differs ever more from families in non-European societies, is also debated within academia.

State of Research

Although the family is a classic subject of social history, there has not yet been an overall account of the history of the family for all of Europe in the second half of the twentieth century. Göran Therborn's impressive new survey on the twentieth-century family is a world history, not a European history, and is limited to three aspects: patriarchalism, marriage, and fertility (Therborn 2004). Two older syntheses, a world history of the family edited by André Burguiére and a history of private life edited by Philippe Ariés and Georges Duby, contain individual chapters on European countries; both were published in the 1980s, however, and thus do not cover the last part of the twentieth century (Burguiére 1987; Ariés and Duby 1993). The historical overviews of the European family by Jack

Goody and Andreas Gestrich, Michael Mitterauer, and Jens-Uwe Krause concentrate on other epochs (Goody 2002; Gestrich et al. 2003). The sociological surveys by John Goldthorpe, Francois Höpflinger, and Martine Segalen are limited to Western Europe or to shorter time periods than the book at hand (Goldthorpe 1987; Segalen 1990; Höpflinger 1997). Nor can national overviews provide an overall picture of the European history of the family; such volumes exist so far only for France, Germany, and Austria (Sieder 1987; Ariés and Duby 1993). Good European overviews have at least been published for individual aspects of family history, though they mostly deal with longer periods of time: an excellent history of women by Gisela Bock (2000), Egle Becchi and Dominique Julia's edited history of childhood (1998), a history of adolescence by Michael Mitterauer (1986), a history of the mother by Yvonne Kniebiehler (2000), and a history of the unwed by Jean Claude Bologne (2004).

Changes to the Family Unit

Two upheavals shaped the history of the family in Europe after 1945. First, the Second World War wrought deep changes in the family. Completely new necessities of cohabitation emerged. This first upheaval was not permanent but short-lived, and it ended during the 1950s with a return to the traditional family. It also did not take place everywhere in Europe but rather only in those countries that were directly affected by the war. The second upheaval, which began in the late 1960s, led to a diversity of family forms that had been unknown until then. This upheaval could be observed in almost all European countries—with significant differences, however, between the West and East, as well as between the North and South.

Postwar Upheaval

During the war and the postwar period, those countries in Europe that had been affected by the war experienced a deep break with the previous family structure, chiefly in the form of five drastic changes of familial cohabitation.

First, new role allocations formed between marriage partners during the period of refugee migrations, bombed-out cities, and difficulty in the day-to-day provision of food, clothing, fuel, and lodging. Normal public services such as schools, kindergartens, and public transportation collapsed. This period of material hardship and its enormous new demands particularly affected mothers. It was mostly they who, in addition to growing vegetables and potatoes or keeping swine and rabbits for meat, stood in lines outside of shops and went to the countryside to forage for foodstuffs. The statistical decline in women's employment in the immediate postwar period is misleading. Wives did not retreat into the private sphere and role of housewife, but instead did the exact opposite: the active tasks of wives outside of the home in the postwar period were far more intense than those before or after. The traditional, mostly masculine income from gainful employment declined in value during this time of need, and the exhausting, mostly feminine benefits of provision for the family gained in worth.

These new role allocations between marriage partners, as well as the inability of those returning from war to fulfill their modified roles as father figures due to injuries or traumatic war experiences, were decisive grounds for marital conflict. "The war fundamentally changed our women: they are more independent, and have also become more cheeky because of it," was a point of view described by a 48-year-old streetcar driver in Berlin in 1946 (*Die Frau von heute* 1946: 17). Quickly carried-out war marriages and life apart from each other during the extremity of war amplified these marriage conflicts even more for many spouses. Divorce rates shot up during the immediate postwar period in almost all war-affected European countries, and indeed only in these countries, decreasing again everywhere thereafter. They are only marginally noticeable in Figure 1.1 below (Flora 1987: 182ff.).

Second, in the aftermath of the war incomplete families were also unusually prevalent, whether due to war death, husbands' long war captivity, or the breakup of war marriages. "Single-mother families," which as a rule occurred involuntarily, were therefore more numerous in the postwar period than previously or subsequently.

Third, the postwar period also offered new roles and freedoms to young unmarried women. As they had better career opportunities and wanted to make up for the adolescence they had missed because of the war, they felt less bound to traditional familial norms and the traditional female lifestyle than the generations before and after. They lived in an unusual situation: they met a relatively low number of young men of their age, who, if they were young occupying soldiers or young war veterans, were often likewise disassociated from traditional familial norms. In many European lands the number of out-of-wedlock births rose and did not fall again until the 1950s (Flora 1987: 160ff.). One Berliner said, on her experience in Berlin as a young unmarried woman: "One was so independent, that one said ... it'd be better, to be alone, you'd actually get along better" (Meyer and Schulze 1984: 127). A 19-year-old Berliner salesman in 1946, surprised by this development, opined that "[m]any of the young women today don't seem to have a right footing any more" (*Die Frau von heute* 1946: 17).

Fourth and furthermore, the independence and responsibility of young people and even children, within and outside of the family, was particularly great during the immediate postwar period. It was not only while fleeing after the war or as returnees from war captivity that youth were forced to depend on themselves much more. Older children and adolescents also had more responsibility within the family than they had before or would thereafter. They participated intensively in the procurement of food, coal, and firewood, whether on excursions to forage for food in the countryside or through thievery as a result of destitution. Due to the frequent absence of parents they also took part in garden work and animal husbandry, as well as in housekeeping. This new independence among young people could lead to conflict, primarily with fathers, who had often not witnessed the development of their young sons and daughters and returned from war with prewar conceptions of family or who transferred military command hierarchies on the family. "My father," wrote one Berlin girl about the year 1948, "could have stayed away. At that time he was unnecessary for us, so to speak, because we got along well enough. … It's harsh, to say something like that, but we were completely self-reliant, even through the war. He was a quasi-obstacle for us, because now the paternal parenting began, which was completely useless" (Meyer and Schulze 1984: 128).

Lastly, the postwar period also often meant a break with the nuclear family that had developed everywhere in Europe in the nineteenth and early twentieth centuries. Familial intimacy had fallen by the wayside, and not only in the extreme situation of flight and displacement. The extreme housing shortage also contributed to this, in that families no longer had private housing and multiple families lived together in a house or even in a single apartment, sharing the kitchen, bathroom, and garden and jointly looking after the children and procuring food, clothing, and fuel.

These exceptional familial circumstances make the postwar period an uncommonly ambiguous epoch in family history that stirs controversy among historians. On the one hand, historians view it as a time of new prospects that fundamentally set the course for the family unit. The greater equality and independence of wives, the cohabitation of unmarried partners, the rapid dissolution of marriages that no longer functioned, and the autonomy of the woman in the single-mother family as well as the new lifestyles of young unmarried women are seen, primarily, as an indication of the new roles for women. From this point of view, the cohabitation of multiple families established new solidarities. The path to politics also became easier for women, above all at the local level. Women were involved in important decisions at a national level too, however, for example in the implementation of the constitutional equal rights article in western Germany. Although these new forms of familial cohabitation vanished again after the immediate postwar period, they were firmly established in the minds of those involved and were mobilized again in the 1960s and 1970s.

On the other hand, these new forms of familial cohabitation are regarded as a short-lived, special situation in the history of the family. They occurred—or so it is argued—not voluntarily, but under the extreme necessities of flight, displacement, and the collapse of economic and public supply systems during the war and postwar period. In addition to this, the National Socialist regime in Germany had already urged a disentanglement of youth from the family. Contemporaries therefore seldom took pleasure in these new familial forms after the Second World War and quickly gave them up again as the economy and the public systems returned to normal.

The Return of the Traditional Family

The 1950s and early 1960s were a time of return to the traditional family in three senses: the return to traditional marriage and to the extremes of gender roles, with clear divisions of labor and separate emotional worlds for husbands and wives; the return to the intimate nuclear family; and the return of parental authority with regard to children and adolescents.

Several indicators mark this return to the traditional family. Divorce went into decline again throughout Europe. The marriage rate was high, and marriages were taking place at an earlier age. The birthrate climbed or at least stabilized. A baby boom, within the traditional two-parent family, became apparent in large parts of Europe. Overall, out-of-wedlock births declined significantly (Flora 1987: 162ff.).

The return to the traditional family was also unmistakable with regard to familial cohabitation. Parental authority was once again strictly enforced, and different gender roles were accentuated in child rearing. Marriages in which the woman stayed at home began to gain importance. If women worked in the 1950s, it was predominantly justified by economical necessity, rarely by an interest in career. Furthermore, the home was the woman's primary domain. The intimacy of the family was reestablished. Massive residential construction created apartments and privately owned homes for nuclear families everywhere in Europe, and there was no provision for close contact or cooperation between families. The arrangement of separate children's rooms strengthened the self-containment of the family even more. This went hand in hand with children's return, bit by bit, from play areas outside of the home. New long-lasting consumer goods—the automobile, refrigerator, and corner sofa in particular—were familial consumer goods that built no new bridges between families. Earlier differences in milieu between bourgeois, proletarian, and rural families diminished as a result.

The traditional family also dominated public discourse, particularly in Western Europe. In a broad consensus of most political parties, churches, and public opinion as well as academia, the traditional two-parent family was viewed as the model family in the early 1950s and 1960s. Family policy supported this tendency as a rule.

Admittedly, it is often overlooked that the 1950s and 1960s family was not simply a return to the pre- and interwar periods; rather, the family evolved in various regards. Though contemporaries made much of the return to the traditional family, a different kind of family had come about. Work outside of the home by married women and mothers increased during the 1950s and early 1960s. This period was the breakthrough to careers for mothers. The marriage with the wife staying at home was not forced back through public debates or familial ideals, but rather in familial everyday life. The increasing professional life of married women also gradually led to a different validation of female labor by the working women themselves. Increasingly, women no longer named only economic necessity as their motivation for working but also an interest in having a career.

Educational opportunities for women also improved in the 1950s and early 1960s. The educational prospects for girls and young women in secondary schools and colleges expanded almost everywhere in Europe during this time. At the end of this epoch, in the early 1970s, girls and boys attended secondary schools with similar frequency. The chances of a young woman entering university rose by about a third (see Table 12.2); they were still far removed from equal but had made significant progress in that direction.

The state of civil law and constitutional rights for husbands and wives changed slowly, even though not only the Charter of the United Nations but also an array of postwar constitutions in France, Italy, the Federal Republic of Germany, and Eastern Europe contained provisions for equal opportunity. For the majority of Western European countries, however, subsequent legal reform did not come about until the 1970s and 1980s. It was only in the Scandinavian countries that this equality had already made headway in the interwar period. In Eastern Europe, on the other hand, equal opportunity rights were often also widely developed on paper, but they were frequently not executed because of the limited power of the courts and the limited rule of law (Therborn 2004).

Demographic and familial structures also changed in comparison to the situation in the 1920s or even the period around 1900. The trend toward ever lower numbers of births slowed in the 1950s and 1960s and even reversed in some countries, but birthrates were not as high as in the inter- and prewar periods. Although the divorce rate sank in many countries, as a rule it remained distinctly higher than in the inter- or even prewar period. Likewise, marriage figures remained clearly higher. The traditional model of the lifelong bachelor lost its penetrating power.

Sharp differences broke out between generations. The emerging generation of young people and young adults was shaped by the experience of a unique economic boom and the beginning of mass consumption. This generation was strongly influenced by American and French rock and roll. A "beatnik" culture developed among the young workers and the middle class, and existentialism, with its specific clothing and music, its stars, and its pub culture came into vogue among students. In stark contrast to this stood a generation of parents who had been shaped by the entirely different experiences of hardship in the global economic crisis, the Second World War, and a traditional culture of austerity. In the Federal Republic of Germany, the fact of the parental generation's involvement in the NS regime intensified the generational extremes even more. Although these differences first penetrated public debate in the late 1960s, many families had dealt with them first in the 1950s, instigated by films such as *Night and Fog*, for example.

The public discourse over women and family policy also changed. In the eastern part of Europe a deeper break with the interwar period emerged. A new image of the working woman, one who performed difficult labor as a tractor driver or crane operator, was created within official propaganda. In the western part of Europe the theme of the working woman and working mother was seldom initiated by the government but rather disseminated through the media, in women's magazines and advertising.

Family Change since the Late 1960s

A second upheaval in the European history of the family has been apparent since the late 1960s. This change went in three directions: a singular, dominant marriage model was replaced with a multiplicity of marriage models, under which the hitherto dominant model still existed but no longer predominated; the child-centric marriage became accepted; and the intimate nuclear family gradually opened up.

These new familial lifestyles had some parallels in the postwar period. Despite this, they differed in a fundamental way: they emerged not by necessity in the aftermath of war, but from voluntary decisions during a historically remarkable rise in the standard of living, a widely expanded welfare state, a rapid expansion of the educational sector, and a stable peace in Europe. A clear connection between the postwar period and this second upheaval is lacking for other reasons as well: in the European countries where neither the Second World War nor the consequent ambiguous postwar period in the history of the family took place, similar familial ways of life developed in the late 1960s nevertheless. Sweden, which was spared from the war to a large extent, was even a vanguard and model for the new familial structures. The postwar period was seldom referenced in contemporary public debate over the new familial models.

It can be argued that this change sprang from the student movement of the late 1960s—or that the opposite is true, that the student movement was a result of the upheaval in family values and family life. The liberalization of parenting and that of the sexual lives of adolescents and young adults were indeed counted among the central demands of this movement throughout Western Europe. Yet family life changed at the same time, not later: the divorce rate picked up again in almost all European countries (see Figure 1.1). The number of births out of wedlock rose. The birthrate in many countries, at least in Western Europe, began to plummet, in part due to oral contraceptives. The marriage rate sank a bit later (Flora 1987: 145ff.), this time not in a short cycle such as had occurred in the postwar period, but rather as the beginning of a longer trend that continued into the 1970s and 1980s. At heart, the demands of the student movement revolved primarily around teenage and young adult ways of life and around the restrictions imposed upon them by their families as well as by the state and public moral standards. In contrast, the change in family was more comprehensive and also modified the parental phase of life and the aging process. All of this points to the student movement being a part of, and even an intensifier of, a broader social upheaval, but not its cause or avant-garde.

The Diversity of Marriage Models

Relationships between marriage partners gradually changed throughout Europe starting in the late 1960s. A new plurality of marriage and family models gradually emerged, supported by many developments: educational expansion and the much improved qualifications of men as well as women; the modern welfare state that held the family back by acting as a protective social guarantor and at the same time adjusted to the new family structures, sustaining them in the process; better healthcare provisions and birth control; employment for mothers, which gave women their own

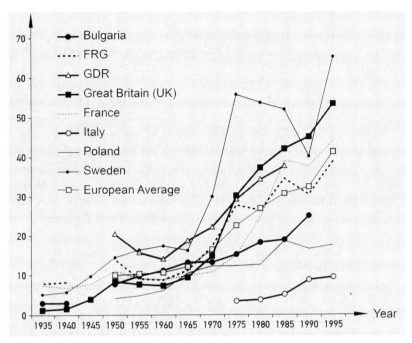

Figure 1.1 Divorce Rates in Europe, 1935–1995
(divorces per 100 marriages, 3-year average)
Source: *UN Demographical Yearbook*, vol. 3 (1951)

income and an individual life plan and thus also more autonomy; the decline of the family economy; the weakening of control by professional, social, and regional milieus; the increasingly intense transnational transfers of marriage and family models; and changes in attitudes and family and vocational values, including further establishment of the love marriage. Eight marriage models gradually came into being.

The first model involved marriages contracted directly before parenthood. Traditional engagement, upon which the future spouses planned to marry and during which they did not live together, decreased more and more. It was replaced by a period of cohabitation and intense mutual acquaintance with one another under the growing demands of the modern marriage for love. This test period did not always look the same legally. The young adults often entered into a "marriage without a marriage certificate," which is largely accepted, at least in the northern part of Europe today. Young adults' surroundings, parents, and landlords, as well as public opinion, adjusted to this new form of cohabitation before parenting relatively quickly, and for this reason the marriage rate sank somewhat. Europe has developed into a special case with a particularly low inclination toward marriage since this period in particular. To a certain extent, young adults married only to quickly divorce if they were not compatible. The rise in the divorce rate in the 1970s and 1980s had in part to do with the prevalence of this test phase before parenthood proper.

A second marriage model was the family with children in which both parents worked. This model was not a complete novelty, as a minority of European families had lived this way for a long time. In the 1950s and early 1960s, however, mothers employed outside the home outnumbered those working in the home. This model was no longer exceptional or born of necessity, but rather a normal life plan that a majority of Europeans followed. European societies adapted to this marriage model by and by, and realigned raising children, familial values, family policy, kindergartens, after-school care, schools, cafeterias, and rental agreements to this new marriage model.

"Marriage without a marriage certificate" became the third new marriage model: families with children in which the parents lived together but formally remained unmarried, thus creating a partnership—not just a period of preparation before parenthood. Perhaps better referred to as a "family without a marriage certificate," its historical development has not been statistically recorded for Europe as a whole. It appears, however, to have been on the rise in the 1970s and 1980s in the northern part of Europe, particularly in Sweden. The jump in out-of-wedlock births, which in Western and Central Europe increased on average from 6 percent in the 1970s to 13 percent in 1990, was evidence of this (Höpflinger 1987: 90; Therborn 1995: 291). European societies also gradually adjusted to these "families without marriage certificates," above all with regard to right of name as well as family, rental, and inheritance law.

A fourth new marriage model was the "patchwork family," in which children from the different marriages of the husband and wife lived together and often simultaneously maintained close relationships with the other parent outside of the household. This family model has become more important, as the divorce rate throughout Europe increased after the 1960s and the high postwar divorce rates were exceeded by those of the 1980s (see Figure 1.1). The cohabitation of parents and children from different marriages had a precursor in European families through the nineteenth century, however. Half-siblings often lived together, though at that time it was because a parent, usually the mother, had died young. What was new, then, in the second half of the twentieth century, was that the cohabitation of half-siblings was due to the biological parent's voluntary decision and furthermore that the children often had close relationships with the biological parent that lived outside the family household.

The fifth new family model with children was more dramatic: the single-parent family, which also became more prevalent after the 1970s. The large majority of these single-parent families were single-mother families. The primary reason for the surge was the rising divorce rate, due to which only one parent remained with the children and, at least formally, did not marry again. A part of these single-parent families came about as an intentional way of life.

A sixth, radical alternative to the family gained currency after the 1970s and 1980s: the percentage of those who never wanted to marry or start a family during their lifetimes increased. Research on the family is united in concluding that a growing, though difficult to establish, part of the population turned away from the role of parent. At first glance this looks like a revival of an old European tradition: up until the early twentieth century a considerable portion of the population remained unmarried and was counted among the particularities of the European family. But the new lifelong renouncement of starting a family fundamentally differed from this: it had nothing to do with the rigid old-European state prohibition of marriage—a form of poverty reduction—nor with a retreat from the secular world into the seclusion of cloisters. Rather it was without exception voluntary and admittedly often due to career constraints. This forgoing of parenthood meant something different from its old-Europe predecessor, and did not necessarily mean a forgoing of partnership.

Lastly, there are two additional, previous marriage models that did not disappear but underwent change. First, the lifelong marriage remained intact. Though it did indeed lose its position as the dominant model, it was not fully replaced by the other marriage models. It did, however, change. The position of the wife became stronger as family law was reformed in most European countries and wives were granted the same rights as their husbands to make decisions regarding parenting and contracts, which became ever more important in a mass consumption society. With greater life expectancy, the lifelong marriage also lasted longer. The "third age," the stage of life of full physical and mental activity after parenthood and after employment, became an increasingly longer part of this lifelong marriage and sustained the economic sectors of tourism, spas, museums, classical concerts, and operas.

Another traditional marriage model was maintained, though it also changed: the joint management of a business. This model also plummeted in importance after the 1970s, but instead of disappearing completely it took on an altered form. It had existed most frequently in the craft trades, retail trade, and agriculture but was also found among the liberal professions, in the households of professors or pastors. The weight of this marriage model had already diminished considerably by the time of the economic boom, as many such small businesses in commerce were abandoned and then as the wives of farmers, craftsmen, and retail traders as well as pastors and professors increasingly followed their own professional path. Yet this marriage and family model was preserved in many service industries—restaurants and hotels, gas stations and repair services—as well as in the liberal professions and in couple-managed medical practices and architectural and law firms. Wives certainly possessed the same education as their husbands in increasing numbers and pursued careers as well. The marriage of two doctors or of attorney and judge to a large extent replaced the marriage between doctor and medical assistant or between the attorney and wife whose law studies had been interrupted by marriage.

These distinctive new patterns in marriage and family were seldom explained by religion, political views, or social milieu. They were largely based on individual living conditions. Familial options and freedoms broadened, as did the associated risks.

This diversity also had its boundaries. Some trends had an impact on all of these marriage models: the decline in marriages, which had reached their peak around the middle of the twentieth century (Therborn 2004); the decrease in number of children and family size, and with this also a fundamental alteration of the parent-child relationship in all marriage and family models; the reduction of infant mortality, the end of disproportionately high maternal mortality, and generally longer life; the cultivation of the love-based marriage as an ideal—a marriage based on personal affection, sexual satisfaction, and partnership and no longer on social position, income, and the same religious affiliation; and the raising of children as the focal point of marriage.

Parent-Child Relationships

Relationships between parents and children also changed after the late 1960s. Demographic changes played an important role in this. Children grew up in significantly smaller families, with significantly fewer siblings and increasingly even as only children. At the same time, a growing number of children experienced loss and replacement of a parent, and sometimes siblings, through divorce and remarriage.

But it was the emergence of the child-centered marriage that primarily changed the relationships between parents and children. Although children had always been central to marriage, they now became the center of the parents' emotional life, and parental care was what gave meaning to the relationship between couples (Harding, Philipps, and Fogarty 1986: 121; Nave-Herz 1988: 98ff.). Parents' attitudes regarding parenting changed. The aim of parenting was no longer only to prepare children for life and to provide the best possible job prospects and educational opportunities. More than before, parents—not only mothers but fathers too—also sought their own happiness and self-realization in parenting. The declining number of children in the family contributed to this trend. The demands of parenting, both the ones parents set for themselves and those that were set for them by the people and conditions around them, increased considerably in the process.

An important effect of this child-centered marriage was a new economic market, consumption because of and for children. The supply of children's furniture, toys, clothing, food, bikes, and car seats as well as children's media and technology expanded and replaced homemade wooden horses and dollhouses. On the one hand, this new child-based consumption made children independent, as they became the prospective buyers and often knew the products better than their parents did. It also led to a loss of intuitive experience, however, in favor of thoroughly second-hand, controlled experiences. At the same time, spouses in child-centered marriages increasingly elaborated and discussed parenting, creating a market for the growing supply of parenting books and magazines.

It is not possible to determine exactly whether parenting models became unified after the 1960s in Europe or a new variety of parenting values emerged. There is little comparative research on the parental values of European parents from the 1950s through the 1970s. Nevertheless, it is astounding that only a single parental value, honesty, was supported by a clear majority of those asked in surveys on values in Europe since the 1980s. No other value—neither tolerance, nor good behavior, nor a sense of responsibility, politeness, self-control, hard work, thrift, religiosity, patience, or imagination—was favored by a majority of European parents (Harding, Phillips, and Fogerty 1986: 20f.). A new and broad diversification of parental values, similar to that with familial models, may stand behind this, but little is known with certainty.

The Opening of the Nuclear Family

Lastly, the family's relationships with the outside world changed after the 1960s—whether with neighbors across the street, extended family, or public institutions and the state. These changes often did not begin exactly in the late 1960s but were either introduced later or went back to the 1950s and early 1960s. Moreover, these tendencies do not always go in a single direction, but rather are thoroughly inconsistent.

Rudimentary family events such as birth and death were increasingly transferred out of the family apartment or house, no longer always occurring in the presence of, or in close spatial proximity to, the family, and taking place without the earlier rituals, last words, and deathbed good-byes. Once purely family affairs, these events now took place in hospitals together with strangers who were specialists in birth and death—doctors, nurses, and midwives. Counter-tendencies such as the home birth, the hospital birth in the presence of a spouse, or dying at home were on the rise, but not prevalent.

Furthermore, family members spent ever larger parts of their days and their lives outside the family. More and more, children and adolescents went to day care, kindergarten, and all-day school. Family life consisted of only a few hours in the late afternoon and evening, and on the weekend. In countries with few all-day schools, affluent parents developed intensive afternoon programs outside of the home, including sports, museum courses, and music lessons. In some countries, children also spent less and less summer vacation time in the parental household or with extended family, instead attending camps or language schools outside the family. While raising children, the mother in particular spent less time with the family and more time at work, A similar development marked the end of life: after parenthood, it became rarer and rarer for married couples to live within their son's or daughter's family circle. More often, they lived in individual households or in retirement homes, and in the "fourth age," that of mental and physical deterioration, were increasingly in nursing homes and hospitals.

A third trend was that the now smaller family finally and noticeably opened up to non-relatives, and to friends in particular. Comparisons in surveys from different points in time show that after the 1960s the family home was increasingly opened up to family friends and neighbors or friends of the children and teenagers. Invitations to play with other children and to dine together became more common, as did social outings and shared vacations. Polls after the 1960s show that the family that was closed to the outside decreased in value and that the contacts between family and friends gained appreciation, though admittedly with wide variations within Europe. In the middle-class apartment, the previous separation between family intimacy and the public blurred. Formerly the parlor had been reserved for visitors and was rigidly separated from the private section of the apartment. In the second half of the twentieth century, the living room with its corner sofa and television became both the family meeting place and the room for receiving guests.

A fourth tendency was that the modern welfare state weakened the insular nature of the family and autonomous personal planning. Beginning in the 1950s (see Chapter 10) the welfare state influenced basic familial decisions more than ever, including those concerning the time that was spent with family. It influenced marriage and the number of children through aid money for families; the employment of wives through kindergarten and all-day schools; the decision to retire and to enter a retirement or nursing home. It was only in times of crisis, such as the postwar period or, in Eastern Europe, during the period after the upheaval of 1989–91 that this trend weakened and the family regained the decisive voice in such decisions.

The fifth trend saw the seclusion of the family further invaded by the growing influence of the media and of public institutions on the family's everyday life and intra-familial relationships. Television, films, and computer games, children's books, kindergartens and schools, and family counseling and therapists influenced parenthood, children's attitudes to parents, and relationships between marriage partners. New models and core values prevailed. External influences on the family were admittedly nothing new, yet they had changed in character: personal influences from local society—the neighbors, priest or pastor, teacher, doctor, shop owner, and hairdresser—were replaced by impersonal influences via the media. Moreover, these influences invaded the family without the possibility of reciprocity once allowed by, for example, supervision by neighbors or extended family, in which the parents were simultaneously involved in the supervision of other families and family members. On the other hand, the families could more easily decide for themselves which of these impersonal influences to absorb—which children's books, psychological counselors, and TV films they took a look at and which they rejected.

Alongside these trends of opening, there were also tendencies toward closure within the family unit after the late 1960s, three of which were significant. The first was closely related to the establishment of the mass consumption society (see Chapter 3). The introduction of durable consumer goods strengthened the seclusion of the family in particular: the private home instead of a rented apartment, children playing in their rooms rather than in the street with other children, the private washing machine instead of public laundries, grocery shopping less often due to the prevalence of refrigerators and freezers, driving in private cars rather than walking or taking public transportation, household radio and television instead of the theater or radio and television in pubs, and record, cassette, and CD players instead of public concerts. All of these acquisitions in the mass consumer society strengthened the private closure of the family and thinned out contacts and social events outside of the family.

A second tendency in the closing off of the family was the domestication of the husband. The increase in free time through the reduction of work hours (see Chapter 2), the do-it-yourself movement, and the other masculine domestic activities that arose out of it gave husbands greater presence in the family living space and weakened their prior tendency toward the purely masculine company of coworkers. This trend was strengthened even more by the loosening of ties to social milieus (see Chapter 7). Class-specific and generally masculine forms of socializing such as labor and trade unions, taverns, and music halls, as well as petit bourgeois and middle-class forms of socialization such as men-only round-tables and club culture, as well as the salons and café visits of middle-class women, declined in the 1960s and 1970s. In contrast, the new and increasing neighborhood and street festivals, church and school functions, and carnivals became occasion for familial social outings.

The third trend in the seclusion of the family emerged under the dictatorships of the eastern part of Europe until 1989–91 and in the right-wing dictatorships in Spain, Portugal, and Greece through the early 1970s. In these dictatorships, families often closed themselves off from the state and from political organizations within an environment shaped by repression and control and thereby created a ring of trust. These regimes resorted to a gamut of methods and institutions to breach this family seculusion— from kindergarten and schools to youth and party organizations to social integration at the workplace and the recruitment of family members into secret service organizations—though mostly to no avail.

Whether the trend of the opening family carried more weight than its countertrend of the new closed-off family is not easily determined. On the whole, however, the opening up of the family most likely prevailed in most European countries, and before 1989–90, at least in Western Europe. But family intimacy was certainly in no way destroyed—intimacy within the family as well as individual privacy within the family remained important values.

Controversies

These changes in the family led to lively controversy. On the one hand, they stoked fears that the family unit was increasingly deteriorating and that a growing part of society was living without familial ties. That at the end of the twentieth century a considerable number of adults never married, that a significant percentage of marriages ended in divorce and the divorced often never remarried, that a large portion of children experienced the divorce of their parents, and that more and more of the elderly lived without any help from their children and also died alone, was viewed as indicating a historically unique and profound crisis of the family.

On the other hand, it was also argued that Europeans saw the family as the most important pillar of their lives, and that the welfare state and high standard of living gave individuals increasingly more freedom to pursue family life as they saw fit. To be sure, these new freedoms also came with problems. The familial future became less predictable and life planning more difficult. Some of the new marriage models—for example, the single-parent family brought about by divorce—were by no means always voluntary. New social inequalities emerged; many single-parent families fell into poverty. In the fourth age, help from adult children often determined whether life ended in the new loneliness of hospitals and nursing homes. Constraints, inequalities, and loneliness had also been prevalent in earlier families, however. From this perspective, the family did not really deteriorate in the second half of the twentieth century, but it did fundamentally change.

Convergences and Divergences

Divergences

In contrast to other social fields, familial forms within Europe in the second half of the twentieth century diverged strikingly. Moreover, differences between individual countries did not diminish during this time, whether looking at the birthrate and child mortality, the divorce rate, out-of-wedlock births and single-parent families, parenting values, or state benefits for the family and child care.

Huge differences can be detected between those lands affected by and those spared from the war. Much of what most deeply changed the families in the countries affected by the war—the war deaths of fathers and the war widows' single-parent families; the rape of mothers, the long-term effects of which were examined very little; the obliteration of entire parts of families through the genocide of the NS regime; the displacement, evacuation, and bombing of families and the painstaking act of regaining footing in foreign surroundings; the evacuation of children and the separation of families during the war; the breakup of family intimacy; the high marriage and divorce rates and the high rate of births out of wedlock during and after the war—was not present in those countries spared the war. These divergences were temporary in nature, however, and had long faded by the end of the twentieth century.

A second divergence that first emerged in the second half of the twentieth century is seen in family differences between Western Europe and communist Eastern Europe. The nearly forty years of Soviet rule did not bring about a uniform communist family; the differences between the individual Eastern Bloc countries were too great for this to occur. Yet several similar trends within families and the life courses they chose stand out. Women and mothers who worked were on average more common in communist countries than in Western Europe, though not much more so than in Scandinavia and Great Britain. The professional lives of women in Eastern Europe differed less from those of men than in Western Europe, again with the exception of Northern Europe. Women did not, however, have equal rights, and they remained scarce in the top political, economic, and management positions. The roles of men and women also continued to differ within the family.

The course of the family also developed differently in Eastern Europe. The marriage rate was higher and the age of marriage lower than in Western Europe. The mothers were younger, the distance between generations shorter, and the birthrates considerably higher than the Western European average. At the same time, life planning was also different. Families were not first started after education and entry into the workforce, but rather often during education.

Four political reasons in particular account for these common trends among the communist countries of Eastern Europe. First, the extensive communist planned economy needed women and mothers as manpower in its massive workforce and hence supported them, and was further strengthened through the socialist and liberal European heritage that demanded equality between men and women; meanwhile, natalistic policies to increase the birthrate, which would ensure a large workforce in the long run, primarily consisted of workplace-based nurseries and kindergartens, maternity leave, and family-friendly social policies. Another reason was the predictability of the course of family life due to the almost complete protection from unemployment and the provision of social welfare that was fully planned from above (see Chapter 10 on the welfare state). Third, the long-neglected housing policies often meant that early marriage was the only way to receive a private apartment. Finally, in a totally different spirit, the founding of a family was a retreat from repressive communistic policy.

The family structures found in Eastern and Western Europe did not immediately converge after the breakdown of the Soviet empire. Due to the collapse of social welfare and the job market, the family in Eastern Europe was more necessary than ever before. Though there were broad variations between the individual countries, the number of divorces and birthrates dropped everywhere. The former GDR was a particularly dramatic example. These new East-West differences gradually began to disappear later on, in the 1990s.

A third, longer-lasting divergence that continues to have an effect today emerged out of the changes to the family unit after the late 1960s. In no way did the diversity of family models develop uniformly throughout Europe. There was, however, no attempt to classify this diversity in a regional typology as occurred in other areas of social history such as work, values, social conflicts, or the welfare state (see Chapters 2, 4, 9, 10). Three roughly distinguishable family patterns from the second half of the twentieth century first became apparent in the late 1960s: a Northern European, a Central and Western European, and a Southern and Eastern European pattern.

The Northern European family pattern, most prevalent in Scandinavia but also in parts of Great Britain, the Balkans, and Russia, was characterized by a particularly strong move away from the lifelong civil marriage. Particularly frequent divorces (see Figure 1.1), out-of-wedlock births and single-parent families, relatively high birthrates, somewhat low infant mortality, strong individual parenting values, particularly high employment among women, and a notably well-developed welfare state as well as a significant tolerance within society and politics for new family forms can be noted in this pattern. As a whole, diversity among family forms developed in this part of Europe in particular combined with plenty of social certainty, high employment, and rather high birthrates.

A different Central and Western European family pattern prevailed in countries such as Hungary, Czechoslovakia, the GDR, the old Federal Republic of Germany, France, the Netherlands, Belgium, Switzerland, and Austria. In this part of Europe similar tendencies toward diversity of family forms emerged as they had in the North, though the trends were considerably weaker. Divorce rates (see Figure 1.1), single-parent families, births out of wedlock, and "families without marriage certificates" increased, but to a far lesser extent than in the North. They were also as a whole acknowledged less by society and political policy. Female employment in the West lay somewhere in the middle, lower than in the North and also lower than in the East before 1989. State social security was also highly developed for the most part, with the exception of Switzerland. These countries experienced a dramatic drop in birthrates after the baby boom of the 1950s; then, beginning in the 1980s, the number of births stabilized at a midlevel plane lower than that in the North, with the exception of France, whose birthrate is among one of the highest in Europe.

Lastly, there was the family pattern that developed in Southern and Eastern Europe outside the USSR. The traditional family was largely preserved in this part of Europe. Divorces (see Figure 1.1), out-of-wedlock births, and single-parent families were significantly rarer than in the other parts of Europe and were rejected more by society as a whole. Female employment, with regard to the noncommunist countries, was rather low and was rarely accepted. In the Eastern European countries female employment decreased in part at a high rate after 1989–90. Birthrates also dropped significantly in these Southern and Eastern European countries and in 2000 were the lowest in Europe. The services provided by the welfare states in these relatively poor countries were limited. In Southern Europe, Spain, Portugal, Greece, and to some extent Italy followed this pattern, as did Romania and Bulgaria in Eastern Europe as well as Central European Poland.

Three frequently stated perceptions could no longer be reconciled with these patterns of development. Catholic countries no longer consistently had higher birthrates than Protestant countries or countries of mixed denominations in the second half of the twentieth century. The factor of religion seemed to have become less important. Two Catholic countries, Ireland and France, reached the highest birthrates in Europe, but other Catholic countries in Southern and Eastern Europe had particularly low birthrates. Furthermore, birthrates did not sink, as often believed, with increasing female employment and with the deterioration of traditional family values. Northern Europe, with its high numbers of women in employment and particularly extensive shift away from traditional family values, at the same time had high birthrates—or at least higher than the South of Europe with its traditional family values and weak showing of female employment. And finally, no fully uniform pattern of development that was considerably different from Western Europe's emerged during the communist era in the eastern part of Europe. On the contrary, the contrasts were sharper between the GDR, Hungary, and Czechoslovakia—which had close links with the Western European development patterns—and East Central and Eastern European countries like Poland, Romania, and Bulgaria, which more resembled the Southern European development pattern.

Similarities and Convergences

The most important convergence concerning the family in Europe was the rapprochement of the familial course of life, which began not after 1945 but as early as the nineteenth century. The first important point in family life, entering school, became more uniform with the final establishment of literacy throughout Europe. The illiteracy rate in a number of Southern and Eastern European countries was still considerable in 1950. School attendance as a part of life was absent in part of the population (see Chapter 12). But by 2000, this discrepancy had almost completely disappeared. The next important point in family life, marriage, first markedly aligned in the 1970s: Europeans married at an increasingly similar age. In 1950, the average age of marriage for women still diverged widely; the extreme cases were Ireland at 28 and France at 23 years old. In 1975, the opposite ends of the spectrum, Ireland at 25 and Hungary at 21, were already somewhat closer in proximity. With the growing diversity of marriage models, however, the increase in differences was renewed after the 1980s (Kaelble 1987: 20; Höpflinger 1997: 108). By 2000, the extremes were again as far apart as in 1950, particularly in Sweden, with an average of 30 years old, and in Poland, where the average age of marriage is 24.

The age difference between men and women also shifted. In 1950, husbands in some European countries were still noticeably older than wives, for example in Denmark, Greece, Ireland, or Italy. These countries followed a marriage model in which the husband had to hold a secure economic position that was often achieved later in life, or in which his dominance was to be ensured by his being considerably older. In other countries, such as Spain, Portugal, the Federal Republic of Germany, and Switzerland, in contrast, the age of marriage for men and women was already very similar by the middle of the century. This difference within Europe diminished as well (Eurostat 1984: Figure 7; Höpflinger 1987: 16; Höpflinger 1997: 108f.; Council of Europe 2005). Furthermore, the ages of parenthood in Europe converged, while fertility rates and number of children during the mother's lifespan became more similar (Höpflinger 1987: 119; Höpflinger 1997: 111; Coleman 2002; Saraceno 2004). And lastly, the stage of life *after* parenthood became increasingly similar in length, while life expectancy in Europe also aligned somewhat (Coleman 2002).

A further convergence, at least among the Western European countries, occurred with family policy. After the Second World War, most Western European countries adopted family policy in accordance with similar basic principles, even though substantial differences remained in the details: a similar civil law equality between parents in raising children; similar public programs for kindergartens and the education of kindergarten teachers; a similar setup of full-day schools, child benefits, and tax breaks for parents with children; protection for pregnant women and exemption from work during pregnancy and directly after giving birth. This occurred primarily though the transfer relationships between the individual European governments.

European Hallmarks

The British and Austrian social historians Peter Laslett, Richard Wall, and Michael Mitterauer developed the thesis of the "European Family" (Wall, Robin, and Laslett 1983; Mitterauer 1986; Mitterauer 2004). The core of European family hallmarks consists in this: in contrast to Japan or

Russia, for example, in Europe young married couples do not marry into the families of their parents or in-laws but rather found their own households. The cohabitation of three generations in one household is thus more rare in Europe than elsewhere. Furthermore, the age of marriage in the European family is particularly high for both men and women, because founding one's own household requires considerable financial means or professional independence. Due to the higher age at marriage, the birthrates in European families are also lower than elsewhere. Traditionally, the number of individuals who remained unmarried was also especially high in Europe, since not all young adults were able to bring together the financial resources to set up their own household, and governmental obstacles to marriage existed into the nineteenth century.

Certain ways of life were also part of the modern European family. The European family shielded itself more than others from extended family, neighbors, and community as well as the state. Family intimacy was more developed. Spousal relationships were stronger, as determined by the ideal of the love-based marriage. Parent-child relationships were formed not only by strong emotional bonds, but also by an exclusive parental responsibility for raising children as well as a greater orientation on the part of the children toward the parents. Separation from one's family of origin in young adulthood was extensively anticipated in European family life, in part during the early modern period through separation from the family in youth and adolescence by attending a boarding school or working as an apprentice, servant, or maid, but also in part through a distinct crisis during adolescence (Mitterauer 1986).

Until the late nineteenth century, this tightly delineated European family was not found throughout Europe, but rather primarily in the North and West: in Great Britain, Northern France, the Benelux countries, Scandinavia, and German-speaking countries. Only in the late nineteenth and twentieth centuries did this family model begin to spread throughout Europe. As it did, the distinct lines of its image softened but remained recognizable. In the latter half of the twentieth century, the three-generation household was much less common than it was in Russia or Japan, the age at marriage was considerably higher than in the United States, and the birthrate was noticeably lower than elsewhere, whether North and South America, Asia, or Africa (UN 1992: 304ff.).

The European family particularities do not consist solely of the aftereffects of this European family, which in comparison to other civilizations faded more than anything in the second half of the twentieth century. European characteristics seem also to have emerged with the new diversity of marriage and familial models. The divorce rate in Europe until now has remained distinctly below the US rate; this is true even in the European countries with a particularly high number of divorces. The highest divorce rates in 1990 in Europe were on average 41 percent, and even in Northern Europe most were still under 45 percent, as opposed to the US at 54 percent. On the other hand, the divorce rates in Europe were clearly higher than in almost all Asian countries, including in modern societies such as Japan, Singapore, Korea, and Hong Kong (Höpflinger 1997: 111; UN 1992: 319f.). One former and remaining characteristic is the single-parent family, which developed according to a similar pattern in many European countries; 11–17 percent of all families in Western and East Central Europe in the 1980s had only one parent. The prevalence of this pattern in Europe, including the extreme European example of Denmark, has always been lower than in the US, whose percentage of single-parent families came in at 24 percent around 1980. Conversely, the share of single-parent families in Japan was significantly lower, 4 percent in 1983 (OECD 1990: 29). The number of out-of-wedlock births was also considerably lower in Europe than in the US, though at the same time many times higher than in Asia (Coleman 2002).

Thus it would not do full justice to European family history to speak exclusively of the differences and divergences within Europe. While they are indeed obvious, alongside them are also noticeable convergences as well as distinct characteristics of the European family that differentiate it from the non-European family.

References

Ariès, Ph., G. Duby, A. Prost, and G. Vincent, eds., *History of Private Life, Volume V: Riddles of Identity in Modern Times*. Cambridge 1991 (French: *Histoire de la vie privée*. Paris 1987).

Becchi E. and D. Julia, eds. *Histoire de l'enfance en occident*. 2 vols. Paris 1998.

Bock G. *Women in European History*. 2009.

Bologne J.C. *Histoire du célibat et des célibataires*. Paris 2004.

Burguière A., C. Klapisch-Zuber, M. Segalen, and F. Zonabend, eds. *A History of the Family, Volume II: The Impact of Modernity*. Cambridge 1996 (French: *Le choc de la modernité*. Paris 1987).

Coleman D.A. "Populations of the Industrial World: A Convergent Demographic Community?" *International Journal of Population Geography* 8 (2002): 319–344.

Council of Europe. *Recent Demographic Trends 2004*. Strasbourg 2005.

Die Frau von heute 2 (April 1946): 17 (survey).

Eurostat. *Demographic Statistics*. Luxembourg 1984.

Flora P. *State, Economy, and Society in Western Europe, 1815–1975*, vol. 2. Frankfurt a.M. 1987.

Gestrich A., J.-U. Krause, and M. Mitterauer. *Geschichte der Familie*. Stuttgart 2003.

Goldthorpe J.E. *Family Life in Western Societies. A Historical Sociology of Family Relationships in Britain and North America*. Cambridge 1987.

Goody J. *Geschichte der Familie*. Munich 2002. (English: *A Family in European History*. Oxford 1999.)

Harding S., D. Phillips, and M. Fogerty. *Contrasting Values in Western Europe: Unity, Diversity and Change*. Palgrave Macmillan 1986.

Höpflinger F. *Wandel der Familienbildung in Westeuropa*. Frankfurt a.M. 1987.

Höpflinger F. *Haushalts- und Familienstrukturen im europäischen Vergleich*. In S. Hradit and S. Immerfall, eds., *Die westeuropäischen Gesellschaften im Vergleich*. Opladen 1997, 97–130.

Kaelble H. *Auf dem Weg zu einer europäischen Gesellschaft: Eine Sozialgeschichte Westeuropas, 1880–1980*. Munich 1987.

Kniebiehler Y. *Histoire des mères et de la maternitè en occident*. Paris 2000.

Meyer S. and E. Schulze, *Wie wir das alles geschafft haben*. Munich 1984.

Mitterauer M. *A History of Youth: Family, Sexuality and Social Relations in Past Times*. Oxford and New York 1992.

Mitterauer M. "A European Family in the 19th and 20th Centuries?" In H. Kaelble, ed., *The European Way: European Societies during the 19th and 20th Centuries*. New York 2004, 140–160.

Nave-Herz R., ed. *Wandel und Kontinuität der Familie in der Bundesrepublik Deutschland*. Stuttgart 1988.

OECD. *Lone-Parent Families: The Economic Challenge*. Paris 1990.

Saraceno C. "The Reproductive Paradox of 'Weak' and 'Strong' Families in Contemporary Europe." *WZB Jahrbuch* (2004): 347–374.

Segalen M. *Die Familie: Geschichte, Soziologie, Anthropologie*. Frankfurt a.M. 1990.

Sieder R. *Sozialgeschichte der Familie*. Frankfurt a.M. 1987.

Therborn G. *European Modernity and Beyond: The Trajectory of European Societies, 1945–2000*. London 1995.

Therborn G. *Between Sex and Power: Family in the World, 1900–2000*. London 2004.

UN. *Demographic Yearbook* 44 (1992).

Wall R., J. Robin, and P. Laslett, eds. *Family Forms in Historic Europe*. Cambridge 1983.

Chapter 2

LABOR

State of Research

Surprisingly, labor—as opposed to the family—is not one of the popular topics within social history. For this reason we cannot refer to a survey of Europe or a historical analysis of the major labor history trends in Europe during the second half of the twentieth century. There are substantially relevant historical surveys and book chapters from sociologists Martin Heidenreich (Heidenreich 2004) and Göran Therborn (Therborn 1995), but these, at most, go back only to the 1970s, not the entire second half of the twentieth century. The overview articles by historians who focus on the history of labor, such as those by Josef Ehmer (Ehmer 2001) or Frans van der Ven (van der Ven 1972), deal very little with the second half of the twentieth century. Jürgen Kocka provided a sketch of what such an overview of the history of labor could look like (Kocka 2000; 2010). Not even specialists in subjects that currently pique the most interest in the history of labor, such as unemployment and women in the workplace, have produced European surveys of this era.

The situation does not look much better for the individual European countries. Only France has two surveys on the history of labor, by Oliver Marchand and Claude Thélot (Marchand and Thélot 1997) and Alain Dewerpe (Dewerpe 2001). Likewise, only a few European countries have overviews on the specialty themes within labor: France and Great Britain each have only one book about the history of unemployment (Salais et al. 1986; Whiteside 1991), and Germany and Great Britain each have just one book on the history of women in the workplace (Frevert 1986; Blackman 1992). All of these accounts, moreover, cover only the period up to the 1980s. Other important topics—such as the change in structure in the labor force, biographies of earning, the qualifications for and down-grading of jobs, and the changes in labor in the industrial, service, and knowledge-based society—are still waiting for surveys on the national and European levels alike.

Labor around 1950

Labor dramatically changed in Europe following the end of the Second World War. Content, hierarchy, professionalization, prestige, payment, working conditions, technology, and even the distance between work-place and home changed so greatly that the work environment in 1950 is often difficult for modern-day Europeans to comprehend.

In the 1950s, Europe was still predominantly agricultural. According to estimates from the International Labor Office in Geneva, of the 181 million gainfully employed Europeans at the time (excluding the USSR and Turkey), 66 million were still working in agriculture, in contrast to only 61 million working in industry and 54 million working in the service sector (ILO 1986, vol. 5: 9, 123). Only Belgium, Great Britain, Germany, Austria, Switzerland, Sweden, and Bohemia had already become indus-trialized countries. In contrast, large European lands such as Italy, Spain, and Poland were still agricultural countries, as were smaller countries in the South and East as well as the outermost northern and western parts of Europe. Even in France industrial work and agricultural activities were still pretty evenly divided. Schoolbooks that place industrialization in the nineteenth century impart a false image with regard to the history of Eu-rope as a whole. The situation in the 1950s was certainly no longer com-parable to the situation in 1850, when industrialization still looked like an adventure with an open ending and, to many Europeans, like a threat. By 1950 it was completely clear what industrialization looked like and what its advantages and disadvantages were, as now there were industrial-ized countries in Europe serving as models. But the complete industrial-ization of Europe as a whole still lay ahead.

Labor in the 1950s was often hard manual labor. At that time, the important branches of business were still far from the mechanization that would mostly be complete by 2000, leading to different types of arduous work. Strenuous manual labor, often already combined with the opera-tion of machines, was still crucial to many workplaces at the time: in ag-riculture as well as in construction, in mining and the steel industry, in the hauling industry as well as in households. This hard physical labor and the illnesses that resulted from it shortened life expectancy. Paintings and sculptures at the time often represented this toil, whether idealizing or criticizing it.

Moreover, family work was also quite common in the 1950s—particularly on farms, in handicraft workshops, and in the retail and hauling industries. Not only married couples but also their parents, adult sons and daughters, teenagers, and at times even children worked together in family-owned businesses. For a substantial part of the European population, family work was still a life prospect outside of industry, large agricultural firms, banks, department stores, and insurance companies, or work in state-run administration, education, and enterprises. Family labor looked fundamentally different from labor in other parts of the economy. Such work was without salary, often without special training, and outside of the job market, and it was moreover dictated by familial hierarchies of authority and familial work values. Economic independence, which was otherwise often threatened, had great value in family businesses. This form of labor remained untouched by labor conflicts and was, as a rule, seldom safeguarded by state social security.

Additionally, women's employment was also still fundamentally different from men's work. Men were usually expected to be employed throughout their entire working life. For women, however, a career was still seen largely as an exception. They were usually gainfully employed only before or instead of being married, in wartime to replace the men, or in emergency family situations when a husband had died or was seriously ill, handicapped, or unemployed. Therefore, women were usually employed in subordinate positions. In the 1940s—during the Second World War and in the postwar period that followed—when many women had to support themselves, these exceptions and emergency situations occurred en masse.

Finally, in the 1950s the countries that had been most affected by the war could still feel its effects on labor, even though they had clearly diminished. Trends in labor were unusually heterogeneous in these countries during the war and the postwar periods. Many lost their jobs or access to their occupations—sometimes during the war because of the years as a soldier, prisoner, forced laborer, or concentration camp prisoner, sometimes during the postwar period due to years as refugees or exiles. Many had to reorientate themselves to the new work situation; some gave up, while others were given better chances than they had had before. During the postwar period many women returned to their roles as housewives and left their jobs outside the home, but many war widows were forced to accept working life. Above all, the postwar period also meant a reevaluation of domestic and external work in those countries most affected by the war. It was not uncommon for activities like small farming, foraging trips, or black market businesses to be a more important means of livelihood than a regular job. These were temporary phenomena, however, that generally did not change labor in the long run.

Labor During the Period of Prosperity in the 1950s and 1960s

During the economic prosperity of the 1950s and 1960s, fundamental changes affected various aspects of labor—in particular productivity and salaries, industrial employment, jobs, unemployment, women in the workplace, family business, the division between working and not working, and ultimately the debate about labor.

Productivity and Salaries

During the postwar period of the 1950s and 1960s, productivity in labor increased extraordinarily quickly. Angus Maddison estimates that from 1950 to 1973, economic growth per capita increased by around 4 percent yearly in the western part of Europe and close to 3.5 percent in the eastern part. Growth rates in this period were much faster than those in the interwar period and the later years from 1973 to 1989, when the growth rate was 1.8 percent in Western Europe and even fell to −1.1 percent in the eastern part of Europe (Maddison 2001: 126). Productivity rapidly increased not only in industry but also, and particularly, in agriculture. This was only possible because a well-trained workforce was available in Europe at the same time that a deficit in streamlining in comparison to the US—caused by the collapse of the European economy during the two world wars—had emerged and could now be made up for. Because of this abnormally high rise in productivity, the salaries and wages of this period increased substantially. Actual earnings increased two- to threefold in Western Europe between 1950 and 1970 (Mitchell 1993: 185ff., 843f.).

The Dominance of Industrial Activity

In the quarter century from 1950 to the early 1970s, the industrial sector grew to be the biggest employer in Europe (Figure 2.1). This epoch was the climax of the industrial society. Although the industrial sector had already reached this place of dominance in countries such as Great Britain, Germany, Austria, Switzerland, Belgium, Sweden, and Bohemia, industrial activity in Europe as a whole became predominant only during this

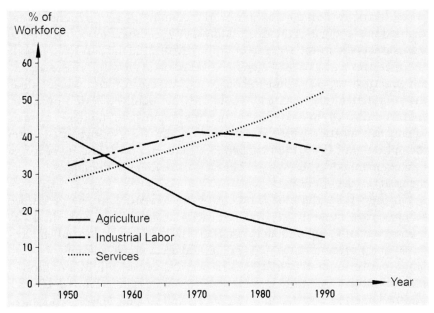

Figure 2.1 Employees by Job Sector in Europe, 1950–1990
Source: ILO, *Economically Active Population 1950–1020*, 5 vols, 5th ed. (Geneva 1997), 115.

time. According to estimates by the International Labor Office, in 1970, 83 million of the 204 million gainfully employed Europeans (apart from the Soviet Union and Turkey) were working in industry and only 41 and 80 million in agriculture and the service sector respectively. To the extent that the statistics can be compared, industrial activity dominated in the USSR as well: 44 million worked in industry, only 30 million in agriculture, and 43 million in the service sector. Turkey at that time, however, was still far from a dominance of industrial activity: 11 million worked in agriculture, 3 million in industry, and 5 million in the service sector (ILO 1986, vol. 4: 174; ILO 1996, vol. 1: 222).

This dominance of industrial activity was based on the traditional growth industries—coal mining, steel, machine construction, and the chemical and electrical industries—which experienced a rebirth during this time in the old industrial countries of Europe. From this emerged a new, dynamic branch of industry: the auto industry and its many supply industries. The auto industry had its beginnings during the interwar period, but it was not until the 1960s that the car became a mass product in Europe. This dominance of industrial activity was a Western European model for the periphery countries that were making their way toward it during these two decades: Southern Italy, Spain, Finland, and Ireland based their industrial policy on this model and set up and supported industrial enterprises. In the eastern part of Europe, the communist governments industrialized and reorganized the economy using the same model. Industrial labor, especially in the large steel mills, chemical plants, and automobile factories, was regarded as the engine of economic growth, prosperity, and full employment. According to European planners in West and East alike, the poor agricultural countries could only be rebuilt into rich industrial countries through industrial activity. This employment model continued to prevail after the age of the industrial society was long over. Even after the upheaval of 1989, industrial employment and the founding of industrial companies was seen as the best way to abate mass unemployment in the eastern part of Europe.

On the whole, the establishment of the industrial society proceeded at a fast pace because economic growth was abnormally high. In 1950, Europe was still predominately agrarian. By 1970, the industrial employment sector predominated and agricultural areas employed only one-fifth of the entire workforce. In 1980, the service sector, with 102 million of the 218 million gainfully employed Europeans (apart from the USSR), was the largest sector. In contrast, only 86 million people were working in the industrial sector, and only a minority of 30 million worked in agriculture (ILO 1986, vol. 5: 9, 123; ILO 1997, vol. 4: 213ff., not including the USSR European successor states and Turkey).

The process of industrialization had lasted much longer in the old European industrial countries, whereas in the new European industrial countries a fast tempo was the norm. The transition from an agrarian to an industrial and then to a service society took place over only a few decades. Many Europeans experienced the entire process during their lifespan. This rapid change had its price, however. Many Europeans lost their jobs and were unable to find new careers. Former farmers, handworkers, and retail dealers were forced to take jobs that were seen as a social downgrade or were forced to retire, often with low incomes and in precarious economic positions. In addition to these victims of rapid change, there were also victims of the collapse of the European empires—refugees from European colonies, war refugees, and those affected by the border adjustments after the Second World War. They too were often in danger of being socially downgraded. These downgrades could have been much worse without the extraordinary economic growth of the 1950s and 1960s as well as the high state revenue and social welfare.

Changes in the Workplace and to Working Life

The workplace changed considerably during the period of prosperity, especially in industry. Setting aside the many jobs that do not transform quickly and limiting the discussion to modern work, it could be said that in the quarter century of European economic prosperity, important elements of industrial work noticeably went into decline. Manual labor that was supported by machines but not structured or replaced by the machines receded. Groups within industrial companies that were relatively self-governed and managed by powerful foremen, who made decisions regarding work management and even about salary and hiring and firing, were increasingly rare. Family-managed work decreased. All this was pushed back by other elements of industrial work, however: complex production with more rigid divisions of labor was on the rise, together with distinct hierarchies that were designated mostly by men. Monotonous assembly line work, considered the most modern form of labor, became more important and considerably reinforced the often clearly visible differences between skilled and unskilled workers, craftsmen, staff, and management levels. Highly organized labor unions and strikes became trends in industrial labor. This hierarchical, rigidly divided, and often so-called Tayloristic industrial labor was in no way new; rather, it had begun during the interwar period. But it was not fully developed until the period of prosperity, when the necessary investments had been made. At the time, this work was often seen as the most conceivably modern labor—the end-all and be-all in the history of labor.

During this period a lifelong, professional career, decided on during school and lasting the next forty or fifty years, prevailed in both the industrial and the service sectors. Social security was also based on this type of career. This professional résumé replaced the less formal moving from job to job among the unskilled, often even the seasonal side jobs for farmers in industry and the temporary work for women before marriage. It also displaced the curriculum vitae of an entire generation who had been thrown off their career tracks, often due to the global economic crisis and the war, and tended to have unusual résumés as a result.

Low Unemployment

One outcome of the economic prosperity of the 1950s and 1960s, an abnormally large demand for workers, resulted in abnormally low unemployment in Western Europe. In some countries, such as France and Great Britain, it had already been low in the 1950s. In other countries, for instance West Germany, it did not fall until the late 1950s. In a few countries, such as Italy, Yugoslavia, and Ireland, unemployment remained high. But in general, unemployment in most European countries had never been as low as at this time (see Figure 2.4). To the extent that comparison is possible, not even the last period of prosperity in Europe—the two decades before the First World War—had seen such a drastic drop in unemployment. These low unemployment rates were also extreme in comparison to non-European national economies; Europe came out on top in comparison to the high unemployment in the US at that time. Europe was not far behind Japan, a model country, and even reached a similarly low unemployment level. Later developments in unemployment were measured against the low unemployment rates of the 1950s and 1960s.

Female Employment

Women's work also changed during this time of prosperity. At first glance, these changes were insignificant: the total number of working women in the 1950s and 1960s in Europe only increased from 33 percent in 1950 to 36 percent in 1970. Two developments account for this slow increase. First, the secondary and university education of women was greatly expanded during this time (see Chapter 12). As a result, women entered the workforce later and the number of young working women sank. Second, at the same time, the development of social welfare slowly began to take hold (Chapter 10), and as the retirement age of women slowly sank, the number of women over 60 in the workplace dropped.

Both developments operated completely differently in the various European countries. They were more than compensated for by a development that shot up women's employment: the number of employed married women and mothers rose sharply at this time. Women increasingly worked not only before marriage or because they were unmarried, but now also during marriage.

This development is most apparent in the professional résumés of women, which can generally be tracked only roughly, without consideration for part-time work and promotion opportunities. The working lives of women clearly shifted between 1950 and 1970 (see Figure 2.2), albeit with significant national differences, which will be addressed later in the chapter. In the early 1950s, many women pulled out of the workforce after marriage to care for their small and school-aged children; only a small number returned to professional life after this. Only about two-fifths of women stayed gainfully employed, and they increasingly left the workforce after the age of 50. In contrast, around 1970 young women under 20 were working noticeably less because they were in school longer, after which more of them remained employed. At this point, almost two-thirds of women between 30 and 50 were employed. For the first time employment was normal for this stage of life. Women aged 60 and over left the workforce more often in 1970 than in 1950, as care for the elderly, includ-

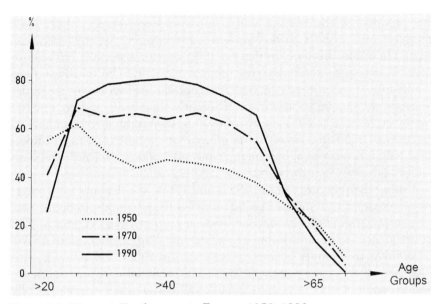

Figure 2.2 Women's Employment in Europe, 1950–1990
Source: ILO, *Economically Active Population: Estimates 1950–2010*, 5 vols (Geneva 1996), vol. 5, 79.

ing pension funds, had greatly improved (ILO 1997, vol. 5: 80; see Figure 2.2).

The Decline of the Family-Run Business

The huge demand for laborers during the economic prosperity led to the decline of the family business. The European economy was made up of two parts in the nineteenth and early twentieth centuries, the so-called dual economy. Its first component, modern, individual wage labor, dominated in industry and in most of the service areas. It was increasingly bureaucratic, industry-determined for quite some time, overwhelmingly male, and orientated to individual accomplishment and lifelong careers. The social relationships between employees essentially depended neither on family nor ethnic group nor regional origin. The weighty role of unions had made strong national social security and national industrial relations a part of this modern wage labor since the pre- and interwar periods.

Alongside this, the second component of family business continued to exist, governed by the previously described and completely different rules. These two economic sectors were, as Burkhardt Lutz argued, closely connected with each other. Family businesses did not merely consume the products of the modern employment and conversely deliver their products and services to the modern economic sectors; they also sent their workforce, primarily in times of prosperity or seasonally but also for several years at a stretch, into the modern economy. The transition from family business to wage pay had its price and quite often meant social descent, as the qualifications for social ascent were missing and because the family business, if it was kept up as well, took substantial time and effort. In times of economic crisis the traditional family business was an important buffer, however, taking the unemployed workforce from the modern sector and carrying it through to the next economic upswing.

During the prosperity of the 1950s and 1960s, the demand for workers was so great and the modern welfare state so attractive that in many parts of Europe family business declined, and with it the dual economy. The consequences were drastic but remained invisible until the late 1970s. The buffer that family business represented in times of economic crisis was irretrievably gone. Unemployment hit the social state and the newly formed unemployment insurance hard, and partly as a result continually increased after the 1980s (Lutz 1984).

The Division between Working and Not Working

During the prosperous period of the 1950s and 1960s, the line between working and not working altered radically. Of course, not everything changed: employment was still regarded by Europeans as the focal point of their lives. A career remained central for personal development, societal contacts, prosperity, and social security.

On the other hand, what did change was the period in which Europeans pursued gainful employment. The number of hours worked per week in the industrial sector (for other areas of the economy there are no comprehensive European data) in Europe fell, according to estimates by the ILO, from an average of about 46 hours per week in 1955 to about 42 in 1970. This development could not be clearly observed in the 1950s, since in some European countries the weekly number of hours worked fell while in other countries, like Great Britain, France, and Czechoslovakia, they increased. It was not until the 1960s that the number of work hours dropped everywhere in Europe (see Figure 2.3).

The use of time after work changed as well. Leisure time was often used as a time of regeneration before working again, as in many jobs the intensity and tempo of labor increased. The commute to work often became longer. Increasing consumption also occupied more time, not only for the purchase of consumer goods but also for the care and repair of houses, cars, and appliances. Educational requirements increased: not only per-

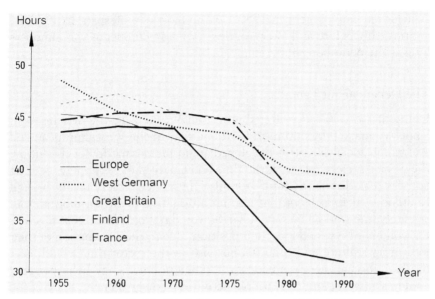

Figure 2.3 Industrial Weekly Work Hours in Europe, 1955–1990
Source: *ILO Yearbook* 1957: 189ff.; 1963: 266ff.; 1971: 468ff.; 1978: 328ff.; 1987: 676ff.; 1992: 730f.
(The European average is calculated from this data, which includes only some of the European countries and changed, and as such should be interpreted with caution.)

sonal continuing education claimed time, but the ever-longer education for children often also required support from parents.

In relation to the year, the number of weeks worked decreased after the 1950s and 1960s. This was not a completely new development (Maddison 2001: 347), but for the majority of Europeans the interruption of work for two or more weeks a year for the purpose of a holiday trip did not begin until the 1960s. Before this, vacations to spas, the seaside, or the homes of relatives in the countryside were more a part of the middle-class lifestyle.

In relation to lifetime, the division between working and not working became also much clearer after the 1950s for the majority of Europeans. On the one hand, as already mentioned, not only women in Europe, but also European men were entering the workforce increasingly later. In 1950 over 80 percent of Europeans started working before the age of twenty; by the late 1970s less than half began so early. This did not mean that the Europeans worked any less at this age, but the work was usually a part of their education or training, which consisted of considerably more learning material and more difficult exams. On the other hand, Europeans were retiring earlier because of better pension systems for the elderly. In 1950 close to half of Europeans were still working after the age of sixty, compared to only one-third by the late 1970s (ILO 1986, vol. 4: 26).

Altogether, employment in 1950 took up most of a lifespan. In 1970, by contrast, life before and after working for many Europeans was almost as long as the period of gainful employment.

The Debate about Labor

In the first two decades after the Second World War, the debate about labor was marked by optimism for the future. In the West, European and Australian social scientists developed an auspicious model for the future: the service society, which at the time had emerged in only a few societies but was regarded as the future for all. The service society meant an end to arduous manual labor, but also an alternative to tiring, monotonous assembly line work. The service sector would not only be seen as recourse for workers who would lose their positions due to the automation of their jobs in agriculture and industry, but also as the sector that would meet the basic human needs of education, religion, emergency help, personal contacts at work, and recreational activities. The greater the share of the workforce employed in this sector, the more humane the society would become. The most important ambassador of this model in Europe was Jean Fourastié, who titled his book *The Great Hope of the 20th Century* (Fourastié 1949; see also Häußermann and Siebel 1995). In the 1960s and 1970s this model was broadened into models of progress that incorporated other dimensions of labor, such as the emergence of office work, process-controlled production, economic and societal planning of new information technology, and fundamental alterations in societal and political power. The American sociologist Daniel Bell was the most famous author to develop such global labor models for progress (Bell 1990).

Labor after the 1970s

Labor in Europe changed dramatically after the 1970s. These changes were ambivalent, making the last quarter of the twentieth century seem in part economically difficult and in part dynamic. This epoch was difficult primarily because of growing unemployment and increasingly irregular employment résumés in which gainful employment was interrupted by unemployment, continuing education, career change, or family leaves of absence. It was a dynamic era because it brought about the transition to a service society but also because of the development of women's employment into modern-day lifelong employment. The terms that society used to express perception of change also altered: much of what was viewed in the 1960s as modern labor has been seen as traditional since the 1990s.

Rising Unemployment

Rising unemployment heralded an era of economic difficulty. Unemployment increased in Western Europe primarily after the late 1970s. It rose in the European Union from 6 percent in 1980 to 7 percent in 1990 and 8 percent in 2000, and was even a bit higher at times: 8 percent in 1985 and 9 percent in 1995 (OECD 2000: 42ff.; see Figure 2.4 for all of West Europe). Not only did it grow during every economic lull; it also was no longer relieved during times of economic upswing. Unemployment became a fixed element of everyday life in the eastern part of Europe following the upheaval of 1989–91. In most countries it affected young adults more than older adults. In some European countries women were more affected than men, though the statistics are sometimes difficult to decipher, as women are less likely to file for unemployment than men (OECD 1999: 46ff.). The growing unemployment was also tied to a slow increase or even stagnation in real wages, at least within industry (Mitchell 1993: 185ff., 843f.).

This increase in unemployment was owed to a combination of factors: a decline in agricultural and industrial employment, changing résumés as well more frequent transitions between different jobs, and new com-

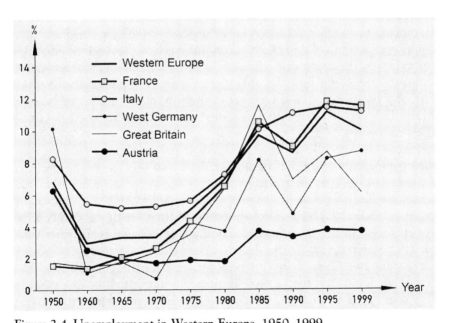

Figure 2.4 Unemployment in Western Europe, 1950–1999

Sources: for 1950, B.R. Mitchell, *International Historical Statistics: Europe, 1750–1988* (Houndsmills 1992), 162ff. (not completely comparable with the following data); for 1960–99, OECD, *Historical Statistics*, different editions, graph "Unemployment."

petition from mostly Asian industry and service companies. The new expectations placed on the modern welfare state and its unemployment insurance, and the altered life plans of women, who no longer left the job market if they became unemployed, played a role, as did the previously mentioned decline in family business.

The Workplace and the Résumé

The workplace also changed work life in several ways after the 1970s, whereby again, only the change in cutting-edge technology was taken into account and not the average workplace. Greater flexibility in automated production allowed the production of large series of similar products on the production belt to shift to a new variety of products. The elaborately organized, divided labor production with routine, uniform tasks on the conveyer belt made way for a somewhat larger variety of tasks, performed individually as well as in groups. The clear lines of division between those employees who were better paid, performed individual tasks, and had more favorable working conditions, and those workers with uniform jobs who enjoyed less prestige and less favorable working conditions in the workplace, faded along with the strict hierarchies of command. More work dealt with the development, adjustment, and inspection of extensive automated production facilities. Labor-saving technologies, in particular computers, were used in industry, economic services, and public administration. New demands were made of employees: flexibility, commitment, innovation, and ingenuity became more important than punctuality, loyalty, and obedience. These changes in the workplace did not all happen in the 1970s, but began earlier in some instances and in others not until the 1980s and 1990s.

These changes all influenced the employment résumé. Lifelong employment with a one-time training at the beginning went into decline. Changes in occupational activity, due to regularly occurring new and additional training as well as temporary unemployment or employment pauses, increased. The level of school and career qualifications rose in general. The future of individual employment became increasingly unclear. Long-term employment decreased and fixed-term contracts became more common. These changes were controversial among social scientists. Some predicted that the normal, lasting, uninterrupted professional life was coming to an end and would be replaced by frequent professional reorientation, additional training, and time-outs. Other social scientists forecast that the irregular résumés would remain a minority in the future as well. In any case, the public social security system was faced with new challenges, as until then it had functioned on the assumption of regular employment résumés. In many European countries, this also weakened unions because they likewise depended on lifelong careers and long-term memberships in the trade unions (see Chapter 9).

Service-Oriented Society

The employment structure in Europe changed fundamentally after the 1970s. The era of the industrial society approached its end as industrial labor, no longer the most common occupation, faced persistent decline. Industrial productivity increased so rapidly that production continued to climb even as employment simultaneously dropped. Europe became a service-oriented society (Figure 2.1).

Two areas accounted for this expansion of employment in the service sector: economic services such as banking and insurance, along with self-employed attorneys, engineers, and architects; and civil services. Service occupations were no longer exclusively urban but expanded into rural areas as well. They also gave new impetus to the professionalization of white-collar jobs. Industrial employment did not disappear completely, however. Even after the 1970s industrial jobs were important in Europe and remained an important target for economic policy. Industrial settlements were critical instruments of economic reconstruction in the formerly communist parts of Europe after 1989–90. Service-oriented society was not implemented rapidly everywhere in Europe, but by 2000 every European country was predominantly a service-oriented society.

Dynamics of Female Employment

Lastly, female employment eventually also became more dynamic in the last quarter of the twentieth century. Despite economic difficulties, it continued to increase after the 1970s. Between 1970 and 2000 the percentage of gainfully employed women in Europe increased on average by 36 percent to 43 percent. This trend can be seen more clearly in graphs showing the life work of women. On average, only two-thirds of women between the ages of 20 and 50 were employed in 1970, whereas in 2000 about 80 percent of all female Europeans were employed. These levels approached those recorded among men, of whom up to over 90 percent were employed, more clearly than in the 1950s and 1960s, though women's résumés were still usually shorter. Women were entering professional life increasingly later, after longer and better training and education. A growing majority of women worked until between the ages 50 and 60. As mentioned previously, they also retired earlier from working life (ILO 1997, vol. 5: 80; see Figure 2.2).

Divergences

As in the case of the family, there were considerable differences among European societies with regard to labor. In the second half of the twentieth century, the differences concerning women's jobs, and furthermore, differences between the center and periphery, the free-market West and the communist East, and various business cultures were especially pronounced.

Female Employment

The differences in female employment did not primarily depend on business culture or the general state of economic development, but much more on familial models, social security, and educational and employment policy. Patterns of women's employment can be distinguished in four regions of Europe.

In the first region, the eastern, communist part of Europe before 1989, female employment had already rapidly increased in the 1950s and 1960s. Here an overwhelming majority of women were employed, in higher proportions than in all of the Western European countries, as the labor-intensive planned economy required a substantial workforce. However, and just as in other European areas, women remained behind men in income and career opportunities. Specialized résumés developed very early: women frequently went to work immediately after school, before the age of twenty, as the educational sector was no longer rapidly expanding. They rarely interrupted their careers to be mothers, as the care of small children was ensured. They also continued working into older age because retirement pay was low.

A second region of female employment was Northern Europe, especially Scandinavia and Great Britain, where female employment was more common than in other countries in Western Europe. It increased more slowly than in Eastern Europe, however, and was connected more with governmental policies of full employment than with an economic labor shortage. In the 1990s female employment in this region was as common as male employment, but résumés looked much different from those of their counterparts in Eastern Europe: the employment of women from youth to young adulthood declined more as education and training were extended, and professional life ended earlier because the modern welfare state was being built up—in Scandinavia even more so than in Great Britain.

The third region included Southern European countries such as Italy, Spain, and Portugal. In these countries female employment likewise increased after the 1960s but essentially only during the period before marriage. The number of working women between 20 and 50 years old grew very slowly and did not exceed more than two-thirds of women. In Turkey not even half of all women worked, and female employment remained far lower than in almost all other European countries. Only a few wealthy countries such as the Netherlands, Luxembourg, Austria, and Switzerland had similarly low rates of female employment.

The fourth region of women's employment was made up of the wealthier continental Western European countries like France, the former Federal Republic of Germany, and Belgium. Here, as in Northern Europe, the increase in the number of women entering the workforce before marriage lagged because of the extension of education. The number of women in the workplace after marriage increased in contrast to the southern part of Europe, though more slowly than in the North. Women also left professional life earlier because of the development of the welfare state.

The differences between these four regions diminished near the end of the twentieth century. Female employment increased throughout Europe as social security, training, and familial models in the different countries became more similar (ILO 1997, vol. 1: 197, vol. 4: 50ff.).

Divergences between the Center and the Periphery

The working world was marked by clear distinctions between the economically dynamic center of Europe and the periphery in the South, East and far North. Labor was in high demand in the center of Europe, whereas unemployment dominated in the peripheral countries. Until the 1970s the center and the periphery of Europe had also differed in industrial work, which was the biggest employment sector in the dynamic parts of Europe but remained considerably less significant in the outer countries of Europe. Professional résumés also differed: in the central part of Europe not as many youth and young adults were working because their education tended to last longer than that of their counterparts in the peripheral countries. As a result, millions of Europeans from the peripheral countries immigrated to the central countries. This migration reached a high point in the 1950s and 1960s (see Chapter 7). These extremes certainly did not emerge in the second half of the twentieth century but had already formed during the industrialization of the nineteenth century. They lingered until the 1960s as industrial work in the center of Europe experienced a kind of second boom in the flourishing mining, iron and steel, chemical, and electronics industries, and experienced a new surge in the expanding automobile industry. However, with the implementation of service-oriented work and reduction of the extremes between the center and the periphery of Europe, these differences gradually weakened after the 1970s.

Divergences between Western Europe and Communist Eastern Europe

A third divergence of labor emerged between the Western European free market economy and the state-run planned economies in the Soviet sphere of influence after the Second World War. In Eastern Europe, labor looked considerably different from its Western European analogue. New forms of labor were centrally planned and implemented according to the Soviet model and under considerable pressure from above. The industrialization and implementation of industrial labor were among the central goals of this economic planning. In contrast to the West, in countries that were already industrialized, like the GDR or Czechoslovakia, the industrial economy was completed and the missing industrial branches—for example, the iron and steel industries in the GDR—were developed. The model of the industrial economy remained the main goal, even after the service sector gained the upper hand in Western Europe as of the 1970s. Czechoslovakia and the GDR were industrial societies in which nearly half of those employed worked in the industrial sector, and they remained such until 1989–90.

In Eastern Europe, industrialization was implemented in a more labor-intensive economy and with less productivity growth than in Western Europe. Because the demand for labor was always sizable, there was often less pressure to perform well in the workplace than in Western Europe. As the labor requirements were not met by immigration from other countries as they were in Western Europe, they were met from the beginning of industrialization, as mentioned earlier, by drawing on another large workforce: women. Among the many special traits of Eastern European labor was a stronger workplace-centered society. Services that were normally found in residential areas in Western Europe were often offered at or through the workplace: day care, canteens, holiday programs, continuing education, visits to the theater and concerts, health care, at times even the sale of consumer goods. The workplace, with its work groups called "brigades," was thus different from Western Europe workplaces and more than just a place of work. The residential area by contrast was less important. Eastern Europe also officially had no unemployment. Of course, these differences should not be overly simplified. There were also differences in labor within the Western free market economies as well as among the economies in Communist Europe, but the East-West extremes ran deep.

These differences did not simply disappear in 1989–90, but they did change rapidly. The transformation crisis after 1989–90 did not bring about any changes that had not already taken place in Western Europe. The shrinking of industrial labor, the increase in unemployment, the disintegration of tight social connections in the workplace, and the precarious footing of female employment were common developments in Eastern and Western Europe. As a rule, this occurred much more quickly in Eastern Europe after 1989–90; however, the transformation was less socially secured and therefore also more brutal. The changes were thus much more of a shock in Eastern Europe than in Western Europe.

Differences among Western European Businesses

A fourth divergence emerged among Western European nations regarding the management of businesses. For the period after the 1980s, labor sociologists differentiate between the strongly bureaucratized French businesses, with weak unions, a strict command hierarchy, and company-related education and career training; the informal Italian businesses with a Taylorist organization of labor, hierarchically structured but with education and career training that are not tied to the company, and weakened unions; the consensus-driven Swedish businesses with strong cooperative unions; the not consensus-oriented British businesses with unions that were fragmented and weakened by the Thatcher era and an educational system focused on general education as opposed to career training; and finally, the German businesses built on technical competence, with strong, cooperative unions and well-developed career training (Heidenreich 1997, 2004).

Other sociologists do not consider the diversity to be quite as broad, but rather see the key differences as lying between the Anglo-Saxon and the Continental European businesses. Anglo-Saxon businesses operated, it is argued, within liberal free market economies whose educational systems primarily provided general knowledge and deregulated job markets that left business with considerable control. They were oriented toward short-term profit and a competitive transfer of technology. Continental European businesses, especially Scandinavian, Swiss, Austrian, Dutch, Belgian, and German, as well as Northern Italian and French businesses in part, in contrast operated within coordinated free market economies with educational systems that trained specialized personnel. They drew up detailed agreements with trade unions and within the participatory board. Their investment decisions were more oriented toward the long term. Their technology transfer was based on networks between businesses, research institutes, and universities.

These two types of Western European businesses had different advantages for the globalizing world market. Anglo-Saxon businesses were able to react more flexibly and could market successful inexpensive products and services to the world market. The Continental European businesses' advantages lay in the global market for quality products and services that could only be generated with a socially secure, highly qualified workforce. Soskice argues that these differences, which developed among businesses in the 1980s, were critical for European societies because the Western European nation-states lost more deciding power. Their economic, welfare, and educational policies had increasingly less impact and, in the era of globalization after the 1980s, at best only influenced economic development in terms of local investment advantages for business (Hall and Soskice 2001; Soskice 2005: 170f.).

Convergences

Along with these divergences, however, two important convergences developed in the second half of the twentieth century. The first important convergence reflected the easing of the contrast between central and peripheral Europe. The former contrast between predominantly agricultural labor in the peripheral South, East, and North, and the predominantly industrial labor mostly in the wealthier European countries diminished as agriculture was modernized everywhere and as a result abated in the peripheral countries as they industrialized and expanded service-oriented labor. This pattern prevailed throughout Europe. Compared to industry, the nature of service-oriented labor caused fewer regional extremes. At the same time, the contrasts in the education and training of the workforce also diminished. The number of illiterate people in the workplace in peripheral countries decreased significantly, and personnel with secondary education became more common. Immigration from Spain, Portugal, Ireland, Southern Italy, and Greece also went down as a result. The former European periphery became a destination for non-European peripheries (see Chapter 7).

A second fundamental convergence of labor in Europe set in after the upheaval of 1989–90. As already mentioned, the differences between East and West did not disappear immediately because labor in the postcommunist countries was in the middle of a transformation crisis. But these new differences were also dwindling by the beginning of the twenty-first century. Industry's negative growth was no longer as rapid, and unemployment was no longer generally higher than in Western Europe. The Czech Republic with 4 percent and Hungary with 10 percent unemployment were already better off in 1997 than the Western European average. Even the postcommunist countries with higher unemployment, like Poland with 11 percent, were not in as bleak a situation as Spain with 21 percent or Belgium with 13 percent unemployment (OECD 1999: 45).

Hallmarks of Labor in Europe

Despite all the differences within Europe during the second half of the twentieth century, the work environment as a whole was different from that in non-European societies in many ways.

European Industrial Labor

One important European trait was the extent of industrial labor in Europe. Only in Europe did industry become the largest employment sector for a specific period, during the 1950s and 1960s, and for differing lengths of time depending on the country (see Figure 2.1). Thus, the development from an agricultural to an industrial and then finally to a service-oriented society, known in textbooks as the Fourastié or Fisher/Clark Model, occurred in Europe alone. Even after the 1970s, when Europe became a service-oriented society, the unique size of the industrial labor force was preserved. In 1990, 36 percent of the gainfully employed were still working in industry throughout Europe, whereas in Japan it was 34 percent and in the US only 26 percent (ILO 1997, vol. 4: 213ff.; OECD 1999: 42f.). Outside of Europe industrial labor increased during industrialization, but it almost never became the biggest employment sector, whether in more prosperous countries like the US and Japan or in newly industrializing countries such as China, India, and Brazil.

Not every European country followed the Fourastié Model, however—notable examples being the Netherlands, Norway, Denmark, Ireland, Greece, and Portugal. Even in France, where the model was developed, there were no specific periods of industrial society. Overall, however, these countries were exceptions among overwhelmingly industry-oriented European activity. This activity existed in Eastern Europe as well and remained there even longer than in Western Europe.

How can this European peculiarity in the history of employment be explained? An initial factor was the long tradition of the role of Europe as the workshop of the world. Not only did industrialization begin particularly early in Europe; Europe also continuously exported industrial and commercial goods to non-European economies and thus captured a strong industrial position in the world economy that it held onto until the second half of the twentieth century. This intense export activity created more industrial jobs in Europe than anywhere else.

Furthermore, historical factors accounted for the industrially intense labor in the nineteenth and early twentieth centuries. An unusually massive nineteenth-century emigration out of Europe spared European cities the inflated, traditional, often precarious service sector of small retailers, restaurant and stall owners, and merchants. The already-mentioned later age of marriage allowed for a large reservoir of single, mobile young adults, which made it much easier to find workers for the location-bound industries of the nineteenth and twentieth centuries. The European consumer's strong preference for non-standardized, individually rather than mass-produced goods, which could be produced only through relatively high exertion from workers within industry and commerce, was also among these factors, which created more jobs in the industrial sector. All of these factors ebbed during the second half of the twentieth century, which also explains why this European particularity no longer clearly existed by 2000 (Kaelble 1989).

Less Female Employment in Western Europe

A second characteristic within European labor was the lower female employment in comparison to other industrial nations, but also in comparison to the newly industrializing country China. This European trait first developed in the 1960s and 1970s, when female employment in Europe increased more slowly than anywhere else. In 1990 only 40 percent of women worked outside the home in Western Europe (more specifically, in France, Germany, Belgium, the Netherlands, Luxembourg, Austria, and Switzerland), and in Southern Europe only 35 percent did, in comparison to 47 percent in the United States and Russia and even 55 percent in China. Despite the comparatively high level of female labor in Eastern and Northern Europe, at 41 percent, Europe as a whole trailed behind other industrial countries and Eastern Asia. Only in Japan, with 41 percent, were women's jobs so similarly limited. In Latin America, Muslim countries, and India, however, female employment was far more limited (ILO 1997, vol. 1: 47ff.; vol. 4: 47ff.; vol. 5: 46ff.).

This deficit in Europe compared to other prosperous societies is not easy to explain. It had in part to do with the particularly long education of European young women and their later entrance into professional life. The European welfare state and the highly developed pension system also played a role. Women also gave up employment at an earlier age than in other places. These explanations are not enough, though. Even during the professionally active ages of 20 and 60, female employment was established more slowly than elsewhere. In 1990 a quarter of the women in Western Europe and close to a third of the women in Southern Europe remained inactive in the work force (ILO 1997, vol. 4: 47ff.). The model of the pure housewife and mother that was developed among the Western European middle class in the nineteenth century seemed to have found its way into the second half of the twentieth century and was only reluctantly given up by European families and European policy. In non-European industrial countries, such models seem to have lost attractiveness more quickly. Meanwhile, the marginal development of the service sector in Europe, which as a rule offered the best job market for women, could have also limited the spread of female labor.

Clearer Division between Working and Not Working

The comparatively slow increase in female employment is only one aspect of a sharper division between working and not working in Europe. This European peculiarity also consisted of the extraordinarily distinct expansion of not working in the form of leisure time or activity outside the job. The reduction in weekly work hours proceeded considerably further in Europe than in large non-European industrial societies and in newly industrializing countries. Most distinctive was the difference from the United States. In 1950, the US was, for many European tourists, still an envied paradise of prosperity where less working time generated higher salaries. The average workweek within industry in the US was about 40 hours. According to data from the ILO, Europeans in comparison were working an average of 46 hours per week. Not one European country was close to the US workweek—not even the wealthy countries that had been spared by the war, like Sweden and Switzerland. This pattern held throughout the 1970s. Thereafter, however, work hours within industry in Western and East Central Europe were on average shorter than in the US. In 1990 the European average weekly working time was 35 hours whereas in the US it was similar to most countries in East and South Asia—still around 40 hours a week. Only a few European countries had a workweek similar to that in the US (see Figure 2.3).

Life as a whole was more clearly divided in Europe between working and not working. Professional life did not last as long as in other industrial countries or in the newly industrializing countries. On the one hand, Europeans started working later in life: in 1990 only one-third of Europeans between the ages of 15 and 19 were employed, as opposed to half in North America and nearly two-thirds in East Asia. On the other hand, Europeans also left professional life earlier. In 1990 only about half of those between the ages of 55 and 59 who were able to work were employed in Europe, as opposed to two-thirds in the US and East Asia; between ages 60 and 64 it was only one-fourth in Europe versus one-half in the US and East Asia. As a result, a fraction of the gainfully employed population in Europe remained nearly stagnant between 1950 and 1990, increasing only from 46 percent to 48 percent. Europe was outpaced by both North America and East Asia, where the percentages increased from 43 percent to 51 percent and from 44 percent to 53 percent, respectively. Europeans did not work as much as North Americans or East Asians (ILO 1997, vol. 5: 35ff.; OECD 1999: 38; Conrad 1992).

References

Bell D. "Die dritte technologische Revolution und ihre möglichen sozialökonomischen Konsequenzen." *Merkur* 44 (1990): 28–47.

Blackman J. *Economic History of Women in England, 1879–1980.* Hemel Hempstead 1992.

Conrad C. "Old Age in the Modern and Post-Modern World." In *Handbook of the Humanities and Aging,* ed. T. Cole et al. New York 1992, 72–97.

Dewerpe A. *Historie du travail.* Paris 2001.

Ehmer J. "History of Work." In *International Encyclopaedia of the Social and Behavioral Sciences,* ed. N.J. Smelser and Paul B. Baltes, vol. 8. Amsterdam 2001, 16569–16575.

Fourastié J. *Le Grand Espoir du XXe siècle: Progrès technique, progrès économique, progrès social.* Paris 1949.

Frevert U. *Frauen-Geschichte.* Frankfurt a. M. 1986.

Hall P.A. and D. Soskice, eds. *Varieties of Capitalism: The Institutional Foundations of Comparative Advantage.* Oxford 2001.

Häussermann H. and W. Siebel. *Dienstleistungsgesellschaften.* Frankfurt a. M. 1995.

Heidenreich M. "Beschäftigungsordnungen zwischen Exklusion und Inklusion: Arbeitsmarktregulierende Institutionen im internationalen Vergleich." *Zeitschrift für Soziologie* 33 (2004): 206–227.

ILO. *Economically Active Population, 1950–2010.* 5 vols. Geneva 1997.

International Labour Office (ILO). *Economically Active Population: Estimates 1950–1980.* 5 vols. 3rd ed. Geneva 1986.

Kaelble H. "Was Prometheus Most Unbound in Europe? The Labour Force in Europe During the Late 19th and 20th Centuries." *Journal of European Economic History* 18 (1989): 65–104.

Kocka J. *Arbeit früher, heute, morgen: Zur Neuartigkeit der Gegenwart, in Geschichte und Zukunft der Arbeit,* ed. J. Kocka and C. Offe. Frankfurt a. M. 2000, 476–492.

Kocka J., ed. *Work in a Modern Society: The German Historical Experience in Comparative Perspective.* New York 2010.

Lutz B. *Der kurze Traum immerwährender Prosperität- eine Neuinterpretation der industriell-kapitalistischen Entwicklung im Europa des 20. Jahrhunderts.* Frankfurt a. M. 1984.

Maddison A. *The World Economy: A Millenial Perspective.* Paris 2001.

Marchand O. and C. Thélot. *Le travail en France, 1800–2000*. Paris 1997.

Mitchell B.R. *International Historical Statistics: Europe, 1750–1988*. 2nd ed. New York 1993.

OECD. *Historical Statistics* (annual publication).

Salais R., B. Reynaud, and N. Baverez. *L'invention du chômage: Histoire et transformation d'une catégorie en France des années 1980*. Paris 1986.

Soskice D. "Varieties of Capitalism and Cross-National Gender Differences." *Social Politics* 12 (2005): 170–179.

Therborn G. *European Modernity and Beyond: The Trajectory of European Societies 1945–2000*. London 1995.

Van der Ven E. *Sozialgeschichte der Arbeit*, vol. 3: *19th and 20th Century*. Munich 1972.

Whiteside N. *Bad Times: Unemployment in British Social and Political History*. London 1991.

Chapter 3

CONSUMPTION AND STANDARD OF LIVING

Consumption, standard of living, and lifestyle in the everyday life of Europeans changed like no other area of social and cultural history during the long period of peace and economic growth in the second half of the twentieth century. What average Europeans ate and drank, how they lived and dressed, relaxed and traveled, how healthy they were and how educated, how high their standard of living was, and how it improved altered dramatically over the last forty to fifty years of the century. Consumption worked its way into politics and stabilized the Western democracies; it strengthened communist regimes in the beginning and destabilized them in the end. Consumption was always a central theme in public debates about progress and the dangers of modernity. The US model was simultaneously more attractive and more controversial in the history of consumption than in any other area of social and cultural history. The second half of the twentieth century cannot really be understood apart from the history of consumption and standard of living.

State of Research

The history of consumption and standard of living in the nineteenth and twentieth centuries is at once one of the oldest and one of the newest topics within social and cultural history. The first great social history debate in the 1960s was about the standard of living in England—during the industrial revolution, however, not the twentieth century. After a long pause, during which it became more of a theme within the early modern period, interest in the history of consumption in the twentieth century increased. Relevant scholarship included an interesting new survey of Europe by Heinz-Gerhard Haupt (Haupt 2003), an analysis of the Americanization of European consumption by Victoria de Grazia (de Grazia 2005), and a historical account of mass culture by Kurt Maase (Maase 1997). In addition to these, national overviews on the history of consumption were published in several European countries (Becher 1990; Benson 1994; Alonso and Conde 1994; Wildt 1994; Schildt 1995; Tanner 1996; Merkel 1999; König 2000). Each of these accounts is different from the chapter at hand: they are not limited to the second half of the twentieth century and usually only address Western Europe. As of yet, a survey of the far-reaching changes in consumption and standard of living since the Second World War is lacking.

Four questions are examined with regard to the second half of the twentieth century. First, the research examines the mass consumption society in Europe after the Second World War and deals with its aftermath in terms of the standard of living, lifestyle, consumption norms, and discourses. More than in other areas of European social history, the question is whether this upheaval of consumption came to Europe from outside sources, i.e., through "Americanization." The second issue examined is whether the developments within the standard of living and consumption in the second half of the twentieth century were actually a history of progress in material living conditions or whether the quality of consumption and of life suffered. Third is the question of divergences and convergences between the individual European countries and the European particularities of the mass consumption society. The fourth and final issue that is explored is the topic of social disparity within consumption and the standard of living—the social divisions that were drawn through consumption and lifestyle and that, with the development of mass consumption, were partly reduced and partly maintained in another form. The first three of these issues will be covered in this chapter; the fourth issue, regarding the social differences in consumption, will first be dealt with in Chapter 5, on social milieus.

The Emergence of Mass Consumption

The emergence of mass consumption was the most important change in the history of consumption during the second half of the twentieth century. It penetrated all societies in comparable ways, led to similar improvements and costs, was advanced by similar forces, and also mostly encountered similar resistance. The United States was singled out in this historical process because the transition to mass consumption had already taken place there in the 1930s and 1940s. In Western Europe this transition was not completely restricted to the second half of the century either. The signs of mass consumption that were already visible during the interwar period were in part specifically European ones and in part an effect of the mass consumption that was already apparent in the US. But impoverishment after two world wars prevented mass consumption from being established in the main part of Western Europe until the 1950s and 1960s, and it reached the eastern and peripheral parts of Europe only in the 1970s and 1980s.

Five basic developments distinguish the establishment of mass consumption in Europe, as elsewhere. First, the basic nature of the majority of consumer goods changed with the emergence of mass consumption. Individual consumer products that were handmade with little help from machines retreated behind standardized, industrialized consumer products. Not only did the method of production change, but also the ways the consumers handled the product. Consumers could no longer so intensively place their preferences in the selection of products or services, but rather were only able to choose between different standardized classifications by parameters such as size, color, smell, taste, or quality. Even time was standardized, whether for the speed of cars, timetables for public transportation, or the hours of operation for stores and banks. During the infancy of mass consumption selection was still very limited, and as a result the transition to standardized goods was an especially big step. The computer-controlled production and service of the 1980s and 1990s, even with complex products such as cars.

Second, modern mass consumption also meant an international and social standardization of consumption. National and regional traits in consumption were stripped away. Mass consumption emerged from national markets. An international "one market" developed, whether through the worldwide reduction of external tariffs according to the framework of GATT, through transnational economic markets such as the European Single Market or NAFTA, or through the invention of transnational consumers such as those in Europe. Products that were originally symbols of a national consumer culture entered the international market and became an integral component of the consumption of other nations.

Modern mass consumption also particularly meant a shedding of the social distinctions that existed between the bourgeoisie, petit bourgeoisie, and working class, as well as the lower rural class and the rural aristocracy. Consumer items that originally held importance as symbols of social milieu became part of the unified mass consumption. Cars, televisions, cosmetics, gowns and suits, living room and nursery, vacations to Italy—all things that were originally instruments of middle-class social distinction—became goods of mass consumption. Soccer games, lard, schnapps, eat-in kitchens—originally symbols of proletarian culture—also became products of mass consumption and accepted by higher social strata. The social differences between city and country, which remained considerable into the early twentieth century, also significantly disappeared with the breakthrough of modern mass consumption. The pressure to conform in the individual milieus and nations was, in many cases, diminished by an individualistic style of consumption. Economic disparity, which will be further explored in Chapter 6, became less noticeable in daily life.

Social distinctions were certainly still expressed through consumption. But the social differences were subtler: they no longer lay in owning a car, but in what model, no longer in traveling abroad, but on the destination, no longer in a living room with a corner sofa, but in the brand of the furniture and the pictures. Some of the wealthy in Europe withdrew from ostentatious public consumption. The fine differences in consumption transformed in part to a secret code for insiders, to symbols within group identities that could no longer be recognized by outsiders. New subtle social distinctions, such as differences between generations, age groups and life phases, ethnic groups, and political milieus, as well as those within the upper classes, the economy, and the academic milieu, were erased by consumption.

A third important feature of the establishment of mass consumption was the change in private household expenses. These changed because on the one hand income soared, particularly in the 1950s and 1970s, and on the other hand the prices of many agricultural and industrial products fell due to an extraordinary increase in productivity. The percentage of private household expenses devoted to food and clothing declined for these reasons. These costs lost their dominant role and left considerably more room for other household expenses (see Figure 3.1); hence the share of income allotted to household appliances and entertainment, transportation, education, living, vacation, and recreation increased proportionately.

Fourth, the breakthrough of modern mass consumption was connected to the commercialization of consumption. The relationship between consumers and the producers of consumer products changed because of this. Above all, consumers' direct contact with producers of goods, such as the farmers at the local markets and the craftsmen in their shops, dwindled away to a large extent. The production of goods within the home, particularly of food and clothing, was driven back by products made outside the home like canned goods, frozen foods and TV dinners, and meals served in fast food restaurants and office, factory, and school cafeterias, as well as by the manufacture of clothing. The familial way of life and privacy changed with this. Eating meals together as a family was no longer as common. On the other hand, products such as furniture, radio, television, and record and CD players strengthened the realm of family and privacy.

Changes in the trade of consumer goods were a further significant contribution to the commercialization of consumption. Trading firms concentrated operationally as well as spatially and became large-scale enterprises. Supermarkets and warehouses sprang up inside and outside city centers, primarily because of the transportation revolution. The clientele of the warehouses expanded. Mail-order companies tapped into a broad mass of customers. Commerce no longer reacted only to consumer wishes but created new consumer groups like children, youth, or singles, and new markets, for instance tourism and do-it-yourself products. Commerce influenced customers with new tools such as marketing, opinion surveys, advertising, and new sales methods. It secured continuous demand through ever changing fashions and the planned obsolescence of goods.

Fifth and finally, the discourse about and attitude toward consumption fundamentally altered. The media in which this discourse took place also changed: it was conducted not only in newspapers, brochures, and discussions but also on the radio, television, and Internet—and only then did it reach a large portion of the population. Advertising acquired an intensity and accuracy that would have been inconceivable before. The image of consumers was transformed. The clear gender differences that shaped advertising before the establishment of mass consumption blurred. The segmentation of customers into social milieus likewise decreased within advertising; rather, an international type of customer was created, and national prejudices were evoked less often.

Furthermore, the debates about consumption changed. In the 1950s and 1960s, visions of a future of unmitigated buying bliss, satisfaction of consumer tastes, and free consumer choice were propagated and discussed throughout Eastern and Western Europe in different ways. At the same time, mass consumption and the American model were strongly criticized. Pessimistic fears regarding the freedoms of the individual, as well as the much remarked-on lifestyle and consumption of intellectuals and the educated class, played a big role. Both perspectives gradually changed after the 1970s and 1980s. The optimistic visions for the future lost their attractiveness in the face of the limits of growth, finite energy supply, and endangered environment, as well as imminent new epidemics and growing unemployment. The term *mass* consumption, which had fundamentally resonated with the pessimistic critique of consumption, gradually receded and made room for the critique of consumer *products*. Criticism about consumption concentrated more and more on questions as to the quality of products: whether they were good for one's health, conserved the environment, and saved energy.

Ultimately, the attitude toward consumption altered. Material consumption, along with internal and external security, was considered a high priority among Europeans into the 1960s and 1970s. This had to do in part with a return to normality after the hardships of war and the immediate postwar period, and in part to the opening of a completely new world of consumption to many people from the middle and lower classes thanks to rapidly increasing income, which improved nutrition, clothing, dwellings, and leisure activities in an unprecedented way. This consumer euphoria was often tied to traditional European values such as frugality, the reuse and repair of goods, and aversion to consumer credits and disposable products. These values had been cultivated in the earlier European economy of scarcity and material want during the economic crisis and war, as well as during the postwar period, and were reinforced by the traditional malnourishment in some peripheral regions of Europe. Even in the boom they were not given up so quickly. Consumption patterns were still strongly tied to social milieus. The concept of "materialistic values" (see Chapter 4) only inadequately reflects this attitude toward consumption.

During the course of the 1970s and 1980s these attitudes changed gradually. Along with the fulfillment of material consumer preferences, opportunities for political and personal development gained a higher priority, as did human relationships. The concept of "postmaterialism" (see Chapter 4) does not quite capture this attitude because it was not a renunciation of material needs. The *individualization* of lifestyle was also part of the change in attitude toward consumption. It benefited from two developments: the newer, greater, but not uncontroversial freedom of the individual that came about from the decline of spending constraints on the food and clothing that were necessary for existence; and the diminishment of ties to social milieus, along with their consumer constraints and requirements for food, clothing, habitation, and travel.

These changes in attitude toward consumption were often perceived in Europe as a contrast between generations. The older generation was often still influenced by the deprivation that had lasted through nearly twenty years of global economic crisis, world war, and postwar recovery. Although this generation was fascinated by the new mass consumption and the jump in standard of living, it considered mass consumption as something extraordinary and retained a basic skepticism that was expressed through pessimistic criticism of consumption, and through traditional frugality. The younger generation, in contrast, grew up with consumption and the standard of living of the 1950s and 1960s. To them, being a consumer no longer meant struggling for scarce consumer goods but instead referred to choosing from a surplus of goods and getting the best possible quality for the best possible price on one's own limited budget. It also meant being entertained by ever more elaborate advertising without being overpowered by it. Consumption was admittedly limited for this generation due to the constraints of the traditional energy supply, growing pollution, increasing unemployment, and the limits of the welfare state. The conflicts with the older generation were often severe, and the contrasts between the generations' experiences of consumption were greater than ever before or since.

Improvement in the Standard of Living after 1945

Along with the establishment of mass consumption, an additional significant topic during the second half of the twentieth century was development in the standard of living. At first glance, the question as to whether the standard of living improved during this time seems easily answered. The Europeans' social situation improved impressively during these fifty years of economic prosperity, peace, international economic opening, social reform, and medical advances. No other period of European history boasts such an increase in the standard of living. This change was especially felt in those countries that suffered destruction and the collapse of normal accommodations during the war. But whether the standard of living was continuously and in all areas improved, and whether the quality of life continued to increase, are in no way as clear.

Income

Private consumer spending, which the OECD has evaluated for Western and Central European countries since 1960, is strong evidence of the improvement in the standard of living in the second half of the twentieth century: it climbed continuously in Europe throughout that period, though the increase did slow after the 1970s. The growth of actual income in Eastern Europe was more restrained before the oil crisis, yet according to evaluations by the OECD it increased drastically in the 1980s, often shrank during the transformation period, and did not increase again until afterward (OECD 1997: 58; OECD 2000: 56; UN 1992: 293).

Changing Household Expenditures

Whether the standard of living improved for Europeans depended not only on the level of income, but also on what and how much was obtained for the money. The question here, then, is whether average Europeans were consistently required to spend their income largely on vital necessities like food, clothing, and housing, or whether part could also be used for other necessities like social security, health care, education, culture, and individual self-development. If ever there was an era in which a transition from having to meet the most important of life necessities to having freedom to shape an individual life was to be experienced by the majority of Europeans, it was the second half of the twentieth century, with its huge increase in income. Did the private expenditures for vital necessities like food, clothing, and habitation actually go down during this period, thus resulting in more freedom for the fulfillment of other necessities?

The share of expenses for food and clothing fell noticeably after the 1950s. The decrease in the expenditures for food is particularly impressive. In 1950, private households in the Western part of Europe spent

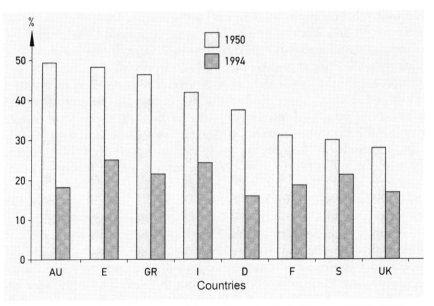

Figure 3.1 Food Expenditures for Private Households in Europe, 1950–1994
(Food expenditures as percentage of household expenses)
Sources: for 1950, A.S. Deaton, "The Structure of Demand 1920–1970," in C.M. Cipolla, ed., *The Fontana Economic History of Europe*, vol. 5 (Glasgow 1976), Figure 4 (selection: all large countries and smaller countries with extreme value in terms of food); for 1994, Eurostat, *Consumers in Europe: Facts and Figures* (Luxemburg 2001), Figure 1.14; the figure uses license plate country codes.

38 percent of their budgets on food, in 1970 the percentage was still 31 percent in the former EC, in 1979 it was 26 percent, and by 1994 it was 19 percent, only half of what it had been in 1950. Similar trends can be found in the eastern part of Europe. In Hungary, for example, the percentage of food expenditures fell from 39 percent to 27 percent between 1960 and 1989. In the GDR the percentage for blue- and white-collar households fell from 49 percent in 1961 to 41 percent in 1985. Meanwhile, there were great differences between the individual countries of Western Europe: in wealthy countries, food costs in private households were much less onerous than in poorer countries, in the 1950s as well as the 1990s. Yet there was no European land in which the percentage of expenditure for food did not drop considerably (see Figure 3.1; Andorka 1992: 87; Schwartau and Vortmann 1989: Figure 4). As a result, the European household was considerably less burdened.

Similarly important was the reduction in household costs for clothing. In 1950 private households in Western Europe spent an average of 13 percent of their budgets on clothing, in contrast to the EC in 1979 with just 9 percent and in 1994 only 7 percent—just over half of what it had been in the 1950s. Significant differences were not discernible between the individual countries in Western Europe. In the long run, the period after the Second World War was therefore a clear break. The percentage of expenditures for essential goods in private households had never before sunk so quickly nor disposable income been so available.

Admittedly, this is not the entire picture. The costs of other essential goods and services, above all for housing but also for transportation and health care, did not go down in any way. To the contrary, they rose markedly in all European countries after the Second World War. In 1950, private households in Western Europe spent just 7 percent of their budgets on rent (excluding heating), in 1970 the percentage had reached 11 percent in EC countries, in 1979 it was 20 percent, and in 1994, 25 percent was spent on housing, including electricity and heating—exponentially more than in 1950 (see Figure 3.2). These numbers do exaggerate the increase a bit, due to change in the definition of housing costs. But the burden that housing costs imposed on private households increased considerably. The increase was not the same in all countries, but there was no country where the cost of housing did not increase. This trend seemed, however, not to have occurred in the eastern part of Europe before 1989. In Hungary and the GDR, for example, the percentage of expenses for housing was kept at the low level of 4 percent through governmental subsidies. In Western Europe such proportions were common in 1950.

Like the cost of housing, the cost of transportation also climbed. The percentage of the household budget allotted to transportation was 11 per-

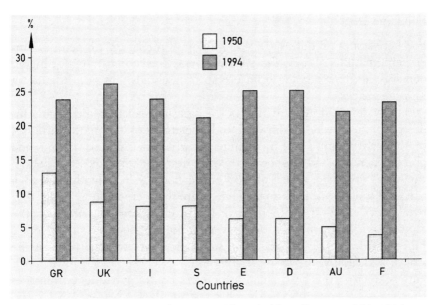

Figure 3.2 Housing Expenses for Private Households in Europe, 1950–1994
(Housing expenses as percentage of household budgets)
Sources: for 1950, A.S. Deaton, "The Structure of Demand 1920–1970," in C.M. Cipolla, ed., *The Fontana Economic History of Europe*, vol. 5 (Glasgow 1976), Figure 4 (selection: all large countries and smaller countries with extreme value, based on housing); for 1994, Eurostat, *Consumers in Europe: Facts and Figures* (Luxemburg 2001), Figure 1.14; the figure uses license plate country codes.

cent in 1970 for EC countries, increasing to 13 percent in 1979 and 15 percent in 1994—again with marked differences between the individual countries. This share rose in the eastern part of Europe as well; in Hungary, for example, it went from 4 percent in 1960 to 9 percent in 1988 (Deaton 1976: Fig. 4; Eurostat 1977: 164f.; Eurostat 1985, vol. 1: 94ff., vol. 2: 160ff.; Eurostat 2001, Fig. 14.1; Andorka 1992: 87; Schwartau and Vortmann 1989: Fig. 4).[1] What Europeans saved on food and clothing was consumed for the most part by the rise in costs of habitation and transportation. The latitude for nonessential necessities had in reality increased only to a limited extent.

Improvement in the Core Areas of Consumption

A complete picture of the quality of the standard of living cannot be taken from private household expenses. Three other areas central to consumption should also be singled out: food and diet, housing, and health care.

Food and Diet

Food consumption during the second half of the twentieth century fundamentally differed from that of earlier eras due to better supply, higher demand, and outsourcing from private households, but also because of new drawbacks.

The widespread malnutrition of the agrarian society and the early industrial society were left far behind. Deficiencies of important nutrients, particularly vitamins and trace minerals, which had shaped the pre- and postwar periods, had disappeared. Apart from the direct postwar period, there was no longer a lack of food or a deficiency in individual areas of the food supply within Europe. There were three crucial reasons for this: the historically unusual increase in the productivity of agriculture; the rapidly continuing internationalization of the food supply for the average European, including imports from subtropical and tropical parts of the world; and finally, the new pressure group composed of nutritional scientists, doctors, teachers, social insurances, and reformed food industries that pressed for healthier foods. The food supply was better, broader, and more diverse than ever before.

Demands regarding the quality of food also increased. Expectations of the processing, refinement, and aesthetic appearance of food and its packaging grew. Behind this lay not only the sublimation and aesthetization of consumption—the new expectations in the appearance of products were also connected with the fact that consumers rarely bought now from the producers at markets or directly at the farm, but through a complicated network of distribution. Because of this they needed new references regarding the quality of the product. The product label or store chain, as well as the product's appearance, was increasingly viewed as a decisive clue to the quality of the product. Advertising increased these expectations of quality and appearance even more.

Decisions about the preparation of food were also relocated outside the sphere of private households more than in earlier periods. Fewer Europeans were eating their main meal at home, and more instead chose in canteens, cafeterias, or fast food restaurants. Meals within private households as well more often consisted of partially or fully prepared, canned, or frozen foods. Institutional kitchens and the food industry increasingly influenced what and how Europeans ate.

The change in diet also had its disadvantages. The unusual increase in agricultural productivity and the food industry depended largely on the massive use of fertilizer, pesticides, and veterinary drugs, leading not only to damage to the soil, rivers, and sea but also to poisonous chemical residues within the food itself. Additionally, there was the danger of supernutrition with all its risks and consequences. High amounts of sugar, fat, and calories in general, as well as the increasing intake of alcohol and nicotine, led to physical damage and illness. Life expectancy therefore did not increase as much as the advances in the supply of food could have allowed. General nutritional knowledge clearly lagged behind the state of nutritional science. Private households, industrial kitchens, and the food industry rarely took advantage of the diversity within the food supply, and day-to-day meals long remained more monotonous, nutrient-poor, and thus also more unhealthy than necessary. Overall, however, in comparison to the malnutrition during the agricultural and early industrial societies, the advances without a doubt outweighed the disadvantages.

Housing

The quality and security of housing likewise improved during the second half of the twentieth century. The quality of apartments rose significantly. In the southern and eastern parts of Europe during the immediate postwar period, only some apartments had access to electricity, fresh water and drainage systems, and toilets and bathtubs. This standard of living, which had been reached earlier in Northern and Western Europe, largely became the norm throughout Europe over the course of the second half of the twentieth century.

The size and use of housing units also improved, and the number of dwellings increased considerably in most European countries. The everyday stress of high-density housing environments was thus clearly reduced. The number of inhabitants per dwelling noticeably sank after the Second World War. At the end of the century every European, statistically speaking, had a room of his or her own. Europeans also lived in increasingly roomier spaces and could develop more within their housing. An individual private sphere in housing opened up not just for the upper classes but also for average Europeans. At the same time, many apartments had just one or two rooms, which meant that an increasing number of singles had a better chance of having their own, self-contained dwelling place.

Housing security also improved noticeably, meaning it was protected from termination of lease or a forced change of apartments. The percentage of homeowners, whose housing security was particularly high, increased in most European countries. At the same time, tenancy law in many countries was significantly changed in favor of the tenant.

For many Europeans the selection of apartments expanded with the expansion of automobile use. The high number of Europeans living outside of cities of over a million inhabitants profited the most from this.

This improvement certainly also had its disadvantages, the most important constant problem being that the housing market did not substantially ease up as a whole. Housing remained expensive, and an increasing percentage of people's growing income had to be spent on housing, though there were periods of less strain on the housing market and more affordable prices. Additionally, reasonable housing was easier to find in economically weaker regions of Europe, where some units were even destroyed due to vacancy. But in the dynamic, attractive regions and metropolitan areas of Europe, the housing situation remained strained throughout the entire second half of the twentieth century.

Furthermore, the automobile revolution was not without disadvantages. The spatial concentration of shopping centers and schools and the greater distances between home and work led not only to higher costs for transportation but also to more time spent in cars or public transportation on the way to work, school, public offices, and shopping. Social isolation among housewives in commuter towns, workers during their commute, children when not in school, and the elderly grew extensively. What the Europeans gained in quality of housing, individual privacy, development, and security, they paid for with money, time, and energy. Growing social isolation was not uncommon, yet in the end progress won out here as well.

Health Care

Health care likewise improved considerably in Europe during the second half of the twentieth century. Private and public expenses for health care increased markedly. According to data from the OECD, health expenses multiplied between 1970 and 2000 in most Western European countries. They also grew proportionately to gross national product. In 1970, the expenses were still between 4 percent and 6 percent in Europe; by 2000, however, they were between 8 percent and nearly 10 percent (OECD, according to Eurostat 2002: 397ff.). During this time of limited public budgets, public expenditures for health care increased more slowly than private expenditures and also developed inconsistently. In most countries they increased and were higher than in wealthy non-European countries. But they also sank in some countries, such as Denmark, Sweden, Ireland, and Italy. The health care system expanded as a whole, and the number of doctors and pharmacies increased in most countries. The number of practicing doctors in proportion to the population doubled or tripled in the time between 1970 and 2000 alone. The market for pharmaceutical products also expanded. Medical progress drastically cut the amount of time patients spent in the hospital, in some countries by half and in others down to even a third. As a result, hospital beds were overall noticeably reduced in proportion to the population (Eurostat 2002: 319ff., 330ff., 354ff.).

Life Expectancy

As a result of the huge private and public expenses for health care, but also thanks to medical innovations and improved nutrition and housing, the kinds of terminal illnesses Europeans suffered also changed. Europe, like North America and Japan, entered into the third phase of epidemiological transition during the second half of the twentieth century, leaving the first two phases behind. In the first phase, already long past, plagues and famine had been responsible for the deaths of many Europeans and life expectancy was very short; in the second phase, pandemics and infectious diseases decreased and the death rate was lower. In the third phase, degenerative diseases, in particular circulatory illnesses and cancer, were the leading causes of death. But many Europeans also died from illnesses that had to do with lifestyle, i.e., the use of alcohol, tobacco, and other drugs, as well as environmental contamination and traffic accidents (Eurostat 2002: 266ff.).

Life expectancy increased with the improvement in the standard of living. The European average (excluding the Soviet Union) between 1950 and 2000 increased from 69 to 79 years for women and from 62 to 73 for men. This development was more rapid than in the US, but slower than in Japan (see Table 3.1). Life expectancy in Europe was consistently longer than in the Arab world, South Asia, Latin America, or Africa, as well as in comparison to Turkey and the USSR or CIS. This continuous increase was among the unspoken expectations of Europeans of this era. Most assumed they would live longer than their parents and grandparents provided there was no war.

European life expectancy did not, however, unusually increase during the second half of the twentieth century, as one would have expected given the massive growth of real income and educational opportunities (see Chapter 12). In most European countries it was the first, not the second half of the twentieth century that was the period of substantial increase in life expectancy. In the first period life was extended on average about twenty years (aside from the Soviet Union), though a bit longer for women than for men. In the second half, by comparison, it was extended by only an additional ten years. This image of a slower development in the

Table 3.1 Life Expectancy for Men and Women at Birth, 1900–2000

		1900	1950	1960	1970	1980	1990	2000
Europe	M	46	64	68	69	70	72	73
	W	48	69	73	75	77	79	79
Western Europe	M	47	65	68	69	71	74	75
	W	50	70	73	75	78	80	81
Japan	M	44	62	67	71	74	76	77
	W	49	66	72	76	80	82	84
US	M	48	66	67	68	71	72	74
	W	51	72	74	75	78	79	79
USSR / CIS	M	31	61	63	64	63	61	60
	W	33	67	71	74	74	73	73
Turkey	M	—	42	51	56	60	65	67
	W	—	45	54	60	65	70	72

M= Men; W=Women

Source: for 1950–2000, unless otherwise noted, United Nations, ed., *World Population Prospects: The 2000 Revision*, vol. 1: *Comprehensive Tables* (New York 2001), 74ff. (respective average of five-year interval after the given date, for 2000 the average of the five years before); for 1900, *UN Demographic Yearbook 1948* (New York 1949), 514ff. (Belgium, Bulgaria, Denmark, Finland, France, Italy, the Netherlands, Norway, Austria, Russia, Sweden, Spain, Czechoslovakia, USA); *UN Demographic Yearbook*, special issue: *Population Aging and the Situation of Elderly Persons* (New York 1993) (Germany 1900, GRD 1950–1980, GDR 1950–1980, Ireland 1900, Switzerland 1900, Czechoslovakia 1950–1990, Hungary 1900); Flora, *State, Economy and Society 1815–1975*, vol. 2 (Frankfurt 1987), 96ff. (Germany, England and Wales, Ireland, Switzerland). For "Europe": average of European countries; 1950 is slightly overstated as some countries with lower life expectancy are missing.

second, mostly war-free half of the century remained unchanged, whether looking at the life expectancy of 20-year-olds or 60-year-olds.

The history of life expectancy took an unexpected turn in the eastern part of Europe: it sank. After the 1980s, life expectancy in Russia was shortened by four years for men and one year for women. Life expectancy also dropped somewhat in Bulgaria, Romania, and Hungary for men and stagnated in Czechoslovakia and Poland. In contrast, life expectancy continuously increased throughout Western Europe from decade to decade. This was also true for Turkey (see Table 3.1). The crisis within the communist regimes during the 1980s and the profundity of the transformation in the 1990s led to deterioration in health care, a decline in social security, and increases in poverty, poor nutrition, and alcoholism. Why this downturn affected men in particular and not every Eastern European country must examined more closely.

Divergences and Convergences

Did the advent of mass consumption lessen the differences between European countries or create more? Was a new variety of national styles of consumption established, or did a new European common ground or even European hallmarks emerge?

Divergences

Throughout the history of European consumption during the second half of the twentieth century, there emerged a multitude of national, regional, and local choices of consumption with regard to food and beverages, clothing and housing, and daily routines. These cannot be further explored here, but four important divergences stand out above all.

The first new divergence, which affected contemporary Europeans deeply, even though it vanished again quickly, was between the wealthy countries that had not been affected by war—such as Switzerland, Sweden, and to a certain extent, England with its empire—and those prosperous countries that had been impoverished by the Second World War. This difference was clearly apparent directly after the war, not only with regard to the standard of living but also in the establishment of leading products of mass consumption. However, this divergence had mostly disappeared by the 1950s and 1960s.

A second difference, which had already existed in the nineteenth century, lay between the industrialized, wealthy, modern countries of Europe, where mass consumption was quickly established, and the less industrialized and poorer countries in which mass consumption as a rule spread more slowly. In the 1950s and 1960s, gaping differences still characterized the establishment of leading goods of mass consumption such as cars—larger differences than those today between the wealthier and poorer parts of the world. At that time France and Great Britain were the most motorized countries in Europe with 37 and 42 automobiles per 1,000 people respectively, much more so than industrialized countries affected by the war such as Germany and Austria, with 6–7 cars per 1,000 people. The number of automobiles was even lower in the poorer peripheral countries. In Greece, Yugoslavia, and Hungary there was only 1 automobile per 1,000 people. The differences were similarly large with regard to other important products of mass consumption such as refrigerators, telephones, radios, televisions, and furniture (Deaton 1976: 102ff.; Eurostat 1977; Eurostat 1985; Kaelble 1997: Figure 1-3; Eurostat 2001). Such clear differences were also considerable in Eastern Europe between the wealthy East Central European countries and the low-income USSR (Figure 3.3).

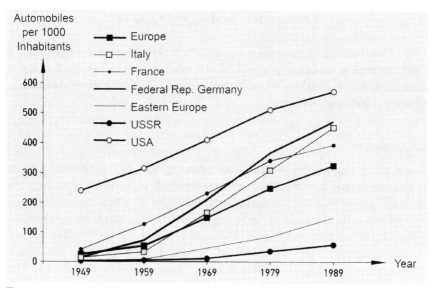

Figure 3.3 Automobiles in Europe, the US, and the USSR, 1949–1989
(Automobiles per 1,000 people)

Source: H. Kaelble, "Europäische Besonderheiten des Massenkonsums, 1950–1990," in H. Siegrist, H. Kaelble, and J. Kocka, eds., *Europäische Konsumgeschichte: Zur Gesellschafts- und Kulturgeschichte des Konsums (18. bis 20. Jahrhundert)* (Frankfurt a. M. 1997), Figure 1.

A third difference in consumption that lasted longer, with deeper effects, was the divergence between Western and Eastern Europe. Before 1989 the eastern part of Europe was not just a delayed consumption society: it followed its own, ultimately regime-forced path to more consumption. Mass consumption was established later; this was true for the spread of cars (see Figure 3.3), refrigerators, washing machines, and televisions (see Chapter 9), as well as the already mentioned changes in household expenses, the reduced contact between consumers and producers, and the spatial and operational concentration of businesses with consumer goods.

Mass consumption looked fundamentally different in Eastern Europe. The state-run supply of consumer goods was not subject to market forces, with the exception of the limited approved rural and handicraft businesses and the more marginal *dacha* production. At first, consumption policies in Eastern Europe held the view that forging their own anti-capitalist path would create a new people, but later the desire to outpace or at least catch up with the consumption standard of the West prevailed. New social inequalities in consumption that were unknown in Western Europe resulted from the privileges held by the milieus close to power regarding the supply of consumer goods.

Additionally, consumption played a special role in the stability of the regime in Eastern Europe. The government aroused high expectations with promises to outpace the standard of living in the West. Unlike in the West, basic goods such as food, housing, and mass transit were highly subsidized. Consumption policies increasingly spiraled into an unstable vicious circle. Subsidization so strained Eastern European economies that many investments could not be made. As soon as subsidization was limited and prices rose, the public protested, having expected the promised improvement in consumption. Investments had to be further deferred, and the quality of the products sank. The way out through investment in the form of credit from the West only led to large debts to the West. In the end, this vicious circle was pivotal to the internal loss of trust in, and collapse of, the regimes.

This divergence between Western and Eastern Europe largely disappeared after the collapse of the Soviet empire. But during the transformation crisis that followed, noticeable differences in consumption and standard of living persisted into the 1990s.

A fourth difference, little researched but often discussed, was between the North and South of Europe. It is difficult to determine exact borders, however. The basic elements of this difference were: more travel by citizens in the North versus more sociability and openness of consumption on the local scale in restaurants, cafes, and bistros among citizens in the South; a special style of housing and furnishings in the North versus the refinement of food and clothing in the South; favoring of home ownership and single homes in the North versus a preference for a rented house in the city center in the South. Many individual goods were also consumed differently—beer in the North, wine in the South; butter and cream in the North, oil in the South; short midday meal and long nights in the North, long midday break and short nights in the South. These differences, as little researched and blurred as they are, also lessened in the second half of the twentieth century, however.

Convergences

Along with these divergences, many distinct convergences with regard to consumption also developed after the 1950s throughout Europe. Such convergences could be found in three categories.

First, many of the divergences discussed above lost their momentum, even if most did not completely disappear. The differences in the aftermath of the war were only temporary and had disappeared by the 1950s and 1960s. Even the stark differences between the wealthy industrialized and poor agricultural parts of Europe were reduced toward the end of the century. The divergences in private household expenses were less severe, especially the expenses for food and housing (cf. Deaton 1976: Figure 4; Eurostat 1985; Schwartau and Vortmann 1989: Figure 4; Eurostat 2001: Figure 14.1; Andorka 1992: 87). The differences in the consumption of the leading consumer goods at the time—automobiles, telephones, radios, televisions, and refrigerators—became much less apparent, especially in the 1980s and 1990s. Just one example was the automobile: around 1990 the countries with the highest density of cars per person, Italy and Germany, had just four times as many cars per person as the country with the lowest density of cars, Poland. In Western Europe the percentage of cars per person was little more than twice that in Eastern Europe (Kaelble 1997). The key countries France, Great Britain, and the former Federal Republic of Germany had already drawn closer to each other in the 1950s and 1960s with regard to consumption (Haustein 2007). This stripping away of differences took place in all industrialized countries, not just the European ones, but it was carried out particularly quickly and completely in Western European societies. The differences between Europe as a whole and other wealthy countries even increased for a time (variation coefficient according to OECD 1982: 14ff.; OECD 1992: 18ff.).

Second, a strong interconnection between the European countries engendered a number of convergences. The selection in supermarkets, furniture stores, warehouses, and restaurants became Europeanized. More and more goods—food, clothing, automobiles, and televisions—came from other countries. The internationalization of consumption that could also be observed in all industrialized countries was primarily a Europeanization of the selection of goods for European consumers. Of course, certain spectacular US goods such as Coca-Cola, jeans, Hollywood films, and fast food restaurants, and certain Japanese products including televisions, CD players, radios, and cars, as well as non-European restaurants and tourist destinations were also part of European consumption. This, however, did not change the dominance of imported goods from European countries, European restaurants, and travel within Europe. There emerged a completely international range of products with multilingual packaging and instructions, to which almost every European country contributed. A European, or rather Western European, consumer was thus created, who accepted European and not just national goods.

Additionally and third, the sense of national differences in consumption also changed. Along with the fully international products, the international market offered Europeans products made in other countries of Europe and labeled so as to indicate their origin with distinct national flair—often contrived by innovative designers, marketing strategists, or restaurant owners. Swedish furniture was sold under Swedish names along with Swedish food. Italian pizzerias were to connect the non-Italian consumer with a taste of Italian life. Creperies, croissanteries, and baguetteries were designed to introduce a French dining experience in city centers and train stations. This placement of national products on the European market meant a complete turnaround for the significance of nationality in consumption. Whereas until the first half of the twentieth century the national pattern of consumption was used primarily for separation from foreigners and for securing a national identity, it tended to change in the second half of the century to a sales strategy toward other Europeans. Consumption lost its role of separation from "the other," and instead became an incentive for access to others, even if this access was often a construction of advertising and marketing and not an actual experience of a different culture. Simultaneously, European consumption homogenized because these national products were sold throughout Europe.

These convergences and Europeanizations of consumption had several causes. The first was the reduction that set in after the 1960s of the extremes between wealthy European countries and the formerly poorer peripheries that had become ever more defined in the nineteenth century. Private incomes differed less among the different European countries, and did so particularly quickly in the Western part of Europe (OECD 1982: 14ff.; 1992: 18ff.). Another reason was the creation of the European consumer market. On the one hand, it was purposely planned with the establishment of the European Community, and later the European Union, by the European governments. On the other hand, European companies seized the opportunity of a common market to gradually create standardized European consumer products and services. The third factor was the expansion of the geographical horizon of personal experience for the average European, in particular after the 1960s. Tourism, business trips, sister city initiatives, student programs, and sometimes intermarriage heightened familiarity with different European countries' consumption to an unprecedented extent for a growing number of Europeans, who then took on consumer patterns from other countries.

European Hallmarks

During the second half of the twentieth century, European hallmarks of consumption were much less visible in comparison with non-European societies than were those of the welfare state, migration, or values. Worldwide trends prevailed in the establishment of mass consumption and the global integration of consumer product exchange and consumption patterns. Nevertheless, consumption and the standard of living still differed somewhat between Europe and other industrial societies in the second half of the twentieth century. Admittedly, these European characteristics are disputed. Some contend that the same worldwide trends and changes took place in Europe and everywhere else. It has also been argued that the Americanization of European consumption wore down any characteristics it had had during the inter- or even postwar period, and that this Americanization was the only real European commonality.

Americanization

The extent of the Americanization of European consumption is debated. Without a doubt, the US pioneered mass consumption. Many developments took place earlier in the United States because the standards of living and consumption were much higher than in Europe. Private households' expenses for essential goods such as food and clothing as a share of the budget dropped much earlier. The new forms of diet—TV dinners, cafeterias, and fast food restaurants—modern housing, and the mobility allowed by the automobile were established much earlier. Because of this, contemporaries perceived European development in large part as imitative of the US model.

Specific American products and styles such as Lucky Strike, Coca-Cola, rock and roll, cartoons like Mickey Mouse, movies and television, novels and nonfiction books, supermarkets, salons, car washes, burger restaurants, and computers conquered the European market. This Americanization did not occur all at once at a zero hour right after the Second World War, but rather reached its full extent in the 1970s.

To be sure, the US model was a central symbol for both proponents and opponents of mass consumption in Europe. "Americanization" was among the key terms used in contemporary criticism of the mass consumption society. But looking back, it is still a misleading simplification to speak of a complete Americanization of European consumption. Modern mass consumption had both European and American roots. The automobile was invented in Europe and was already an integral part of the streetscape during the interwar period. The commercialization of consumption via warehouses and the food industry also began at the same time as in the US, in the nineteenth and early twentieth centuries. Several European variations of fast food vendors such as sausage booths, snack bars, creperies, pizzerias, and *döner kebab* booths were already so widespread that the European criticism of American fast food was surprising to many. Most of the fundamental developments that were often characterized as Americanization after the Second World War had already been established in Europe and, speaking broadly, would most certainly have taken place without the American precursors if Europe had not been impoverished by the two world wars.

Furthermore, the consumption of US products was also ultimately quite limited in Europe. The bulk of European consumer goods were produced in Europe. Many products were imported from East Asian countries, though without talk of an Asianization of European consumption. The most popular products of modern mass consumption, such as automobiles, furniture, refrigerators, televisions, telephones and mobile phones, and record and CD players, did not usually come from the US. The small proportion of American products on the European consumer market was not just a matter of cultural limits and the massive intellectual criticism of American products and sales methods in Europe. Much more pivotal was that Europe had already developed a consumer goods industry that was raring to go after the Second World War and that quickly expanded on the European market after the 1950s.

Conversely, the American lifestyle also Europeanized. European products penetrated the American market after the end of the Second World War—the VW Beetle, European wines and cheeses, clothing and furniture, and specialty restaurants started by European immigrants. It is without doubt, however, that European products did not modernize the American lifestyle as American products modernized the European lifestyle. Nor did they generate fears of modernization or fantasies about cultural repression. The Europeanization of the US is thus not often discussed. "Americanization" was a part of the process of the *reciprocal* permeation of Western Europe, or Europe, and the US by the 1960s at the latest.

Consumption within a Particularly European Context

Despite all the common global or Atlantic trends, the structures of consumption in Europe were different from those in other industrialized countries.

European Style and Variety of Consumer Products

The most noticeable distinctions of European consumption in the second half of the twentieth century concerned a uniquely European taste and individuality of design. This taste differed from preferences in Japan, the US, or Russia. This common European style extended to a vast variety of goods. The countless breads, cheeses, sausages, wines, clothing fashions, furniture and architectural styles, and luxury products in general could be traced back to the Europeans' strong traditional need to emphasize the regional and national as well as the distinctiveness of occupational, religious, ethnic, and social milieus. These historical reasons have certainly lost some force. But the remarkable variety of European consumption remained, though often changed, processed, and marketed; it was greater than in the United States, Japan, and the Soviet Union and fulfilled Europeans' need to be individually unique.

Among these distinctions of European consumption was the European vacation culture, which expanded particularly fast after the Second World War. Europeans developed a different attitude toward work and free time compared to the Japanese or Americans. Whether throughout the day, week, or especially the year, Europeans began to spend a greater proportion of their time outside the workplace after the 1950s and 1960s. The holiday tourism that brought millions of Europeans onto the streets and into trains and planes not only contributed to the considerably stronger integration of European countries after the Second World War, but also took place at a volume never matched by non-European industrialized countries, allowing for a completely new business sector in the service area. It formed an outside image of the mountainous and seaside regions of Europe and led to a special European yearly rhythm in life and familial interaction.

Priorities in Consumption

A second European distinction consisted in private household expenditures, in particular in comparison with the US. Private households in Europe spent more on food and clothing and less on transportation and communication (Herpin and Verger 1988: 108ff.). Compared to Americans, Europeans owned fewer leading products of modern mass consumption such as automobiles, televisions, or telephones (for automobiles see Figure 3.3). Conversely, more books were produced in Europe than in the US (Kaelble 1997: Figure 4). There was indeed a common trend regarding mass consumption in Europe and in the US, but European-American differences definitely remained, particularly in the areas of food, clothing, housing, communication, and transport.

These special priorities in European consumption cannot be explained by income level, as the differences in income between the US and wealthy European countries have become irrelevant in the past two decades. Thus, US consumption did not simply develop further. The differences in consumption had other causes, having to do with European family and labor, with the lower number of working hours in Europe, with the somewhat smaller percentage of employed women and therefore greater importance of the home as the center of their lives, and the intense seclusion of the family from the outside, all of which explain the higher expenses for furniture and housing in Europe. The European-American difference in consumption was also connected to the different European use of space and the higher density of residents in European cities. European households therefore spent less on transportation, automobiles, and communication. But these differences between European and American consumption also had much to do with the enhanced development of the public welfare state and municipal public utilities in Europe, which will be further explored in Chapters 10 and 11. Because of these, expenses for social security, health, education, and transportation were greatly reduced for European households. Finally, the differences may also relate to the still remaining significance of social distinction in Europe and consequent social demarcations via clothing, food, interior design, and reading, which continue to be strong.

European Roots of Mass Consumption

A further European hallmark is evident more in comparison to Asian, Latin American, Arab, and African countries. In contrast to its onset in these societies, mass consumption in Europe did not assert itself as a foreign model that threatened the traditional way of life. Seeing mass consumption as a pure "Americanization" was much less of a reality in Europe than in Japan, India, or the Arabic world.

Discourses about European Consumption

The discourses on consumption into the 1960s across all political camps were more skeptical and critical in Europe than in the US. These European intellectual discourses cultivated a European self-perception in which Europe was set apart from American mass consumption in a positive manner and the European elite seemed more detached from consumption and more idealistic than its American counterpart. In this view, mass culture had less of an influence in Europe, the need to conform was weaker, and individualism and social hierarchies were in less danger from mass consumption than in the US. These discourses tapered off around the 1970s after mass consumption took hold in Europe, whereupon the intellectuals also accepted and took advantage of it. The strong skepticism regarding consumption still remained in Europe, however. It shifted from a basic criticism of mass consumption to a particularly intense European discussion about the quality of mass products in terms of nutrition, environment, health, and enjoyment (Kaelble 1997).

Notes

1. Measured for different expenses: 1950 for 13 countries: Austria, Belgium, Denmark, Finland, France, Germany, Greece, Ireland, Italy, Netherlands, Spain, Sweden, and Great Britain; 1970 for the 9 and 1980 for the 10 member states of the EC; 1994 for

the 15 EU member states. The numbers would change little, however, if each country were looked at respectively.

References

Alonso L.E. and F. Conde, *Historia del consumo in España: Una aproximación a sus origins y primer desarrollo*. Madrid 1994.

Andorka et al. *Social Report*. Budapest 1992.

Becher U. *Geschichte des modernen Lebensstils: Essen—Wohnen—Freizeit—Reisen*. Munich 1990.

Benson J. *The Rise of Consumer Society in Britain, 1880–1980*. London 1994.

Deaton A.S. "The Structure of Demand, 1920–1970." In *The Fontana Economic History of Europe*, vol. 5, ed. C.M. Cipolla and R. Greaves. Glasgow 1976, 89–131.

De Grazia V. "History of Consumption." In *International Encyclopedia of the Social and Behavioral Sciences*, vol. 4. Amsterdam 2001, 2682–2687.

De Grazia V. *Irresistible Empire. America's Advance Through 20th Century Europe*, Cambridge, MA. 2005

Eurostat. *Soziale Indikatoren für die Europäische Gemeinschaft 1960–1975*. Luxembourg 1977.

Eurostat. *Haushaltsrechnungen: Einige vergleichbare Ergebnisse*. 2 vols. Luxembourg 1985.

Eurostat. *Consumers in Europe: Facts and Figures*. Luxembourg 2001.

Eurostat. *Health Statistics: Key Data on Health 2002*. Luxembourg 2002.

Haupt H.-G. *Konsum und Handel: Europa im 19. und 20. Jahrhundert*. Göttingen 2003.

Haustein S. *Vom Mangel zum Massenkonsum: Deutschland, Frankreich und Großbritannien im Vergleich 1945–1970*. Frankfurt a. M. 2007.

Herpin N. and D. Verger. *La consommation des Français*. Paris 1988.

Kaelble H. "Europäische Besonderheiten des Massenkonsums, 1950–1990." In *Europäische Konsumgeschichte. Zur Gesellschafts- und Kulturgeschichte des Konsums (18. bis 20. Jahrhundert)*, ed. H. Siegrist, H. Kaelble, and J. Kocka. Frankfurt a. M. 1997, 169–203.

König W. *Geschichte der Konsumgesellschaft*. Stuttgart 2000.

Maase K. *Grenzenloses Vergnügen: Der Aufstieg der Massenkultur 1850–1970*. Frankfurt a. M. 1997.

Merkel I. *Utopie und Bedürfnis: Die Geschichte der Konsumkultur in der DDR*. Cologne 1999.

OECD. *Short-Term Economic Statistics: Central and Eastern Europe*. Paris 1992.

OECD. *Historical Statistics: 1960–1980*, Paris 1982; *1960–1990*, Paris 1992; *1960–1995*, Paris 1997; *1960–1997*, Paris 1999; *1970–1999*, Paris 2000.

Schildt A. *Moderne Zeiten: Freizeit, Massenmedien und "Zeitgeist" in der Bundesrepublik der 50er Jahre*. Hamburg 1995.

Schwartau C. and H. Vortmann. "Die materiellen Lebensbedingungen in der DDR." In *Deutschland-Handbuch: Eine doppelte Bilanz 1949–1989*, ed. W. Weidenfeld and H. Zimmermann. Bonn 1989, 292–307.

Tanner J. *Fabrikmahlzeit: Ernährungswissenschaft, Industriearbeit und Volksernährung in der Schweiz, 1890–1950*. Zurich 1996.

UN. *Economic Survey of Europe*. New York 1992.

Wildt M. *Am Beginn der "Konsumgesellschaft": Mangelerfahrung, Lebenshaltung, Wohlstandshoffnung in Westdeutschland in den fünfziger Jahren*. Hamburg 1994.

Chapter 4

CHANGING VALUES AND SECULARIZATION

Changing values have garnered a great deal of public interest in recent history. The referendums on the European Constitution and the Lisbon Treaty, the decision on Turkey's accession to the European Union, the wars in Iraq and Afghanistan, as well as the rise of China, India and Russia generated discussions about the historical roots of European values. The change in religious and political values represented by Muslim immigrants has moved the public as much as the "Silent Revolution" of slow historical value changes, the impact of the 1960s, and the new values within the younger generations.

Attention to changing values has likewise changed in the historiography. Around 1970 value change and religiosity were for the most part not seen as important materials in contemporary history. When gone into at all, trends other than those today were at the fore: the loosening of ties to family and milieu, the break with the older Victorian and Wilhelmine values, and secularization. In the early twenty-first century, in contrast, value changes and religiosity have become standard topics of European contemporary history. Now it is more the undiminished strength of family values, the integration into local networks and the new religiosity that are the focus.

State of Research

A range of international analyses written in recent years has addressed value changes and religiosity in Europe. There is, however, still a lack of overviews on the overall European development. The influential social science studies by Ronald Inglehart (Inglehart 1995, 1997) and Henri Mendras (Mendras 1997) cover neither the entire half century between 1945 and 2000 nor all of Europe. There does exist a whole array of overviews on the history of religion, but either they cover much larger periods of time and cannot intensively respond to the final decades of the twentieth century (Marramao 1996; Rémond 2000; Maurer 2002; van Dijk 2004), or they deal with only Western or Eastern Europe (Pickel 1998; Pollack 1998, 2000).

The fundamental question regarding value change and religiosity was very clearly described in these books and essays, however. The question involves whether during this period there really was a departure from the values of family bonds, from meritocratic values at work, and from loyalties in politics; whether a turning away from primary virtues such as diligence, obedience, and discipline can be observed; whether this was a turn toward secondary virtues like thoughtfulness, tolerance, a sense of responsibility, and self-development; and whether the secularization process actually continued to progress. In addition to this, intra-European divergences are also considered. Can two different sets of values actually be picked out in the Europe of the second half of the twentieth century—a Western European set in which personal development, individual freedom, willingness to take risks, democracy, human rights, and international peacekeeping were increasingly accepted; and an Eastern European set of values in which social security, public order, a higher standard of living, and fear of hegemony and of loss of national sovereignty achieved highest priority? Finally, the objective is also to determine whether there were common European values and religiosity in the late twentieth century and by which values Europe was differentiated from non-European societies, as well as where the spatial borders of these common European values lay.

This chapter begins with a concise outline of important concepts and then covers the change in values and religiosity during the various eras of the second half of the twentieth century. It expounds next upon the divergences and convergences among intra-European values and ends by dealing with the characteristics particular to European values.

The chapter is based, inter alia, on the European and worldwide studies of values that were carried out after the 1980s. It attempts to access the development in the period preceding this by scrutinizing the differences between older and younger age groups in these surveys. This method can be utilized for value change, as values are fundamentally developed during adolescence and early adulthood and tend to change little after this. Only broad trends can be detected in this way, however. Apart from this, the chapter is limited to values, norms, and intentions. How they are translated into action must be left unexamined—other chapters in the book provide information regarding this.

Changes in Values and Religiosity

Concepts of Changing Values

The profound change of values in Europe during the second half of the twentieth century resulted in different terms within the social sciences. Here we will take note of four particularly familiar and influential concepts.

The political scientist Ronald Inglehart tried to seize upon this change with the concept of the transition from *material* to *postmaterial* values. Material values rate standard of living, economic growth, and price stability, as well as security from criminality, national security, and the authority of the state, unions, companies, and the church, particularly highly. In contrast, postmaterial values give special priority to individual self-realization, civil social interaction, human rights and international cooperation, commitment to small groups and social movements, individual participation, and often culture and aesthetics. According to Inglehart, the shift from material to postmaterial values took place after the 1960s and 1970s. It occurred slowly, as values generally can only change when values other than those held by the older generation are adopted by a new generation during adolescence and early adulthood, since at an older age values are retained. Ronald Inglehart examined the change of values in Europe as well as worldwide and in doing so analyzed numerous European and global studies on values that have been conducted since the 1980s.

In contrast, the sociologist Henri Mendras, along with many other sociologists, referred to an *individualization process* that took place in a wide variety of national and regional variations. Individualization implied a separation from the strong connection to social milieus. Ties to milieus such as the middle-class, industrial working-class, agricultural, and lower middle-class milieus were weakening, as were bonds to religious and ethnic milieus. Individualization also meant detachment from a single family model—from the values of the lifelong, legalized two-parent family tied to a gender-specific distribution of labor between the husband, who works outside the home, and the wife, who is responsible for housework and raising the children. Instead a whole range of family models and diverse family values were now adopted. Additionally, individualization meant a loosening of the stable, lifelong, unconditional loyalty to large organizations such as the nation, union, and church. New voluntary commitments and bonds to friends, social movements and associations, and free churches and private forms of religion emerged; they were based on individual decisions and as such could be rapidly dismissed and replaced. Commitment remained as a value, but the significance of the permanence of bonds decreased. As a general rule, the shifting of primary educational values was also part of individualization. Supra-individual values such as loyalty, obedience, and discipline weakened, and individual values such as self-development, personal responsibility, a willingness to take risks, and tolerance intensified. Comprehensive social security through the welfare state, better educational opportunities, a favorable labor market (above all for women), and greater geographical mobility were important causes of the individualization process.

The sociologist Gerhard Schulze stated a quite similar value change with his concept of the *hedonistic society (Erlebnisgesellschaft)*, though with this concept he attempted more to capture the division of modern society in this process. This change in values had already taken place in some milieus that were slowly growing. Schulze referred to them as the "hedonistic milieu," "alternative milieu," and "aspirational milieu," as well as the "traditionless worker milieu." In contrast, other milieus fought against this change of values, yet were slowly declining. Schulze called these milieus the "upper conservative milieu," "petty bourgeois milieu," and the "traditional worker milieu." Schulze examined the expansion of the modern milieus and the decline of the traditional milieus with detailed surveys in the 1980s and 1990s. His work was limited entirely to the old Federal Republic of Germany, however. Other social scientists further developed this concept and above all also drew international comparisons (Sinus 2003; Hradil 2006: 285ff.).

The concept of secularization was specially developed for the study of religion and religiosity. Three different processes, which are closely connected but cannot all be covered in the following, are generally regarded as being a part of this. The first includes the reduction of the church's political power, the end of its secular tasks—from coronations through to carrying out of birth, marriage, and death registers—and the loss of massive church assets. This secularization had taken place long before 1945, and the relationship between church and state in Europe took on diverse forms thereafter. One could find the strict separation of church and state, as in France, as well as the multifaceted involvement of churches in governmental social and education programs, as in Germany. Second, secularization is understood to mean a decline in the church's significance in the core values and raison d'être of a society. The original central role of religion in creating meaning in all areas of human life dissolved through this process of desacralization. Different spheres such as economics, politics, art, and science as well as religion differentiated, became independent, and developed their own norms, meanings, values, and vocabularies. If anything at all, only the political sphere still played an overarching role; the religious sphere alone remained for the churches' services and for church charity. This development, however, took place long before the second half of the twentieth century.

Third, secularization is understood as a weakening of the bond to the church, a decrease in church membership and church service attendance, less utilization of the church during personal crises, and dwindling use of ecclesiastic rites in the most meaningful events of private life such as birth, passage into adolescence, marriage, and death. More and more, religion was becoming a private matter. This manner of secularization was likely owed to a number of reasons: the constraints and pressures of politics; societal modernization, urbanization, scientification, and educational expansion as well as social security; and the isolation of the church opposite social and cultural change. It did indeed begin long before the mid twentieth century, yet it experienced a striking continuation in the second half of the twentieth century, which is why it is the primary subject of the following discussion. Values and religiosity did not, however, simply develop straightforwardly in one direction during the half century between 1945 and 2000—the change was more complicated.

The Contradictory Postwar Period

On the one hand the material need of the postwar period forced an orientation toward material values after the Second World War. People needed to secure their very survival and sought to improve their standard of living. This applied also to reestablishing public order, which in many parts of Europe had deteriorated in the immediate postwar period. A strong tie to milieus can be explained by the fact that help in times of distress could be found there; class milieus were just as important as church or ethnic milieus. Membership in churches increased throughout Europe, despite some churches' involvement in propping up dictatorships. The secularization process did not continue, but rather swung more in the opposite direction. Trade union membership also increased as never before or after in European history.

On the other hand, the postwar period was also an era of individualization, albeit one often compelled by circumstance. Young people were less accepting of traditional family hierarchies than at any other time in history. Young soldiers returning from war had, to a large extent, grown apart from family structures. Young women often lived a life detached from their families or at least wished they did, whereby they often came into conflict with their fathers. During the war, wives had become accustomed to independence and often found it difficult to return to the old family values and marriage roles. It was not without reason that existential philosophy, which bemoaned the *geworfensein* of people into their individual situations, was particularly popular during the postwar period.

Changing Values from the 1960s through the 1980s: The Era of Individualization and Secularization

The actual period of the process of individualization, the transition from material to postmaterial values, and the new push toward secularization comprised the decades between the 1960s and 1980s. This era of change cannot be precisely defined chronologically; it also varied from country to country. During these decades political, professional, and familial values as well as religiosity fundamentally changed.

It was value changes associated with individualization that primarily took place during this time, which was characterized by a growing permissiveness. European surveys on values featured an increasingly liberal mindset on topics such as abortion, divorce, euthanasia, homosexuality, and marital infidelity, even in surveys in which it was not a matter of whether those surveyed were themselves involved in these practices. This permissiveness increased in almost all Western European societies, though not in all age groups. An overwhelming majority of older people in 1990 disapproved of homosexuality, divorce, and abortion, while the vast majority of the young accepted them. The older age group that had developed its value set in the 1950s, however, had adopted the change. At the same time, there is no evidence of a particularly eventful age group that in one fell swoop implemented this permissiveness—as, for example, is sometimes claimed for the particularly permissive generation of 1968 (Ashford and Timms 1995: 126).

These trends cannot be understood without noting a second change in values: trust in fellow human beings grew in most Western European countries—not only trust in close family relatives, but also in fellow humans outside the family. This was also a longer process, in which this trust in fellow humans became somewhat greater in each age group. A large majority of the younger age groups possessed trust in human beings. In contrast, mistrust still prevailed among the older age groups, who had experienced the deterioration of help from others during the war and the immediate postwar period (Ashford and Timms 1995: 12).

Trust in others was not prevalent among Europeans overall, however. In only a few countries, primarily those in Scandinavia and the Netherlands, did a majority of people trust others outside their family in the 1980s. In the lion's share of European countries only a minority trusted others.

This civil mistrust had a long tradition in Europe and was strengthened somewhat by the experience of both world wars and the violence brought about by political conflicts. This mistrust in the 1980s existed not only in countries like Germany or Italy that had experienced dictatorships during the first half of the twentieth century, but also in old democracies such as France, Great Britain, and Belgium. It was also true in 1990 of countries such as the Czech Republic, Poland, Hungary, Russia, and Bulgaria, which had a long period of dictatorship behind them. This culture of mistrust first gradually softened among the younger Europeans (Ashford and Timms 1995).

In comparison to the rising level of trust, tolerance toward minorities changed astonishingly little between the 1960s and 1980s. The majority of Europeans in 1980 had no objection to immigrants or to a member of a different religion as a neighbor. This tolerant attitude also remained among the prevailing majority of Europeans across all Western European countries when this question was asked in more detail in 1990 concerning Jewish, Hindu, or Muslim neighbors, and there was particular tolerance with regard to Jewish neighbors. In contrast, the majority of Europeans were far less tolerant of alcoholics and drug addicts. Close to half of Western Europeans, young and old, did not tolerate these neighbors. With regard to alcoholics, significant differences were discovered between Northern and Continental Europe, as very different drinking cultures prevailed in these areas.

Public institutions were regarded with increasingly more mistrust between the 1960s and 1980s in Western Europe—as was surely also the case in Eastern Europe. A small Western European majority mistrusted the army and the state administration as well as parliament, the press, unions, and large corporations. Churches and the welfare system gained the trust of only half of Europeans. Mistrust primarily continued to grow in the 1980s for the army, but also for churches, the courts, police, and parliaments. Only the police and educational system had the trust of a clear majority; trust in the educational system even increased. Overall, however, trust in public institutions dropped. This loss of confidence began not in the 1980s but earlier, being observable in the age groups that had developed their political values in the 1950s and 1960s (Harding et al. 1986: 95; Ashford and Timms 1995: 16, 132ff.).

At the same time Western Europeans gained increasingly more confidence in their own political actions. Petitions and demonstrations, which at least enjoyed the sympathy of a large majority of young people, were most popular. Boycotts met with the approval of a small majority of young people, though a majority of Western Europeans, young and old alike, had little trust in squatting or wildcat strikes. Confidence in personal political actions increased among the age groups whose values had formed in the 1960s and 1970s. Overall, then, while trust in public institutions sank from the 1960s through the 1980s, confidence in fellow human beings and in personal political action rose (Ashford and Timms 1995: 134).

In close connection with the growing trust in others and confidence in personal political action, the family values of Europeans also changed from the 1960s through the 1980s. The familial objectives in raising children between 1981 and 1990 more clearly focused on internally guided values. Tolerance, a sense of responsibility, honesty, and good behavior became the leading family educational values or at least gained considerable acceptance. Externally guided values such as obedience, selflessness, patience, and thrift were indeed retained by a growing minority of Europeans, yet by the 1980s they were far from finding the same acceptance as internally guided values. This change had also been occurring gradually since the 1950s (Harding et al. 1986: 20f., 126; Ashford and Timms 1995).

Values regarding marriage also diversified. The lifelong two-parent family with strict divisions of labor between man and wife gradually lost importance. Perceptions of the role of mothers altered. The majority of Western Europeans—with the exception of West Germans—considered a working mother just as good a mother as a housewife, at least after the children had reached school age. The majority of Europeans also expected wives to bring in income as well. The strict rejection of divorce declined—in 1980, two-thirds of Western Europeans still opposed divorce; by 1990 this number was only about half. This change in values also emerged in the 1960s, and with each new age group the strict opposition eased. By 1990 only a third of Western European young adults opposed divorce. In particular when violence, infidelity, alcoholism, or drifting apart were involved, divorce was as broadly accepted as abortion in 1980. The majority of those in older generations were opposed to extramarital affairs, though for those age groups whose family values were formed in the 1970s this was no longer the case. Acceptance of homosexuality increased (Ashford and Timms 1995).

This change of opinion was not primarily due to Europeans changing their values—laying aside old values and turning toward new ones over the years—but was rather because the younger Europeans' values differed from those of older Europeans. Yet this value change too was not characterized by a unique and deep break between generations or a particularly revolutionary new generation. Rather, it became accepted gradually as tolerance increased among each new young generation. In any case, significant tension between age groups was a part of the changing values from the 1960s to 1980s (Harding et al. 1986: 20f., 126; Ashford and Timms 1995: 63ff., 119ff., 136; Inglehart 1995).

This change had clear boundaries, however. The significance of the family did not decrease in the eyes of the majority of Europeans, but rather continued to increase. Even among younger generations only a minority viewed the family as an outdated institution—and an even smaller minority did so in 1990 than did in 1981. The values governing a good marriage—tolerance, mutual respect, and faithfulness—remained remarkably stable: on this point young and old agreed. In the 1980s in most European countries, family values that contemporary sociologists would classify as traditional, such as parents sacrificing for their children, unconditional love for children, and a preference for the two-parent family over the single-parent family, actually increased, first losing ground only in the 1990s in most European countries. It would thus be incorrect to view the time between the 1960s and 1980s as fundamentally a period of deterioration of family values (Ashford and Timms 1986: 67, 122, 135).

Similarly, work values changed between the 1960s and 1980s. The transformation was interrupted by an important change of trends during the 1980s, however. The practice of employees taking part in the decision-making process had won quite a bit of ground since the 1960s among Western Europeans, being met with considerably more sympathy from younger than from older employees a change in work values that was closely linked with the increasing sense of self-responsibility, growing trust in others, and individual political action. Yet this trend changed among all age groups in the 1980s: sole decision-making by the employer gained more support, and the differences between age groups clearly dwindled. Something similar took place with the meritocratic values at work, which had lost a substantial number of supporters between the 1960s and 1980s. In 1980, younger Western Europeans were still less convinced than older Europeans of the wisdom of the merit principle, but this trend also changed in the 1980s: by 1990 it again clearly had the upper hand, and a greater consensus between age groups existed regarding payment according to merit. Europeans developed ever more decisive ideas regarding their workplace. They were increasingly interested as to whether work was paid well and the workplace safe, whether personal achievements could take place in the workplace, and whether the work climate was good. Their opinions in surveys were increasingly pronounced. In contrast to what some authors believe, however, this did not represent any clear trend toward more postmaterial values. Both material work values, i.e., good pay and job security, and postmaterial work values, such as opportunities for development at work and a good work atmosphere, were of more importance than earlier (Ashford and Timms 1986: 117ff.; European Values Study).

The change in work values also had its limits, however. The workplace remained central in the lives of the majority of Europeans. Work satisfaction changed little, and there were few differences on this count among various age groups. That superiors should not only give orders but also convince workers of their necessity likewise maintained a broad consensus. At the same time, what the decision-making hierarchy should look like in companies remained controversial among Western Europeans. Supporters of the employers' monopoly on decision making were unchangingly similar in number to supporters of the employee-participation approach to company decisions. In contrast, attitudes toward nationalization of the economy or worker self-management remained unchanged among Western Europeans, and supporters did not form a majority in any age group (Ashford and Timms 1986: 134).

This change in values between the 1960s and 1980s is explained in various ways. According to a first interpretation, the change in values was essentially the result of prosperity. Steadily growing incomes, greater job security, more education, and ever better social security created space for individualistic values. As long as prosperity can be safeguarded, individualized values will also remain stable. A second explanation attributes the change in values to political and cultural players, intellectuals, and experts, as well as the media and social movements like the student movement. In this view the shift was not a silent revolution of commoners, but an intentional and successfully provoked value change. A third explanation sees the change in values as the result of a specific historical situation involving not only prosperity but also the generational conflict between the war and postwar generations, as well as the massive influence of the American model.

Lastly, church ties and religiosity also changed from the 1950s to the 1980s. At this time church membership dropped almost everywhere in Europe. Only the number of visitors to mosques grew, though this was not due to a growing religiosity but primarily to immigration and to the immigrants' reaction to the experience of European society. Participation in ecclesiastical rites—regular church service as much as holy day religiosity, baptism, communion, confirmation, church weddings, and funerals—mostly declined even more than church membership. The drop in church-related activities was without a doubt significantly more pronounced in Eastern, communist Europe than in Western Europe, but moving away from the church was also a dominant trend in the West, albeit neither everywhere in the West nor simultaneously or equally dramatically throughout.

This decline in religiosity and in church ties had three main causes. In Eastern as well as Western Europe it had to do with rapidly growing income, the expansion of government social security, better health, and increasing life expectancy, as well as the increasing level of education between the 1950s and the 1980s. As a result of these developments, personal life crises seemed more calculable. The fear of the continuous threat of hardship and death, for which the church offered consolation and help, subsided. As Europeans increasingly accessed advice for practical life questions from the radio, television, press, and family counselors, the clergy lost much of its local moral authority. Psychological, medical, and academic scholars seemed increasingly more competent to Europeans than did the local clergy. Moreover, religious belief was more and more becoming a private matter. In the 1980s, the majority of Europeans still believed in God, life after death, and a soul—yet fewer and fewer entered into a close church relationship or took part in religious rites. Finally, the decline of the church in Eastern Europe had to do with the political repression of the church and with the struggles between church and state—which, however, played out differently in each country and had correspondingly different consequences regarding the move away from the church. In the GDR and Czechoslovakia the effect was far more dramatic than in Poland, for example.

The Other Value Change: The 1990s

The 1990s marked a shift from the previous decades' comfort with the concepts of postmaterialism, individualization, and secularization. The changes in values and religiosity from the 1960s through 1980s did not simply continue in the 1990s; instead they frequently developed in a different way.

First, trust in others and in public institutions changed. Having grown since the 1960s in Western Europe, trust in others sank again in the 1990s in most European countries, including almost all of the large countries like Great Britain, France, Italy, Poland, and Germany. Only in a few, mostly small countries did it rise again. For this reason, a functioning civil society was no longer such a widespread objective. At the same time, direct personal solidarity was highly regarded. In most European countries a majority supported personal help for the elderly, sick, or disabled, though admittedly only a small number of countries did so for the unemployed (Ashford and Timms 1995).

The exact opposite was true of the trust in public institutions, which, reversing the decline of previous decades, increased in most Western European countries. A few large Western European countries like France, Great Britain, and Spain did not experience this trend, however.

It is surprising, meanwhile, that the sinking confidence in others was not reflected in a growing intolerance toward minorities. Quite the contrary, tolerance toward minorities actually increased during the 1990s. In 1999 in both Western and Eastern Europe, a larger majority of Europeans than in 1990 stated in surveys that they were willing to accept a foreigner or person of other ethnicity or skin tone, including a Muslim, as a neighbor. This willingness lessened in only a few European countries, though admittedly, large countries were among them. Tolerance did not mean helpfulness, however. Only a small minority were willing to personally help immigrants in Western and Eastern Europe (Ashford and Timms 1986: 14).

Family values underwent a change in direction during the 1990s as well. Almost all European countries saw a turning away from the close and exclusive child-parent relationship, parental sacrifice for children, and unconditional parental love of children. In the majority of Western European countries, including four of the five largest, Europeans agreed less with these family values. This change was not dramatic, and in a whole range of other countries these values even gained ground, particularly in Eastern Europe. Yet they had less backing in general throughout Europe. The role of women changed more distinctly. The single mother was frowned upon less, and at the same time motherhood was no longer seen as the only role for women. The traditional attitude regarding women's roles lost significance in all the Eastern European and the majority of Western European countries, with the exception of the former Federal Republic and Denmark. This break was sharp, considering that support for this traditional family value had increased in most European countries during the 1980s (Ashford and Timms 1995).

As we saw, a change had already set in with regard to work values in the 1980s. Equality in pay and in the decision-making process among employees was less important to Western Europeans, among whom meritocratic values and the sole discretion of the employer in making decisions gained support while critical interest in the quality of work increased. Management hierarchies were more accepted, but they had to be based on performance, management had to be convincing, and the quality of employment had to be favorable.

Religiosity also changed in the 1990s, albeit not as clearly as the other areas. Three new developments could be observed. First, secularization noticeably weakened throughout Europe. Church attendance did not decrease to the same extent as in the 1980s—rather, it fell in only about half of the countries and increased in the other half. No longer so clearly in decline, belief in God began to grow a bit in most countries, in both the West and East. The number of individuals who considered themselves not religious or nonbelieving did not jump as sharply as it had in the 1980s. Moreover, the traditional churches—Catholic, Protestant, and Orthodox—experienced a revival in the eastern part of Europe during and directly following the upheaval of 1989–91. Church attendance and membership grew again, though admittedly only temporarily and primarily during the transformation crisis that affected the standard of living and social security of a substantial number of Eastern Europeans. Religious conflicts also temporarily returned in the Yugoslavian War. Finally, it was long apparent that the renunciation of church services was not always a renunciation of religion. Europeans turned to Christian sects or Far Eastern religions or converted to Islam, though these conversions and syncretic religions always remained a fringe phenomenon. None of this was a strong indication of a comeback of religiosity or church ties, but it was indeed an indication of the weakening of secularization (Schilling 1991; Pickel 1998; Halman et al. 1999; Pollack 2000; Dobbelaere et al. 2002).

There were also clear continuities in the 1990s. Permissiveness continued to increase throughout European nations in the 1990s, with only the few exceptions of Finland, Lithuania, and Hungary. The changes in family values were far from comprehensive. The values that sustained marriage remained the same: mutual respect and trust were still the central values for a stable marriage, while conversely, it was no longer crucial that marriage partners share the same religion, political views, or social background. The familial goals of child rearing also continued to develop in the same direction as previously. Internally guided values—independence, tolerance, and determination—continued to grow in most countries; externally guided values such as obedience, loyalty, hard work, and thrift continued to be supported only by a minority. However, disruption in the shift from externally to internally guided values was detectable in a few countries, primarily Great Britain and the former Federal Republic of Germany. There were also continuities with regard to work values. In the 1990s, material values like income and job security remained just as important to Europeans as postmaterial work values like personal development in the workplace and work climate. Yet there was no clear shift to postmaterial work values here, as the key conditions—a favorable job market and rapidly increasingly real earnings—no longer applied. A final continuity held for religious values, whose obsolescence was not under threat (Ashford and Timms 1995).

The change in the 1990s had many causes. The ongoing economic difficulties since the 1970s and the related difficulties of forging a career at a time of growing unemployment carried over into values. The significance of family increased for the individual, whereas trust in others and in civil society decreased. The rise in violence in Southeastern Europe could have temporarily deepened this mistrust. On the other hand, the experience of a long period of peace and democracy secured by European governments, along with a drop in violence between states and social movements, had slowly increased trust in public authorities, especially after the fall of the Wall. The long-term experience of the modern welfare state was—despite the critique of the welfare state, which will be taken up in Chapter 10—a further important prerequisite for the increased trust.

Overall, the change of values in Europe between 1945 and 2000 differed from the claims inherent in the concepts of postmaterialism, individualization, and secularization. They explain developments from the 1960s to 1980s quite well, yet for three reasons they give only an incomplete impression. First, they allow for only a poor comprehension of the changes in values in the immediate postwar period and then the 1990s. During the immediate postwar period, individualization trends and the return to religious involvement combined to strengthen ties to milieu. In light of the material hardship and moral depression of the postwar period, this was hardly as contradictory as these concepts would indicate. They also explain the 1990s only with difficulty: although individualization and postmaterialism continued to increase, this period was also characterized by completely different trends, such as growing trust in public institutions, increasing mistrust of fellow human beings, strong family ties, growing sympathy for sole decision-making by employers, and the deceleration of secularization. These concepts often do not even succeed in incorporating all aspects of the value change from the 1960s to 1980s. They overemphasize the renunciation of values, detachment of bonds, and rejection of certain norms and do not tap into the development of new values such as the growing trust in others, growing solidarity and individual responsibility, increasing social commitment, growing interest in the workplace, and the return of religiosity. Finally, these concepts are too often based on the experience of the developments in Western Europe and tend to gauge the values in Eastern Europe as lagging far behind.

European Divergences and Convergences

Divergences

Values and religiosity were a crucial cause of intra-European divergences and geographical divisions in the second half of the twentieth century. Two geographical dividing lines deeply rooted in the history of religion and values in Europe came up again and again in contemporary debates: between the Latinates, or Catholic and Protestant Europe, and Orthodox Europe, and second, between Christian and Muslim Europe in the Balkans and Turkey. These dividing lines were politically explosive—some Europeans even proposed mapping membership in the European Union along such spatial religious lines. In the second half of the twentieth century, however, their significance had waned. Muslim immigrants to Western and Central Europe had become so numerous that the geographical division in the Balkans was far less important than the social lines demarcating the Islamic minority throughout Europe. The geographic line between the Latinates and Orthodox Europe also faded. Divergences in values along this line were no longer recognizable at the end of the twentieth century, even though the church organization and the ecclesiastical principles in the Latinates and Orthodox churches were clearly different.

In the second half of the twentieth century, the Europe of value differences—now even more marked—was primarily, as it had been in the past, a Europe of regional differences. Most European countries—Spain, Portugal, Italy, and Belgium in particular but presumably some countries in the eastern part of Europe as well (similar analyses for Europe as a whole are lacking)—exhibited massive regional differences in values. The extremes between Extremadura and Catalonia, between Calabria and Venetia, between Scotland and Southeast England, between Wallonia and the Brussels region, were greater than those between nations. National borders often were of secondary importance for the respective perceptions of values (cf. Mendras 1997: 137). The marked regional differences were reflected in religiosity and ecclesiastical ties as well as in family and work values. Unfortunately, it is unclear whether these regional divergences continued to increase or whether they lessened over the course of the second half of the twentieth century.

A second geographical division was set between Western and Eastern Europe. It is astounding, however, how weak the differences turned out to be in light of decades-long communist propaganda, education on other non-Western values, and the massive transformation crisis after the collapse of the Soviet empire. After 1989–90 the already-mentioned thesis was often and persistently put forth that the continent was divided between the Western European worldview, where the values of trust in democracy, self-realization, individual freedom, willingness to take risks, secularization, human rights, and international peacekeeping were widely accepted; and the Eastern European worldview, in which social security, public order, higher quality of life, religiosity, and fear of hegemony and of loss of national sovereignty would have been the highest priorities.

But there is little evidence of such grave divergences. It is true that while confidence in political institutions rose in most Western European countries, it sank in Eastern Europe during the transformation crisis of the 1990s. Yet there is no clear difference between a mistrustful Eastern Europe and a trusting Western Europe—quite to the contrary, the important differences existed within both parts of Europe. By 2000 in the eastern part of Europe the mistrust of public institutions in some countries, such as the Czech Republic and Bulgaria, was very high, far greater than in most of the Western European countries. Yet at the same time trust in public institutions in some eastern countries, such as Poland, was far greater than the Western European average and was more similar to the Scandinavian countries.

It is completely correct that in Eastern Europe trust in others, an important prerequisite for civil society, was in most cases considerably less pronounced than in Western Europe (Ashford and Timms 1995). It is also true that intolerance toward immigrants and minorities was particularly acute in some Eastern European countries, such as Poland, Slovakia, Romania, and Bulgaria, and that it was extremely low in some Western European countries, like the Netherlands, Sweden, and Portugal (at least according to Ashford and Timms 1995). Yet in many other countries in Eastern and Western Europe, differences in tolerance toward immigrants and minorities were not apparent. France and Denmark did not differ much from Russia, nor Great Britain from Ukraine, Italy from Belarus, or West Germany from Latvia.

A slight strengthening of family ties was seen in the 1990s in Eastern Europe, most likely as a result of the transformation crisis. But no East-West divides pertained to different familial roles in the previous communist and Western Europe, whether with regard to parenting values, marriage values, parent-child relationships, or attitudes regarding divorce or single mothers.

Inglehart's argument (2000) was generally accurate, given that Western Europe leaned toward postmaterial values, more so than the US and Japan, while Eastern Europe leaned more toward material values—a long-term effect of the difficult material situation in the Soviet sphere of influence and the transformation crisis. Inglehart places Eastern Europe close to Latin American and South American countries (Inglehart and Abramson 1995: Chart 8.1). Yet the tendency to turn away from postmaterialism was just as strong in Western Europe as in Eastern Europe during the 1990s, when in both East and West a majority of those asked refused to be explicitly classified as either "materialist" or "postmaterialist." No divides can be detected between East and West with regard to permissiveness, either: opinions similarly varied as much between the

Czech Republic and Poland as between France and Portugal, and permissiveness increased just as much in Eastern as in Western Europe during the 1990s. Lastly, at the end of the twentieth century material work values, that is, the priorities of income and job security, were not especially more popular in Eastern Europe. Conversely, postmaterial work values such as personal achievement and work climate were no more accepted in Western Europe. Material work values were taken particularly seriously in Hungary, Romania, and Slovakia as well as Italy and Switzerland. These same countries also attached strong significance to the postmaterial side of work. The material side of work was taken less seriously in France, Sweden, and the Netherlands, but also in the Czech Republic and the former East Germany (Ashford and Timms 1995).

Religiosity did increase differently after 1989–90 in Eastern Europe compared to Western Europe. Ties with the church resurged directly after the collapse of the Soviet empire in 1989–91; secularization was thwarted more here in the 1990s than in Western Europe. But the more distinct new European differences ran more along the lines of religious denomination. In predominantly Protestant lands such as the Scandinavian countries, Estonia, and the former GDR, but also in the Czech Republic, a Catholic country, the trend toward secularization continued. In many Catholic countries in both the eastern and western parts of Europe, this tendency was weaker. In contrast, in Orthodox countries like Russia, Romania, and Bulgaria, as well as in Muslim countries such as Albania or within the Islamic immigrant minorities in Western Europe, a new church-oriented clerical religiosity developed in the 1990s (Pickel 1998; Pollack 2000).

Overall, differences in value systems did indeed exist between Eastern and Western Europe, but they were limited and tended to continue to diminish. The East Central European enlargement of the European Union in 2005 was thus not an expansion into a world of foreign values, but rather an opening to a world of comparable values.

Parallels

In addition to these differences, common trends in changing values can also be observed among most European countries. Four such common trends emerged after the collapse of the Soviet empire in particular, although also in part before it.

The first common, yet also contradictory, trend can be found in attitudes toward others. Basic trust in others decreased in most European countries during the 1990s. A common European culture of skepticism regarding others seems to have become stronger everywhere, including against the backdrop of a very skeptical European attitude to the future, which on a global scale was unusually pronounced. Paradoxically, at the same time solidarity, particularly with the elderly and disabled, was strong. There was even a notable shift in the direction of tolerance toward immigrants and members of other ethnicities in a majority of European countries. In any case, fewer and fewer Europeans disliked neighbors who were immigrants or members of a different ethnic group. The skeptical view of others may have encouraged/strengthened solidarity and tolerance toward the disadvantaged and minorities. Notably, this common trend first emerged after the collapse of the Soviet empire, whereas before this divergences tended to prevail.

A second, and again quite contradictory, common trend in the 1990s—as already mentioned—concerned postmaterial values. The divide between the more postmaterially oriented Western Europe and the more materially oriented Eastern Europe did not completely disappear, primarily because of the far lower standard of living and the recent experience of public order disintegrating in Eastern Europe. Unlike in the 1980s, however, the postmaterial focus went into decline in most Western European countries as well. Only in a few countries—Italy, Great Britain, Sweden, Denmark, and Austria—did it continue to increase. Uncertainty as it pertained to the social situation may have had an impact throughout Europe. At the same time, postmaterial work values won ever more favor in most European countries.

A third common trend began to show in the development of family values. The traditional mother, who found her purpose in life in raising children and not in a career, lost as much support in most of Europe as the externally guided child-rearing values of thrift, obedience, religiosity, and loyalty. The working wife, and internally guided values like independence, tolerance, and determination, won ground in most European countries. This common trend did not first appear in the 1990s, however, but before then, though the exact beginning is unclear (Ashford and Timms 1995).

A fourth parallel was present in European religiosity, whose basic development in the second half of the twentieth century was similar despite the enormous and undeniable differences between nations and regions. The immediate postwar period was an era of returning to religiosity and to the church throughout Europe, after which a push toward secularization saw religiosity and ties to the church decrease in Western as well as Eastern Europe. This did not level out the intra-European differences, but it was evident everywhere. Later, a resurgence of religiosity, which was often syncretic, was evident throughout Europe in the 1990s. This resurgence did not reverse the loosening of church and religious ties, but did slow it down in many countries. These common developments could often also be observed in Russia, but not in Turkey (Gerhards 2005).

European Hallmarks

One of the Europeans' greatest mistakes at the end of the twentieth century was the naïve idea that their own shift toward new values—individualization, postmaterialism, and secularization—had taken place throughout the modern world and that European family values, work values, and the European distance from churches had prevailed or must have prevailed in all other modern societies. To the contrary, surveys on global values changes on other continents at the end of the twentieth century showed distinct differences between Europe and other modern societies. The European traits that became recognizable, most of them emerging first in the second half of the twentieth century, though not necessarily long-lasting, did present a quite clear profile by the turn of the twenty-first century.

These European hallmarks were for the most part closely connected with the long-term European orientation regarding values, as most recently referred to by Hans Joas. This orientation is characterized primarily by values such as individual freedom, tolerance, rationality, inwardness, and self-realization. The distortion and control of values that took place during the European dictatorships, wars, and genocides of the twentieth century is certainly also a part of this European orientation (Joas and Wiegandt 2005). The short-term European characteristics at issue here can only be understood and explained through the recent encounters and disputes with non-European societies.

The first European hallmark was the strong propensity for postmaterial values, as pointed out by Ronald Inglehart. Strictly speaking, this is not so much a European, but rather a Western European, hallmark. Inglehart argues that Western Europeans particularly value postmaterial values, more so than North Americans or the Japanese, and in contrast take material values less seriously (Inglehart and Abramson 1995: 128). At the end of the twentieth century, Western European societies seemed to be an avant-garde of postmaterialism. Admittedly, it should be added as a limiting qualifier that postmaterial values in Western Europe lost quite a bit of ground at the end of the twentieth century, and it cannot be ruled out that this European trait will not disappear again. Yet in the late twentieth century it existed without a doubt.

A second European hallmark was European skepticism—regarding the future, science, and often government and other people as well. Almost nowhere, at the end of the twentieth century, were opportunities for the future gauged so skeptically as they were in the majority of European countries. The future looked far rosier in India, the US, China, and Korea than it did in Europe. Only in Japan, some Latin American countries, and Turkey was the future viewed as pessimistically as in Europe. To be sure, Europe had its islands of optimism, primarily in Scandinavia and Great Britain. But these were exceptions. Skepticism toward important public institutions—primarily the government, administration, and churches— was greater in Europe than in most non-European societies, again with the exception of the Scandinavian countries. Similarly great skepticism was evident only in Japan and Korea, as well as in China, at least with regard to churches. And almost nowhere was there so little trust in others as in Europe. In most parts of the world, including North America, China, Japan, and India, trust in others was greater. Only in Brazil and Turkey was mistrust more extensive than in Europe, while in Latin America it was similarly widespread (World Values Study 1981–2000; Therborn 1995: 264–276; World Economic Forum 2004).

This European skepticism had several roots. It had partly to do with the twentieth-century experiences of violent dictatorships whose promises of a brilliant future ended in disaster. These negative experiences are an important element of European identity to this day. Skepticism was weaker only in those European countries without such experience with dictatorship—i.e., the Scandinavian countries and Great Britain. Experiences with the strong, highly bureaucratic and intrusive European state also contributed to this skeptical attitude. European skepticism led to Europeans exercising resistance and defending their individual private freedoms. This produced not only Hobbesian or Machiavellian schools of government skepticism, but also critical attitudes to politics and churches among the citizenry. Lastly, European skepticism also had to do with shattered hopes. After the bitter experiences of two world wars, the extraordinary growth of prosperity and the huge technical and medical advances of the 1950s and 1960s, behind which a forward-thinking government intervention seemed to stand, generated high hopes for future progress. But this optimism reverted to the previous European skepticism with the end of the growth in prosperity and eventual acknowledgment of new epidemics, the boundaries of progress, and energy shortages.

A third European hallmark was its especially advanced secularization, mentioned previously. Ties to the church, participation in church rituals, and private belief in God were distinctly less developed in most European countries—with the exceptions of Poland and Ireland—at the end of the twentieth century than they were in non-European societies. Religiosity was clearly stronger in North, Central, and South America, India, Muslim countries, Africa, and the Philippines than in Europe. Only East Asian countries such as China, Japan, and Korea were secularized to the same extent as Europe (Therborn 1995; World Values Study 1981–2000).

These European hallmarks, however, did not become part of an identification with Europe, as the Europeans could not compare themselves to all of the societies of world. As a rule, these European peculiarities were only found in comparison with very specific societies. At the end of the twentieth century, the Europeans had extensive experience of two societies with which they were very closely interwoven and day-to-day encounters were particularly frequent: the United States and the Arabic world. With regard to the United States, new differences in values developed in the second half of the twentieth century, particularly in the 1990s. Having been obscured during the Cold War, they emerged more clearly after the collapse of the Soviet Union: differences in attitudes toward violence, possession of firearms and the death penalty; the role of the state and the welfare state; consumption and the environment; religion and churches; the future, technological and scientific progress; the nation, international agreements, and international military interventions. These differences, however, took a back seat to the common Western democratic and economic values. With regard to the Arabic world, Europeans were confronted with partially similar and partially different divergences in values. Divergences appeared in attitudes toward violence and the death penalty, as well as religion and secularization, but also toward social values with regard to family, work, and parenting, permissiveness, and tolerance regarding others. Striking differences largely concerned democratic values and the values of civil society.

References

Ashford S. and N. Timms. *What Europe Thinks: A Study of Western European Values*. Aldershot 1995.

Dobbelaere K., L. Tomasi, and L. Voyé. "Religious Syncretism." *Research of the Social Scientific Study of Religion* 13 (2002): 221–243.

Gerhards J. *Kulturelle Unterschiede in der Europäischen Union: Ein Vergleich zwischen Mitgliedsländern, Beitrittskandidaten und der Türkei*. Wiesbaden 2005.

Halman L. et al. "The Religious Factor in Contemporary Society." *International Journal of Comparative Sociology* 40 (1999): 141–160.

Harding S., D. Phillipps, and M. Fogarty. *Contrasting Values in Western Europe: Unity, Diversity and Change*. London 1986.

Hradil S. *Die Sozialstruktur Deutschlands im internationalen Vergleich*. 2nd ed. Wiesbaden 2006.

Inglehart R. *Kultureller Umbruch: Wertewandel in der westlichen Welt.* Frankfurt 1995.

Inglehart R. *Modernization and Postmodernization: Economic and Political Change in 43 Societies.* Princeton 1997.

Inglehart R. "Globalization and Postmodern Values." *Washington Quarterly* (Winter 2000): 215–228 (also at: www.twq.com/winteroo/231Inglehart.pdf).

Inglehart R. and P.R. Abramson. *Value Change in Global Perspective.* Ann Arbor 1995.

Joas H. and K. Wiegandt, eds. *Die kulturellen Werte Europas.* Frankfurt a. M. 2005.

Marramao G. *Die Säkularisierung der westlichen Welt.* Frankfurt a. M. 1996.

Maurer C. *Réligion et culture dans les societes et les états européens.* Paris 2002.

Mendras H. *L'Europe des européens: Sociologie de l'Europe occidentale.* Paris 1997.

Pickel G. "Religiosität und Kirchlichkeit in Ost- und Westeuropa: Vergleichende Betrachtungen religiöser Orientierungen nach dern Umbruch in Osteuropa." In *Religiöser Wandel in den postkommunistischen Ländern Ost- und Mitteleuropas,* ed. D. Pollack, I. Borowik, and W. Jagodzinski. Würzburg 1998, 55–85.

Pollack D. "Einleitung. Religiöser Wandel in Mittel- und Osteuropa." In *Religiöser Wandel in den postkommunistischen Ländern Ost- und Mitteleuropas,* ed. D. Pollack, I. Borowik, and W. Jagodzinski. Würzburg 1998, 9–53.

Pollack D. "Religiös-kirchlicher Wandel in Mittel- und Osteuropa—ein Überblick." In *Säkularisierung in Osteuropa: Ursachen und Folgen,* ed. H. Dähn and R. Rytlewski. Berlin 2000, 83–93.

Rémond R. *Religion und Gesellschaft in Europa.* Munich 2000.

Schilling H. "Nationale Identität und Konfession in der europäischen Neuzeit." In *Nationale und kulturelle Identität,* ed. B. Giesen. Frankfurt a. M. 1991, 192–252.

Sinus Sociovision. *Sinus Milieus International.* Heidelberg 2005

Therborn G. *European Modernity and Beyond: The Trajectory of European Societies 1945–2000.* London 1995, chap. 11.

van Dijk H. "Religion between State and Society in 19th Century Europe." In *The European Way,* ed. H. Kaelble. New York and Oxford 2004, 253–275.

World Economic Forum and Gallup International Voice of the People Survey. *Survey 5.1.2004.*

World Values Study, Official Homepage, *Surveys 1981–2000.*

Part II

SOCIAL HIERARCHIES AND INEQUALITIES

Chapter 5

ELITES, INTELLECTUALS, AND SOCIAL MILIEUS

The second part of this book looks at changes in social inequalities and social hierarchies in Europe, exploring them in different ways. A first approach addresses measurable elements of social position—income, wealth, education, housing, and life expectancy—examining whether inequalities in social position have diminished or become more defined since the Second World War. A second approach focuses on the social distinctions in people's interactions with each other. The term "social distinction" encompasses the various everyday actions people in a certain social milieu use to recognize one another and differentiate themselves from people within a different milieu. Consumer behavior can be included in this, as can everyday manners and rituals, the use of language, contact with high culture, the practice of reading newspapers, vacations, debates, conflicts, values, and norms, as well as membership in clubs and associations. This approach calls into question whether these social distinctions became more or less pronounced after 1945 and whether they increasingly became less noticeable to individuals.

The third approach examines the dispersal of opportunities for mobility, access to education, and occupational opportunities, as well as to high-income, affluent, prestigious positions within society. This approach questions whether opportunities for mobility have expanded since 1945 and how they have been distributed. Meanwhile, a fourth approach covers how the contemporary understanding of inequality and the contemporary debate about social and political inequality have changed. This involves not only the severity of perceived inequality and its causes, but also the dimensions of social inequalaity that are emphasized by contemporaries.

The Elites

State of Research

The research on the history of European elites during the second half of the twentieth century primarily addresses four issues. The first encompasses the continuity or replacement of elites during the political regime upheavals in Europe at the end of the Second World War and after the collapse of the Soviet empire in 1989–90. This frequently examined subject is often politically explosive. For example, the question of whether the Nazi and the communist elite in East Central and Eastern Europe were replaced after 1945 and 1989–91 respectively interests not only academia but the public as well. A second frequent topic focuses on the exclusivity or openness of the elite. Along these lines, research has often dealt with and comparatively traced whether the European elite was more exclusive than the US elite. It also questions whether the European democracies were more open than the European dictatorships.

A third and likewise frequent issue concerns the power of the elite. This includes whether elites were so homogeneous and interwoven that one can speak of a single power elite, as C. Wright Mills did in his classic about the US elite in the middle of the twentieth century, or whether the different members of the elite—politicians, big business owners, top-ranking officials, military brass—not only set themselves apart from one another but also competed against each other for power. Finally, a fourth topic, raised more often in recent years, revolves around the European elite's political and economic potential—their abilities to make the right political and economic decisions and acquire the right education and professional knowledge—around their international competitiveness, and conversely around the danger of incompetence and corruption among the elite. Whether the public trusted or distrusted the elite depended greatly on all of this (Birnbaum 1985; Henke and Voller 1991; Tarrius 1992; Soutou 1994; Berghahn 1995; Bertin-Mourot and Bauer 1996; Bussière and Dumoulin 1998; Schröder et al. 2000; Charle 2001; Frei 2001; Hartmann 2001; Sklair 2001; Hartmann 2003; 2004).

As of yet there is no overview of the history of the elite in Europe, or even Western Europe, as a whole. So far we have summaries only of individual countries, and in the best-case scenario, a comparison of two or three large countries, although even these deal only with specific elites, that is, only the political, economic, or administrative elite.

The term elite refers to those who hold the top positions within a country, that is, the strategic decision makers within politics, the economy, the administration, and the army, as well as in churches, associations, unions, culture, and large research institutes. It is not easy to decide which positions in particular were most powerful and prestigious, as this could differ from country to country or change over the course of the twentieth century. For example, parliamentary delegates made up a part of a country's political elite in democratic Western Europe, but not in communist Eastern Europe because they were not strategic political decision makers there.

The Transformation of European Elites

During the second half of the twentieth century the European elites changed considerably. At the same time, it is important to distinguish between their dramatic, often conflictual replacement through regime upheavals and their slow, unspectacular transformation over time.

Periods of Upheaval

The European elite experienced three dramatic regime-related upheavals during the second half of the twentieth century. The first is the radical change from dictatorships to democracies, especially at the end of the Second World War in Western and East Central Europe, and then again in the early 1970s in Spain, Portugal, and Greece. Second is the emergence of communist dictatorships during the postwar period in Eastern Europe, and third is the transformation from communist dictatorships to democracies at the beginning of the 1990s. The elite in most European countries experienced at least one of these upheavals in the second half of the twentieth century; in East Central Europe and Germany they went through all three. These experiences were absent from only a few European countries—Great Britain, Ireland, Sweden, and Switzerland. A fourth kind of transition from a communist regime to a postcommunist, authoritarian regime seems to have been limited to only a few countries, such as Russia.

The upheaval that took place during the transition from authoritarian and fascist dictatorships to democracies is a particularly sensitive historical theme, as many members of the elite were involved in the strategic decisions, and often crimes, that had taken place during the dictatorships and were thus incriminated as a result. Others, however, had offered resistance or at least not been mere stooges within the regime. In most European countries the elite was in no way completely replaced during the transition from a dictatorship to a democracy. Generally only the highest echelons of politicians were replaced—not those who held higher positions in the administration, judiciary branch, military, economy, or churches. The expertise of these elites seemed to be irreplaceable. Governments also wanted to prevent anti-democratic opposition to the elite and to integrate the old elite into the democracy.

In Germany and Italy almost all of those in the governmental cabinets after the end of the dictatorships had a clean history. There were more newcomers in the German and Italian parliaments at this time than ever before or after (Best and Cotta 2000: 504). Only a few, but all the more controversial, members of the Federal Republic's political elite were suspected of having incriminated themselves by participating in the Nazi regime. Businessmen, top-ranking officials, and professors in West Germany were, in contrast, only temporarily dismissed by the occupying powers and then mostly reappointed during the Adenauer era. In Italy, continuity among the elite in the unoccupied South was especially noticeable during the period between Fascism and the republic. But even in North Italy, which had been occupied by the Nazis, the courts convicted only a few members of the elite who had withstood savage purges. The replacement of elites was impeded not only by the monarch, who soon departed, but also by the allies and even the Partito Comunista Italiano. Meanwhile, in France, from the upheaval of the Vichy regime through to the Fourth Republic, the administrative elite, judiciary, big business owners, and churches likewise remained largely untouched.

The exchange of elites was humane in most countries during the transition from the authoritarian regimes and dictatorships to democracies. It was only in France and in northern Italy, during the fervent cleansing directly after the end of the Nazi occupation, that members of the elite were murdered. Those among the political elite who were found guilty of charges were normally punished by courts, or by special courts for this such as the Nuremberg Court or the Austrian People's Court. These special courts were appointed by their respective governments in the countries that had been occupied by the NS regime, as well as in Austria. In Germany the Allies appointed them. These courts sentenced some members of the elite to death. Most of the death sentences were enforced, although some were suspended, as in the spectacular case of the French marshal Pétain.

During the second governmental upheaval, the establishment of the communist regime in Eastern Europe, the replacement of the elite was comprehensively and disproportionately more violent than during the transformation from dictatorships to democracies. In Croatia, where the dictatorship was directly replaced by Tito's communist regime, not only heads of the Ustascha regime but also members of the religious elite were killed in mass shootings, executed upon decisions by quick military tribunals or show trials, jailed, or banished. In Hungary, the elite in the Horty regime or Arrow Cross Party were either driven from the country in a mass deportation by the Soviet occupiers or charged, and in some cases executed, by the People's Court show trials at the end of the war and beginning of the communist regime. There were no wild purges in the Soviet Occupation Zone (SBZ), but many Germans—not just those incriminated as part of the NS regime—were indiscriminately detained in large Soviet camps with high death rates. Soviet military tribunals and German special courts also undertook the replacement and punishment of the NS elite. Politicians, businessmen, large-scale land owners, and the judiciary, police, and military were more likely to be slated for replacement than were academics and members of the hard-to-replace liberal professions. Despite this, there were continuities among the economic and administrative elite in the eastern part of Europe.

During the third upheaval, the change from communist regimes to democracies in East Central Europe, those in seats of power within politics and the economy were also mostly replaced. Only the religious elite remained in their positions, as they had not, for the most part, compromised themselves. The postcommunist parties brought to power politicians, managers, and high-ranking officials who had acted only in subordinate positions within the communist regime, had not taken part in making strategic decisions, and therefore were not among the elite in the true sense of the word. There was quite a bit of continuity, but little among the elite. The extent of continuity was largely dependent upon whether a functional, qualified replacement elite was available. On the other hand, relatively little continuity was seen in East Germany, where many members of the new elite came from the West and for a long time conveyed the impression that West Germans dominated the population in the East.

This third upheaval was much more humane than the communist regimes' seizure of power. Murders were not committed and death sentences were not imposed—apart from the execution of Ceausescu and his wife in Romania. Court proceedings were rare and took place only in Germany against a few members of the GDR elite, not in other East Central European democracies.

Change among the Elite
The elite not only changed after or due to political upheavals; their structure also changed during the second half of the twentieth century, even in the absence of such massive turning points.

Changes in the social composition of the European elite have been well studied. The social and regional background of parliamentarians and politicians by and large remained constant. Openings for other social strata can be detected only in the first half of the twentieth century; thereafter they were rare. The political competition between communist Eastern Europe, where parliaments were more socially diverse but had no political influence, and the liberal West did not have much impact. Even after the general adoption of women's suffrage in Europe, the number of women among the political elite increased unsteadily. Only in the last two decades of the twentieth century did the number of women in Western European parliaments and in Western governments rise (Best and Cotta 2000).

The professionalization of the European political elite tended to increase their exclusivity, as did their increasing academism and the corresponding drop in the number of members without a university education. Education of this professionalized political elite concentrated mostly on a few subjects that differed from country to country. Professionalization of the political elite also meant more politicians whose careers were purely party- or organization-related, and fewer newcomers from other professions. The number of politicians starting as public officials also increased. Given their abundance in many countries, along with ease of access to careers reliant to some extent on party patronage, public officials were easily launched into political careers. Professionalization also meant an increasing dependence on professionalized preparatory and advisory help from consultants, political advisors, speechwriters, the media, campaign managers, and polling institutes. This professionalization of the political elite admittedly had begun before the second half of the twentieth century, but it gained significant impetus in this period. It was impressively documented in a broadly funded study of the European parliaments in France, Italy, Great Britain, Germany, the Netherlands, Norway, and Finland, albeit with pronounced differences between these countries (Best and Cotta 2000; Best 2003). This professionalization, and the resulting exclusiveness of the political elite in Western Europe, have been seen as important reasons for the crisis in the public's trust of the political elite (Best 2003).

The economic elite changed as well. The practice of family entrepreneurs owning and managing big businesses went into decline in almost all of Europe during the second half of the twentieth century. Managers, who ran the business but were no longer the owners, replaced them. This change among the economic elite was not new but had already begun during the First World War, in particular in Germany, and outside of Europe in the US and Japan. The switch to non-owners' management of businesses had mostly ended by the second half of the twentieth century. This metamorphosis was more than just a change to ownership structures. The promotion of managers also altered the economic elite, as their careers, interaction with other members of the elite, and values differed from those of the family entrepreneur. As opposed to the family owner, managers almost always had a university education. They were better connected to other parts of the elite or at least to other members of the middle class. Social background, marriage, and education linked them in particular with senior officials and professionals. At the same time, they were less likely to come from the economic milieu than were family entrepreneurs. Managers could more easily switch over to other elite positions, particularly within top management, but also in professional politics. This shift was practiced in different ways in different European countries. It was especially common in France, where the term *Pantouflage* was coined to describe it. Lastly, managers' values differed from those of family entrepreneurs. They were less attached to the business, which they did not own. It was not growth in the business so much as salary, career, and the company's share price that indicated their success. Their take on governmental economic policy and on union power was usually more flexible, and their internationality often more distinct, than that of family entrepreneurs.

A final change, this one in Eastern Europe, was the emergence of a socially exclusive, gerontocratic, political elite that for the most part lost the trust of the general population. The political elite in Eastern Europe in the late 1940s and early 1950s was considerably more accessible than was its Western counterpart, but thereafter they became increasingly similar in terms of lack of openness. The GDR's political elite in the 1980s was just as academic as the political elite in the Federal Republic of Germany. Unlike in Western Europe, positions among the elite remained widely closed off to women in Eastern Europe. The change to a new generation was also delayed. Younger politicians rarely made it to top seats of political power. When the Soviet empire collapsed, the considerably more exclusive elite in Eastern Europe suffered an even greater crisis of trust than the one experienced in Western Europe.

Divergences

European elites differed greatly from one another in the second half of the twentieth century and were linked to only a limited extent. Two divergences in particular influenced the history of the elite during the second half of the twentieth century: the aforementioned opposition between the elite in the liberal West and the communist elite after the Second World War, and much older national differences. The educational institutions they attended differed fundamentally in particular. In Great Britain, public schools and the prestigious Oxford and Cambridge Universities, where lifelong networks often developed, continued to dominate the education of the political and economic elite. In France, a large section of the elite was recruited from the highly selective "grandes écoles," among them the Ecole Nationale d'Administration (ENA), which was first established in 1945. Networks of lifelong connections also developed at these schools. Germany, by contrast, forbore to establish such select schools and universities; hence its top-ranking political positions were accessed via other avenues. The prime minister and ministers in Great Britain and France usually came from the upper class, whereas the German chancellor usually came from the middle class (Hartmann 2003).

Convergences

Along with these divergences, important convergences also became evident in the second half of the twentieth century. These convergences had much to do with the elite's similar academic training; with the gradual implementation of democracy and democratic values among the elite in Germany and Italy, later in Spain and Portugal, and finally in East Central Europe; and lastly with the trend toward transnational elites in Europe.

The academic training and professionalization that had set in among the elite by the end of the nineteenth century led to a similar social composition for the political elite as well as the economic and administrative elite. During the second half of the twentieth century an intense academism; a dearth of politicians from the agricultural milieu, whether peasants or aristocrats; and a high proportion of public service officials in top-ranking political positions was observable almost everywhere (Best and Cotta 2000). The career paths of the political elite were similar. Politicians usually entered political office around the age of forty and lived off of politics, having previously held non-political jobs. The percentage of women in politics, which had long been very different from country to country, began to align in the 1990s (Kaelble 1986; Hartmann 2003; Geissler 2006). The significant differences that had still existed during the interwar period between the German economy, which was defined early on by managers, and the French and British economies, which were more characterized by family entrepreneurs, diminished (Kaelble 1986). Around 2000 the vast majority of top European companies were headed by managers. Growing similarities could also be observed among the administrative elite (Page and Wright 1999).

Another convergence was the rise of a transnational European or global elite during the second half of the twentieth century. Its members were top-tier leaders in multinational corporations and transnational science, or representatives of transnational culture, i.e., architects, conductors and directors, soloists, painters, and sculptors.

Little research has focused on the elite directly tied to the European Union—European parliamentarians, commission presidents and commissioners, members of the European council, top-ranking EU officials, judges on the European Court of Justice in Luxembourg, and board members of the European Central Bank, as well as the experts and the top level of the European civil society. It is not yet clear how coherent and intertwined this European elite was and how strong its common values of democracy, international peace, orientation toward a market economy, social security, and the general Europeanization of Europe had become.

European Hallmarks

During the second half of the twentieth century, the European elite exhibited several particularities that distinguished it from the aristocratic, exclusive, and imperial European elite of the nineteenth and early twentieth centuries.

The first was the elites' experience of dismissal and banishment after regime changes. At the beginning of the twentieth century, the European elite's familiarity with such hardships referred largely to the distant French Revolution. However, elites in the great majority of European countries would soon experience them firsthand. Comparative research has not adequately addressed how these episodes were received or how they affected trust in European democracies. There are also no comparative studies that relate European elites to Asian, African, and Latin American elites, who had similar experiences.

A second difference was observable between Europe and the US but far more striking in comparison to Latin America, Turkey, and many African and Asian countries. In Europe the *political* elite became the predominant group of elites during the second half of the twentieth century, while the military elite was increasingly subordinated to and controlled by it. Previously, the distribution of power in Europe among the elites had often looked different: in Germany, Spain, Portugal, and Greece the military elite had much more influence, and may even have dominated for a time; it was only in Great Britain, France, and a few smaller countries that the political elite's place of supremacy was already secure. The political elite also gained increasingly greater influence over the administrative elite. The top ranks of administration were politically staffed, whether according to the proportional representation of parties as was the case in Austria and Italy, according to the government's party line as in Germany and

France, or via connections to governmental circles as in Great Britain or Denmark (Page and Wright 1999). As a result, the administrative elite lost some of its traditional autonomy. The political elite gained clear control over the economic elite in Eastern Europe only during the communist period. In Western Europe the economic elite defended its autonomy and even reinforced it at the end of the twentieth century. Nevertheless, the political elite in Europe often managed to gain more leeway for action vis-à-vis the economic elite than its counterpart did in the US. The political elite's retention and expansion of power compared to other elites during the second half of the twentieth century is therefore an important European trait.

Another hallmark is the creation of a supranational elite in Europe. National governments often designated the heads of the European Commission, the parliamentarians in the European parliament, the judges in the European Court of Justice in Luxembourg, and the directors of the European Central Bank, but this had little effect on the autonomy of their decisions. This European elite acted differently from the national elite: it was more disconnected from democratic control and had a surprising, often publicly underestimated amount of power that originated primarily from negotiations and compromises and less commonly through bureaucratic authority and confrontation. They relied more on the counsel of experts than did the national political elites. Nonetheless they lacked the insignia of a European elite; that is to say, that they had so far developed few symbols and rites and had not established any common educational institutions or common lifelong networks.

The Intellectuals

The term "intellectuals" here means educated individuals who have great influence on the political public but do not consider themselves part of the political, economic, administrative, or religious elite. They also do not exert their public influence through large organizations such as associations, unions, or NGOs. According to Christophe Charle, author of the most important book on the history of European intellectuals, three factors must be distinguished. First, there is the political role intellectuals play as opponents, critics, advisers, and legitimizers of governments and administrations. Second, one must consider the extent of their integration with the political and economic elite and the middle class—the common social circles and marriage networks, common social backgrounds and education, common values and maxims, the extent of their connection to the upper classes, and the amount of latitude they are given. And finally, there is the role of the intellectual as a producer of knowledge that has its own markets, technological innovations, constraints, and legal and cultural rules (Charle 1996; cf. also Lepenies 1985; Ringer 1992; Winnock 2003). These factors assume that intellectuals cannot be understood exclusively as political players or even just as active public critics of the government, and that they are also little understood when viewed only as producers of knowledge with their own markets or simply as a part of the middle class.

An overview of the intellectuals of the current era like the one written by Christophe Charle about the nineteenth century has not yet been produced. The successful books about intellectuals in the twentieth century are national histories. The best-known example, Michel Winnock's history of intellectuals (Winnock 2003), concentrated entirely on France. Even Michel Trebitsch's highly commendable collections on European intellectuals consist primarily of national descriptions (cf. Granjon et al. 1997; Trebitsch and Granjon 1998; Bachoud et al. 2000; Racine and Trebitsch 2004). Intellectuals with European stature and international charisma have yet to become the subject of biographies.

The Transformation of the Intellectuals

European intellectuals underwent considerable change during the second half of the twentieth century. The oft-lamented, but never convincingly proven, decline of the intellectual was a frequent topic. Time and again there were, of course, periods during which the intellectuals' political influence was more limited than it was in their heydays during the Enlightenment, the *Vormärz* and the Revolution of 1848, and the periods after the two world wars, as well as during the 1960s in Western Europe and the 1980s in Central Europe. The present-day early twenty-first century is also no golden age for the intellectual. It is possible, though, that intellectuals will regain political significance again, whether as the initiators of democracy in the parts of Eastern Europe that are not yet democratic, as intermediaries in the climate of increasing distrust between citizens and the national elites in Europe, or through the unclear relationship between the European center of power in Brussels and the still quite inchoate European public.

In fact, three lasting transformations took place during the second half of the twentieth century. First, intellectuals changed as a result of the difficult and often painful reappraisal of their part in the Fascist and National Socialist regimes and communist dictatorships, in which some intellectuals played a malign role. Their involvement as commentators and propagandists of dictatorial ideologies, as well as their entirely new joint responsibility for the stabilization of criminal, misanthropic regimes, is one of the twentieth century's bitter experiences. Coming to terms with the intellectuals' roles during the dictatorships over the course of the Nazi regime was a long, often arduous process during the second half of the twentieth century. In the case of dictatorships within the Soviet empire, the process was usually more rapid and more intense. This charge of intel-lectuals playing a political part was rarely an issue before the First World War or even during the interwar period.

A second important change, one that has seldom been dealt with, had to do with the public. Intellectuals are crucially dependent on access to the public, upon whom their activities depend. Changes among the pub-lic dramatically affected the intellectuals for many reasons. Intellectuals had successfully negotiated access to the media of the nineteenth cen-tury—to publishers, newspapers, and magazines. However, they were in a considerably weaker position with regard to the new forms of media that were created in the twentieth century, such as radio, film, records, and television: the production apparatus was more extensive, and the roles of non-intellectual professions were of significantly more importance. In addition, governments had far more control over access to radio and TV stations. Intellectuals, therefore, often had to bow to the constraints of these new forms of media. Furthermore, it became more difficult for intel-lectuals to live off of royalties. They often had to develop new life strat-egies, either taking on posts within the new media and thus becoming even more subject to these constraints, or procuring positions as teachers, editors, or experts in public service, and as such facing other limitations. It cannot yet be foreseen whether the Internet, with its open access, can give the intellectuals' influence a fresh impetus.

The third change among intellectuals in the second half of the twen-tieth century was their internationalization, which was not a completely new process. The traditional intellectuals of the eighteenth and nineteenth centuries were also international: they knew other languages, communi-cated in the most important language of the time, French, often traveled abroad, and learned from intellectuals in other countries. Their critique of national governments was simultaneously aimed at global politics, as the governments were either global powers like Great Britain and France or played a global role as in the case of Spain, the Netherlands, Belgium, and Portugal. The European Enlightenment of the eighteenth century, a project by intellectuals, was a symbol of their internationality.

This internationality receded in the late nineteenth and early twenti-eth centuries, however. Intellectuals now primarily wrote in their national languages and aimed to influence their own countries. Their critiques ap-plied to the national government, church, and economy. The First World

War was also a war of national intellectuals. Many intellectuals who were driven into exile by the dictatorships of the twentieth century were so tied to their national culture that they had difficulty finding their way in their new surroundings.

The internationalization during the second half of the twentieth century initially looked like a return to the internationality of the pre-national intellectuals in the eighteenth century. Intellectuals again learned to not only read but also speak international languages and could thus engage in spirited dialogue with intellectuals from other countries. Stints abroad in France, Italy, and the US now increasingly belonged among the experiences of the European intellectual as well. But this renewed internationalization was indeed different from that of the eighteenth century. The ties to one's national language, public, and culture certainly did not disappear, but international manifestos, such as the report by the Club of Rome or the manifestos by Habermas and Derrida, became more common. International collaboration between intellectuals increased. Even the subjects of intellectual critique became more international. With decolonization and the end of Europe's global role, the national governments in Europe were reduced to medium powers. Many intellectuals did not stop at critiquing their own govenments but extended their scope to the superpowers of the US and USSR.

Divergences

During the second half of the twentieth century, five different kinds of intellectuals stood out in Europe. Found in every country, each type had a different importance in each. The best-known was without doubt the type for which the term "intellectual" was created: politically engaged generalist. He—or less often, she—was originally closely linked with France and the Paris metropolitan area. This intellectual was half man of letters, half political author, and in no way a specialist. He kept a sharp distance from politics and the political elite, generally did not take a governmental position, and kept a distance from the economy and the church. At the same time he played an influential role in the political public of the country. He almost always belonged to a political milieu, sometimes to a leftist milieu such as that of Jean-Paul Sartre, Simone de Beauvoir, or Pierre Bourdieu, and sometimes a rightist milieu, as was the case with Raymond Aron. Regardless of political leanings, he (or she) always held a certain degree of independence within his own political milieu. He functioned as an individual and also as a member of a school of thought who signed manifestos and influenced certain newspapers, publishers, and book series, thereby developing a lifestyle with preferences for literature, music, and paintings, as well as specific parts of town, restaurants, cafés, and vacation spots. This type of intellectual made his living from the success of his books and articles.

These intellectuals played an unusually important role in French society because in the absence of large hierarchically structured parties, unions, and associations, political trends were oriented toward individuals and informal groupings. This type of intellectual, who in France emerged in the 1880s at the latest with the Dreyfus Affair, was embodied by Emile Zola. Albert Camus, Jean-Paul Sartre, Raymond Aron, and André Gide were its main representatives in the period after the Second World War. Umberto Eco in Italy, Günter Grass and Heinrich Böll in Germany, and T.S. Eliot in Great Britain are all also considered to have been this type of intellectual.

A second type of intellectual was the influential expert who was engaged in the public and in politics. His or her stature relied on expertise in an occupational field, combined with political commitment. This engagement was commonly tied to the political impacts of the given field, whether the debate concerned physics and atomic weaponry, biology and the environment, or history and dealing with the Nazi past. This type of intellectual did not reserve his or her expertise for the professional public but also opined on general policy. During the second half of the twentieth century some internationally known figures of this type of intellectual in Europe were the philosophers André Glucksman and Carl Friedrich von Weizsäcker, sociologists Pierre Bourdieu, Anthony Giddens, and Ralph Dahrendorf, physicist Jens Reich, economist Gunnar Myrdal, and historians François Furet and Hans-Ulrich Wehler. Intellectuals of this second type were much less connected to a political milieu and certain lifestyle than were those of the first type. They did not exploit the devices typically used for political influence, whether manifestos or political journals, nor did they hang out in any particular cafés or bars or embrace a publicly celebrated lifestyle. They usually lived off fees for their expertise, not from book or article royalties, and did not stand in such principled opposition to the government as did the first type of intellectual. This second type could become a government advisor or even minister, or a corporate consultant. Such intellectuals were particularly influential in societies where highly organized party machinery, large unions, and powerful organizations dominated the political public. They offered something that these organizations were usually lacking: expertise.

A third type of intellectual was the politically engaged and influential amateur. These intellectuals did not rely on a base of specialized knowledge like the expert intellectual but were generalists who could give opinions on many political questions. Unlike the first type, they were neither associated with a certain political milieu nor with a journal, institute, or publisher. Instead they were usually loners who stood politically only for themselves and moved among political camps without difficulty, yet the public accorded them authority. They were not in diametric opposition to political or economic power, and generally lived off of their income as writers, or often from their personal fortune. This type of intellectual became rare during the second half of the twentieth century. Arnold J. Toynbee was among this type of intellectual in Great Britain, as was Sebastian Haffner in Germany.

A fourth type of European intellectual during the second half of the twentieth century was the dissident in East Central Europe. Similar to the traditional intellectual, dissidents usually built on tightly knit local networks of political and personal friends. Dissident movements were, to a large extent, circles of friends. Dissidents' authority could rest on their reputation as a writer, as in the cases of Václav Havel and György Konrad. They could also be experts in areas that were crucial to the communist regime, like physicist Robert Havemann or historian Bronisław Geremek. As with the other types of intellectuals, their political engagement was important. They thus stood in an even more fundamental opposition to the regime than the traditional intellectual. György Konrad referred to this as "anti-politics": their role and their authority in public hinged completely on this fundamental opposition to the regime. When the regime disappeared, such an intellectual either lost public authority or needed to develop a new role in the public as a writer or a politician, as Bronisław Geremek and Václav Havel succeeded in doing.

The dissidents also differed from the other types of intellectuals in that access to the official public sphere of their own country was often restricted. Even the critical underground circles in Poland, which sometimes were closer than any to actually being a public sphere, was still very limited. The influence of the dissidents was therefore not dependent on their own country but on their reception in the West. Without the respect of the public in the West, they were seldom important in their own countries. Furthermore, life and work for this type of intellectual was disproportionately more charged and dangerous than for the other types, as they risked death under Stalin and imprisonment thereafter, or had to at least accept a troublesome life of being harassed by the secret police.

The fifth type was the intellectual for which Julien Benda coined the well-known expression "la trahison des clercs" during the interwar period. These were the previously mentioned intellectuals who did not keep a critical and personal distance from the abuse of power, as the other types did, but for whatever motive placed themselves entirely in the service of those in power in the dictatorships or nondemocratic parties. They reproduced and elaborated upon the official political and cultural ideologies, legitimized them, and commonly propagated an illusion of intellectual freedom that made it easier for the intellectual and academic milieu to accept these ideologies. They were usually in close contact with the political elite—indeed, almost in the same social circle—but based their authority on their expertise or their success as writers. The philosopher Martin Heidegger and the constitutional law expert Carl Schmidt hoped to take on roles as prominent unofficial intellectuals for the Nazi regime but were not given any long-lasting opportunities to do so. The author Ezra Pound played the role of a regime supporter in Fascist Italy. The historian Jürgen Kusczynski and the writer Hermann Kant took this role in the GDR.

These intellectuals did not necessarily have to live in the same country as the dictatorship but could also hold their disastrous position within democracies as the public supporters of fascist or communist regimes. Stalinism, for example, received intellectual support of this kind in democratic Western Europe. A remorseful, often dramatic return or conversion to the traditional role of an independent European intellectual was characteristic of this type and, for certain generations of European intellectuals, part of a normal résumé. The intellectual in the service of dictatorships is the most controversial and often tragic type. They actually stood in contradiction to the European tradition of the publicly, politically engaged scholar, but they are a real part of the history of intellectuals in Europe. They should not be confused with the semiofficial party and governmental intellectuals in democracies, as it was possible for these intellectuals to distance themselves more from power and even possible political errors without spectacular acts of contrition or painful personal redemption, as they were not accused of aiding human rights violations, wars, and genocides.

Convergences

Along with these substantial differences there were also convergences among European intellectuals during the second half of the twentieth century. A first similarity had to do with the previously touched on internationalization of the intellectual market and contacts. In comparison to the intellectuals in the first half of the twentieth century—but not those of the Enlightenment—European intellectuals were usually more open to the public in other countries and continents, adopting ideas from outside their own national borders and gaining vital experience in other countries. Exiles returning to Europe after the Second World War took on a pioneering role in this process.

However, this internationalization also had visible boundaries. There were no Europe-wide intellectual book or media markets, and European bestseller lists were not very similar. Only a gradual change can be spoken of. Though it was rare for an intellectual to gain recognition throughout Europe, the Polish historian Bronisław Geremek, the French sociologist Pierre Bourdieu, the British sociologist Anthony Giddens, the German philosopher Jürgen Habermas, and the Italian literature scholar Umberto Eco all had a degree of prominence that came close to this level of European intellectual stature during the second half of the twentieth century.

In a second convergence, the range of intellectuals diminished for political reasons as the last two types of intellectuals, the dissidents and the dependent intellectuals backing dictatorships, disappeared from Europe with the end of the authoritarian and fascist regimes in 1945 and again in the early 1970s, and then finally with the collapse of the Soviet empire in 1989–90. The amateur intellectual also eventually became rarer during the second half of the twentieth century, in part because the importance of professional knowledge increased to such an extent that amateurs could no longer hold their own ground.

A third convergence traces back indirectly to the European Commission in Brussels. The European Commission mobilized many experts for political counsel because its personnel were limited and because it expanded during a period when the "outsourcing" of services and knowledge was part of its philosophy. It supported itself more with the knowledge of experts than did many national administrations. Countless expert committees, reports, white papers, and congresses developed out of initiatives by the commission. Parallel to this, it established an extensive research budget of about 18 billion euros. The goal of this research program was, above all, to create European networks and through them a European expert community. It was certainly not the goal of the European Commission to create European intellectuals, but experts' inquiries and the creation of European networks paved the way for politically engaged intellectuals at the European level.

European Hallmarks

Specific characteristics among European intellectuals have not yet been widely researched because specialists have been more concerned with intra-European national differences. Nevertheless, three traits have emerged in recent history.

A first hallmark: the intellectual was invented in Europe, as it was here that the necessary conditions developed—rivalry between many political centers of power, separation of church and state, and the autonomy of universities and the public sphere. Identification with the role of intellectual was strong within Europe as a result. The public generally expected engaged intellectuals. The distance and autonomy of European intellectuals with regard to political power as well as the economy and the church was particularly pronounced throughout Europe, or at least more so than in the US, Japan, China, or India. Politicians, economists, and the church were aware of the role of the intellectuals, and depending on the situation at hand they were accepted, exploited, or viewed as opponents. Shmuel Eisenstadt has furthermore already referred to intellectuals' distance from power as tracing back to the axial age of antiquity, in which Europe did not differ from China or India, but did indeed differ from Japan (Eisenstadt 2003).

Another hallmark of the European intellectuals was their provincial nature, especially during the second half of the twentieth century. European intellectuals were, with few exceptions, only read on their own continent and mostly only within their own countries, thus differing from a number of US intellectuals who had more opportunity to be read or heard worldwide. This was not only because English became a global language, but also because the US received special attention as a global power and American political intellectuals could have greater impact on their government's more important global decisions than European intellectuals could in their countries. Outside the US during the second half of the twentieth century most intellectuals were as provincial as those in Europe, whether Chinese, Indian, African, or Latin American. The distinction of the European intellectuals consisted in the experience of being relegated from a global role, during the period when Europe was a global center, to a position of being read or heard only regionally or nationally.

A third European hallmark was the bitter experience of dictatorial support and the reappraisal of this fundamental failure on the part of European intellectuals. The intellectuals in North America and India did not have this experience. Those of China, Latin America, the Arabic world, and Japan were certainly also in the service of dictatorships and supported human rights violations and wars, but the expectations of the intellectuals in East Asia, the Arabic world, and perhaps even Latin America were not as high. The European distinction lay in the especially harsh contradiction between the high expectations of intellectuals and their somewhat precipitous moral decline. Working through this contradiction led to a European sensitivity to the moral threat of intellectuals—to a culture of conversion and remorse, but sometimes also to a skepticism about how much opportunity for action intellectuals actually had in dictatorships.

Social Milieus

Social milieus have always been a key topic within social history. The social histories written by authors such as E.P. Thompson, Jürgen Kocka, and Michelle Perrot focus on laborers, the bourgeoisie and petty bourgeoisie (or middle and lower-middle classes), salaried employees, rural aristocracy, and farmers. The research usually concentrated on the development and the peak of these traditional milieus in the nineteenth and early twentieth centuries, however. The second half of the twentieth century has been sidelined. The few sociologists and historians who worked on this later period, like Henri Mendras, Monique de Saint Martin, Josef Mooser, Hannes Siegrist, Christoph Kleßmann, Gérard Noiriel, and Olivier Zunz almost unanimously describe the decline of these class milieus, i.e., the deterioration of the working-class, rural, and aristocratic milieus. Only the development of the middle class and white-collar workers remained controversial (Kocka 1981a; 1981b; Mendras 1984; Mooser 1993; Saint Martin 1993; 2000; Schulz 2000; Siegrist 2001; Noiriel 2002; Zunz et al. 2002; Kleßmann 2007). Examination of these milieus were usuallly limited to one country, though, or in the best-case scenario included the comparison of two or three countries. The works by Jürgen Kocka about the European bourgeoisie, Christophe Charle about European intellectuals, and by Klaus Tenfelde about European laborers and labor movements are exceptions to this rule (Tenfelde 2005; Charle 2007; Kocka 2011). The central question in the following sections is whether these social milieus lost or retained their influence throughout the second half of the twentieth century.

The Middle Class

Opinions differ among historians, sociologists, and intellectuals as to whether the middle class dissolved, changed, or maintained its status as a political player during the last half century. Also debated is whether it remained distinguished from lower classes and was still an internally interconnected milieu. Some maintained that the end of the middle class had come, as stated by Günter Grass in 1988: "The class, that was once called the bourgeoisie no longer exists, it disappeared after the First World War, affected to the core by inflation and National Socialism" (Giroud and Grass 1988: 88ff.). Others thought that the middle class, which included entrepreneurs, those in the liberal professions, high-ranking administrative officials, grammar school teachers, and professors, could hold its own ground. It was held together by publicly confirmed common values and remained more powerful than ever before as a political player (Siegrist

1994, 2001; Wehler 2001; Vogel 2005; Kocka and Mitchell 2011, cf. also Kleßmann 1994; Berghahn 1995; Mendras 1997; Jessen 1999; Joly 1999; 2000; Zunz et al. 2002; Kocka 2004; 2011). These opposing positions seem less contradictory when a closer look is taken at the ways in which the middle class changed after the 1950s.

Changes to the Middle Class: The 1950s and 1960s

The European middle class changed significantly during the second half of the twentieth century. Three different epochs within this time period can be distinguished: the 1950s and 1960s, which were a period of re-stabilization for the bourgeoisie; the late 1960s to the 1980s, an era of fundamental change; and the 1990s, a period of consolidation for this altered bourgeoisie.

For the middle class, the 1950s and 1960s were an era of restabilization following a deep crisis that had placed its members face-to-face with real threats. It had first entered this crisis of confidence with the onset of the First World War and the Great Depression. It was under attack, not only by the labor movement but also by many disappointed intellectuals and critics among its own ranks, for it had not managed to create an efficient economy, international peacekeeping, or an integrated, stable society. Furthermore, parts of the middle class had experienced a severe existential crisis during the war and the Nazi occupation of Europe, when large numbers of the Jewish middle class were murdered or expelled. Even the non-Jewish middle class in countries like Poland were purposefully decimated by the Nazi regime. In addition to this, members of the bourgeoisie in many European countries lost their possessions—the "raison d'etre" for this milieu—as a result of bombings and displacement. In the countries where the daily food supply collapsed during the immediate postwar period, the social distinctions of the bourgeoisie often collapsed as well. Even middle-class women had to forage, cultivate small gardens, and trade carpets, furniture, pianos, and other normally bourgeois wares with farmers for food. After the Second World War, members of the bourgeoisie who had profited from and collaborated with the Nazi regime were discredited among sections of the public. Furthermore, communist governments in the eastern part of Europe systematically tried to do away with the bourgeoisie as a social milieu during the 1950s and 1960s. A final threat to the bourgeoisie was posed by decolonization, which ended many promising career opportunities overseas.

Despite, or because of, these crises, the bourgeoisie in Western Europe stabilized in the 1950s and 1960s. The unique economic boom during this period, the stable peace in Western Europe, and the Cold War strengthened confidence in the bourgeoisie. The labor movement no longer fundamentally criticized the bourgeoisie. Critics among their own ranks became quieter. A new belief in progress and the future came into being, from which the bourgeoisie also profited.

This restabilized bourgeoisie was still very similar to the bourgeoisie of the nineteenth and early twentieth centuries. This could even been seen in language; "bourgeoisie" and "middle class" were still terms used in everyday speech. The economic foundation of the bourgeoisie continued to be solid: family and self-owned businesses were established considerably more frequently than today. In particular in France and Great Britain, the replacement of family-run businesses by manager-run businesses in large concerns was still to come. The bourgeoisie still set itself far apart from the rest of society, i.e., from the working-class milieu, farmers, the petty bourgeoisie, and salaried employees. Property was still a clear social line that divided them from the rest of society. The distribution of wealth was considerably more unequal than today (see Chapter 6), and the possession of resources still played a special role in upper middle-class wealth. The rentier, an important historical figure in the bourgeoisie who lived only from his wealth and had no clear career, was still plentiful, at least in countries like France and Great Britain, as opposed to Germany, where he had already been widely edged out due to inflation and the devastation of war. A broad, milieu-conscious, industrial working class and the petty bourgeoisie generally still stood opposite the bourgeoisie.

Academic education also distinguished the bourgeoisie from those in lower social classes. Only a small number of adults attended university (see Table 12.1). The percentage of university graduates among all of the gainfully employed adults of the time—including the graduates from the pre- and interwar periods—was even smaller still. An elitist middle-class consciousness supported by an exclusive academic education was thus not yet a contradiction to reality. Furthermore, clear social lines of division were still being drawn through consumption. Whether a family was part of the middle class was clear by its lifestyle: whether they owned a car or television, what books they read, whether they vacationed abroad, what clothing they wore, and of course whether they had servants.

Moreover, the European middle class continued to have a common core set of values that was also often publicly touted. This was especially true of middle class family values: the clear allocation of roles between the employed husband and the wife, who was limited to the tasks of a housewife; the intense devotion on the part of the parents, and especially the mother, to the children; the seclusion of the family from the outside; the rational, frugal lifestyle of the private household; the considerable importance of family for the passing on of wealth; special middle-class transitions between phases of life; and special rituals for introducing daughters to society. Significance was placed on education, especially higher education and the education of an elite, on individual merit and self-control, on career and work as the center of life, on the central role of professional autonomy from the state, and on autonomy as entrepreneurs as well as in liberal careers such as professor and priest. Also of considerable importance were the autonomy and individualism of the artist and intellectual and, finally, the fundamental postulate regarding the equality of human beings at least before the law, the call for human and civil rights for everyone, and the demand for parliamentary control of the government and administration.

Beyond this, the internal interconnection of the middle class still existed, in part through exclusive marriage circles, in part through the common academic education and the traditional educational canon, and in part through an intense social life and connections maintained via pubs and clubs, middle-class manners, and common meeting places like the opera, theater, concerts, and museums. The middle class recruited overwhelmingly from within its own class. This interweaving and the social lines of division were not only lived out but also desired. The middle class was completely aware of its singularity and for the most part wanted to remain a special social class.

The Late 1960s to the 1980s

The middle class began to change beginning in the late 1960s, however. Another middle class gradually emerged, one that differed greatly from the traditional European middle class. The tension that had previously existed between the middle class and the working-class and rural milieus continued to decrease with the arrival of this new bourgeoisie. Little remained of those two milieus, so the fear of revolting workers and contempt for backward farmers that had characterized the middle class in the nineteenth and early twentieth centuries, and that was still present in the 1950s and 1960s, by and by lost their points of reference.

During this period the middle class outgrew its bounds as a small, refined social milieu minority. Middle-class jobs expanded rapidly, and the European middle class jumped from a middle class that encompassed only a small percentage of society to a middle class comprising one-third to one-half of the population, if the percentage of students in the younger generation is taken as a basis (see Table 12.1). This trend persists to the present; should it continue, the share of those belonging to the middle class will soon be higher than the percentage of industrial workers in the traditional industrial society around 1900. This massive middle class in the making could rise to over 100 million people in Europe. The consequences for social behavior, self-image, and the place of the individual have been little considered and studied even less.

Additionally, the lines of social division by which the middle class had distinguished itself from the lower classes through lifestyle, education, and wealth blurred and changed. Servants disappeared from private households, and car ownership, televisions, dining and children's rooms, travel abroad, suits, gowns, cosmetics and perfume, books, restaurants, butter, wine, and champagne were no longer middle-class specialties. These visible social lines were replaced by less obvious differences in choice of car manufacture, vacation destination, perfume, brand of clothing, or wine region. The differences were often so subtle that only insiders were able to recognize them.

The academic education that had been a clear middle class social distinction going into the 1950s was increasingly less suitable as such. Higher education had been expanding since the late nineteenth century and now reached a new dimension. In many European countries close to half of those born in any given year had attended university by 2000 (see Chapter 12 on education). In the process of this expansion, universities lost their previously exclusive character. The lines once drawn within educational systems in some European countries, for example in the Grandes Écoles in France or the Oxbridge universities in England, were no longer social distinctions of the middle class but rather lines drawn within the middle class itself. Furthermore, the educational gap between university graduates and the rest of society was distinctly smaller. While university graduates during the immediate postwar period faced a society in which few had progressed beyond elementary school, in the 1970s and 1980s the middle levels of education between university and elementary school fanned out. Stopping at mere elementary education became increasingly rare. The previous enormous social gap between the small minority of those who were academically educated and those who had an elementary education or were even illiterate was part of the past.

Property also lost some of its power as a means of social distinction. It was no longer only the middle class that possessed property; others now owned houses or cars, and had life insurance, mortgages, and bonds. The distribution of wealth remained unequal, but it did even out a bit (see Chapter 6 on social inequality). The social consequences of property ownership changed in particular. The majority of the population achieved the social security that property had given the middle class, which fundamentally distinguished those with a middle-class lifestyle from the "have-nots" in a different way: instead of security through wealth, they obtained security through the welfare state. At the same time, the rentier typical of the late nineteenth and early twentieth centuries, who lived off of his own wealth but had no career, became increasingly less common after the Second World War.

With this outward blurring of social lines, the social divisions within the middle class became more clearly visible, especially with regard to consumption and lifestyle. Individual professional groups within the middle class often distinguished themselves from each other by car make, vacation spot, clothing, and choice of newspaper, music, furniture, reading material, leisure activities, restaurants, and bars. Pierre Bourdieu's study of social distinctions quite impressively showed examples of the internal differences among the higher classes in France during the 1980s, which were not fundamentally different from those in other European countries (Bourdieu 1984: 212). Whether the bourgeois marriage pool and sociability opened somewhat has not been sufficiently analyzed.

In addition, middle-class values changed. Work, achievement, career, literacy, and an academic education were of course still highly appreciated, but family values shifted. The previous contrasts between male and female roles diminished. Equality in male and female education and employment became accepted in the middle class, even if women did not always choose to pursue a career. In 2000 more women studied at European universities than did men (see Chapter 12). The roles of the father and mother were less in opposition to each other. The separation between male and female senses of sociability changed as women joined male social environments and altered them. A variety of family models were lived out within the middle class, as was also the case in other parts of society. The middle-class family clearly lost influence. It no longer had a supporting role in the passing on of wealth to the next generation, as family-run businesses became less common within the economy and in the liberal professions. The role of the family in children's choice of partner or career diminished. We know too little about other values, especially the importance of nation, state, governmental authority, and democracy, among the European middle class.

Finally, the European middle class became more internationalized than it had been before the mid twentieth century. Not only entrepreneurs, but also high-ranking officials and scholars became more international in their fields, though this was rare among doctors and lawyers. At the same time, the internationalization of the middle class meant something other than what it had meant in the first half of the century. Internationalization was no longer so strongly associated with colonial domination, European empires, or occupation during war, but instead was related to international trade and export, international organizations, and the

European Union, as well as the internationalization of education and research.

The 1990s

The 1990s brought little change but rather marked a continuation of the trends from the 1970s. One development became more distinct than before, however: the crisis that had continuously accompanied the European middle class since the First World War, albeit in different forms, began to subside, in that it no longer had a life-threatening enemy. The power of the middle class was more boundless than ever, at least in comparison to the nineteenth and early twentieth centuries. The nobility was no longer a serious rival for political power; even in the last refuges of nobility—diplomacy and the army—members of the nobility had sunk to a limited few since the middle of the twentieth century. The labor movement's strength had continually decreased since the 1970s, dramatically in countries like France, Great Britain, and Italy, and more slowly, but still noticeably, in countries like Germany and Austria (see Chapter 9 on social movements). The alternative of a society without a middle class vanished into thin air with the collapse of the Soviet empire, and an economic and intellectual middle class slowly developed in East Central European societies. All in all, middle-class influence was now seen as a norm that no one thought to shake up within his or her own society or anywhere else in Europe.

A previously little-known threat stood in opposition to the middle class, however, just as it did for the rest of society. Not even the middle-class milieu was protected from joblessness or fears regarding a shortage of middle-class careers for their descendants. Academic success no longer necessarily led to professional and career success. That one's grown daughters or sons could honor the middle class value of professional success and the family's position within the middle class could be maintained was no longer a given. The middle class fear regarding the social decline of its sons and daughters increased.

European Divergences and Convergences

Until 1989–90, the divergences among the middle class in Europe did not recede during the second half of the twentieth century—an era of a new fundamental difference, the likes of which had not existed since the emergence of the middle class in the late eighteenth century. In the western part of Europe the middle class restabilized during the 1950s and

1960s. In the eastern part, in comparison, the previously mentioned significant injuries that the Nazis had inflicted upon the European middle class were augmented by the communist regimes' extensive measure to do away with it. The fact that one half of this Europe had a middle class and one half did not was an especially harsh new difference.

Furthermore, the differences that had affected the European middle class in the nineteenth and early twentieth centuries remained in effect during the second half of the twentieth century. Jürgen Kocka differentiates between three types of European middle class in each period. First came the wealthy, successful, strong Western European middle class, which was tightly interwoven with an open, commercialized aristocracy in social descent, and whose educated middle class—with the exception of France—was relatively weak and did not advance until later. Second, there was the Central European middle class, which came into financial success only later on, excluded by an aristocracy that was politically powerful primarily east of the Elbe, secured by privilege, and less commercialized. The educated members of this middle class were notably distinguished early on, politically influential, and oriented toward a strong state. And third, the Eastern European middle class: likewise excluded by a strong aristocracy, it was less financially successful and less distinguished as an educated middle class, and above all was less coherent and far more ethnically fragmented than the Western and Central European middle class (Kocka 1988).

These long-term differences continued to have an effect during the second half of the twentieth century. The economic and the educated middle class held different importance in society. The English and the West German middle class were quite different during the 1950s and 1960s. The German educated middle class still had much higher expectations of its own position within society, had a particular approach to advancement through education, and pushed for a more distinct boundary between itself and the lower social classes than did, say, the British educated middle class, which had not gone through a crisis of confidence as the German middle class had after the Nazi regime (Vogel 2005). The previous differences between the French and German middle class remained, in many cases. The lifestyle of the West German middle class was more withdrawn and less ostentatious than that of the French bourgeoisie. It was less pretentious with its wealth, less intensely interconnected through common elite schools like the Grandes Écoles, and somewhat more accepting of social climbers (Kaelble 1991a,b).

Nevertheless, the second half of the twentieth century was not just an era of divergences; convergences were also noticeable. The developments that changed the middle class in the late 1960s took place throughout

Western Europe. Middle-class careers expanded everywhere, and social distinctions between the middle and lower classes receded, developing into more subtle social differences. Family values were similarly affected. The former differences in the relationships between aristocracy and middle class played almost no role because the aristocracy in Central and Western Europe had lost its former importance. Ethnic distinctions within the middle class became weaker in Eastern Europe and a bit stronger in Western Europe. The reemerging middle class in Eastern Europe was much less ethnically divided, as ethnic groups no longer played as big a role after the Holocaust and the displacement that took place after the war. At the same time in Western Europe there came about a new Indian, Chinese, and Turkish middle class that was less integrated with the indigenous middle class. These developments marked a gradual convergence between an ethnically divided middle class in Eastern Europe and an ethnically homogeneous middle class in Western Europe.

European Hallmarks

The middle class was a special European feature that developed not in all European societies, but only in important and formative ones. To be sure, the occupational groups that made up the middle class existed elsewhere, but the European distinction lay in the previously mentioned interweaving of these professional groups through common social, economic, and political values and norms that were spread and propagated through public discourse.

A European hallmark during the second half of the twentieth century was the experience and memory of displacement, expulsion, or even liquidation by the communist regimes, as well as by the Nazi regime in its own countries and the lands it occupied—an experience not shared by the upper social rungs in either North America or Japan. This experience for the European middle class, which stood in great contrast to its unique heyday during the nineteenth and early twentieth centuries, faded noticeably in the 1990s and was rarely still recalled.

The Working Class

In contrast to the middle-class milieu, historians and sociologists rarely disagree about *whether* the working-class milieu weakened and instead argue, at most, about *when* it happened (cf. Mendras 1986; Fridenson 1990; Kaschuba 1991; Moser 1993; Berger and Broughton 1995; Schildt 1996; Hübner 1999; Berger and Compston 2002; Noiriel 2002; Tenfelde 2005;

Kleßmann 2007). The traditional European working class primarily had three functions. First, it was an "emergency milieu" of mutual solidarity, in case of unavailability or inadequacy of state- or church-based aid in times of personal crisis, the death of a family member, serious illness, unemployment, or poverty in old age. Second, in a society where the bourgeoisie and petty bourgeois excluded workers from education, social actitivies, and social respectability, the working-class milieu afforded its members a lifestyle promoting self-respect and dignity. Their educational establishments, music halls and chanson culture, holidays and demonstrations, restaurants and getaways, special clothing, and consumption revolved around societal self-respect and worth. And lastly, the working class was also the supporting level of the labor movement, the union movement, and the socialist parties (Tenfelde 1988).

In no way did these three functions always coincide, however. The working-class milieu was not consistently socialist, but was also often conservative, linked strongly to the church and sometimes open to the radical right. Conversely, the socialist movement was supported not only by the working class but also by other social milieus, including salaried employees and the petty bourgeoisie as well as intellectuals. The working class had furthermore been deeply politically divided into a socialist and a communist milieu during the interwar period and then again during the Cold War in the more powerful European countries. The political uniformity of the working class should therefore not be overrated, and the social foundation of the socialist movement in Europe should not be oversimplified. Nevertheless, the emergence of the European working-class milieu largely explains why socialism first existed as a mass movement in Europe and why the European model was then borrowed and changed in other parts of the world. Vice versa, the decline of the working class also explains why the union movement has lost much of its earlier strength in the last few decades.

It is undisputable that an industrial working-class milieu still existed in the 1950s and 1960s. Industry was the foundation of this milieu, and industrial work was at its peak throughout Europe at this time. Only during this period was the industrial sector the largest employment sector in Europe overall. It was also then that it first superseded the agrarian sector because the European periphery in the South, East and North of Europe industrialized during this period, in part through planned economies and in part through the free market, while at the same time the old industrial countries continued to have a strong industrial sector (see Chapter 2 on labor).

The European working-class milieu gradually receded for several reasons beginning in the 1970s and 1980s. A first, economic reason was the already-depicted decline of industrial employment throughout Western

Europe. This decline was usually not dramatic, but it was clearly noticeable. According to estimates by the International Labor Office, industrial employment fell from over 50 percent to just over 40 percent in the 1970s and 1980s, especially in Northern and Western Europe. According to estimates by the OECD, industrial and trade activity was still at 38 percent in Western Europe in 1960, but by 1999 it was only at 29 percent (OECD 1985: 36; 2000: 40; ILO 1997: 214ff.). The percentage of workers in a narrower sense sank even more. Meanwhile, structural changes further weakened the working class. The number of indigenous, skilled, male industrial workers went down. Instead the number of unskilled, female, and foreign workers, who were less responsive to the previous working class's way of life, increased (Mendras 1986: 35 ff.; Noiriel 2002). The new immigration from the Eastern and Southern Mediterranean changed the European working-class milieu in particular.

Another change affecting the working class was the rise in real income, primarily since the boom of the 1950s and 1960s. This increase led to a considerably better standard of living and housing, to better nutrition, clothing, furnishings, household appliances, leisure time, and vacations for the worker. The threat of complete destitution subsided from workers' everyday lives. As a result, the practical everyday solidarity in emergency situations—one of the former working-class culture's basic functions—became less imperative. At the same time, the improvement in the standard of living also meant that the social lines dividing the working class from the bourgeoisie and lower middle classes with regard to consumption were less clearly drawn and that the exclusion by others, as well as the segregation imposed by the working-class milieu itself, became less noticeable in everyday life. Proletarian traits that once had strongly distinguished working-class from middle-class households diminished: the kitchen as the central point of the home was increasingly replaced by the living room with its corner sofa and wall units, as was the norm for the rest of society. The diet by which a blue-collar household was immediately recognized during the first half of the twentieth century—reliant on such staples as lard, potatoes, pork, beer, and hard liquor and generally lacking in fruit—began to resemble that of the rest of society or, conversely, was sometimes imitated by the other classes. Proletariat clothing—caps and overalls—disappeared and was replaced with work clothes or standard apparel from department stores that other classes purchased as well. The differences in essential household expenses came to a minimum. Skilled laborers' households in France in the 1950s still spent about half of the household budget on food, double the percentage for professional households. By 1980 this share had fallen to only a quarter—about one and a half times as much as the food allocation in professionals' households

(Herpin and Verger 1988: 114). The introduction of the compact car and along with it the vacation, department stores and supermarkets for everyone, mass residential construction, and many new consumer goods functioned as a social equalizers.

Another crucial cause of the decline of the proletarian working-class milieu was the creation of the modern welfare state, which was first implemented after the war (see Chapter 10 on the welfare state). It considerably improved social security in individual life crises such as disease, death of a parent, unemployment, and poverty among the elderly. It also contributed considerably to the fact that the everyday solidarity of the former proletariat working-class culture was no longer as urgently necessary as it had been. Older, nongovernmental, voluntary insurances for individual occupational groups like the *Mutuels* in France were pushed to the sidelines by the more centralized social security after the Second World War. The everyday pillars of the older proletarian working-class milieu lost importance as a result.

The exclusion of the children of laborers from secondary and higher education decreased. Working-class children's chances of snagging a spot in a university in Europe around 1950 were still unimaginably poor: not even one in 100 working-class children made it to college. But by 2000, on average in Europe, just over one of every ten blue-collar children went on to higher education. This did not yet amount to equality of opportunity, but it was a definite improvement. The increase in the percentage of working-class children among students, which on average remained low, was not as critical to this change as was the enormous expansion of the number of students and universities (see Chapter 12).

Urban expansion after the Second World War likewise eroded the proletarian working-class milieu. City growth during the late nineteenth and early twentieth centuries had led to a spacial separation of social milieus—to completely working-class districts, and sometimes even to almost entirely working-class cities in Europe. After the 1950s and 1960s, by contrast, city planning managed to blur these old social lines of division in city districts (see Chapter 11 on cities). Laborers no longer lived together exclusively with other laborers.

Meanwhile, the new forms of media and the new leisure industry marginalized the old proletariat leisure culture. The media that emerged after the interwar period and were not tied to a particular milieu—for example radio, film, television, records, and paperbacks—blurred not only the social lines dividing the bourgeoisie from lower social classes but also the lines dividing the working from the upper classes. Attempts by the labor movement to insulate the milieu, for example proletariat radio, movies, records, and paperbacks, proved unable to take hold and had largely failed since the interwar period (see Chapter 8 on media). The lines dividing milieus broke open in sports as well. Soccer, once a primarily proletariat sport in England, also became popular outside of the working class. Established local activities that spanned the milieus, such as carnivals or district festivals, increased, and new ones were created.

At least in Germany, political decisions also contributed to the decline of the working-class milieu. The sharp division between the social democratic and communist subcultures during the Weimar Republic had already had a negative effect on working-class culture. The destruction of the labor movement culture or its retreat underground during the Nazi regime weakened it even further. After the Second World War the Social Democratic Party of Germany and the unions in West Germany decided not to reestablish the multitude of former workers' associations. Within the remaining labor movement culture, older organizations like the Workers' Welfare Association, the Workers' Samaritan Federation Germany, and Neue Heimat (New Home) largely lost their former identity as pillars of the working-class milieu and like many others became charitable organizations or apartment building contractors.

Divergences

The working-class milieus in Western and Eastern Europe differed the most from each other before 1989. These divergences fundamentally changed thereafter, however. During the 1950s and 1960s, social distinctions in Eastern Europe were significantly more marginal than in the West for several reasons. The prominent social divisions that still existed in Western Europe had disappeared with the repression and ousting of the upper and lower middle classes in Eastern Europe. Furthermore, in the East public luxury consumption and demonstrative social distinction through cars, travel abroad, food, and clothing receded and were replaced by a commonality of want due to the centralized state control of consumer goods. Educational opportunities for working-class children were purposely improved throughout Eastern Europe, and the clear social divide caused by the exclusion of blue-collar children from academic education faded considerably. Many members of the new power and economic elite came from the working-class milieu and symbolized the improved opportunities for advancement. Social demarcations based on property diminished upon the socialization of businesses and the devaluation of home ownership. The welfare state in Eastern Europe afforded quite a bit of social security, and the labor-centered society offered workers many amenities not previously accessible to them, including vacations, other cultural programs, and continuing education courses.

But these East-West differences changed considerably during the course of the 1970s and 1980s. The working-class milieu was generally preserved more in Eastern Europe than in Western Europe. A deciding factor in this was that industrial employment did not decrease in Eastern Europe and the industry sector and its share of jobs were retained. Immigration of foreign workers was also much less common. Furthermore, in Eastern Europe the increase in real income was smaller and opportunities for consumption fewer; social delineations blurred more slowly as a result. The head start on social security there faded away with the implementation of the modern welfare state in Western Europe. Social contrasts after retirement were sharper in the East than in the West. Educational opportunities improved more slowly in the East, as secondary schools and universities did not expand as quickly; thus, working-class children in the 1980s in Eastern Europe usually had fewer opportunities for higher education. Finally, the bourgeoisie's former social distinctions were replaced by new social distinctions that were just as formidable as the old ones. The cadre and intelligentsia defined themselves through travel abroad; separate, more affordable shopping opportunities; and better access to governmental vacation and cultural programs.

The Rural Milieu

A third milieu that shaped the European societies of the nineteenth and early twentieth centuries and still existed during the postwar period also eroded over the last decades of the century: the rural milieu. The decline of this milieu had not only economic causes, but societal and political causes as well (cf. Kaschuba and Lipp 1982; Huebscher 1983; Moulin 1983; Mendras 1984; Brüggemeier and Riehle 1986; Gervais 1987; Erkner 1990; Humm 1999; Bauerkämper 2002; Patel 2009).

In many cases the economic basis of the European rural milieu during the postwar period and the 1950s was still primarily economic self-sufficiency. European peasants did not usually manage their farms according to the principles of profit maximizing and sale of their products on the market; rather, they primarily produced for their own use. As well as consuming quite a bit of the food from the farm themselves, they made most of their own clothing, procured their own means of heating, and carried out repairs to their own houses and equipment for the most part by themselves. They did not even necessarily relinquish the building of houses to construction companies but were often autonomous in this as well. They sold a portion of their products on the market or to cooperatives, of course, but the principle of self-sufficiency was still dominant and shaped their entire method of operation.

This method of operation differed greatly from work in cities, where by contrast there was no clear division between work and leisure. Agricultural work meant continuous demands, admittedly with individual work rhythms regarding the intensity of tasks throughout the day, the week, and especially the year and throughout life. A lack of specialization was still characteristic in agricultural work. Peasants were generalists who raised crops and livestock, produced a multitude of products in so doing, and at the same time were competent to perform a wide range of repairs. Because of this marginal specialization, peasants obtained little formal training. Education was rudimentary and sometimes completely nonexistent, and occupational knowledge was passed down within the family or learned through practical tasks as a farm hand. Agricultural management also always meant heavy physical demands on the entire family: at an early age children were incorporated into the work process, as were housewives, unmarried family members, and the elderly.

Farmers' extensive self-sufficiency and special operating methods led to unique ways of life. Through to the postwar period, the rural standard of living was much lower than the urban standard of living, with the exception of the class of wealthy peasants. Homes' facilities for drinking water supply, electricity, bathing, and heating were generally lower than the urban standard. In 1970, half of the farms in the French region Ille-et-Vilaine were still without running water. One-third of the farmhouses had only one room, and more than a quarter had dirt floors (Huebscher 1983). A peasant's diet was often unilaterally oriented toward products from his own land. In contrast to the nineteenth century, peasants tended to have poorer health than city dwellers because their food was often unhealthy and medical treatment from doctors was usually insufficient. Life expectancy in rural areas was thus usually shorter than in cities. Real income in the country—difficult to calculate because of the extensive self-sufficiency—often seemed to be lower. For all these reasons, rural households were unable to keep up with urban consumption, especially the acquisition of new, long-lasting goods like household appliances, radios, televisions, records, books, and, of course, vacations.

Social contacts for rural families looked very different from those in city households. Especially in regions with single farmsteads, rural life was strongly characterized by social isolation, and bonds among family were strong. The rate of occupational inheritance, and with it the continuity of the rural way of life and rural poverty, was high. In France in 1953, 60 percent of peasants' sons still became peasants. The isolation of rural life led to fewer chances to escape or advance socially because there were few opportunities for education or information about other careers. Marriage pools were also extensively limited to rural families. The quota of unmarried people was high and likewise perpetuated the limited chances of leaving the rural milieu (Huebscher 1983).

Decimated after the 1950s by a historically unique transformation, the rural milieu today lingers only as a fringe phenomenon within European agriculture. This deep upheaval has, as of yet, unfortunately only been sparsely researched. More intensive research about this dramatic change in European society has been conducted by historians only for France and by ethnologists for Germany.

The causes of the rural milieu's decline were largely economic. The traditional farm with its high degree of self-sufficiency was replaced by modern agricultural enterprises that were managed as businesses, producing relatively few products according to the principles of profit maximizing and selling their products on the market like every other producer. This new type of farm was capital-intensive and was operated in line with modern accounting principles. On one hand, the extraordinary increase in Western European agricultural production after the Second World War was part of the establishment of the modern farmer. Productivity figures for vegetables as well as livestock skyrocketed more quickly than ever before in the history of European agriculture, even more quickly than productivity within industry. During this historically unique rise in productivity, Western Europe not only attained self-sufficiency in terms of agricultural production but also became one of the most important agricultural exporters in the world. On the other hand, the number of agricultural employees sank rapidly throughout Europe even as, for the first time in history, the number of agricultural businesses also noticeably shrank. The last decades of the century were a unique period of upheaval with regard to the mode of operation, productivity, and number of businesses in European agriculture.

This upheaval had far-reaching effects on work models within agriculture. Those whose livelihoods were in agriculture were now, in contrast to the peasant production managers, similar to those who were outside of agriculture in the trade and service industries: they were specialists in the production of specific agricultural products. Their education became longer and often incorporated secondary education in addition to an elementary education. Farmers often also had vocational training, remaining on the cutting edge of knowledge about their particular production areas through continuous training and advisory services. Unlike peasant agriculture in earlier days, farming was a career. A farmers's professional tasks no longer fundamentally differed from those in the industry and service sectors. The relationship between business and family changed as a result. Increasingly fewer agricultural businesses remained family businesses, at least in the traditional sense of all family members regularly working for their own company.

The rural way of life changed radically. Rural real income climbed steadily in most Western European countries. The farmer's standard of living came into alignment with the standard of living among city dwellers. The quality of living conditions was no longer as noticeably different. The availability of drinking water and electricity resembled that in urban households, as held true for bath and toilet facilities. Agricultural households were as integrated into the market as urban households, buying not only industrial goods but also food, clothing, heating supplies, and furniture from the market. Differences in the use of durable consumer goods like refrigerators, televisions, washing machines, and freezers completely disappeared in the century's later decades. Rural households were even better equipped than urban households with certain durable goods that were especially important for life in the country, like automobiles or freezers (Huebscher 1983).

The rural lifestyle also changed fundamentally: the former social isolation of peasants was broken thanks to the automobile, and the center of many activities relocated from villages to small cities, admittedly to the decisive disadvantage of age groups that could not use cars, including adolescents and the elderly. Deep interfamilial conflicts about family life emerged—or at least this was reported in France—centered in part on the farmer's economic behavior and in part around the relationship of the family to the agricultural business. More and more, rural children left the farms. In 1977 only one-third of farmers' sons in France chose a career in farming; another third became laborers. More surprising is that one-third became white-collar employees, civil servants, tradesmen, and merchants, and close to every twentieth farmer's son advanced into a higher class. Marriage pools also opened up, and marriages between farmers and urban dwellers and between farmers and women with other careers became considerably more common (Huebscher 1983: 496; Moulin 1988: 254). Whether the farmer's way of life and village life still differed from city life after this upheaval in rural life and business, through which farmers became a small minority in most villages, is controversial. In any case, the differences between rural and urban life decreased.

The Petty Bourgeoisie

The milieus discussed above held sway in European society and politics, but no less influential was a fourth milieu: the petty bourgeoisie or lower middle class, encompassing independent tradesmen, retailers, innkeepers, truckers, and fishers. Geoff Crossick and Heinz Gerhard Haupt have elaborated five traits in particular that characterized this milieu from the nineteenth century into the 1950s and 1960s (Crossick and Haupt 1998; cf. also Winkler 1972).

Economic independence and the desire to run one's own business were significant characteristics of the petty bourgeoisie. Lower middle–class autonomy relied heavily on property, with its economic opportunities for profit and its social security. Like the middle class, or upper middle class, the petty bourgeoisie differed from laborers and low-wage employees by dint of property. They differed from the bourgeoisie, however, in that their values were opposed to bureaucratic careers as civil servants or salaried employees as well as to careers in education as teachers and professors. The petty bourgeoisie was furthermore economically fixed at a local level for the most part—a trait also in opposition to the economic middle class. Its clientele was usually local or came from the rural surrounding areas. The threat of superior competition from large companies was also an influence on the petty bourgeoisie after industrialization and the development of larger industrial firms and commerce. For craftsmen the threat was large industrial producers; for retailers, the department store, store chain, and shopping center; and for carriers, the train or postal service. This competition was not usually based on the petty bourgeoisie's home turf but came from the big cities and capitals, or from abroad. At the same time, the economic independence of the lower middle class was in constant danger due to their dependence on credit, whether in the form of bank loans to their businesses or the extension of credit to customers. The petty bourgeoisie thus always combined economic independence with property ownership and the security it provided, but its position was also precarious, subject to the risks posed by larger companies and the financial weaknesses of its own clientele.

The petty bourgeoisie was affected by social mobility to a far greater degree than is generally accepted. Studies on the nineteenth and twentieth centuries alike have shown time and again that by no means did family business traditions among the petty bourgeoisie necessarily prevail through several generations. Quite to the contrary, the petty bourgeoisie was distinguished by high social mobility in different directions: members of the petty bourgeoisie came from other social classes more frequently than did peasants, workers, or members of the middle class. Conversely, the sons and daughters of the lower middle class seldom remained in this social milieu, a significant variance from the pattern of children born to peasants. Many descended socially into the working class, but many also advanced. The petty bourgeoisie was an important milieu of origin for the educated middle class, businessmen and entrepreneurs, as well as for those in liberal professions, senior civil servants, teachers, and professors. The petty bourgeoisie résumé was shaped by many changes, including shifts from being financially independent to being wage-dependent. The lifespan of small businesses was not generally very long. Even though long-lasting family businesses only survived within a small higher social level, they strongly defined the public image of the petty bourgeoisie.

The family played a central role for the petty bourgeoisie. Lower middle–class businesses worked intensively with familial resources, tending to be family businesses operated by a married couple and employing children and other family members. In the absence of an inexpensive family workforce, the family economy among the petty bourgeoisie was often uncompetitive and unable to survive crises. Relationships between married couples and between parents and children were shaped by business in a special way among the petty bourgeoisie. The share of work between husbands and wives varied according to the country. In some countries, like France, the wife took charge of customer relations while the *patron* was rarely visible in public. Family life and family business, small business, and the private familial household were often closely intermingled. Furthermore, apprentices and assistants were often integrated within the family in lower middle–class businesses, which resulted in especially close ties and responsibilities as well as conflicts.

The petty bourgeoisie developed an individual culture that was dominant in small cities. This culture supported itself with sport and gun clubs, song and music associations, and book clubs and conferences. Lower middle–class culture imparted a set of values centered on the family, individual wealth, personal trust, independence, and local identity. Political values and attitudes were also a feature of the petty bourgeoisie and, in contrast to the social and economic aspects of the lower middle class, varied greatly from country to country. The lower middle class played a large role in the labor movement in some countries; in others it was a decisive basis for political liberalism; in yet others it supported political conservatism. In German lands it was also a social foundation of the rise of the Nazi movement. The political culture of the petty bourgeoisie, which was important everywhere, depended largely on the respective national environment.

How much the petty bourgeoisie tried to separate itself from the working-class milieu is controversial. Some historians argue that the social lines dividing it from the working class were a core issue within the petty bourgeoisie. Other historians argue that the lower middle class, as the milieu of bartenders, retailers, and craftsmen, was strongly integrated with the working-class milieu, representing an important network for the working-class milieu and even often advancing to become political spokespersons for the labor movement. Early socialist parliamentarians were not uncommonly innkeepers or retailers.

This traditional European lower middle–class milieu did not disappear as dramatically as did the rural milieu, but it did fundamentally change during the second half of the twentieth century. The number of small businesses decreased considerably throughout Europe, and the number of lower middle–class households also dropped. The petty bourgeoisie's social mobility also changed. Workers had better opportunities for advancement, and more social climbers came from the rural milieu. The middle class recruited more from other parts of society. The lower middle class became more feminine, as many boutiques and stores were run by women and not by families. Family ties became weaker in general. The family business, in which parents and children or other family members worked together, became considerably less common. It survived the longest in the lower middle–class milieu of immigrants. The petty bourgeoisie, who were numerically weak, no longer influenced local culture as strongly—especially when immigrants made up a large part of the lower middle class. Above all, the petty bourgeoisie lost its former political significance as a foundation for conservative or liberal parties.

Summary: The End of a European Hallmark?

Social milieus changed significantly in Europe during the second half of the twentieth century. The previous working class of mostly urban industrial workers, which still existed into the 1960s, significantly declined in Western Europe during the 1970s and in Eastern Europe in the 1990s. The peasant milieu that was often encountered in Europe in the 1950s shrank away to only a small remainder. The petty bourgeois retailers, independent craftsmen, innkeepers, transport carriers, and fishers were likewise no longer as numerous in 2000 as they had still been in the 1950s. It was only the ranks of middle class and salaried employees that did not decrease, but to the contrary expanded. By 2000, the middle class shaped European society more than ever before as its former opponents in the spheres of social influence and political power—the aristocracy and organized labor in particular—now wielded only weak remnants of their former clout and were no longer actually societally opposed to the middle class. At the same time the upper middle class changed considerably. A small elitist middle class had become a broad mass middle class that no longer separated itself so distinctly from the lower classes socially or in terms of differing values, especially in family life and politics, as it had around 1950.

Had a striking European hallmark dissolved in the process? Did the unique European world of social milieus, which were dependent on each other for their social distinctions and severe tensions, now belong to history? The social distinctions between these different milieus in Europe had undoubtedly eroded by the end of the twentieth century. Of course, many institutions, buildings, and ways of life characteristic of these social milieus were preserved. There were still strong unions in Europe after the decline of the working-class milieu, and as a result also stronger business associations and other employment relations than in non-European societies. Also lingering were labor parties. Though their social base was increasingly shifting to other classes, these parties still strove to use the previous dividing line between wage laborers and the rest of society as a political camp.

At the same time, there were still middle-class parties that attempted to cash in politically on the old appeal of the middle class. Most European countries retained the institution the middle class had once used to draw and maintain a line of social distinction from the lower classes: the state-run university, and in some European countries, like France and Great Britain, even elite secondary schools and colleges. And European sociedty was still replete with the instruments the bourgeoisie had once used to form social lines: the refinement of food, beverages, clothing, taste in interior design; and education in the areas of art, music, film, and literature. The buildings related to former social milieus were firmly present: middle-class residential areas as well as working-class districts and peasant villages still existed, giving European cities and villages a completely different silhouette compared to settlements in North America or Japan. Most notably, however, citizens were no longer so bound to social milieu as they had been from the nineteenth to the mid-twentieth century. Important social divides blurred within European society as social milieus changed.

However, social inequalities, social distinctions, and barriers to social mobility only changed, without diminishing. Between the upper and lower classes, inequalities, social distinctions, and obstacles to mobility remained as distinct as before. In no way did the extremes of upper-class luxury and poverty disappear—to the contrary, both actually intensified at the end of the twentieth century. The boundaries to educational opportunities and advancement for the lower and middle classes were preserved, as were the privileged opportunities that allowed those born into the higher classes to remain there. The decline of lifestyles particular to the former milieus and the social divides between them did not create an egalitarian society. More importantly, European societies developed special traits regarding social inequalities and social mobility. The next chapter will cover these.

References

The Elite

Bach M. "Europa als büorkratische Herrschaft: Verwaltungsstrukturen und bürokratische Politik in der Europaischen Union." In *Europawissenschaften*, ed. G. F. Schuppert, I. Pernice, and L. Haltern. Baden-Baden 2005, 575–611.

Bertin-Mourot B. and M. Bauer. "Vers un modèle européen de dirigeants? Une comparaison Allemagne/France/Grande-Bretagne." *Problème séconorniques* 2, no. 482 (1996): 18–26.

Best H. "Der langfristige Wandel politischer Eliten in Europa 1867–2000: Auf dem Weg der Konvergenz?" In *Oberschichten – Eliten – Herrschende Klassen*, ed. S. Hradil and P. Imbusch. Opladen 2003, 369–400.

Best H. and M. Cotta. *Parliamentary Representatives in Europe 1848–2000: Legislative Recruitment and Careers in Eleven European Countries.* Oxford 2000.

Birnbaum P. *Les élites socialistes au pouvoir: 1981–1985.* Paris 1985.

Bresc H., F. D' Almeida, and J.-M. Salmann, eds. *La circulation des élites.* Paris 2002.

Bussiere E. and M. Dumoulin, eds. *Milieux économiques et intégration européenne en Europe occidentale au XXe siècle.* Arras 1998.

Charle C. "Légitimité en peril: Eléments pour une histoire cornprarée des élites te de l'état en France et en Europe occidentale (XIXe–XXe siècle)." *Actes de la Recherche* 116–117, special issue "Histoire de l'état" (March 1997): 39–52.

Charle C. *La crise des sociétés impériales, Allemagne, France, Grande-Bretagne (1900–1940): Essai d'histoire comparée.* Paris 2001.

Frei N. *Karrieren im Zwielicht: Hitlers Eliten nach 1945.* Frankfurt a. M. 2001.

Geissler R. *Die Sozialstruktur Deutschlands.* 4th ed. Opladen 2006.

Hartmann M. "Class-Specific Habitus and the Social Reproduction of the Business Elites in Germany and France." *The Sociological Review* 48 (2000): 241–261.

Hartmann M. "Nationale oder transnationale Eliten: Europäische Eliten im Vergleich." In *Oberschichten – Eliten – Herrschende Klassen*, ed. S. Hradil and P. Imbusch. Opladen 2003, 273–298.

Hartmann M. *Elitesoziologie: Eine Einführung.* Frankfurt a. M. 2004.

Henke K.-D. and H. Voller, eds. *Politische Säuberung in Europa: Die Abrechnung mit Faschismus und Kollaboration nach dem Zweiten Weltkrieg.* Munich 1991.

Herzog D. "Der moderne Berufspolitiker: Karrierebedingungen und Funktion in westlichen Demokratien." In *Eliten in der Bundesrepublik*, ed. Hans Georg Wehling. Stuttgart 1990, 28–51.

Kaelble H. "The Rise of the Managerial Enterprise in Germany, c. 1870–c. 1930." In *The Development of Managerial Enterprise*, ed. K. Kobayashi and H. Morikawa. Tokyo 1986, 71–86.

Page E.C. and V. Wright. *Bureaucratic Elites in Western European States: A Comparative Analysis of Top Officials.* Oxford 1999.

Schröder H.W., W. Weege, and M. Zech. *Historische Parlamentarismus-, Elitenund Biographieforschung.* Cologne 2000 (HSR, Attachment Nr. 11).

Sklair L. *The Transnational Capitalist Class.* Oxford 2001.

Soutou G.-H. "Les élites diplornatiques françaises et allemandes au XX siècle." In *Eliten in Deutschland und Frankreich im 19. und 20. Jahrhundert,* ed. R. Hudemann and G.-H. Soutou. Munich 1994.

Tarrius A. "Circulation des élites professionnelles et intégration européenne." *Revue européenne des migrations internationales* 8 (1992): 27–56.

Ziegler D., ed. *Grossbürger und Unternehmer: Die deutsche Wirtschaftselite im 20. Jahrhundert.* Göttingen 2000.

Intellectuals

Bachoud A., J. Cuesta, and M. Trebitsch, eds. *Les intellectuels et l'Europe.* Paris 2000.

Charle C. *Vordenker der Moderne: Die Intellektuellen im 19. Jahrhundert.* Frankfurt 1996.

Eisenstadt S. N. "Transcendental Vision, Centre Formation and the Role of Intellectuals." In *Comparative civilizations and multiple modernities.* 2 vols. ed. S.N. Eisenstadt. Leiden 2003, vol. 1, 249–264.

Granjon M.-C., N. Racine, and M. Trebitsch, eds. *Histoire comparée des intellectuels.* Paris 1997.

Lepenies W. *Die drei Kulturen, Soziologie zwischen Literatur und Wissenschaft.* Munich 1985.

Racine N. and M. Trebitsch, eds. *Du genre en histoire intellectuelle.* Paris 2004.

Ringer P. *Fields of Knowledge.* Cambridge 1992.

Trebitsch M. and M.-C. Granjon, eds. *Pour une histoire comparée des intellectuels.* Paris 1998.

Winnock M. *Das Jahrhundert der Intellektuellen.* Constance 2003.

Bourgeoisie

Berghahn V.R., ed. *Quest for Economic Empire: European Strategies of German Big Business in the Twentieth Century.* Oxford 1995.

Bourdieu P. *Die feinen Unterschiede.* Frankfurt a. M. 1984.

Charle C. "La bourgeoisie en Europe au XXe siècle." In *Encyclopedia of History,* ed. J. Winter (forthcoming 2007).

Giroud, F. and G. Grass. *Ecoutez moi: Paris-Berlin, Aller-retour.* Paris 1988.

Herpin N. and D. Verger. *La consommation des française.* Paris 1988.

Jessen R. *Akademische Elite und kommunistische Diktatur: Die ostdeutsche Hochschullehrerschaft in der Ulbricht-Ära.* Göttingen 1999.

Joly H. *Patrons d'Allemagne: Sociologie d'une élite industrielle 1933–1989.* Paris 1996.

Joly H. "Kontinuität und Diskontinuität der industriellen Elite nach 1945." In *Grossbürger und Unternehmer: Die deutsche Wirtschaftselite im 20. Iahrhundert,* ed. D. Ziegler. Göttingen 2000, 54–72.

Kaelble H. *Nachbarn am Rhein: Entfremdung und Annäherung der französischen und deutschen Gesellschaft seit 1880.* Munich 1991a, chap. 9.

Kaelble H. "Die oberen Schichten in Frankreich und der Bundesrepublik seit 1945." *Frankreich-Jahrbuch* (1991b): 63–78.

Kleßmann C. "Relikte des Bildungsbürgertums in der DDR." In *Sozialgeschichte der DDR*, ed. H. Kaelble, J. Kocka, and H. Zwahr. Stuttgart 1994, 254–270.

Kocka, J. *Industrial Culture and Bourgeois Society: Business, Labor, and Bureaucracy in Modern Germany*. New York 1999.

Kocka J. "The Middle Classes in Europe." In *The European Way: European Societies in the 19th and 20th Centuries*, ed. H. Kaelble. New York and Oxford 2004, 15–43.

Kocka, J. and Mitchell, A. eds. *Bourgeois Society in 19th Century Europe*. Basingstoke 2011.

Mendras H. *La seconde révolution française 1965–1984*. Paris 1986.

Mendras H. *L'Europe des européeens: Sociologie de l'Europe occidentale*. Paris 1997.

Saint Martin M., de. *L'espace de la noblesse*. Paris 1993.

Saint Martin M., de. "Vers uns sociologie des aristocrates déclassés." *Cahiers d'histoire* 45 (2000): 785–801.

Siegrist H. "History of Bourgeoisie, Middle Classes." In *Encyclopedia of the Social and Behavioral Sciences*, ed. N.J. Smelser and P.B. Baltes. Amsterdam 2001, 1307–1314.

Vogel R. "Bürgertum oder Akteure der Zivilgesellschaft? Bildungspolitische Interessenpolitik von Grossunternehmern und Hochschullehrern in Britannien und Westdeutschland (1945–1965)." Dissertation HU Berlin 2005.

Wehler, Hans-Ulrich. "Deutsches Bürgertum nach 1945: Exitus oder Phönix aus der Asche." *Geschichte und Gesellschaft* 27 (2001): 617–634.

Zunz O., L. Schoppa, and N. Nawatari, eds. *Social Contracts under Stress: The Middle Classes of America, Europe, and Japan at the Turn of the Century*. New York 2002.

Working Class

Berger S. and D. Broughton, eds. *The Force of Labour: The Western European Labour Movement and the Working Class in the 20th Century*. Oxford 1995.

Berger S. and H. Compston. eds. *Policy Concertation and Social Partnership in Western Europe*. New York 2002.

Fridenson P. "Le conflit social." In *L'histoire de la France*, vol. 3: *L'état et les conflits*, ed. V.A. Burguière and J. Revel. Paris 1990.

Geissler R. *Die Sozialstruktur Deutschlands*. 4th ed. Wiesbaden 2006, chap. 9.

Hübner P. *Arbeiter in der SBZ – DDR*. Essen 1999.

ILO. *Economically Active Population*. 5 vols. Geneva 1997.

Kaschuba W., G. Korff, and B.J. Warneken, eds. *Arbeiterkultur seit 1945: Ende oder Veranderung?* Tübingen 1991.

Kleßmann, C. *Arbeiter im 'Arbeiterstaat' DDR. Deutsche Traditionen, sowjetisches Modell, westdeutsches Magnetfeld (1945 bis 1971)*. Bonn 2007.

Mendras H. *La seconde révolution française 1965–1984*. Paris 1986.

Moser J. "Arbeiter, Angestellte und Frauen in der nivellierten Mittelstandsgesellschaft." In *Modernisierung im Wiederaufbau: Die westdeutsche Gesellschaft der 50er Jahre*, ed. A. Schildt and A. Sywottek. Bonn 1993.

Noiriel G. *Les ouvriers dans la société française XlXe–XXe siècle*. Paris 2002.

OECD. *Historical Statistics, 1960–1983*. Paris 1985.

OECD. *Historical Statistics, 1970–1999*. Paris 2000.

Schildt G. *Die Arbeiterschaft im 19. und 20. Jahrhundert*. Munich 1996.

Tenfelde K. "Vom Ende und Erbe der Arbeiterkultur." In *Gesellschaftlicher Wandel, Soziale Demokratie: 125 Jahre SPD*, ed. S. Miller and M. Ristau. Cologne 1988, 155–172.

Tenfelde K. "Arbeiter, Arbeiterbewegungen und Staat in Europa des 'kurzen' 20. Jahrhunderts." In *Arbeiter in Staatssozialismus*, ed. P. Hübner et al. Cologne 2005, 17–34.

The Rural Milieu

Bauerkämper A. *Ländliche Gesellschaft in der kommunistischen Diktatur: Zwangsmodernisierung und Tradition in Brandenburg 1945–1963*. Cologne 2002.

Brüggemeier B. and R. Riehle. *Das Dorf*. Frankfurt a. M. 1986.

Erkner P. *Ernährungskrise und Nachkriegsgesellschaft: Bauern und Arbeiterschaft in Bayern 1943–1953*. Stuttgart 1990.

Gervais M. et al. *La fin de la France paysanne: de 1914 à nos jours*. Paris 1987.

Huebscher R. "Destruction de la paysannerie?" In *Histoire des français XIX–XXe siècles: la société*, ed. Y. Lequin. Paris 1983, 483–529.

A. Humm. *Auf dem Weg zum sozialistischen Dorf? Zum Wandel der öffentlichen Lebenswelt in der DDR und der Bundesrepublik Deutschland 1952–1969*. Göttingen 1999.

Kaschuba W. and C. Lipp. *Dörfliches Überleben*. Tübingen 1982.

Mendras H. *La fin des paysans*. Paris 1984.

Moulin A. *Les paysans dans la société française de la révolution à nos jours*. Paris 1988.

Patel, K. *Europäisierung wider Willen. Die Bundesrepublik Deutschland in der Agrarintegration der EWG 1955-1973*. Munich 2009.

Petty Bourgeoisie and White Collar Employees

Crossick G. and H.-G. Haupt. *Die Kleinbürger, Eine europäische Sozialgeschichte des 19. Jahrhunderts*. Munich 1998.

Kocka J. *Die Angestellten in der deutschen Geschichte 1850–1980: Vom Privatbeamten zum angestellten Arbeitnehmer*. Göttingen 1981a.

Kocka J., ed. *Angestellte im europäischen Vergleich*. Göttingen 1981b.

Moser J. "Arbeiter, Angestellte und Frauen in der nivellierten Mittelstandsgesellschaft." In *Modernisierung im Wiederaufbau: Die westdeutsche Gesellschaft der 50er Jahre*, ed. A. Schildt and A. Sywottek. Bonn 1993.

Schulz G. *Die deutschen Angestellten seit dem 19. Jahrhundert*. Munich 2000.

Winkler H. A. *Mittelstand, Demokratie und Nationalsozialismus*. Cologne 1972.

Zunz O. et al., eds. *Social Contracts under Stress: The Middle Classes of America, Europe, and Japan at the Turn of the Century*. New York 2002.

Chapter 6

SOCIAL INEQUALITIES
AND SOCIAL MOBILITY

The changes depicted in the divisions and hierarchies among social milieus convey only part of the history of social inequality in Europe. This chapter covers two additional central changes: in inequality in individual social status, and in individual opportunities for mobility, primarily with regard to career mobility, social advancement, and decline.

State of Research

Although social inequality and social mobility are closely connected theoretically, they have usually been separated in the historical research. In theory, it can be argued that social inequality and opportunities for social mobility are alternative options. Societies with significant inequality and strict hierarchies are normally seen as tolerable only if they also offer significant opportunities for mobility, education, and advancement. If such prospects are lacking, as a general rule either conflicts emerge for better opportunities and more social equality, or potential social climbers emigrate. In contrast, insignificant opportunities for mobility are generally more accepted in societies with little inequality or hierarchy. These alternative options are only rarely examined together in research on European history, however.

No overview has yet been published on the history of social inequality and opportunities for social mobility in Europe since 1945. As it is almost exclusively sociologists and economists who treat these topics, historians will benefit from a brief explanation of key terms and research methods in sociological and economic research.

The Transformation of Social Inequality

Not all aspects of social inequality can be addressed—only income and wealth can be surveyed reasonably well for a sufficient number of European countries since 1945. The trajectory of inequality in living arrangements, health care, life expectancy, and threat of criminality can be surveyed only poorly for all of Europe since 1945. This section is therefore limited to changes in income and wealth distribution. One additional aspect of social inequality that can be tracked, educational opportunities, is addressed in Chapter 12.

As in the other chapters, the following section involves the book's two key questions. First it will trace long-term developments in income and wealth distribution since the Second World War to explore whether differences were intensified or alleviated over the past fifty to sixty years. It is primarily economists interested in history who have examined this question. Then it will address a question that, though less often pursued by economists, is here a central theme: European hallmarks.

Indicators of Income and Wealth Distribution

Previous research findings on the development of income and wealth distribution can only be understood when the indicators that have been worked with are known. This is why they are being covered for the general reader—the rushed reader can skip this section.

In order to understand literature about income and wealth distribution, it is necessary to understand the basic idea of measures of distribution. The most important measure of distribution arranges income recipients or wealth holders according to their amount of income or wealth. In Figure 6.1, for example, income recipients are organized by amount of income on the horizontal axis; their percentage share of national income is plotted along the vertical axis. The characteristic distribution curve emerges through this. The diagonal in this figure is the fully illusory condition of complete equality. The deviation in the curve indicates the degree or historical change of inequality in distribution. When the curve

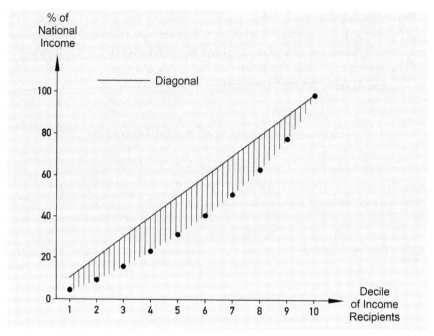

Figure 6.1 Income Distribution in the Federal Republic of Germany, 1969–1998

moves further from the diagonal, inequality increases; when the curve nears the diagonal, inequality lessens.

If multiple societies or the same society at different points in time are to be compared, it is difficult to differentiate between these curves visually, and a precise comparison is not possible. It is for this reason that the curve was recorded as an indicator, a single statistic: the Gini coefficient. It represents the ratio of area between the curve and diagonal (the hatched area in Figure 6.1) and the area in the triangle formed by the 45-degree diagonal and the horizontal and vertical axes. The Gini coefficient would be zero with absolute uniform distribution of income or wealth and would be 1 with absolute inequality of income and wealth—two values that never occur. An increase in the Gini coefficient points to an increase in inequality; a decrease in the coefficient indicates a decrease in disparity. Differences in inequality between various societies are also easily readable through the Gini coefficient.

A disadvantage of the Gini coefficient is that it reduces a complicated process to a single numerical value. To more adeptly differentiate, the so-called decile and quintile are brought in. These measurements also order income recipients by amount of income, dividing them into groups of 10 (decile) or 20 (quintile) percent and then calculating the percentage of national income each group receives. If the percentage of the top decile, i.e., the top 10 percent of income earners, rises and the percentage of the lowest decile, or lowest 10 percent of income recipients, sinks, income inequality has intensified. Table 6.1 uses this measurement of income distribution. As for the distribution of wealth, in which a great deal of wealth is concentrated among a small minority, this measurement is even more differentiated. The percentage of wealth for the richest 5 percent or even 1 percent is tracked. Table 6.2 includes this distribution measurement for wealth distribution.

It should be noted that there is a second often-used measure of distribution that is not oriented toward the extreme cases of absolute inequality and equality but that on the contrary measures the deviation from the average, to determine levels of poverty. Those households whose income is considerably lower than the national average—for example, about half of the average income—are considered poor.

Lastly, it is important to pay attention to the kind of income examined in the distribution of income. Gross income, from which tax and social security contributions have not yet been deducted, provides a less realistic picture than net income. Individual income, or the income of individual persons, independent of whether they live in a single or family household, provides a less realistic view than the so-called equivalent disposable household income, in which income is recorded by household and not by individual person. In this case, tax and social security contributions are also deducted and further financial burdens due to children or other dependents are taken into account according to certain rules. The distribution of household income and equivalent disposable household income are usually significantly less equal, but more realistic.

The Development of Income and Wealth Distribution

Research on the development of income distribution since the Second World War has been shaped by a thesis that is often referred to as the Kuznets curve, named after the American Nobel Prize winner Simon Kuznets (Kuznets 1967). The Kuznets curve implies that inequality of income distribution intensified during industrialization, when the rich received an ever increasing percentage of national income and the poor an ever smaller part, and that after industrialization, including in recent decades, a counterdevelopment—a reduction in income inequality—began: the portion of national income held by the rich decreased again and the portion of national income among the poor increased. So far we know little about the first part of the Kuznets curve, the period of intensification of income inequality, as this development has only been verified for a few countries (Kraus 1981; Lindert and Williamson 1985). In comparison, the second part of the Kuznets curve, the reduction of income inequality, has been substantiated for an impressive number of European and non-European countries. This part of the Kuznets curve also affects the period since the Second World War. For Denmark, the former Federal Republic of Germany, Finland, France, Great Britain, the Netherlands, Norway, Austria, Hungary, Sweden, and Switzerland, a clear reduction in income inequality from the interwar period through to the 1970s has been recorded, as it has for Canada and Japan as well (see Table 6.1). Those with the top earnings in all of these countries now account for a smaller share of the national income. Table 6.1 shows this for the top 10 percent of income recipients. At the same time, the poorest gained a larger proportion of national income, as can be seen in Table 6.1 for the lowest 20 percent. In contrast, the middle-income group changed little overall and is therefore not included in the figure. Among the industrialized countries, so far as they have been examined, there was no country in which the opposite, an increase in income differentials, was clear and recognizable in the longer term. The development stagnated only in the US. This trend of attenuation in income differences certainly lasted for different lengths of time in different countries. The extent of the attenuation also varied by country, and in the end quite different income differentials remained. Yet the trend can be seen almost everywhere; for this reason the Kuznets curve has been the focus of attention in research.

It is not only the abstract, statistical aspect of national income that reflects this tendency. The easier-to-classify income differentials between social groups, qualifying groups, and careers, as well as men and women, have also diminished somewhat over the past few decades. These income differences have been examined less often, however, and are more difficult to track Europe-wide.

The discussion to date about the Kuznets curve primarily revolves around explanations as to why income inequality has lessened. Over the course of the debate, two broad camps have crystallized. One side primarily emphasizes political factors—changes in the political distribution of power and new political decisions. The other side, however, attempts to explain the reduction of income inequality with reference to the workforce and the development of the workforce.

First, with regard to the political explanations for the reduction of income inequality in the industrialized countries, two far-reaching societal changes in particular are cited again and again. On the one hand, it is argued that the balance of power shifted between employers and unions during the course of the twentieth century. The influence of trade unions after the Second World War became far greater than it had been during the interwar period, aside from short periods of exception such as the hey-

Table 6.1 Income Distribution in Europe, the US, and Japan
(Personal income before taxes 1910–1970 or disposable income 1980–1990)

a. Top 10 percent of Income 1910–1970 or Top 20 percent 1980–1990

	1910	1920	1930	1940	1950	1960	1970	1980	1990
Europe									
Belgium	—	—	—	—	—	—	—	35.1	35.6
Denmark	—	38.9	39.9	36.8	28.6	27.3	32.0[b]	—	—
Germany[a]	40.5	—	36.5	36.0	36.0	39.4	33.7	35.3[b]	36.4[b]
Finland	—	50.9	48.3	38.3	32.8	30.5	30.2	31.4	31.9
France	—	—	—	—	36.2	34.0	29.3	38.4	38.4
Great Britain	—	—	—	38.8	33.2	29.1	27.5	35.6	38.2
Netherlands	—	—	—	—	36.1	31.8	29.5	34.7	34.7
Norway	29.8[b]	—	38.2[b]	—	28.6	27.2	24.7	32.8	33.3
Austria	—	—	28.4	—	22.6[b]	24.9	24.7	—	—
Sweden	—	39.2	44.5	33.7	28.8	25.9	24.0	30.8	31.8
Switzerland	—	—	—	—	37.3	37.8	32.3	—	—
Hungary	—	—	—	—	—	20.2	15.9	18.6	20.9
Non-European Countries									
US	—	—	—	—	28.9	27.0	28.4	37.3	39.8
Japan	—	—	—	—	—	25.2	23.2	—	—

b. Lowest 20 percent of Income

	1910	1920	1930	1940	1950	1960	1970	1980	1990
Western Europe									
Belgium	—	—	—	—	—	—	—	4.2	4.2
Denmark	—	1.4	0.2	0.1	4.6	4.2	3.9	—	—
Germany[a]	—	—	—	—	—	1.8	3.9	10.5[b]	9.6[b]
Finland	—	—	—	—	0.1	3.5	2.1	4.5	4.3
France	—	—	—	—	—	2.8	3.8	3.1	3.0
Great Britain	—	—	—	—	—	9.7	5.6	3.5	2.5
Netherlands	—	—	—	—		2.2	2.4	4.4	4.1
Norway	3.8[b]	—	2.1[b]	—	0.6	2.0	4.8	4.1	3.9
Austria	—	—	—	—	4.6	4.2	4.9	—	—
Sweden	—	1.7	—	3.2	4.6	6.3	8.4	4.0	3.3
Switzerland	—	—	—	—	0.1	2.4	9.5	—	—
Non-European Countries									
Japan	—	—	—	—	—	7.8	8.7	—	—
US	—	—	—	4.1	3.7	3.7	3.8	2.1	1.9

Footnote a. 1950–1970 only in the former Federal Republic of Germany
Footnote b. Break in comparability

Notes: The dates of data vary by country. The years listed in the table are only approximate. Actual dates could be plus or minus four years.

Sources: For all Western European countries 1910–1970 (aside from France): see P. Flora et al., *State, Economy and Society in Western Europe, 1815–1970*, vol. 2 (Frankfurt a. M. 1987), 641 ff. For all other countries, 1910–1970: M. Sawyer, "Income Distribution in OECD Countries," *OECD Economic Outlook, Occasional Papers* (July 1976): 27 ff; for 1980, 1990: A.B. Atkinson et al., *Income Distribution in OECD Countries* (Paris 1996), 49; Germany, 1980–1990: I. Becker, "Zur Verteilungsentwicklung in den 80er und 90er Jahren," *WSI-Mitteilungen* 3 (1999), 210 (equivalent disposable household income, thus only comparison of trends is possible); Hungary, 1962–1987: R. Andorka et al., *Social Report* (Budapest, 1992) 75 (household income; no showing for the lower income groups).

day of the Front populaire in France or the years under the Weimar Republic until 1930 in Germany. The increasing pressure by the unions, so the argument goes, significantly boosted the employee's share of national income, and income inequality was noticeably reduced as a result.

It is also suggested, however, that the trade unions' strength and negotiating power were too diverse in the different industrialized countries to explain the internationally universal and long-term trend in income inequality reduction. That France, a land with notoriously weak unions, showed a more distinct reduction in income differences than did the former Federal Republic of Germany, where unions' negotiating power was notoriously strong, seems to belie this argument (for unions see Chapter 9).

The second political explanation revolves around a different secular, political turning point, namely the emergence of the modern welfare state after the Second World War (for more on this see Chapter 10). It is argued that the welfare state, with its social security and guarantee of a minimum income for the entire population, as well as its coupling of pensions and wage continuation, contributed considerably to the average income, to the extent that the share of national income for the poorest within the population noticeably increased. Differences between average incomes and the incomes of welfare recipients and retirees lessened after the 1950s and 1960s with the emergence of the modern welfare state. The share of income received by the poorest people increased markedly (see Table 6.1). The welfare state does indeed explain why the income for the poorest improved, but the chief objection to the argument is that it fails to explain why the income of the wealthiest worsened. It should also be kept in mind that ultimately, the modern welfare state after 1945 brought about a redistribution of income between the labor force and retirees but hardly changed the income distribution among those employed. Nonetheless, this argument offers a partial explanation for the Kuznets curve.

The arguments that try to explain the decrease in income inequality through developments in the job market and workforce look very different. The first influential explanation was elaborated by another Nobel Prize winner, Jan Tinbergen. He was one of the first to substantiate and analyze the trend in the reduction of income inequality between the 1930s and 1950s with an international comparison of primarily North America and the northern part of Western Europe (Great Britain, the Netherlands, Sweden, Denmark, Germany) (Tinbergen 1978). His argument was that the twentieth century, and particularly the period since the Second World War, was shaped by a race for educational expansion, i.e., between the growing supply of highly qualified manpower on the one hand and the growing demand for highly qualified manpower due to the technological advances in the economy on the other. For long periods of the twentieth century, up until the point of his research, this race had clear results: the supply of highly qualified labor grew more rapidly than the need for it. For this reason, higher incomes did not increase as quickly as the national income as a whole. The percentage of higher income within the national income therefore decreased, and the differences in income softened further. Tinberger's argument certainly remains current, as the expansion of the educational sector has continued through to the present and the supply of university graduates has exceeded demand, with the exception of a few small segments of the academic job market (see Chapter 12). That almost all university graduates were nonetheless employed in the decades of economic prosperity through to the 1970s was quite crucial with regard to the impact of this surplus of university graduates.

A second, completely different argument is based on the development of the workforce. The percentage of salaried employees increased quite a bit in all industrial societies over the course of the twentieth century. At the same time, the percentage of the self-employed among the labor force decreased. The differences in income among salaried employees were far less distinct than those among the self-employed. The establishment of wage-earner and salaried employee societies in Europe thus led to a decrease in income differences, although more in the mid-range incomes than between the rich and poor.

A third argument originated with Peter Lindert and Geoff Williamson (Lindert and Williamson 1985), two economic historians who comprehensively and internationally proved the second part of the Kuznets curve, the reduction of inequalities in income. They also saw the leading causes in the job market and in the development of the workforce, and they provided three explanations.

First, the differences in income within industrialized societies abated because the enormous disparities in income between the modern, dynamic, and therefore high-income industrial sector and the traditional areas of agriculture and service were eliminated. This was due in part to the drop in traditional employment and in part due to the increase in productivity and with it the increase of income within agriculture. Williamson and Lindert found a second explanation for the decrease in income differences in the shrinking reservoir of cheap labor in the modern industrialized countries: the unskilled workforce became scarcer and thus better paid, reducing the differences in income. The international migration of cheap labor from non-industrialized, low-income countries, according to Lindert and Williamson, did not balance out this contraction of the cheap labor reserve. The workforce reservoir of women was also more heavily used in Northern and Eastern Europe after the 1950s (see

Chapter 3). Third, the workforce's qualifications continuously improved after the Second World War. The old system, marked by the sharp contrast in education between a tiny minority of university graduates and an overwhelming number of those who had only completed primary school, vanished. Through a deep-reaching and often underestimated change in the education of the workforce, a completely different society emerged with many levels of education, among which high school graduates constituted a relatively large group (cf. Chapter 12). This differentiation of educational opportunity also clearly advanced the reduction of income inequality. Lindert and Williamson particularly stress the irreversibility of these three developments. In their eyes, the trend of income inequality reduction was also irreversible, and a renewed intensification of income inequality was not expected (Lindert and Williamson 1985).

This is exactly what occurred, however, over the last twenty years of the century. The trend in income distribution reversed in the 1980s and 1990s. The Kuznets curve leveled out, the reduction in income inequality ended, and in most European countries an opposite trend set in. Differences in income intensified again, primarily in the upper- and lowermost income groups. For a large number of European countries—Belgium, Germany, Finland, France, Great Britain, Norway, Sweden, and Hungary—as well as for the US—it has been shown that the upper income groups (in Table 6.1, the top 10 percent of income recipients) reaped a growing percentage of the national income, while the lowest income groups (in Table 6.1 the lowest 20 percent of income recipients) received only a sinking share of the national income. A.B. Atkinson's work in the "Luxemburg Study" exposed this new trend in particular (Atkinson 1996). These changes, though of varying intensity in different countries, were clearest in Great Britain and the US as well as in Hungary even before 1989. In contrast, this trend could not be observed at all among the top income groups in the Netherlands, whereas in Germany it had set in by the 1970s but was less visible by the 1990s (Becker and Hauser 2003: 83ff.). It should be kept in mind, however, that the income definitions in this study are in part different from those that are used in the Kuznets curve. The period of observation is still new, and it remains to be seen how long this trend will last.

The tendency toward more inequality has also been supported by studies on poverty. A new poverty emerged among the unemployed, single-parent families, immigrants, and young adults and pushed the traditionally poor—the unskilled worker, the rural domestic helper, the home worker, small-scale farmers, and the elderly—into the background (Atkinson 1982; Leibfried 1991; Hauser 1993; Leibfried and Leisering 1995). Examinations of poverty carried out throughout Europe, such as the poverty report by the German government, the "Poverty in Britain Report," and studies by INSEE in France, ISTAT in Italy, and the Andorka Group in Hungary, show a clear increase in poverty since the 1980s—the major challenge presented by the more recent development in social inequality.

The increase in income differences has various economic, social, and political causes. They have not yet been sufficiently examined, however. Five aspects appear to play important roles. First, the Kuznets curve was based on a comparison of historical epochs that were particularly advantageous for it, but that were also exceptional historically. The Kuznets curve supports itself mostly by a comparison of two extreme situations in economic history—the 1930s and 1940s, during the modern industrial society's worst economic crisis and the most devastating war in modern Europe, and the 1950s and 1960s, a unique period of prosperity. It is rather questionable whether the Kuznets curve would be supported by the comparison of normal periods in economic history.

Second, most explanations of the drop in income inequality did not rely on long-term factors and as such could not take effect over the long term. The unions' negotiating power did not continuously increase. Completely to the contrary, a significant weakening of workers' organizations became apparent in a number of European countries after the 1980s, as much so in a country with traditionally strong labor unions, like Great Britain, as in a country with weak unions, such as France (see Chapter 9). The welfare state, an additional cause for the earlier attenuation in income differences, was dismantled to a large extent in the 1970s and thereafter publicly entered a state of crisis (see Chapter 10). Thus no impulse toward a further reduction in differences of income could come through this avenue. Likewise, there can be no question of any further drop in the reservoir of cheap labor and continuous rise in cost for unskilled laborers. Quite to the contrary, there was a massive immigration of cheap labor—in Europe primarily from Eastern Europe and the Southern and Eastern Mediterranean, and in the United States primarily from Latin America (see Chapter 7). In the industrialized countries, differences in income thus increased again between the high-income locals and low-income immigrants.

It was not just the short-term reasons for the reduction in disparity that were inapplicable. Third and conversely, a series of economic reasons for an increase of income differences emerged. The most effective cause was the growing unemployment, which had continuously increased in almost all of Europe since the 1980s and by the end of the 1990s hovered around a disastrous 10 percent of those gainfully employed. This unemployment led to considerable and continuously growing income losses among the poorest income groups. In most European countries the income level of the unemployed fell and lagged behind general income developments. A further cause of increased income inequality affected the opposite end of the spectrum: wealth that had been accumulated during the period of prosperity, which was often bequeathed in the 1980s and 1990s, yielded a secure income during a period of increasing real estate and bond values for the class of the well-off and wealthy, thus helping to account for the increase of income share for the top earners in the 1980s and 1990s. The disproportionately increasing salaries for executive managers were an additional reason, though this did not pertain to all European countries. The economic factor Tinbergen cited as reducing income disparities also changed. The expansion of the educational sector overshot the demand for educated workers even farther than during the prosperous period of the 1950s and 1960s, and unemployment rose among university graduates. The job markets for university graduates just beginning their careers split: those in job markets with extreme demand started with very high salaries and increased the percentage of income among the high-income earners. Those in job markets with an oversupply of university graduates, in contrast, muddled through with lower salaries and temporary contracts or were unemployed. These sharp differences in income among academically trained job seekers also intensified income disparities.

A fourth, more social reason for the growing inequality in income had to do with the changes in families and marriage models (see Chapter 2). Two different, new models inadvertently contributed to the income inequalities. On the one hand, single-parent families, usually headed by single mothers and often created by divorce, clearly increased. These families were an important component of the new poverty and added to the decrease in income among the poorest part of the population. Another model, in comparison, strengthened the percentage of top incomes: marriages without children, in which both partners earned income, thus producing a high household income. This type of marriage had increased since the 1960s and 1970s and accounted for a part of wealth and income growth in the 1980s and 1990s. These households were prevalent among the top fifth of income earners and strengthened the proportion of high incomes (Atkinson 1996; Becker 1999).

A fifth cause had to do with the changes in the interventionist state. As of the 1980s, the interventionist state unintentionally propelled the rising income inequality in two ways. On the one hand, service transfers, such as retirement and unemployment benefits, welfare, child allowances, and family tax credits, which had significantly increased and provided the poorest strata of the population with a somewhat larger share of income, were cut or did not grow at the same rate as the general income level.

The income of these transfer service recipients and their percentage of total income dropped as a result. On the other hand, the interventionist state had also supported the increase in the percentage of the top income. The higher incomes experienced broad tax relief during the 1980s and 1990s, in part as a result of a conscious governmental relief policy, in part through tax evasion. Many European governments certainly expected their tax relief measures to result in increased investment, more jobs, and reduced unemployment. Increasisng inequality was accepted as the price paid for more jobs, in the hope that in the longer term less unemployment would again moderate the loss of income among the poor. So far, this hope has seldom been realized.

Wealth Distribution

The Kuznets curve is used in analyzing the distribution of not only income but also wealth. Because it has not been examined for many countries, we cannot review its development as exactly as with income distribution, but we can give a rough estimate of any trend.

A few general notes are necessary here as well. Wealth distribution concerns a completely different aspect of material living conditions than income distribution. It includes the living situation of only part of the population, as only the taxed, and thereby only the greatest wealth is included in the statistics. Most of the analyses used as a basis here deal with just under half of the population. Furthermore, the social inequalities are far sharper with regard to wealth than to income. In the British case in the 1950s, for example, the richest 5 percent of wealth holders had at their disposal more than two-thirds of the British national wealth (Table 6.2). In contrast, the top 10 percent of British income earners received only approximately one-third of the national income (Table 6.1). Wealth distribution therefore includes not only a smaller part of the population, but also a much steeper level of social inequality in particular.

The Kuznets curve seems to be even more convincing with wealth distribution than with income distribution in the second half of the twentieth century. The reduction of social inequality was even more clear and impressive. Very clear declines in the concentration of wealth were proven in the top wealth in France, Great Britain, Sweden, and Switzerland as well as the United States. The concentration of wealth in the hands of the richest percent was halved between the 1910s and 1920s and the 1970s. The decline in the concentration of wealth among the top 5 percent was not quite so rapid but was still striking. Admittedly, we do not know how it developed in many countries. But this mitigation of concentrated wealth is verifiable in countries as different as Great Britain, Switzerland, and France (see Table 6.2). Likewise, sharp declines have been recorded in the amount of asset shares in the hands of the most affluent fifth of wealth owners in the old Federal Republic of Germany—from 78 percent in 1973 to 63 percent in 1998 (Hauser and Becker 2003: 22). This reduction in the concentration of wealth could already be detected during the interwar period, but it primarily set in during the period of prosperity in the 1950s and 1960s. It also wore away at the historically biggest differences with regard to the concentration of wealth in Europe (cf. Table 6.2).

This mitigation of the concentration of wealth had economic, social, and political causes. The primary cause of the "deconcentration" of wealth was the fundamental changes to household expenditures during the establishment of mass consumption (see Chapter 3). Household expenditures on immediate needs such as food and clothing fell, while the expenditures on living, education, transportation, and social security rose.

The jump in all these expenditures had repercussions on the distribution of wealth. Expenditures on living went not only into rent, but also to an increasing degree into apartment or home ownership. Expenditures on transportation went not just toward fares but toward buying cars, which in turn changed the structure of assets and liabilities. Expenditures on social security went more and more into life insurance and bonds; education expenditures went in part into educational savings plans and educational endowment insurance. These new household expenses altered the distribution of wealth, broadened the number of smaller wealth holders, reduced the weight of productive wealth, which was always particularly concentrated, and increased the weight of forms of wealth such as home ownership, life insurance, and bonds as well as ownership of long-lasting consumer goods that were far less unequally distributed. Additionally, after the Second World War personal ownership of productive property dropped significantly—another effect of the decline in agriculture.

A second, political cause can be seen in the government reinforcement of this wealth "deconcentration" in an entire range of European countries. In some countries, like Great Britain, the concentration of wealth was moderated through property and estate taxes that were introduced after the Second World War (Atkinson and Harrison 1978). This factor should not be overestimated at the European level, however. A number of European countries, such as France, levied few to no taxes on property and nonetheless experienced a sharp reduction in the concentration of wealth. In comparison, the policies for the accumulation of wealth—subsidies and tax relief for home ownership as well as for life insurance—may

Table 6.2 Distribution of Wealth in Europe and the US, 1902–1979

a. Share of wealth in the total assets of the most affluent 1 percent of wealth holders

	1902–1913	1920–1929	1930–1939	1950–1959	1960–1969	1970–1979
Europe						
Belgium	—	—	—	—	28 %	—
Denmark	—	—	—	—	—	25 %
Germany (West)	31 %	—	—	—	—	28 %
England and Wales	—	61 %	54 %	45 %	31 %	32 %
France	50 %	45 %	—	31 %	—	26 %
Sweden	—	50 %	47 %	33 %	24 %	21 %
Switzerland	—	—	—	—	43 %	30 %
US	—	36 %	28 %	28 %	29 %	25 %

b. Share of wealth of the most affluent 5 percent of wealth holders

	1902–1913	1920–1929	1930–1939	1950–1959	1960–1969	1970–1979
Europe						
Belgium	—	—	—	—	—	47 %
Denmark	—	—	—	—	—	47 %
Germany (West)	51 %	—	—	—	—	—
England and Wales	—	82 %	77 %	71 %	56 %	56 %
France	80 %	65 %	—	53 %	—	45 %
Sweden	—	77 %	70 %	60 %	48 %	44 %
Switzerland	—	—	—	—	63 %	53 %
US	—	—	—	—	—	43 %

Sources: H. Kaelble, *Auf dem Weg zu einer europäischen Gesellschaft: Eine Sozialgeschichte Westeuropas, 1880–1980* (Munich 1987). Additionally: Sweden: R. Spånt, "Wealth Distribution in Sweden 1920–1983," in: E.N. Wolff, ed., *International Comparison of the Distribution of Household Wealth.* (Oxford 1987), 60 (1920, 1930, 1951, 1966, 1975); Switzerland: W. Ernst, *Die Wohlstandsverteilung der Schweiz* (Diessenhofen 1983), 204 (1979).

have been more important as they supported forms of wealth that were less concentrated (Becker 1999).

An opposing factor that decelerated the "deconcentration" of wealth became active around the 1970s, however: longer life expectancy led to less frequent distribution of wealth due to death and inheritance. At the same time, the birthrate went down, as then did the number of heirs decades later. The end of the rapid increase in real income made the private accumulation of wealth more difficult. As a result, the deconcentration of wealth took hold in only a few countries, like Germany (Glatzer and Hauser 2002). Meanwhile, wealth concentration held steady or increased somewhat in most countries. Good comparative studies remain to be undertaken regarding the changes in the distribution of wealth in Europe.

European Commonalities of Inequality

European commonalities of inequality in income and wealth distributions are not immediately apparent, as the individual countries differed considerably. In the second half of the twentieth century, the Scandinavian countries had the lowest income disparity. In contrast, it was particularly sharp in Great Britain and the Southern European countries, whereas in France, Germany, and East Central Europe it lay somewhere in between (Sapir 2004: Figure 8.1). Five European commonalities stand out, however.

First, it is clear that the intra-European differences in income distribution, as in the case of the distribution of wealth, played out within a limited stratum in the second half of the twentieth century. The top 10 percent of income earners never had at their command, so far as has been examined until now, substantially less than a quarter or more than a third of the national income. Only Hungary before 1989–90 falls outside of this spectrum. Another example: during the same period, the richest 1 percent of wealth holders never owned more than a third or less than a fifth of all wealth. It is not possible to speak of similarity in the statistical sense, but the extent of the differences is nevertheless limited. In other areas of society the intra-European differences were more extreme.

Second, the Kuznets curve and its reversal were particularly pronounced in Europe after the Second World War. The US seemed to follow the curve less because a few fundamental factors reining in the re-intensification of income disparity in Europe took different forms in the US. The mitigation of income differences remained weaker in the US because the welfare state was not built up as much and the poorest social strata received less financial assistance. Another reason, however, was that in the US, the extremes between poor small-scale subsistence peasants and craft and small retail businesses on the one hand, and the modern industrial and service sectors on the other were never so extreme that their disappearance could so noticeably reduce differences in income as in Europe. The re-intensification of income disparity from the 1980s on remained weaker in the US because this society was spared Europe's high unemployment rates. Moreover, the welfare state's transfer services did not plummet as sharply in the US as they did in Europe because they had never been as high.

Third, despite the re-intensification of differences in income, the distribution of income in Europe remained somewhat less disparate than in the US. This was not reflected in the highest incomes, which were similarly distributed in the US and Europe. But the share of income for the poorest income earners did clearly remain higher throughout the entire second half of the twentieth century than in the US. This European hallmark evolved gradually after the Second World War and has been preserved through the end of the century. It existed in Western as well as Eastern Europe, yet also in New Zealand, Canada, and Israel. It was not the case in the US, Latin America, or the Middle East including Turkey (Bertola 2010; Bertola et al. 2006). A key reason for this is the more fully developed and maintained European welfare state.

The situation between Europe and Japan was the complete opposite. The distribution of income in Japan during the second half of the twentieth century was distinctly less disparate than in almost all of the European countries for which we have information. The poorest income group in Japan received a greater share of the national income, and the wealthiest income group received a smaller share than almost everywhere in Europe. Although many comparisons were drawn between Europe and Japan over the last two decades of the twentieth century, these differences remain little discussed. They can be associated with the far lower unemployment in Japan, the flat Japanese business hierarchies, the Japanese consensus society, and the Japanese dual economy. Yet we are still waiting for a good explanation of this European characteristic compared to Japan.

Fifth, the distribution of wealth in Europe during the second half of the twentieth century did in principle undergo the same development as in the US: the concentration of wealth was watered down somewhat. The European peculiarity lay in the far more substantial reduction in the concentration of wealth in the European countries that have been studied to date, compared to the US. A European hallmark meanwhile disappeared. Directly after the Second World War, the concentration of wealth in European societies like those in Great Britain, France, or Switzerland was substantially higher than in American society, but this European peculiarity seems to have died out during the course of the second half of the twentieth century. The establishment of the modern consumer societies with their long-lasting consumer goods, along with the increase in the standard of living during the period of prosperity in Europe, allowed the European and American societies to become more similar.

Social Mobility

Research on the history of social mobility following the Second World War primarily pursues two questions. On the one hand, it is interested in whether the prospects for social ascent within European societies improved or remained unchanged and whether the dangers of relegation intensified or remained secondary. One the other hand, it deals with the classic question preoccupying social scientists like Alexis de Tocqueville and Werner Sombart as early as the nineteenth century: whether the social prospects for advancement were better in the US than in Europe, and whether the US's edge remained, reemerged, or disappeared after the Second World War.

Research on the history of social mobility has specific focal points and blind spots. It concentrates on the actual ascents and descents and rarely covers the ideas and myths of the rise and fall. Additionally, it deals with social ascent and descent primarily as *professional* advancements and is less interested in other forms of rise and fall that could be gauged by income, property, education, or lifestyle. These other aspects are, at best, summarized by blanket statements and examined as rise and fall between social strata. The research also concentrates to a large extent on men and only occasionally looks at the ascent and descent of women. It additionally primarily focuses on the wealthier, industrial part of Europe and devotes very little attention to the periphery.

The history of social mobility since the Second World War is primarily studied by sociologists. Historians have yet to contribute anything worth mentioning. The sources that historians normally employ for historical surveys of social mobility in the nineteenth and early twentieth centuries—civilian status files, public opinion polls, and personal files from companies and public administrations—are increasingly more difficult to access due to the tightening of privacy protection during the period since the Second World War.

Research on social mobility has developed its own vocabulary and a multitude of methods for measurement, which cannot be explained in this chapter due to space considerations. They do not necessarily need to be known in order to understand the key results of the research. Only one method will be expanded upon, as it has become formative for the *history* of social mobility in the twentieth century: the cohort analysis, which was developed by sociologists. A sociological survey concerning a specific period of time is used for the cohort analysis. Respondents are ordered by age group, and changes affecting different age cohorts are equated to historical developments. If the rate of social ascent is low among the older and high among the younger participants, it is inferred that upward mobility increased in recent history. This method is problematic, as the social mobility among the various age cohorts are not neatly separated but can be influenced by the same historical contexts. Certain major events like war, crises, and periods of prosperity affect different cohorts simultaneously. Another problem with cohort analysis is that the data on the older participants is often less precise than the younger participants', as the past is more distant. For these reasons, only rough trends can be deduced from the cohort analysis—its seemingly exact, statistical findings should not be overstressed.

Changes in Social Advance and Descent

The changes in social advancement and decline in modern industrial societies during the nineteenth and twentieth centuries have long been debated. Two basic positions are generally taken: one, the more optimistic argument that professional mobility increased with the gradual establishment of the modern industrial society, whereupon social advance, as well as social decline, became more common; and two, the more pessimistic idea that with the emergence of large corporations, huge bureaucracies, defined professional careers, and regulations by the welfare state, social ascent and descent became ever more rare in comparison to the transitional phases within European history and the industrial revolution in particular.

Neither of these positions has been confirmed by the research on the development of social mobility since the Second World War. Its main finding is that the frequency of both social advancement and social decline changed little, and that there is no identifiable tendency toward either the opening or closing of European societies. The most recent and comprehensive study of this kind, by Erickson and Goldthorpe, makes this particularly clear. The study compares seven Western and Eastern European countries—Great Britain, France, Ireland, Sweden, Hungary, Poland, and Germany—a very diverse range of countries that, taken together, are home to a substantial number of Europeans. Based on a survey from the early 1970s, it compares the years of birth between 1905 and 1940, dealing with those gainfully employed between the 1930s and 1960s. The study examines social mobility between generations, between fathers and sons, and between seven major occupational groups (Erikson and Goldthorpe 1992). This comparison of European countries, to date the most sophisticated and comprehensive by far, does indeed show changes in the mobility rates for individual countries, but not for these countries as a whole (cf. also Almendinger and Hinz 1997; Müller 2001).

Of course studies of this kind have their limits, the greatest for this chapter being that they masterfully use a multitude of surveys from the early 1970s for comparison, but only cover the early part of the second half of the twentieth century. Drastic social changes during this era that are covered in other chapters, such as the industrial society's transition to a service society, the rapid expansion of education, immigration, and the reduction of major occupational groups including manual labor, which must have had sharp effects on social mobility, were just beginning to gradually emerge and reached full swing only later. Yet even Erickson and Goldthorpe registered clear changes in the mobility of a dwindling, though once massive, occupational group: farmers. Overall, however, it is still too early to evaluate the trends in social mobility for the entire second half of the twentieth century. We have to wait until the sociological surveys from the 1980s and 1990s are comparatively analyzed.

By contrast, the few studies on the social mobility of women—until now the stepchild of historical mobility research—have verified more pronounced changes since the Second World War. These studies conclude that educational opportunities for women considerably improved from the 1940s on, whereupon the educational prospects for young women eventually became almost indistinguishable from the opportunities for young men (see Chapter 12 also). According to this research, women's professional prospects also improved, although they admittedly still differed greatly from men's. Despite the improvement in women's professional and social mobility opportunities, the playing field between the sexes remained uneven in the area of professional prospects (Handl 1988; Federspiel 1999).

Convergences

Whether or not European societies have become more similar in terms of social advance and decline over the last few decades than they were in the early twentieth or even nineteenth century cannot be precisely answered yet, as research has rarely posed this question until now. Nevertheless, a string of indicators point to similarities among European societies during the 1960s and 1970s. Erickson and Goldthorpe's study visually gives the impression that the mobility rates within European societies were neck and neck, and that the social mobility rates in the 1950s and 1960s became even more similar (Erickson and Goldthorpe 1992: 74). Among birth cohorts in 1910, European soceities' differences were considerably greater than among the birth cohorts in 1940. In a detailed comparison of Great Britain, France, and Sweden, Erickson and Goldthorpe suggest that social advance and decline in Great Britain and France approximated each other for decades, until the early 1970s (Erickson and Goldthorpe 1992). Paired comparisons between the Federal Republic of Germany and France in the 1960s and the Federal Republic and Great Britain in the 1970s had similar findings (Mayer 1980; König and Müller 1986). The tenor of these studies is that the social advances and declines in these societies resemble each other, even if the analyses naturally concentrate on the residual differences because they are more intellectually appealing.

The United States' Lead in Opportunities for Social Advancement

Europeans began discussing the better opportunities for social advancement in the US long before the Second World War. In the 1830s Tocqueville returned from a trip to the United States, which at the time was still a small country with only a few million residents, with the impression that the opportunities for advancement were much better there than in "old Europe." Since then, most of the big names among European social scientists have commented on this advantage in the United States. The debate continued after the Second World War. In 1947, Simone de Beauvoir returned from a visit to the US with a very skeptical opinion: "The 'push to the top' that characterized American life, in which generations upon generations among the lower classes raised themselves up a rung in society, is almost complete" (de Beauvoir 1999: 311)." In contrast, Ralf Dahrendorf saw the United States' lead only two decades later as still in existence and unflappable. He very resolutely retained the opinion "that both claims, that the mobility process within American society had barely altered throughout its history and that there were no more prospects for advancement in America than in Europe, are so far completely unfounded. Much still speaks for the immediate experience of every visiting traveler in America, that this land makes advancement possible for those that would have remained stranded in Europe's rigid layered structure" (Dahrendorf 1968: 78).

While the debate continued with undiminished intensity, social scientists began for the first time to empirically test this thesis. Seymour Martin Lipset provided the first important attempt at this (Lipset and Bendix 1959). He argued that there was no evidence at all for a noticeable American prominence with regard to opportunities for social advancement. Mass mobility and the rate of advance for workers in nonmanual jobs were roughly the same in all industrial societies. According to Lipset, the more industrialization set in throughout the world, the more the similar the opportunities for promotion were.

This first attack on the image of the United States' edge over Europe with regard to opportunities for social mobility was heavily criticized. It was first charged that the indicators it had utilized were much too broad, and that the simple ascent from manual to nonmanual jobs revealed very little about the advances or backwardness of opportunities for forward social mobility. Other American sociologists showed that the prospects for promotion in the upper classes, primarily among the academic professions, were considerably greater in the US during the 1950s and 1960s than in Europe, and that in this sense there was in fact a lead in advancement in the US. Numbers regarding stronger growth of the university sector in the US confirmed this argument, even if the European and American educational systems are not easily compared (see Chapter 12). The second serious objection to Lipset's argument was that industrialization did not simply lead to an alignment in social mobility. Studies on Europe and America in the late nineteenth and early twentieth centuries, that is, after the actual industrial revolution, proved the opposite—some prominence in advancement in American society (cf. Kaelble 1983). And last, the argument was made repeatedly that the purely statistical examination of mobility rates only deals with part of the history of social mobility. A different, more significant part of the history of social mobility, one with more political consequences, was the Americans' belief in the great opportunities for advancement in their society—the faith in the myth of going from rags to riches. This myth constituted an important part of the American identity and contributed considerably to American workers being less class-conscious, as well as more willing to organize trade and labor unions, than the European workers.

Recent research on the period since the Second World War has indeed confirmed Lipset's findings to a large extent. In a comparison between Sweden, Great Britain, and the US, Erickson and Goldthorpe come very close to the core of Lipset's results for the early 1970s. As opposed to Lipset, however, they found a multitude of differences between the US and European societies and an absence of support for the idea that industrialization had leveled out differences in mobility among modern societies. In their very detailed study, which utilized many more refined indicators than Lipset's, they showed that the United States' perceived edge in advancement was unsubstantiated (Erickson and Goldthorpe 1985). A special European path of less mobility and opportunity for advancement was not confirmed for the 1970s in comparison with the US. It remains to be seen whether this finding would be valid if other non-European industrial countries, like Japan, were also considered and the last two decades of the twentieth century were examined as well. It also remains to be seen whether the results would look different if the rates of mobility for all of Europe were evaluated, and the lopsided comparison were not drawn between the entirety of the United States and individual European countries that are often smaller than New York. This question is certainly not closed—but current research does not confirm a distinct social immobility in Europe.

Conclusion

Overall, a distinction must be drawn between two completely different eras of social inequality and mobility in the second half of the twentieth century. In the first era, between the 1950s and 1960s, differences of income and wealth clearly decreased in most European countries. This has been documented for Western Europe and is assumed to be the case for Eastern Europe as well. The wealthy received somewhat less and the poor somewhat more of the national income. Women's income approached men's. It can be assumed that social differences in quality of life and inequalities in health care also decreased due to increasing income and the establishment of the modern welfare state and modern health care sector, even though Europe-wide studies of this are lacking. At least illnesses due to poverty like tuberculosis, cholera, and typhus decreased in the epidemiological transition. The carefully drawn lines between social milieus were no longer as clearly defined. At the same time, educational opportunities improved considerably, primarily for women but also for the lower social strata. The traditional pattern of sharp extremes between a small academically educated minority and a large mass of primary school graduates disappeared. High and mid-level educational qualifications increased (see Chapter 12). Opportunities to advance did not improve during this era, however. The time of new opportunities for promotion in Eastern Europe after the social system upheaval and the removal of the old economic, political, and cultural elite remained a politically burdened intermezzo. This stagnation in possibilities for social advancement was mostly tolerated, however, in light of the reduction of social inequality.

This development reversed from the 1970s and 1980s on. The reduced inequality in the distribution of wealth disappeared in most European countries. Rising inequality set in in Eastern Europe and intensified after the collapse of the Soviet empire. Differences in income became more pronounced throughout almost all of Europe, including between men and women in the business sector, the largest occupational sector by far. Differences in the likelihood of unemployment likewise increased, often also between the sexes. New forms of poverty emerged among the unemployed, single-parent families, immigrants, and drug addicts. We do not know how other areas of social inequality—in housing, health care, or protection from crime—developed throughout Europe as a whole, but they clearly depended significantly on income and the welfare state. Given that increases in income remained marginal and the general expansion of the welfare state had ended, it cannot be ruled out that these other social inequalities also began to increase again. Differences in educational opportunity, however, continued to shrink, most distinctly for women. For the lower classes and new immigrants they diminished to a lesser extent and not everywhere.

We do not yet know whether the opportunities for social advancement improved overall in Europe. They became worse in the eastern part of Europe in the 1980s. The opportunities for social ascent that were blocked by the social climbers of the 1950s were a decisive internal reason for anti-regime protests at the end of the 1980s. How these opportunities developed in Western Europe is unclear. Had they increased, the increase in social inequalities would have been more tolerable. A decrease in chances to advance socially would have been one of the reasons for the moroseness, pessimism about the future, and growing mistrust of the political and economic elites in Europe from the 1980s and 1990s onward.

References

Income and Wealth Distribution

Andorka R. et al. *Social Report*. Budapest 1992.

Atkinson A.B. *The Economics of Inequality*. 2nd ed. Oxford 1982.

Atkinson A.B. et al. *Income Distribution in the OECD Countries*. Paris 1996.

Atkinson A.B. and A.J. Harrison. *The Distribution of Wealth in Britain*. Cambridge 1978.

Becker I. "Zur Verteilungsentwicklung in den 80er und 90er Jahren." *WSI-Mitteilungen* 3 (1999): 205–214 and 5 (1999): 331–337.

Becker I. and R. Hauser. *Anatomie der Einkommensverteilung: Ergebnisse der Einkommens- und Verbrauchsstichproben 1969–1998*. Berlin 2003.

Bertola G. "Inequality, Integration, and Policy: Issues and evidence from EMU." *Journal of Economic Inequality* 8 (2010): 345–365.

Bertola G., R. Foellmi, and J. Zweimueller. *Distribution in Macroeconomic Models*. Princeton 2006.

Flora P. et al. *State, Economy and Society in Western Europe, 1815–1970*. Vol. 2. Frankfurt a. M. 1987.

Glatzer W. and R. Hauser. "The Distribution of Income and Wealth in European and North American Societies." In *Changing Structures of Inequality: A Comparative Perspective*, ed. Y. Lemel and H.-H. Noll. Montreal 2002, 187–217.

Hauser R. "Armutszonen und Armutspolitik in der Europäischen Gemeinschaft." In *Lebensverhältnisse und soziale Konflikte im neuen Europa*, ed. B. Schäfers. Frankfurt a. M. 1993, 218–231.

Hauser R. and I. Becker, eds. *Reporting on Income Distribution and Poverty: Perspectives from a German and a European Point of View*. Berlin 2003.

Kaelble H. *Auf dem Weg zu einer europäischen Gesellschaft: Eine Sozialgeschichte Westeuropas, 1880–1980*. Munich 1987.

Kraus F. "The Historical Development of Income Inequality in Western Europe and the United States." In *The Development of the Welfare States in Europe and America*, ed. P. Flora and A.J. Heidenheimer. New Brunswick 1981, 187–236.

Kuznets S. *Modern Economic Growth: Rate, Structure, and Spread.* New Haven 1967.
Leibfried S. "Towards a European Welfare State? On Integrating Poverty Regimes into the European Community." In *Social Policy in a Changing Europe*, ed. Z. Ferge et al. Westview 1991, 227–259.
Leibfried S. and L. Leisering. *Zeit der Armut.* Frankfurt a. M. 1995.
Lindert P. and J.G. Williamson. "Growth, Equality and History." *Explorations in Economic History* 22 (1985): 341–377.
Sapir, A. et al. *An Agenda for a Growing Europe.* Oxford 2004.
Sawyer M. "Income Distribution in OECD Countries." In *OECD. Economic Outlook, Occasional Papers.* July 1976.
Tinbergen J. *Einkommensverteilung: Auf dem Weg zu einer neuen Einkommensgerechtigkeit.* Wiesbaden 1978.

Social Mobility

Almendinger J. and T. Hinz. "Mobilität und Lebenslauf: Deutschland, Grossbritannien und Schweden im Vergleich." In *Die westeuropäischen Gesellschaften im Vergleich*, ed. S. Hradil and S. Immerfall. Opladen 1997, 247–285.
Beauvoir S. de. *America Day by Day.* Berkeley 1999.
Dahrendorf R. *Die angewandte Aufklärung: Gesellschaft and Sociology in America.* Frankfurt a. M. 1968.
Erickson R. and J.H. Goldthorpe. "Are the American Rates of Social Mobility Exceptionally High? New Evidence on an Old Issue." *European Sociological Review* 1 (1985): 1–22.
Erickson R. and J.H. Goldthorpe. *The Constant Flux: A Study of Class Mobility in Industrial Societies.* Oxford 1992.
Federspiel R. *Soziale Mobilität in Berlin des 20. Jahrhunderts.* Berlin 1999.
Handl J. *Berufschancen und Heiratsmuster von Frauen.* Frankfurt a. M. 1988.
Kaelble H. *Social Mobility in the 19th and 20th Centuries: Europe and America in Comparative Perspective.* Leamington Spa 1985.
König W. and W. Müller. "Educational Systems and Labour Markets as Determinants of Worklife Mobility in France and West Germany: A Comparison of Men's Career Mobility, 1965–1970." *European Sociological Review* 2, no. 2 (September 1986): 73–96.
Lipset S.M. and R. Bendix. *Social Mobility in Industrial Society.* Berkeley 1959.
Mayer K.U. "Berufstruktur und Mobilitätsprozess." In *Soziale Indikatoren im internationalen Vergleich*, ed. H.-J. Hoffmann-Nowotny. Frankfurt a. M. 1980, 97–134.
Müller W. "Social Mobility." In *International Encyclopedia of the Social and Behavorial Sciences*, ed. N.J. Smelser and P.B. Balthes. Amsterdam 2001.

Chapter 7

MIGRATION

International migration and the resulting minority groups in Europe underwent a revolution after the Second World War. No longer a continent of worldwide emigration, Europe became instead a leading immigration destination, at times attracting more migrants than the enduring immigrant haven of the United States. This development ushered in massive transformations in the social structure, migrants' occupations, and the understanding of migration and immigration policy. Migration and the resulting minorities became highly political topics that defined election campaigns and assumed an important place in government statements and in social movements. In the process, the European view of the United States' immigration model altered, as did the external perspective of Europe as a continent of immigration.

State of Research

General historical research tends to underrate, rather than overrate, the significance of international migration. It is often overlooked that the wealthy western parts of Europe, without intending or desiring to do so, became a global destination of immigration in the second half of the twentieth century. The state of specialized literature in this area is much better than that regarding other topics discussed in this volume. A number of publications on the history of migration in Europe are available, chief among them the excellent overview by Klaus J. Bade on the long-term perspective of migration in Europe from the eighteenth century to the present (Bade 2000). Alongside this are the sociological and polito-logical European overviews of the period after 1945, published respectively by Heinz Fassmann and Rainer Münz, by Rainer Ohliger, Karen Schönwälder, and Triadafilos Triadafilopoulos, and by Sarah Collinson (Collinson 1993; Fassmann and Münz 1996; Ohliger et al. 2003). Finally, world history overviews by Dirk Hoerder, by Timothy Halton and Jeffrey Williamson, and by Stephen Castles, integrate migration in Europe into a global context (Hoerder 2002; Castles 2003; Hatton and Williamson 2005).

Regarding changes in migration since 1945, two seldom-considered yet important continuities should not be forgotten. First, immigration from peripheral, partially industrialized parts of Europe was nothing new but had begun with industrialization in the second half of the nineteenth century. This continuity is often overlooked in countries such as Germany because the immigration of the late nineteenth and early twentieth centuries was interrupted by the two World Wars. Continuities in other European countries, such as Great Britain, France, Belgium, and Switzerland, where the number of foreign workers fell only slightly during the interwar period, are in contrast much clearer and more the general rule in European development.

Second, despite heavy immigration, almost all European countries consistently maintained into the 1990s that they were not immigration countries. Legally, most of the immigrants remained foreigners. The only breach in this tightly closed phalanx against immigration policy was the legal right of EU citizens to work and reside in every other EU country. This provided only economic rights, however. The central political civil right—the full right to vote—and thus immigration in the fullest sense remained elusive, even for EU citizens in other EU member states.

Postwar Period

In no era of the twentieth century were Europeans more on the move than during the war and postwar eras. At no other time was migration associated with such force, inhumanity, and suffering. However, as normal labor migration was also ongoing in both the postwar and the prewar periods, forced migration and labor migration are not always easily distinguishable.

Forced Migration

Above all, forced migration in the aftermath of the war shaped the postwar era. Four forms of forced migration pushed millions of people in Europe out into the streets.

Millions of displaced persons—workers who had been forcefully recruited for the NS wartime economy—returned to their homelands after the war and sometimes migrated yet again if they were persecuted in their homelands. By the war's end, on German territory alone there were around eleven million foreign forced laborers and prisoners of war who had been incorporated into the economy, in particular from Poland, the Soviet Union, and France, but also from Belgium and the Netherlands (Bade 2000: 299). Even when these forced laborers returned shortly thereafter to their homelands, the experience of the forced labor lived on in the memories of many French, Dutch, Belgian, Polish, and Soviet citizens and influenced policy regarding Germany in the decades after the Second World War.

A second forced migration in the war's aftermath was the massive re-migration of millions of prisoners of war, concentration camp survivors, deportees, evacuees, those forced to resettle, and those who had fled the bombings. After the war most of them returned to their families and their homelands or, if communist rule in Eastrn Europe or other political reasons precluded a return to their homelands, migrated overseas. Jews who had survived the concentration camps remained at first in camps in Germany and then immigrated, mostly to the United States. Millions of prisoners of war returned to their families in the late 1940s; in Germany, they numbered around five million. A considerable share of the numerous evacuees similarly returned to their homelands. Added to these were the forced evacuees from German cities who had been brought to the countryside; evacuated children in Great Britain who had been brought to shelters for children before the German bombardment; and evacuees and refugees in France, the Netherlands, and Belgium who had fled from the bombings, the war zones, or the German occupation. In Germany alone, they are estimated to have numbered around ten million (Bade 2000: 299). This forced migration remained a dramatic experience in the memory of Europeans for decades. Its later effects have not been fully investigated.

Far more closely studied are the permanent consequences of a third forced migration following the Second World War. As a result of the redrawing of borders at the war's end, many millions of refugees and exiles were forced to leave their homes or flee to the West to escape communist rule. Their numbers included German refugees and exiles from the former German regions newly incorporated into Poland and Russia, Polish refugees from formerly Polish regions of what was now Russia, German refugees from northern Czechoslovakia, Hungarian refugees from Romania and Slovakia, Italian refugees from Yugoslavia, Finnish refugees from the southeastern part of Finland that had been lost to the Soviet Union, and refugees from the newly communist Poland, Czechoslovakia, Hungary, Romania, and Bulgaria, as well as the Soviet-occupied portion of Germany. In Germany alone they came to 12 million refugees; in Poland, 3 million (Bade 2000: 299f.). This migration in turn left behind many traces. In the case of West Germany, the millions of refugees and indigenous Germans were deeply divided, and not only socially: a number of these refugees organized themselves separately along political lines as well. They formed their own party, which received 6 percent of the votes in its first national election in 1953 and formed a faction within the Bundestag. Social barriers arose between exiles and nationals in other countries as well. The integration of these refugees in the period directly following the war proved a challenging task.

Finally, a fourth migration caused by political force, which has similarly been quite closely examined, was smaller in number but politically and culturally very significant: the remigration of political exiles and the technicians and scientists emigrating to Allied countries who constituted Germany's "intellectual reparations." Of the many politicians, academics, and artists who fled from the NS regime to Western and Northern Europe, Turkey, the Americas, and China, only a few returned to Germany and Austria permanently or for regular periods of time after the war. Among them were personalities who would become exceptionally influential, such as the politicians Willy Brandt and Bruno Kreisky, the poet and dramatist Bertolt Brecht, and the German academics Ernst Fraenkel and Jürgen Kuczynski. The sometimes voluntary, sometimes forced migration of scientists and technicians to the arms industries of the US, the USSR, Great Britain, and France was small in number, but these migrants were important to their countries of immigration, above all in the development of rocket construction (Ciesla and Judt 1996).

Labor Migration

In addition to the forced migration of millions and associated suffering caused by the war, normal migration was part of the postwar period. Just as before the war, this migration was concentrated in the wealthier parts of Europe. By the end of the postwar era in 1950, almost 1,800,000 foreigners were working in France, close to 400,000 in the smaller country of Belgium, approximately 300,000 in the even smaller country of Switzerland, and almost 30,000 in Luxembourg (Table 7.1). Even by today's standards this was significant, yet it was only a third to half the number of employed foreigners living in these countries at the beginning of the 1970s, that is, after the long economic boom of the 1950s and 1960s created enormous demand for labor. This normal labor migration, as previously stated, looked back on a long tradition in these countries. The geographical origin of this foreign labor force in the postwar period looked roughly the same as in the decades before.

Another "normal" component of migration in the postwar era, a new wave of emigration to the prospering Americas, was above all an escape from the miserable material situation in a Europe that was destroyed by war and held an uncertain future. Some of these migrants were related to soldiers through transatlantic marriages; yet another flow consisted of often surreptitiously escaped Nazis, war criminals, mafia-like war profiteers, and other fraught supporters of the dictatorships. In West Germany, emigration reached its highest point in 1949. More than 270,000 people left the western zones in this year alone, almost 170,000 of them headed to the Americas—the United States above all, but also Canada, Brazil, and Argentina. Even during the historical peak of emigration from Germany in the 1880s, the annual outflow was never much greater than it was in 1949. Similar developments affected the other traditional emigration destinations: Great Britain, Spain, Sweden, and Italy. This wave of emigration, however, was a phenomenon of the postwar era: by the early 1950s, emigration to the Americas had already begun to abate. This last great wave of European emigration to date has since dwindled to nothingness.

The Boom of the 1950s and 1960s

In the history of migration and minorities, as elsewhere, the economic boom of the 1950s and 1960s was a return to normalcy and a step out of the shadows of the war. However, even as it advanced the development of migration, the economic boom simultaneously altered it.

The direct consequences of the war on migration had already disappeared before, or at the very least during, the boom. The displaced persons, forced laborers within the NS economy, and concentration camp survivors either permanently remigrated or migrated onward. Only a few remained behind. The majority of refugees and evacuees integrated economically during the boom. Integration certainly did not mean simply fitting into the existing society. Refugees, like the locals, not only made do within the new society but also actively created it and were often a driving force of the boom. They established companies, seized upon initiatives in academics and politics, and by settling permanently even created a new mix of religious denominations at the local level, which contributed significantly to the mutual acceptance of denominational milieus and of the church.

Of course, some refugees were unable to overcome the traumatic experience of their escape and social decline, or were excluded by locals. Yet the most spectacular sign of a politically nonintegrated refugee minority, their political party within the Federal Republic, the Bund der Heimatvertriebenen und Entrechteten (BHE), had already fallen below the 5 percent stipulation by the third national election in 1957. Even the Ministry for Expulsion Affairs dissolved in 1969. What remained were interest groups of evacuees that in part preserved tradition and in part demonstrated their opposition to the de facto drawing of boundaries in East Central Europe. They were only ever able to organize some of the evacuees and refugees. Integration in the 1950s and 1960s proceeded just as swiftly in other parts of Europe, to which large numbers of evacuees had immigrated after the war (Benz 1992; Benz 1995; Ther 1998; Schulze 2001).

Labor Migration

Meanwhile, the economic boom of the 1950s and 1960s introduced a new period of massive labor migration from Europe's periphery to its industrialized center, bringing this type of immigration again to predominance and changing it in various ways.

During the quarter century of the economic boom, the number of foreign workers in countries of immigration climbed more steeply than ever before or ever since. In Western Europe this number tripled between 1950 and 1970. The current percentage of foreign workers (not including the foreigners who live but do not work in the respective country) is mostly a legacy of rapid immigration during the economic boom. By the end of the boom, around 1970, there were close to ten million foreigners in Western Europe. Immigrants were particularly numerous in Switzerland, and in France, Sweden, and West Germany, they made up around 5 percent of the population. These statistics are certainly not fully representative, as not all immigrants were registered as foreigners. Immigrants from the former colonies of Great Britain and France or ethnically German immigrants from Eastern Europe in West Germany could easily become citizens and therefore do not appear as foreigners statistically. Migration did not take place throughout Europe but was constrained to the economically dynamic parts of Western Europe. Few immigrated to Southern Europe—Spain, Portugal, Italy, or Greece—or to Finland, as these countries were still too poor to have work for immigrants (see Table 7.1). In the eastern section of Europe, no significant immigration was planned or permitted.

Immigrant Background and Social Structure

As was the case previously, the labor migrants in the 1950s and 1960s predominantly came from elsewhere in Europe, mainly the European pe-

Table 7.1 Foreign Residential Population in Western European Countries, 1950–2000
(in thousands and as a percentage of the total population)

Country	1950		1970/71		1982		1990		2000	
	Thousands	(%)	Thousands	(%)	Thousands	(%)	Thousands	(%)	Thousands	(%)
Germany (1)	568	1.1	2,976	4.9	4,667	7.6	5,338	8.4	7,297	8.9
France	1,765	4.2	2,621	5.1	3,660	6.7	3,607	6.3	3,263	5.6
Great Britain	*	*	2,000	3.6	2,137	3.8	1,904	3.3	2,342	4
Switzerland (2)	285	6.1	1,080	17.4	926	14.4	1,127	16.7	1,384	19.3
Belgium	368	4.3	696	7.2	886	9	903	9	862	8.4
Netherlands	104	1	255	1.9	547	3.8	692	4.6	668	4.2
Austria	323	4.7	212	2.8	303	4	482	6.2	758	9.3
Italy	47	0.1	*	*	312	0.6	469	0.8	1,388	2.4
Sweden	174	1.8	411	5.1	406	4.9	484	5.6	477	5.4
Spain	93	0.3	148	0.4	183	0.5	279	0.7	896	2.2
Greece	31	0.4	15	0.2	60	0.6	173	1.7	*	*
Denmark	*	*	*	*	102	2	161	3.1	259	4.8
Norway	16	0.5	76	2	91	2.2	143	3.4	184	4.1
Portugal	21	0.2	32	0.4	64	0.6	108	1.1	208	2.1
Luxembourg	29	9.8	63	18.5	96	26.3	109	28.2	*	*
Ireland	*	*	137	4.6	232	6.6	80	2.3	127	3.3
Finland	11	0.3	6	0.1	13	0.3	26	0.5	55	1.1
Lichtenstein	3	21.4	7	33.3	9	34.1	11	38.1	11	37.5
Western Europe (3)	3,785	1.3	10,728	3.2	14,685	4.2	16,085	4.5	19,208	5.2

* No available data

Notes: (1) 1950–1990, West Germany; since 1991, East and West Germany. (2) Not including seasonal workers. (3) Only countries listed with available data are compared.

Sources: 1950–1990, H. Fassmann and R. Münz, eds., Migration in Europa: Historische Entwicklung, aktuelle Trends und politische Reaktionen (Frankfurt a. M. 1996), Figure 1.1; 2000, OECD, Trends in International Migration: Continuous Reporting System on Migration 27 (2002): 295.

riphery. The traditionally strong immigration from Eastern Europe, however, was almost entirely blocked by the Iron Curtain. In 1968 more than two-thirds of the foreigners in France were still Europeans, mostly from Spain, Italy, Portugal, Belgium, and even Poland; only about a quarter of the immigrants originated in Africa, mostly Algeria. Europeans similarly still prevailed by far within West Germany's foreign labor force at the end of the boom in 1970. Four-fifths of the immigrants were European in origin, mostly from Italy, Yugoslavia, Greece, and Spain. Only around a sixth came from Turkey. According to an estimate by the European Community, in 1969 a solid quarter of the foreign labor force came from member states of the EC, and an additional quarter from other European countries that joined the European Community afterward, namely Spain, Greece, and Portugal. At that time, only a small minority, around one-fifth, came from the Muslim Mediterranean countries: Turkey, Algeria, Morocco, and Tunisia (*Données Sociales* 1981: 47; Flora 1983: 43; Werner and König 1984, Figure 8).

In this period of expanded hiring of foreigners, the social structure and attitudes of both European and non-European immigrants still differed starkly from those of native citizens. Even in the 1970s the immigrants were still disproportionately uneducated or poorly trained, predominantly male, and far more likely than locals to be young, unmarried adults. Surveys in the 1950s and 1960s revealed that immigrants for the most part wanted to work only temporarily in the immigration countries and then return to their homelands (e.g., *Données Sociales* 1981: 49, 58). Thus the immigration in the 1950s and 1960s was, much more than in future decades, a migration of young, male laborers who came without a family and intended to stay in the industrialized countries of Europe for only a limited time.

Immigration at this time was thus unusually inexpensive for the public sector. Immigrants stayed mainly in inexpensive company-owned lodgings, placing far less strain on the housing market and requiring a lower level of public housing subsidies than they would later on. As foreigners still rarely came with family, few foreign children attended the schools, so the costs for teachers and special school materials were still marginal. Most of all, though, the foreign labor force contributed more to, and drew far less on, the social security system than citizens did. Only a small percentage of foreigners were elderly and received pension payments.

Immigration Policy

Similarly, the policy on the foreign labor force in the 1950s and 1960s differed decidedly from that in the period to follow: in most of the European countries, the concept of foreign policy was to create a mobile manpower reserve that could be quickly dismantled and sent back to its home countries. The European public seldom discussed permanent integration of foreign workers, and xenophobic right-wing extremist political movements demanding rapid expulsion of foreigners were still rare. In a number of European countries, however, policies favored quick, open immigration for special groups: in France, for French immigrants from Algeria; in Great Britain, for British immigrants from the collapsing Commonwealth; in Belgium and the Netherlands, for the returning European migrants from the Congo and Indonesia, and in West Germany, for immigrants from the GDR or Germans from Eastern Europe. A sharply divided policy of a mobile labor force reserve composed of foreigners and an open immigration policy toward millions of other immigrants was thus characteristic of a significant part of Western Europe. This contradiction rarely attracted attention.

Immigration policy in the 1950s and 1960s primarily remained within a national framework. Seldom was foreign policy coordinated within the European Community. Previous differences in naturalization policy thus remained quite clearly in place. France, with its traditionally low birthrate and its economic need for immigration, continued to have relatively high numbers of naturalizations. Germany, Switzerland, Austria, and Sweden, with their traditionally high birth and emigration rates, had in contrast only very small numbers of naturalizations.

The 1970s and 1980s

The 1970s and 1980s represent a profound turning point in Europe's history of immigration. First of all, the increase in immigrants slowed with the end of recruitment throughout Europe in 1973–74, whereupon the number of foreign workers increased only slightly. In many countries, for instance Switzerland, this number even sank noticeably. Nevertheless, the number of foreign residents increased. Between 1970 and 1990, the number of foreign persons in Western Europe climbed from around 11 to 16 million. The increase was particularly sharp in West Germany, the Netherlands, and Austria, and modest by contrast in Great Britain, Switzerland, and Sweden (Table 7.1). It was primarily family members that made up the increase in foreigners now.

In this way, the lifestyle of foreign residents increasingly began to fundamentally resemble that of nationals. Immigrants now lived more and more in families. As a result, they too made social welfare benefit claims. Their children used school facilities. The workday increasingly resembled that of citizens. The economic segmentation of work done by immigrants, i.e., the initial concentration in manual, primarily unskilled labor in agriculture, the building industry, and the service industry's dirty work, eroded somewhat. Foreign employees now increased in most industry and service branches. Education for immigrant children improved (see Chapter 12). A foreign petty bourgeoisie consisting of retail merchants, travel agency owners, and repairmen emerged, as did even a foreign middle class of entrepreneurs, doctors, engineers, and writers—not in all immigrant groups, but certainly in sizable ones.

Thus the societies of Indians in Great Britain, Algerians in France, and Turks in Germany increasingly differentiated themselves into their own social classes, coming closer to being complete societies and beginning to resemble their local native societies in the process. It was only occupations within public administration, the justice system, the army, and universities and schools that still widely remained closed to foreigners. The character of immigration changed: whereas unskilled manual laborers could immigrate for a few years and then be replaced by other immigrants, this principle of rotation was not as easily deployed for occupations requiring higher qualifications, as the relevant knowledge and language skills, could not be learned in a short period of time. For the host countries, immigrants were often difficult to replace. Meanwhile, immigrants themselves increasingly entertained the prospect of a long or even permanent stay.

New immigrants' regions of origin decisively changed in the 1970s and 1980s, with non-Europeans carrying more weight in particular. Push and pull factors were simultaneously at work here. The decisive pull factor was that migration from the former European periphery—Spain, Portugal, Greece, Yugoslavia, and Ireland—no longer met the European economy's demand for labor, as the periphery was developing rapidly and emigration from these countries decreased. Thus, in the 1970s and 1980s, the foreign labor recruitment to the Muslim, Eastern, and Southern parts of the Mediterranean, and in part also to the former colonies of a few European countries. Adding to this were push factors such as the growing population pressure in Africa and the Middle East, the growing economic rift between Africa and Europe, reductions in the costs of transportation and especially air travel, and the need to escape from a growing number of cruel dictatorships and genocides. As a result, the new differences arising between individual European countries often hinged on the national differences within their colonial pasts.

Another outcome of this non-European migration was the emergence of a new variety of religions in Western Europe, including Islam with roughly 20 million followers in Europe as of 1990, of whom 8 million were native Muslims from the Balkans and Bulgaria, an inheritance of the Ottoman Empire, and around 12 million were Muslims who had immigrated to Western Europe. In Western European countries that did not have two primary Christian denominations, Islam became the second-largest religious group. It was far more important than the other non-European religions among immigrants. This new religious plurality brought a new cultural diversity to European daily life; however, it also generated new tensions due to differing lifestyles and religious organizations.

A new form of migration remained almost unnoticed. Instead of the poor migrating to Europe's wealthy regions, the new development played out between wealthy countries as managers, researchers, intellectuals, and students as well as retirees migrated to the South. This form of migration is poorly understood. We know only that educational migration increased and that the number of foreign European students at European universities increased in the years between 1980 and 1995 alone from around 120,000 to close to 350,000 (see Chapter 12 on education). We also know that migration within European countries was not merely the migration of poor Sicilians to Germany or unskilled Portuguese workers to France, but also that of British students to French universities, French managers to the Netherlands, and Dutch retirees to Tuscany. We do not know exact numbers for the whole of Europe, however.

Immigration policy changed fundamentally with the onset of Europeanization in the 1970s and 1980s. A halt to the immigration of foreign workers was coordinated and simultaneously carried out in most European Community member states in 1973–74. The number of foreign workers grew only slightly or stopped growing completely almost everywhere in Europe from that point on. At the same time, the European Community's labor market was increasingly liberalized for EC citizens. The Single Market project in 1986 lowered the hurdles for Europeans who wanted to work in other EC countries and in particular for those who wished to start businesses. The mutual recognition of academic degrees had been instigated even before the Bologna declaration of 1999. Moreover, the European Union gradually gained authority in immigration policy through the Schengen agreement, the Maastricht treaty, and in particular the Amsterdam treaty (Bade 2000).

Finally, the politicizing of the topic of immigration increased dramatically and intensified in two directions. On one hand, policy proposals favoring immigrants' social and political integration in Europe and a departure from a pure labor force reserve policy multiplied. The reasons for this push toward integration policy were not only of a humanitarian nature. The experience of the 1970s and 1980s unmistakably showed that the immigration of foreigners was not temporary. It also became clear that the European economies could no longer do without foreign workers. The wide range of relevant proposals fell roughly into two camps with different objectives: complete linguistic, social, and political integration of foreigners into the respective country, which would turn foreigners into normal Frenchmen, Belgians, or Britons; or an acceptance of the respective society's basic values whereby immigrants could meanwhile maintain their language, lifestyle, and culture without being forced to fully integrate into their adopted society. The spectrum of suggestions for the practical integration of immigrants was therefore quite broad, from policies for improving immigrants' material standing and education to the communal right to vote and bilingual school education to the offer of swift, uncomplicated naturalization upon the decision to permanently stay in the country of immigration. Policies regarding immigrant integration concerned controversial issues, such as the conflict over wearing a headscarf as symbol of Islam in France, or the ruling on crucifixes in the classroom in Germany. Immigration policy became a focus of political campaigns.

At the same time, tendencies toward political xenophobia and demands for the rigorous deportation of foreigners and complete closure of the borders certainly grew in strength. Xenophobia became an important campaign topic. New radical right parties, such as the National Right in Great Britain, the Front National in France, and the Republicans in Germany, ran campaigns founded almost entirely on xenophobia and were even represented by some members of the European Parliament.

The Late 1980s and 1990s

New developments in the late 1980s and 1990s emerged out of the upheaval of 1989–90. The development trends during this period were not altogether new and continued three previous tendencies in particular.

Continuities

The slowed growth of foreign workers that had begun in the early 1970s continued, at least according to official statistics (see Table 7.1). Yet at the same time the foreign populations of many Western European countries continued to increase, primarily due to an influx of families. There is substantial evidence, however, that the stagnation in the number of foreign workers was an illusion. Illegal workers, who were not represented in official statistics, increasingly settled in Europe as the Eastern European and Chinese borders opened and the economic gap between Africa and Europe grew. Millions of illegal immigrants worked in Europe. There would have therefore been de facto significantly more foreign workers in Europe in the 1990s than in the 1970s and 1980s, when the borders of the communist regimes in Europe and East Asia were still heavily controlled and emigration was extremely difficult. The increase in educational migration—studying in other European countries—meanwhile carried on as it had in the 1970s and 1980s.

A third continuity in the late 1980s and 1990s was the ongoing dismantling of barriers to mobility within the European Union and settlement in other member countries: the slow process of educational standardizations and mutual recognition of diplomas, the laborious opening of professional examinations and career-related controls, the slow acceptance of social security systems for other Europeans, and the federal bureaucracies' complicated chore of familiarizing themselves with this new form of immigration. European Union policies, the Single Market project during the presidency of Jacque Delors, and the EU's new treaties promoted this dismantling of mobility barriers, as did pressure from the immigrants themselves, who learned through their own practical experiences with migration.

New Developments

The late 1980s and 1990s also brought new developments in the history of migration in Europe. A first, and certainly temporary, development was a massive influx of political refugees and asylum seekers, which was in part associated with the collapse of the Soviet empire, the dictatorship in Romania, and the Yugoslavian civil war, and in part with the accumulation of brutal dictatorships in Africa and the Middle East. European countries faced new kinds of decisions, as these immigrants generally did not wish to settle down in their new environment but rather wanted to return to normal lives in their home countries as soon as possible. Politically, it was hotly debated whether the asylum seekers should be eligible to become long-term residents. The flood of asylum seekers in general turned into an important political topic at times.

A second new development was the return of the traditional East-West migration that had been a major trend in intra-Europe migration in the nineteenth and early twentieth centuries. It had been largely suppressed by communist rule in Eastern Europe but resumed after the collapse of the Soviet empire. However, this was not simply a repetition of the earlier form of migration to the Western European centers of industry and agriculture, which was no longer very attractive, or a form of the traditional educational migration to Western European universities. The new East-West immigration was not only an economic migration, but also often a political escape from the areas where postcommunist dictatorships and civil wars emerged.

Furthermore, the new East-West migration was much more seldom a Jewish emigration than in the nineteenth and early twentieth centuries, as a large number of Jews had been killed in the Holocaust, and Israel and the United States had become more attractive destinations for Jewish migration in any case. Finally, compared to times before the Second World War, the new East-West migration was much more intensely part of a brain drain, an emigration of highly qualified individuals from Eastern Europe to the West. Some of these migrants aimed to temporarily work at unskilled jobs in agriculture, construction, and private households, but some represented a definitive movement of highly qualified individuals to European and American institutes of higher education, and often a bitter loss for Eastern European countries.

A third new development was the non-European migration to what was earlier the European periphery: Spain, Portugal, Italy, Greece, Ireland, and Finland, where this new immigration began in earnest in the 1990s (Table 7.1). The immigrants came partly from Eastern Europe, that is, from Russia, Ukraine, and Romania, partly from the southern Mediterranean and the Middle East, and partly from Sub-Saharan Africa, frequently in the form of illegal, high-risk immigrants being exploited by human traffickers and arriving via sea. This migration was a sign that the former gap between the dynamic center and the developmentally backward periphery of Europe had closed and that prosperity was increasing within these peripheral countries as well.

A fourth development was not completely new but was more manifest in the 1990s: the emergence of a transnational milieu of immigrants who lived in various countries and thus did not see themselves simply as emigrants in one country and as minorities in another. These immigrants lived in international family relationships through which they maintained connections to cities in various counties, were equally familiar with different cultures, mastered two or more languages, and often possessed passports from two countries. These transnational milieus developed within various classes of European society, in the international expert milieus with their international research institutes, international business milieus, and international labour milieus. They were bridges for international understanding and transfers. They connected European countries to each other, but also often connected Europe with non-European societies.

Divergences and Convergences

Divergences

A first and older contrast existed between industrialized, high-growth, affluent European countries, in which immigrants had been finding work since industrialization, and the preindustrial, poorer, peripheral, more agrarian European countries, which were often a source of migrants but had rarely been a destination of immigration. Up until the 1980s, Italy, Spain, Portugal, Greece, and Ireland were part of this periphery.

A second, new contrast emerged after the Second World War between the immigration countries of the West and the communist countries in the East, which, as their national borders were increasingly hermetically controlled after the communist takeover, largely remained without immigrants. This broke the long tradition of international immigration within Eastern Europe to the industrial regions in the Czech Republic, GDR, and Hungary, as well as immigration from Eastern Europe to the West, in particular to Germany and Austria, but also France. While the number of foreigners in Western European industrialized countries reached an unprecedented height, nation-states in Eastern Europe let in only very few foreigners, who often were "ghettoized" and subject to forced seclusion. This set Europe on a course toward profound social differences. Not only the structure of those gainfully employed, but also the attitude toward foreigners and perception of the nation diverged. Significant migration could be seen only within the Soviet Union, especially the migration of Russians into the Soviet Union's non-Russian western and southern republics and, in European territory, primarily to Estonia, Latvia, and Ukraine. This migration certainly differed from that in Western Europe. As immigrants from the dominant republic into the subordinate republics, these migrating Russians enjoyed a status completely different from that of immigrants from the periphery in Western Europe.

A third intra-Europe difference that only existed among the immigration countries was likewise partly old and partly new: the differences in the geographic background of the immigrants. Since the second half of the nineteenth century, each immigration country had generally had its own profile of European immigrants that changed little even as late as the 1980s. In France, immigrants largely came from the Iberian Peninsula, Spain, and Portugal; in the former Federal Republic of Germany and Austria, in contrast, they primarily came from Yugoslavia, Greece, and Turkey; in Great Britain they mostly came from Ireland; and in Sweden they often came from Finland.

Drastic new differences in the backgrounds of non-European immigrants emerged after the Second World War. In several countries, non-

European immigrants largely came from former colonies: in France, immigrants came from the Maghreb and francophone Africa; in Great Britain they hailed from the Caribbean, India, and Pakistan; in the Netherlands there were many from Suriname. West Germany, in comparison, had no such postcolonial immigration. Turkey, the origin of most non-European immigrants, was never a German colony. The massive immigration from Eastern Europe, however—from the centuries-old regions of German emigration and influence in Russia, Poland, and Romania—is rightly viewed as a residual effect of the collapsed, informal, and imperial influence of Germany in Eastern and East Central Europe.

A fourth European difference that is often overlooked concerned not international but rather internal migration within the respective countries. The height of internal migration, and thus also of urbanization, did not occur simultaneously throughout Europe. Part of Europe experienced this in the period after 1945—France as well as Italy, Spain as well as Ireland and Finland—and internal migration, or migration from the country into the cities, was never so extreme as during the 1950s and 1960s. This, however, was not the general rule in Europe. In other countries, especially the old industrialized countries such as Great Britain, Sweden, and Belgium, as well as Switzerland and even Germany (if the massive flight and displacement after 1945 is disregarded), the high point of internal migration lay in the "long nineteenth century" up to the First World War.

Lastly, an important, particularly spectacular, and often discussed fifth divergence consisted in the sharp contrasts between the national immigration policies as well as educational, social, and community policies, which cannot be traced individually here. Here, too, previous contrasts from the nineteenth century mixed with new divergences from the period after 1945. The best-known former divergence, which was apparent as early as the nineteenth century, was the diverse character of citizenship. It was either based on the citizenship of the parents, on *ius sanguinis*, and thus excluded children who, though born to foreign residents, had grown up in the country of immigration as foreigners themselves; or it was based additionally on the place of birth, on *ius solis*, and thus facilitated naturalization for the children of foreign expatriates. Prime examples of this intra-Europe contrast, even into the 1990s, were France, which combined *ius sanguinis* and *ius solis* and had a long tradition of naturalization, and Germany, which used only *ius sanguinis* and was therefore much more closed off to immigrants. France's citizenship law came about during the Napoleonic era, when the birthrate in France had declined to an unusually low level and a strong need for immigration arose simultaneously. On the other hand, the German citizenship law originated in the early twentieth century, when European nationalism was increasingly ethnic and Germany was still an emigration country. After the Second World War, Germany's citizenship law was no longer appropriate for the time, and resulting changes had muted the stark French-German contrast by the 1990s.

A much less widely known but fundamental and old difference in immigration policy was the non-European validity of national European citizenship law, a topic that may seem surprising at first glance. The textbook image of the complete establishment of the nation-state in Europe in the nineteenth and early twentieth centuries conceals the fact that citizenship, a central instrument in distinguishing one nation from others, was in no way identical to the nation in all European countries. Citizenship in the European colonial empires not only served as a means of demarcation for the nation, but was also applicable to those living outside the national territory in the colonies, and in fact also to the indigenous populations in the colonies. In contrast, citizenship in noncolonial European countries was generally limited to the citizens of the national territory. This sharp intra-European contrast became clearly visible only upon the collapse of the colonial empires, when many Indians, Pakistanis, Algerians, black Africans, and Surinamese immigrated to the European mother countries with their European passports. A sharp divide emerged between European countries with citizens of color and European countries without minorities of color.

Convergences

At the same time, convergences in migration caused Western European societies to more closely resemble one another. A first convergence was that many of the divergences just described abated in the 1990s. The difference between the industrialized, wealthy countries with many immigrants and the peripheral countries without immigrants grew less obvious after immigration to the peripheral south of Europe—Italy, Spain, and Portugal—began in the 1990s. The difference between Western Europe, with its robust immigration, and Eastern Europe, with its minimal, strictly controlled immigration, also declined in the 1990s, as East Central Europe now experienced immigration as well. Despite many differences, immigration became a common European experience.

The social structure of immigrants was also similar. No longer just the single workers without families that had migrated throughout Europe in the 1970s and 1980s, it now included many family members as well. Immigrants had gone from holding only specific, mostly unskilled jobs to working in a broad spectrum of occupations, becoming members of the petty bourgeoisie and the middle classes. Beyond this, there was a trend across Europe toward a growing religious plurality, and an increasing number of Muslims in particular. Furthermore, the pattern of immigration was similar in most Western European countries: a sudden increase in the number of foreigners in the 1950s and 1960s, mostly as a result of labor immigration; a coordinated halt in recruitment to most Central European counries in the 1970s and 1980s, and thereafter a decelerated increase in the foreign labor force, immigration being largely restricted to family members.

Finally, diminishing policy differernces between individual countries marked a clear convergence. The prime European difference between French and German immigration policy begame less defined in the 1990s, as Germany eased naturalization and France made it more difficult. Much exchange and transfer regarding immigration law lay behind this. First and foremost, however, was that immigration policy within the EU member states, as mentioned before, gradually began to Europeanize starting in the 1970s. A single immigration and asylum policy for the European Union was initiated in the 1990s. As a result, immigration policy in the EU became Janus-faced. On one hand, foreigners from other EU countries were increasingly treated on equal terms and less often perceived as foreigners in most EU member states. On the other hand, the European Union continued not to view itself as an immigration civilization. The European Commission, meanwhile, tended to see itself as such, at least more so than the national governments. The basic contradiction between the actual substantial immigration of foreigners and the denial of immigration policy was a European common ground.

European Hallmarks

At the same time, unmistakeable differences in immigration and the new minorities distinguished Europe from other industrial societies like the US, Japan, and the USSR. A first European hallmark was the dramatic upheaval mentioned at the beginning of the chapter, which no other civilization has experienced within such a short period of time: in the nineteenth and early twentieth centuries, Europe was the source of a global, massive emigration unique within world history and more significant than emigrations from China, India, or the Arabic world. Then, in the second half of the twentieth century, Europe became one of the most important centers of immigration, just as important as the US or the Middle East and far more significant than Russia, Japan, or South Africa. Of course, Europeans did continue to emigrate in the second half of the twentieth century, and immigration to Europe did not always remain at the same level. Still, this upheaval was like no other. It was accompanied by a decisive change in Europe's understanding of itself and a fundamental change in Europe's attitude toward others.

An additional, often forgotten European hallmark also exists, though it contrasts only with North America and not with the old civilizations in Asia and Africa: the juxtaposition of existing, territorial minorities connected to a specific region, such as the Muslims in the Balkan belt of Albania, Bosnia, Macedonia, and into Southern Bulgaria, with immigrant minorities who mostly lived in cities, sometimes shaping a certain part of the city but never connected to any one region. Traditionally, the territorial minorities were most frequently in the eastern part of Europe, had existed under socialist cover, and then experienced a renaissance after 1989–90. These minorities were common in the western part of Europe as well, for example in the Basque country, Scotland, Corsica, or Frisia. In contrast, the immigrant minorities were most frequently in Western Europe, but also emerged in Eastern Europe, before 1989–90 mostly as Russian minorities in the European Soviet republics, and after 1990 as new immigrant minorities. Minority conflicts in Europe thus also looked different from those in the US: they were not only a matter of immigrant minorities who developed their own self-image, organized, and attempted to assert the rights of their members in the political public. Instead, they also simultaneously represented older traditional conflicts of nationality that were based on very different grounds, had come about since the nineteenth century in particular, and claimed control of entire regions politically and culturally. In North America, this occurred only in the form of Native American reservations.

One should not overlook a new European hallmark that emerged in comparison with the US after the Second World War. In the first half of the twentieth century, the North American and European immigrants still came from similar regions—mostly from Italy, Poland, and Ireland. They were at any rate European, and were generally members of Christian churches. This similar immigration reinforced the coherence of the Atlantic region. From the 1960s onward, however, the regions of origin of immigrants to Western Europe and the United States increasingly differed. Immigrants to the United States now mostly came from Latin America and Asia, whereas immigrants to Europe largely came from the southern and eastern parts of the Mediterranean. An additional fundamental difference emerged as a result. While immigration to the US essentially led to a strengthening of the diversity of Christian denominations, Europe experienced much heavier immigration by Muslims. In 2000, around 10 million Muslims lived in the large countries of immigration in Europe—France, Germany, and Great Britain—and in Europe as a whole there were approximately 20 million Muslims, in part long established residents and in part immigrants. In the US there were only around 4 million. Old European-American similarities with regard to immigrant background and religion thereby became less pronounced.

Finally, the Europeans also adopted a particular attitude toward immigrants in political terms. On the one hand, the Western European countries' opening of their borders to foreigners was unique in modern world history: through a full integration among European Union members, the borders of wealthier countries were completely opened to peripheral European countries as well. The Common Market and the common EU citizenship that was gradually coming into being in principle did away with every type of limitation to migration within the European Union. For these reasons, migration to another EU country became easier for EU citizens than the former trend of migrating to the United States, the classic immigration destination of the late nineteenth and early twentieth centuries, which kept its immigration under strict control. On the other hand, with respect to foreigners outside of the EU, Europe still refused to see itself as a land of immigration. Despite a strong public movement in favor of quicker naturalization, most European governments stayed with a policy of tightly controlled immigration and limited naturalization.

References

Bade K.J. *Europa in Bewegung: Migration vom späten 18. Jahrhundert bis zur Gegenwart.* Munich 2000.

Benz W. "Fremde in der Heimat: Flucht, Vertreibung, Integration." In *Deutsche im Ausland—Fremde in Deutschland,* ed. K. Bade. Munich 1992, 374–386.

Benz W., ed. *Die Vertreibung der Deutschen aus dem Osten.* Frankfurt a. M. 1995.

Castles S. *The Age of Migration: International Population Movements in the World.* 3rd ed. Houndmills 2003.

Ciesla B. and M. Judt, eds. *Technology Transfer out of Germany after 1945.* Amsterdam 1996.

Collinson S. *Europe and International Migration.* London 1993.

Donnés Sociales: Edition 1981. Paris 1981.

Fassmann H. and R. Münz, eds. *Migration nach Europa 1956–2000.* Frankfurt a. M. 1996.

Flora P. *State, Economy, and Society in Western Europe 1815–1975,* vol. 1. Frankfurt 1983.

Hatton T.J. and J.G. Williamson. *Global Migration and the World Economy: Two Centuries of Policy and Performance.* Cambridge 2005.

Hoerder D. *Cultures in Contact: World Migration in the Second Millennium.* Durham, NC, 2002.

Ohliger R., K. Schönwälder, and T. Triadafilopoulos, eds. *European Encounters: Migrants, Migration and European Societies since 1945.* Aldershot 2003.

Schulze R. *Zwischen Heimat und Zuhause: Deutsche Flüchtlinge und Vertriebene in (West-) Deutschland 1945–2000*. Osnabrück 2001.

Ther P. *Deutsche und polnische Vertriebene: Gesellschaft und Vertriebenenpolitik in der SMZ/ DDR und in Polen 1945–1956*. Göttingen 1998.

Werner A. and I. König. *Ausländerbeschäftigung und Ausländerpolitik in einigen westeuropäischen Industrielstaaten*. Nuremburg 1984.

Part III

SOCIETY AND STATE

Chapter 8

THE MEDIA AND
THE EUROPEAN PUBLIC SPHERE

The following five chapters cover the relationships and tensions between society and state. They approach these topics from two different perspectives. The first two chapters deal with nongovernmental players that impacted the government and public administration, the media, and the public, as well as social movements and civil societies. The three chapters after this discuss the opposite, the exertion of influence by the government on society in three large societal areas: social security, city planning, and education.

The media shaped society and culture during the second half of the twentieth century more than ever before. It also influenced daily routine and individual privacy, family values, work values, and the values of everyday human interaction more than previously. It also influenced private consumption more, as the advertisements within the media were more polished and better informed about the customer. Media also played a considerably more important role in Europe's political public. Political controversy and public image, parliamentary debates, and public speeches took place more often in the media, especially on television. Media was often seen as an independent "fourth estate," an essential pillar of modern democracy, though it was also sometimes viewed as a threat, if a major company controlled the media and the diversity of opinion in the media was no longer safeguarded.

Not only did the media influence society more, but society also influenced the media. Opinion polls and viewing figures made media increasingly dependent on society. Interest groups, social movements, networks, churches, businesses, cities, and universities exerted influence on the media and professionalized their public relations. It was not only journalists who had their say in the media. Members of different social groups wrote articles, appeared in talk shows, were interviewed, and wrote letters to the editor. Independent media experts from the new media and communication sciences criticized and influenced the media as well. At the end of the twentieth century the Internet gave citizens much more autonomy and participation than classical media had provided.

During the second half of the twentieth century the media internationalized to a great extent. This process took place in very different ways with different consequences. The internationalization of *products*, especially music, TV films, and feature films; the internationalization of formats of *presentation* in the media, political magazines, TV shows, quiz shows, talk shows, news agencies, and advertisements; the internationalization of *media ownership*, the development of larger international media groups that did not often affect the national character for commercial reasons; and finally the internationalization of the *audience*, the transnational audiences of several national and international medias were developments that ran different courses and required specific observation.

This chapter addresses two themes. On the one hand, it discusses the social history of European media, the impression of societal actions through the media, and societal power of the media, as well as the history of media users, their choices, and their resistance in the world of mass media. On the other hand, it addresses the history of the European public sphere, including the expert public and cultural scene, viewing the public as having critical political potential and presenting a stage for the presentation of power.

State of Research

The history of the media is not an established theme within social history. Only in recent years have social historians and media scholars begun to write primary contributions on it (Requate 1999; Schulz 2000; Wilke 2000; Schanze 2001; Schildt 2001; Weisbrod 2001). So far the history of media has been understood above all as national history (Hickethier 1998; Marssolek 2001; Charle 2004; Chartier and Martin 2005). With the exception of one chapter of a book (Sassoon 2006) no European history of the media since 1945 exists, not even for individual forms of media, and for film are there only two European histories (Sorlin 1994; de Grazia 2005).

Research on the European public sphere has also intensified in recent years, especially studies by social scientists, who almost exclusively conduct media analyses of the present. The involvement of historians has been marginal up to now (Eder and Kantner 2000; Gerhards 2002; Kaelble 2002; Requate and Schulze Wessel 2002; Trenz 2002; Klein et al. 2003; van den Steeg 2003; Meyer 2004; Risse 2004; Wessler 2004; Peters et al. 2005). A historical overview of the history of the European public sphere after 1945 does not yet exist.

The Postwar Period

The postwar period, the time between the end of the war and the early 1950s, marks a sharp break in media history in the majority of European countries. In countries that had experienced dictatorships, almost all forms of media had to be replaced. In Germany, Italy, and Austria almost none of the important broadcasting corporations, newspapers, or magazines date to before this founding period. Important newspapers and broadcasting corporations were developed or redeveloped in Western countries that had been occupied by the Nazi regime. In France, *Le Monde* in 1944, *Les Temps modernes* in 1945, *Radio France Internationale* in 1945, and *Critique* in 1946, as well as the *Telegraaf* in 1949 in the Netherlands, were all reestablished. Plurality of opinions and greater autonomy among journalists in Western Europe replaced the centralized control of the media that had existed under the dictatorships and occupying regimes. Upon the communists' seizure of power in Eastern Europe, the publishing, cultural, and broadcasting scenes there also changed, though in a different direction. New, mostly communist newspapers and magazines tied to the government were started, the existing press became politically standardized, and the diversity of opinions was dismantled.

The postwar era was a boom period for the media. The number of readers and listeners increased. Newspaper circulation rose, broadcast listeners became more numerous, and more books and records were sold than ever before. This audience boom can be explained by the interest in political information after the oppressive period of dictatorship and occupation, the demand for more and different entertainment, and slowly growing spending capacity. Meanwhile, the media were undergoing a limited internationalization as a European integration of media was attempted and the American AFN, heard regularly, gained great influence among youth especially, becoming part of the lifestyle by which they tried to distinguish themselves from older generations. It would be an exaggeration to speak of Americanization at that time, however, because European enterprises controlled not only the press and broadcasting in Europe, but film and music as well. After the Second World War the media remained nationally organized to a large extent; international media groups did not yet play a role within Europe.

The postwar period was also simultaneously affected by continuity. Technical innovations were rare. New types of media were not created. For the most part, the mass press had already been developed before the First World War, as had radio, film, and records during the interwar period. At least in Western Europe, the division into private and public media continued to exist. The press, books, music, and film continued to be private and therefore mostly eluded state control. Broadcasting remained public and was checked by the government and sometimes by civil society differently from country to country. Above all, however, the postwar period was only to a very limited extent a period of new media men and women, new publishers, and new journalists, and the ascent of some spectacular media entrepreneurs is deceiving. The majority of journalists and publishers had already had their careers during the interwar period and had worked in media under the dictatorships in Germany, Austria, and Italy. In these countries they adjusted to democracy sometimes out of conviction, but sometimes opportunistically.

There was some evidence of a European public sphere during the postwar period. The debate about Europe and its distinctions from the US or the USSR was lively and attracted not only Europe enthusiasts like Henri Brugmans or Denis de Rougemont, but also many important intellectuals of the time, like Thomas Mann, T.S. Eliot, and Simone de Beauvoir. Historians wrote in particular about the history of the idea of a unified Europe. The College of Europe, established in 1950 in Bruges to educate European experts, was meant to build an important premise for a European public.

During the postwar period European symbols were also created. The European Movement, which created a European flag with a green "E" on a white background, which has since been forgotten. The present-day European flag with twelve stars on a blue background appeared in 1950 and was adopted by the Council of Europe in 1955. The first European stamps emerged. European posters, usually a bouquet of the national flags, were often printed. Europa and the bull were used in caricatures and represented in paintings and sculptures. Meaningful historical figures were elevated from national to European symbols, especially Charlemagne, whose name was used for the international Charlemagne Prize of Aachen that has been awarded since 1950. European political rites were created, for instance the signing of European treaties in prestigious palaces and the opening of borders between European countries by young Europeans. Many of these symbols and rites were created within civil society and social movements, rather than by governments and international organizations.

The international European culture scene developed almost explosively. Most of the larger European cultural festivals were created at this time. In 1945 the Salzburg Festival, which had been reduced to a military propaganda event for the NS regime, was newly established. The Locarno Film Festival, the Karlovy Vary Film Festival, and the Bregenz Festival were created in 1946, which also marked the reemergence of the Venice Biennale after its cessation during the war. In 1947, the Avignon Theater and Music Festival, the Cannes Film Festival, the Edinburgh Music Festival, and the Edinburgh Film Festival were established. In 1950 the Berlin Film Festival, in 1953 the San Sebastian Film festival, and in 1955 the Documenta in Kassel began. In addition to all this, a Europe-wide media platform for broadcasting and television, the European Broadcasting Union, was established in 1950 and launched "Eurovision" in 1954. Many Western European countries belonged to it. Unlike the European Coal and Steel Community, it did not emphasize the economic, but instead the cultural integration of Europe. Eurovision broadcast big concerts, sporting events, competition for the European Song Contest, and a few significant political events like the coronation of Queen Elizabeth II. With similar goals, in 1954 Robert Schuman and Denis de Rougemont established the European Cultural Foundation, which was meant to support cultural integration and which financed transnational European art projects first in Geneva and later in Amsterdam.

The emerging European public sphere had clear limitations. These new symbols of Europe were not widely circulated. No important Europe-wide media were created during this period. The new transnational cultural public remained limited to a small circle and did not develop into an actual, political public sphere. The national media reported about European proceedings and events from a national perspective and placed their own national politicians and national interests first. National debates, conflicts, decisions, and political personalities remained dominant. The European expert public sphere remained weak. Only a small minority of social scientists, historians, and lawyers worked on Europe. Cultural festivals wanted to be international but not necessarily European. It should also not be forgotten that there was no European decision-making body that could be criticized, supported, or influenced by a European public sphere at that time. Absent the contrast of a political center of power, the European public sphere was incomplete.

The 1950s to the 1970s

The period between the 1950s and 1970s, a time of economic boom and various societal upheavals discussed in this book, was also a period of revolution in the history of the media, as television set in as the new key mass medium in Europe. It is estimated that in 1955 close to every sixteenth European and nearly every seventh Western European household—but almost no Eastern European households—owned a television. In 1965, televisions were present in nine out of ten Western European households but still only very few Eastern European households. By 1975 over a third of Eastern European households also had televisions, and in 1985 almost all European households had televisions. The television became a form of mass media in Western Europe during the 1960s and in Eastern Europe by the 1980s.

Compared to the US, Europe was late in implementing the television, even though it was technically prepared to do so much earlier. The main reason was that it was not until the economic boom of the 1950s and 1960s that Western Europeans had enough spending capacity to afford this medium (see Chapter 3 on consumption and standard of living) and that the Western European governments had enough financial power to invest in public television broadcasters. Only in the 1970s did the communist governments competing with the West first realize television's importance for political propaganda and regime stability.

Television very quickly became a key medium because it connected moving images, news, and live reporting in many competing programs. It was a key medium for entertainment as well as for political information. The cinema, which had experienced its heyday during the 1950s with forty to fifty thousand cinemas, was forced back by television, although with considerable differences within Europe. While the cinemas in Southern Europe and in France survived, and the number of cinemas even increased in Eastern Europe, by the 1960s movie theaters were beginning to fold in the northern part of Europe, i.e. in Great Britain, Scandinavia, West Germany, the Netherlands, Switzerland, and Austria. By the 1980s and 1990s, movie theaters were closing throughout Europe as audiences shrank, despite the creation of multiplex cinemas with many screens (see Table 8.1). In line with this trend, the production of films for the broad masses had already clearly decreased in Western Europe by the 1970s. US production survived this crisis far better, embraced cost-efficient production, internationalized content, and in the 1970s began to conquer the European market. It was first during this time that the films most watched and internationally successful in Western Europe were overwhelmingly American. European films for the general population were usually only

Table 8.1 Media in Europe, 1955–1995

Year	Books	Cinema	Radio	Television	Newspapers	Magazines
1955	124,886	44,391	66,240	8,568	1,949	/
1965	198,162	48,992	102,703	58,560	1,851	/
1975	265,277	53,964	158,987	116,810	1,499	6,018
1985	362,166	/	246,032	154,333	1,600	7,266
1994	470,531	27,119	351,802	219,050	1,792	4,488

Source: *UN Statistical Yearbooks*, Years: 1957; 1960; 1966; 1967; 1968; 1977; 1978; 1981; 1985/86; 1988/89; 1993; 1994; 1995. Books: number of new releases and reprints; cinema: number of theaters (1994, not 1995); radio: number of radio receivers (in thousands) (1953, not 1955; 1986, not 1985); televisions: number of television sets (in thousands) (1956, not 1955); newspapers: number of daily newspapers (1965: without the ca. 700 local newspapers only counted during this year in the Federal Republic); magazines: number of magazines.

national successes. From this time on, one can speak of an Americanization of European cinema and television. This caused a deep upheaval for European film with effects that can still be seen today. It was only with intellectual films for a small, academic audience that European, and chiefly French, film producers remained strong and successful.

In contrast, television presented little threat to other media: radio, newspapers, books, magazines, and theater. Quite to the contrary, they have grown at approximately the same rate since the 1970s, when television took root (see Table 8.1). Positioned to profit from growing purchasing power during the economic boom, they had advantages that the television did not have. The invention of the transistor radio, for instance, made this medium portable; it could be listened to in the car or at the beach and had better quality reception with the VHF band. Radios became so inexpensive that each member of the family could tune in to his or her own radio program; thus, as opposed to television, the decision about which radio program to listen to was no longer an issue of power within the family. Compared to television, radio production was faster and better targeted to particular audience milieus: local and regional audiences, housewives, young people, and those interested in culture.

Newspapers repeatedly experienced periods of crisis but always recovered, and in the long term they withstood competition from television (cf. Table 8.1) for several reasons. They could be taken anywhere—buses, waiting rooms, and so on—and they appealed to a local audience more than television. Special journals devoted to a multitude of areas in life, from teen to women's magazines, golf to hobbyist magazines, sports papers to architectural periodicals, all emerged. Also, newspapers' financial basis—subscriptions, commercial advertising, and private ads—differed from television's and was not threatened until the 1980s, upon the rise of TV advertising and the Internet. Investigative journalism developed more intensely in newspapers than it did in television; substantive coverage of political and economic scandals, such as the Spiegel Affair, remained more the domain of newspapers.

Taken together, these developments had several far-reaching social and political consequences. The media strengthened the retreat to domestic privacy from everyday publicity on the street and in bars. Originally barroom pursuits, listening to the radio and watching television became private activities. Records were listened to at home. The family gathered for evenings in front of the television instead of meeting with others outside of the home. The domestic daily routine, especially in the evenings, was strongly shaped by television. It was not only the media, but also other long-lasting consumer goods like the car and the refrigerator that enforced this return to domesticity and to the nuclear family. Furthermore, the media strengthened the youth culture, which was breaking away from the culture of older generations, especially through radio broadcasting, transistor radios, and records. Music was central to this generation. It was first through the media that rock, and later pop music, became mass cultures spreading to small towns and rural areas and were no longer phenomena specific to large cities.

The media additionally encouraged the individualization process. Mass media provided information about very different values, lifestyles, milieus, and cultures, about clothing, public appearance, morals, and debates. It became easier to compose an individual lifestyle and value set. Finally, mass media also spread political and social information. It became easier to gain social recognition through better information. Users of the modern mass media could join in the conversation. At the same time, modern media strengthened the societal and political consensus, because not only the public but also the private media needed to address middle-of-the-road tastes and political opinions to be accepted by their audience and by broadcasting and television companies. It is therefore difficult to decide which came first: the stronger demand for political and cultural information as well as entertainment, or the larger supply by the mass media. The media's negative influence is apparent with regard to the rising inclination to violence, decreased social contact, and declining responsibility for family and the social environment.

At the same time, society's exertion of influence on the media was amplified. The importance of audience numbers and opinion polls for television constantly increased. The professionalization of influence on the media became more established. The student movement purposely used the media, especially television, to publicize political actions, a tactic that was taken over and further developed by later social movements.

In contrast, the internationalization of the media remained limited during this era. Neither the media ownership nor the audience became recognizably international. Only the Americanization of the media in Western Europe intensified. European television productions often assumed the same formats—the quiz show, the talk show, the TV magazine—used in American television, which had a head start and thus functioned as a model. Furthermore, an Americanization of products developed from the 1970s on. US films began to dominate European movie theaters and TV channels because they were offered cheaply, the US film distribution societies dominated the market, and the US had a long-standing technical monopoly on satellite broadcasting. The American broadcast station AFN remained influential in a number of European countries. European media seldom reflected international, European influence Radio Luxembourg being a notable exception. Americanization was admittedly restricted to these areas. Neither the press nor radio nor television programs were Americanized, and documentary films too remained a European domain. The Cold War eventually led to an internationalization of the media, especially for broadcast radio. From the 1950s on, Western European radio stations such as the Voice of America, Radio Liberty, Radio Free Europe, Radio France Internationale, BBC World Service, and Deutsche Welle were broadcast beyond the Iron Curtain to listeners in Eastern Europe, just as Eastern European stations conversely broadcast to a Western European audience.

This internationalization was so limited, however, that there was no resulting impetus for the European public sphere. This developed little, even though after several enlargements the purview of the emerging European decision-making center, the European Community, encompassed nearly two-thirds of the European population (not including the USSR) by the beginning of the 1980s and, what is more, Western European societies increasingly assimilated to one another. The media rarely reported about Europe and continued to come from a primarily national perspective, placing national politicians and national themes at the forefront of their reportage about European decisions. A European media had still not emerged. The first attempt at a European radio and television platform, the previously mentioned European Broadcasting Union, entered a period of crisis during this era because the US controlled the new worldwide television transmission technology, satellite broadcasting, and therefore called the shots.

Intellectuals usually withdrew from the debate about Europe's culture and society, partly because the European Coal and Steel Community and the European Economic Community were too economic, not cultural enough, too conservative, too much like public authorities, and too narrow geographically. For some, they derived insufficiently from below or from a social movement. Intellectuals also often thought in terms of different geographical areas. During the Cold War the confrontation between the Atlantic West and the Eastern European–Soviet region was central. A common European space no longer seemed to be a cultural or political reality, given the seemingly permanent division of Europe. Europe played a marginal role in the many visions for the future that were discussed and popular at the time. The US, or in other visions the USSR, played the central role. Public spheres of European experts only rarely formed. Historical science began to internationalize during this period, but the predominant new international approach was the comparison of nations. Historians did not commonly see Europe as a whole.

This period did not yield many new European symbols. The European stamps that had been released since the 1950s were more exercises for designers in the beginning; later they displayed European landscapes, artworks, discoveries, and scholars. Furthermore, every country produced its own national European stamp. Common European stamps were few. The symbols that the Council of Europe created—Europe Day on the 5th of May (1964) and the Anthem of Europe (1972)—remained widely unknown. European memorials and the European interpretation of significant historical personalities were established but not substantially enhanced. No architectural structure was publicly designated as a symbol of Europe by Brussels or in Strasbourg. The most famous public political rituals were painstaking compromises made by exhausted circles of European politicians after long nights of negotiations, or dry group photos of state and government leaders lined up like sardines in a can. The presidents of the European Commission remained as unknown to the European public as European parliamentarians, even after the first European election in 1979, in which about two-thirds of the population voted. The international political rites that did have a strong, emotional effect on the European public remained bilateral: for example, the meeting between de Gaulle and Adenauer in the Reims Cathedral for the conclusion of the Elysée Treaty.

Theaters, museums, and concerts likewise Europeanized only to a certain extent. Translations between European languages, as measured by book production, did not become noticeably more common. The bestseller lists remained different from country to country. Very few books became Europe-wide bestsellers, and those that did were often by American and not European authors. No effective European cultural and educational policy had yet emerged from the EEC, the Council of Europe, or the European governments. Numerous international, often bilateral, cultural meeting centers were created at this time; the German side alone established the Villa Zuccari in Florence, the Villa Vigoni in Menaggio, the German Historical Institutes in Paris and London, and the exchange program at the Academy of the Arts in Berlin, for example. International film, theater, and music festivals became more numerous. The international book fair in Frankfurt experienced a considerable revival. However, this cultural scene did not give rise to a common European cultural public in which intellectuals, artists, and patrons enjoyed Europe-wide prominence, nor to a European audience that read the same bestseller list, heard the same intellectuals speak, listened to the same music, and watched the same European films. For the most part, a European cultural public sphere was neither extant nor wanted on the cultural scene.

Internationalization and Europeanization after the 1980s

The third era within the history of the European media and public had quite a different appearance. The 1980s brought about three fundamental changes: more media privatization, more internationalization of the media, and more of a European public sphere.

The privatization of television and broadcasting considerably changed the landscape of European media. Throughout much of the 1980s, private television and broadcasting played only a marginal role in Europe. By 2000, most viewers and listeners watched and listened to private television and radio. This privatization led to a sizable expansion in choices of media, a larger variety of radio stations, and a larger variety of media that had always been private, like newspapers and magazines, books, music, and films. This range of media variety was so wide because no displacement process or crowding out developed between the different forms of media through privatization; rather, all areas of media expanded—not only television, but radio, theater, newspapers, and magazines as well (cf. Table 8.1). Even cinema was on the rise again during this era. However, privatization did not result in improvement of the quality of television and radio stations; nor did consumers' direct participation increase. The advance of privatization should also not be overestimated; this privatization was not complete anywhere in Europe. Public stations still existed almost everywhere, and conversely important forms of media, print, music, and film production had already been private to a large extent beforehand.

The increased variety of media forms resulted not only from privatization of public media but also from fundamental technological changes. The production of texts and images, and later of music, changed through rapid advancements in electronic data processing. Books, newspapers, and magazines could be produced more easily and inexpensively because they were no longer prepared through the division of labor at typewriters and desks, but on the computer monitor of a single person. The increasing variety in the range of media had a lot to do with easier, more inexpensive, yet still high-quality copies of texts and images, and later of music, through machines for copying and reproduction, and the Internet. Media enterprises lost some control over the distribution of their products. New data carriers for text and images emerged: in addition to paper and records, disks and CDs were used for text, images, and music, and videos and DVDs for films. These new data carriers often had a short lifespan of only one or two decades, but they increased the variety of the media supply.

A much different form of privatization was the shifting of the border between public and private, more specifically between public media and private exchange. This shift is still under way, so its impact is not yet clearly visible. The large variety in the range of media—not only television but also radio, print, and music—strengthened the return to privacy because all of these forms of media are not usually heard, watched, or read in public, but rather at home. At the same time, the Internet not only opened a new kind of public sphere within the home but also carried the private sphere into the public via Internet forums and magazines, chat rooms, self-made websites, Internet shopping, and politically mobilizing e-mails; that is, via a new kind of public amusement, but also a new form of economy and politics. The home became the public sphere.

The second important change during this epoch was the internationalization of the media, along with its products, proprietors, and audience. To the public, this media internationalization primarily meant a continued internationalization of texts, images, music, TV, and films as well as music CDs and specialized journals. Europeans' consumption of international media was more frequent. Public international media like the BBC World Service, Radio France Internationale, and Deutsche Welle expanded their audiences in Europe, as was also the case with private international media like the *Financial Times*, *Le Monde*, the *Neue Zürcher Zeitung*, El País, the *Metro*, and the American CNN.

This internationalization of media had different causes. It was partly a result of the internationalization of media ownership and the attendant effect of media privatization. Private media companies did not remain national companies, but rather developed into international media groups like Bertelsmann, Time Warner, Sony, and Murdoch. Public television and radio establishments had not internationalized to this extent. The internationalization of the media was also politically desired, an outcome of the recently instituted European Union media policy. Furthermore, media internationalization resulted from technological changes. Cable and satellite dishes both increased the variety of television channels available to audiences and made the medium more international, as transmitting stations from other countries became considerably easier. Arte, BBC, and CNN gained an international audience because of this.

The international distribution of texts, images, and music also became extraordinarily easy and cheaper as well thanks to the Internet and, to some extent, the automatic telephone and fax machine. Internet distribution, unlike the transport of goods, faced very few national borders capable of stopping information. The few governments that wanted to establish national Internet boundaries, as was the case in China and Saudi Arabia, had to negotiate complicated special contracts with providers, the efficiency of which is not yet clear. Of course it should not be overlooked that the Internet did not necessarily always internationalize content—it could also be used to strengthen regional or local identities.

This era eventually eventually decisively boosted the development of a European public sphere. Intellectuals began to discuss Europe even before the fall of the Wall. The impetus came from intellectuals like Richard Löwenthal, Edgar Morin, Rémi Brague, Jacques Derrida, Jürgen Habermas, Anthony Giddens, György Konrad, and Bronisław Geremek. The decline of the Soviet empire and the end of the division of Europe, the enlargement of the European Community, which increasingly represented Europe as a whole, and the upturn in European integration under Jacques Delors, as well as the rise of East Asia and the end of the classification of the globe into first and third worlds all fueled this fresh spate of debate about Europe.

During this era there also emerged a European public sphere of experts, who developed networks in conferences, journals, and memoranda and had influence on the European Union's decisions. Economists, lawyers, and political scientists were particularly active in such endeavors. Historians who worked transnationally changed their perspective. International series like *Europa Bauen* and new paperback books about European history examined Europe as a whole. The Groupe de Liaison of European historians and the network established by René Girault in 1989, "Identités européennes," came into being. Furthermore, historians devoted more intense scrutiny than before to transfers, integration, cultural encounters, and mutual images between Europe and non-European societies.

At the same time, new symbols of Europe were instituted, sometimes successfully: the cardinal red European passport, the European flag with twelve stars on a blue background that was adopted by the European Union in 1986, the European anthem, Europe Day on 9 May, and since 2002 the most broadly circulated European symbol, euro notes and coins. The architecturally prominent seat of the European Parliament was erected in Strasbourg, and a European district emerged in Brussels next to the European Commission's Berlémont high-rise and the European Parliament and Council buildings. A mythology regarding the European Union's founding fathers was created primarily around Robert Schuman and Jean Monnet, but also in part around Winston Churchill. National war memorials like Verdun were reinterpreted as European monuments to peace. The fall of the Wall, which could have been an entirely German event, became an event for European retrospection. Plans were laid for European museums in Brussels and Aachen, as well as for important places of remembrance for hundreds of thousands of visitors. The constitutional treaty project was to stand as another important European symbol.

Unlike in the postwar period, most of these symbols did not come from below—that is, they did not arise from social movements but were initiated from above by the European Union. Furthermore, not all of these symbols were successful. Europe Day and the European anthem remained as unknown to Europeans as the European district in Brussels or the parliament building in Strasbourg. European stamps were issued less often. The constitutional treaty failed in 2005. Nevertheless, during this era European symbols were more widespread than ever before.

The national media became Europeanized in three ways. First, news about the European Union became more common in national media because the European Union's decision-making power spread to increasingly more fields in the 1990s. The EU developed into a powerful decision-making center and became an object of public criticism. The campaigns for numerous European referendums introduced European themes to the media, which discussed not only advantages of the EU but also its weaknesses. In any case, the media reported much more often about the European Union and excited a great deal of interest among readers. European news became so important that the various European national media agencies often ran the same European headlines at once. News was also increasingly presented differently, less from a completely national perspective and more from a European perspective. The European Union in general became more important in the media than it had been from the 1950s through the 1970s, and not at the cost of news from the rest of the world, but at the cost of news from other European countries (Eder and Kanter 2000; Gerhards 2002; Kaelble 2002; van den Steeg 2003; Meyer 2004; Risse 2004; Peters et al. 2005).

Media interest in the European Union did not continuously grow, of course. In some respects a renationalization can even be spoken of. The responsibilities of the European Union did become more extensive and increasingly affected the population's everyday life, but it was often national heads of state and government—not EU representatives—who explained and interpreted the European Council's decisions to the press, usually purposely in front of the national flag. At the European level, civil society usually kept out of the public mobilization of citizens and thus did not thwart these trends (see Chapter 9).

Second, the internationalization of private and public media that was mentioned earlier also contributed to Europeanization. True, this internationalization led in many directions, to Americanization or toward Asian or global trends within the European media. But the Europeanization of the European media was at least one direction of development. The BBC, RFI, *Financial Times*, *Le Monde*, and Deutsche Welle were read, watched, and listened to more than ever before.

Third, numerous efforts have advanced the project of establishing a transnational European media. The best-known venture—the German-French television channel *Arte*, which has been on the air since 1992—has always had European ambitions. In addition to this, Euronews, a European news station that is carried by about twenty public-service European television broadcasters, has presented European news in several European languages since 1993 and claimed to have reached close to 8 million viewers by 2005. Meanwhile, the private transnational European media projects Eurosports, The European, Liber, and Café Babel have enjoyed various degrees of success. Of these three developments, the most important to date has been the Europeanization of the content presented by national media, as it has reached the most readers, listeners, and viewers.

The cultural scene also changed after the 1980s. Theater, film, music, and culture festivals expanded considerably, even if they did not fundamentally change in nature. New projects were created, like the Theatre Odéon européen in Paris, initiated by French Minister of Education Jack Lang and since 1983 directed by Giorgio Strehler. Film and theater festivals, among other cultural festivals, became central to local politics. Intercity competition not only became considerably livelier as of the 1980s but also centered on culture, science, and sport rather than focusing on industrial settlements. The cities taking part in this competition were more willing to finance these cultural festivals and had more influence regarding the events. The profession of cultural manager came into being, and as a result the new educational discipline cultural studies was created.

The European cultural scene was certainly more international than it was consciously European, but starting in the 1980s it was also influenced by the beginning of the European Union's cultural policy. The European Union had made statements on European culture since the 1970s and continued this in the 1980s with a statement on the "European cultural area" in 1980 and the European Cultural Charter of 1989. Also in the 1980s, the European Union first took on functions in cultural policy, signing the Single European Act in 1986, expanding its competencies with the Maastricht and Amsterdam Treaties, and proceeding to take relevant decisions in the 1980s. It began to regulate the prices of books and influence author rights. It organized several cultural programs like Kaleidoskop, Ariane, and Raphael, which were combined in the Culture 2000 project in 2000. They all had the goal of strengthening integration between national European cultures, albeit with a very small budget of less than 200 million euros. The best-known project in this program is the competition for the title of European City of Culture, or European Capital of Culture as it has been called since 1999, which the European Union has awarded to nearly thirty Western and Eastern European cities since 1985.

Of course, the European public sphere was not developed in terms of the national public sphere. There have even been countertrends since the 1990s. Later European Commission presidents were unable to mobilize the European public as Jacques Delors had done with the Single Market project. Voter participation in European elections sank continuously, a sign that the European parliament was not successful in positioning itself within the European public sphere. A contradiction emerged: on the one side was the deepening and enlargement of the European Union as carried out by politicians, European officials, and European experts; on the other side was the perception of Europe held by its citizens, which found its expression in the "no" to the constitutional referenda in France and the Netherlands in 2005. Still, the indications of a European public sphere discussed above have overall become stronger since the 1980s.

Divergences and Convergences

The divergences and convergences between European societies were also altered by the changes to media and the public. In the first decades after the Second World War, the media in the periphery of Europe still differed markedly from their counterparts in the wealthier parts of Europe. The fundamental requirements for developing both the media and the public to consume them were largely lacking in poorer European countries. Illiteracy was still prevalent, the standard of living was low, and rural subsistence agriculture was still widespread. Not only print media, but also radio and television were therefore much less common in peripheral countries like Portugal, Spain, Greece, the Balkans, Bulgaria, Romania, and Turkey than in Western Europe and East Central Europe, and also less common than in the USSR. In 1970 the distribution of newspapers, radios, and televisions in these countries was at most still only half of the European average, and not uncommonly considerably below even this (UN 1983: 422ff.). The public sphere in these countries was usually more oriented to word of mouth, local, and dependent on personal encounters. In a number of countries the public was restricted and deformed by dictatorship. This inter-European divergence diminished gradually during the 1980s and 1990s as illiteracy was eliminated (see Chapter 12 on education). Dictatorships fell, and mass media, especially radio and television, became so inexpensive that they were part of the minimum standard of living in Southern and Eastern Europe.

A second fundamental divergence formed after the Second World War between the liberal public sphere in the West and the public sphere in communist Eastern Europe. This divergence was not just a contrast between *the* western and *the* eastern public, but rather existed in different tensions and interactions between the various publics and the governments. Western Europe had autonomous public spheres made up of various individual, partly interwoven, political, economic, scientific, cultural, and religious public spheres, as well as public spheres of experts in every country. The governments and national administrations, as well as media owners, did try to influence the public. But the public sphere was able to preserve its autonomy and, if necessary, enter into conflict with the governments. Governments did not earnestly try to unify the multitude of various public spheres. These public spheres in Western Europe had European, Western, and global dimensions. The governments of larger countries and international organizations, such as the United Nations and the World Bank, also tried to influence these public spheres, which protected their autonomy with the support of intellectuals, experts, and international civil societies.

In each country in Eastern Europe, in contrast, the government and national party created, controlled, and staged a comprehensive, unified, official public sphere. Governments accomplished this through their monopoly of information and censorship. However, an anticipatory, internal censorship also played a role: a certain amount of seemingly free criticism was allowed, but attacking the government's monopoly of power was impermissible. Similarly, an internal, highly controlled public sphere that was closed to the outside world contributed to the appearance of a monolithic public, as did repression of unaccepted journalists and intellectuals. "Counter publics" opposing these controlled official public spheres began to emerge in the 1960s and 1970s, relying on journals, books, flyers, initiatives, art exhibitions, illegal meetings, readings, and seminars to sustain their small groups of supporters. Counter publics discussed not only themes that were forbidden by the government but also forms of public spheres that had more freedom. They were not uniform but consisted of different religious, academic, and artistic groupings. Counter publics saw themselves in part as purely national and in part as transnational spheres. In any case, they were connected with the public sphere in the West.

Finally, Eastern Europeans developed private communication networks. These were not fully organized public spheres with political goals and their own media but rather formed during free time in bars or at workplaces, and tended to foduc on suggestions to improve living standards. Though large parts of the populace supported them, they became politically relevant only upon the collapse of the Soviet empire (Beyrau 2000; Niedermüller 2002). The fundamental difference between the Western and Eastern public spheres thus lay not in the density of media forms or in the previously mentioned delay in the implementation of new forms of media like television, but in the governments' very different exercise of control over public spheres and the publics' differing abilities to criticize the government. This intra-European divergence disappeared with the fall of the Soviet empire.

Finally, a new difference in the role of the government in the internationalization of the media developed as of the 1980s. This divergence was especially visible between France and Great Britain, but could also be found among other European countries. The internationalization of the media in France largely consisted of initiatives by the French government, which organized a systematic media Europeanization that tended to align with the European Community. Strengthening Europe with respect to the US's media supremacy was an essential part of this policy. These governmental initiatives were supported by countries whose languages— French, German, and Italian—were not international and therefore faced difficult linguistic limits in regard to the internationalization of the media in Europe, which meanwhile could not advance without massive governmental support. The most established projects were the European Broadcasting Union, Eurovision, and later Arte; the European Cultural Charter, and local projects like the Théâtre européen de l'Odéon, the Cannes Film Festival, and the theater festival in Aix-en-Provence.

The British internationalization of the media, in stark contrast to this, was able to rely on its expanding global language, English. It consisted mostly of an international expansion of existing national British media and the BBC World Service, and the internationalization of the audience for British publishers and newspapers, of which the *Financial Times* was the most successful example. The British path was not primarily targeted at Europe but at the enormous English-speaking audiences in North America, India, Africa, and Australia. Europe was usually more of a sideshow. Governmental help and state-run initiatives were limited, and as a result not many international film, theater, or music festivals were initiated or subsidized by the state. The French and British methods cannot be cleanly separated from each other. French international media policy worked with national French media like Radio France Internationale or *Le Monde*, which expanded its international clientele and had a large non-French audience. Conversely, Great Britain also took part in media initiatives by the European government. But the basic trends differed between the countries.

European Hallmarks

European media development in the second half of the twentieth century sometimes followed worldwide trends that, though led by the US, were implemented similarly on every continent, in cinema and television as well as cyberspace. However, a number of distinctly European characteristics are discernible.

Public radio and television broadcasters overseen by the government and civil society were, and remain in the twenty-first century, a European peculiarity. Unlike the state-run broadcasting and television establishments in many Asian, African, and Latin American nations, they were able to protect their autonomy from the government. The ways of doing so were secured differently in each European country, but the government mostly did not control them. At the same time, and unlike public broadcasters in the US, they remained alongside private free or commercialized radio and television despite maintaining great autonomy from the market. This autonomy played an important role in the quality of broadcasting and television and has been preserved for the foreseeable future as well, despite the rapid rise of the private sector since the 1980s.

The self-image of those working in media was also different in Europe. This applied to journalists as well as to the intellectuals and experts who did not live from the media but through it. Pure investigative journalism, which emerged in the US during the nineteenth century and enjoyed great success in uncovering the huge scandals of the second half of the twentieth century—e.g., the Watergate scandal—did not take hold as strongly on the European continent as it did in the US. There was not a single European model that mirrored investigative journalism, but instead several models of journalism careers. The independent "worldview" journalist, as was developed in the German and French weekly newspapers *Die Zeit* and *Nouvel Observateur*, had far greater importance in Europe than in the US. Party-affiliated, milieu-based, religious, and trade union journalism also played a bigger role in Europe than it did in the US, as parties and unions were more strongly founded on a solid membership base and also used the media to hold this firm foundation intact. Even as ties to political and social milieus loosened through the individualization process (see Chapters 4 and 9), party-affiliated and religious journalism remained important in stabilizing the rest of the milieus. Pure ideologists and propagandists must also be counted among European journalists, developing in European dictatorships throughout most of the twentieth century and found in its second half among the communist dictatorships in particular, but also within the Iberian right-wing dictatorships. Even though this propaganda journalism for the most part disappeared from Europe with the end of the Franco and Salazar regimes and the collapse of the Soviet empire, it inescapably remains one of the dark sides of European history.

Furthermore, the traditional medium of the book was much more developed in Europe than in the US or Japan. In 1985 about 700 books per resident were produced in Europe as a whole. The US and Japan produced only about half of that, and Latin America, China, and the Arabic world produced even less (Kaelble 1997). This European edge cannot be explained by the reading intensity in Northern Europe alone. Even in Southern Europe, where the media, as mentioned before, were much less prevalent for some time, the population read more books compared to the US. In everyday life, Europeans attached far greater importance to this classic medium than did Americans, Asians, or Arabs.

This had much to do with Europe's different political history. Modern democracies replaced Europe's Ancien Régime during the eighteenth and nineteenth centuries through a political mobilization of the population, in which print media played an important role. No such Ancien Régime ever existed in the US. The European experience with dictatorships and occupations in the twentieth century, from which few countries were spared, increased the importance of printed media because criticism of these dictatorships was for the most part produced via the medium of print, in particular books, in addition to newspapers. Printed media were also more important in the everyday life of Europeans because they were a supporting element of an especially developed sense of privacy for the individual and the family, of separation from the state, and of the creation of a domain of trust and solitude (see Chapter 4 on values). The reading material in books and newspapers was the key component to this privacy and its special communication with the outside world.

A fourth characteristic within the history of the European media and public is their transnationality. With few exceptions, the European media generally surpass the US media in coverage of countries and areas outside their own territory. A transnational public, as was already discussed, developed only in Europe. This special European transnationality within the media also had several causes. In part it reflects Europe's national small scale, which forces citizens to become more informed about the other nations that are encountered time and again. It also has to do with European integration and the rising importance of an international center of power, the European Union, in Europeans' everyday life. But the distinctive European experience with the media in dictatorships also played a role. An important element of dissidents' strength in communist Eastern Europe was their presence in the media outside of their own national space, especially in Western democracies. Without this transnational Western public, dissidents in Central Europe would never have gained prominence in their own countries. Europeans learned that the media outside their own country also count.

A fifth characteristic was that after the collapse of the European colonial empires, Europe became a vital global platform for the media and the public. Europe led the world in both production and exports of books and newspapers. In 1998 Europe exported $5.8 billion worth of books, or 54 percent of world exports, whereas the US exported $2.1 billion worth of books, only 20 percent of world exports. Europe had a 69 percent share of world exports of newspapers and magazines while the US had only 14 percent (UNESCO 2000b: 14, 18). Nowhere else at that time were so many books translated into so many languages and exported as in Europe. Eighty-eight percent of all book translations worldwide were published in Europe (UNESCO 2000a: 375). Europe's global role was related to the fact that as an educator, Europe led the world alongside the US and attracted nearly as many international students (UNESCO 1993: 3, 335f.; 1999: II, 486–488).

Europe's global role in the media was also associated with the high numbers of tourists to Europe. During the second half of the twentieth century Europe became the greatest tourist magnet in the world by far. A substantial, though not precisely definable, part of this tourism was cultural tourism: visits to museums, concerts, old city centers, castles, and churches. Of course Europe's global role in media differed fundamentally from the US's because there was no superpower behind European culture. European culture thus received less attention but also less of the criticism superpowers attract. It would be unrealistic to view Europe as a passive, culturally polluted victim of American and Asian media culture. Europe's post-decolonization role in the global media and the international public differed greatly from the part it had played during the colonial period.

Notes

1. Estimates based on the UN Statistical Yearbook (1957–1995), under the general assumption that the number of households is about one third of the population.

References

Beyrau D. "Die befreiende Tat des Wortes: Dissens und Bürgerrechtsbewegungen in Osteuropa." In *Samizdat: Alternative Kultur in Zentral- und Osteuropa*, ed. W. Eichwede. Bremen 2000, 26–37.

Bösch F. *Mediengeschichte*. Frankfurt 2011.

Charle C. *Le siècle de la presse (1840–1939)*. Paris 2004.

Chartier R. and H.-J.Martin, eds. *Histoire de l'édition française*. 4 vols. Paris 2005.

Eder K. and C. Kantner. "Transnationale Resonanzstrukturen in Europa: Eine Kritik der Rede vom Öffentlichkeitsdefizit." In *Die Europäisierung nationaler Gesellschaften*, ed. M. Bach. Wiesbaden 2000, 306–331.

Gerhards J. "Das Öffentlichkeitsdefizit der EU im Horizont normative Öffentlichkeitstheorien." In *Transnationale Öffentlichkeiten und Identitäten*, ed. H. Kaelble, M. Kirsch, and A. Schmidt-Gernig. Frankfurt a. M. 2002.

Grazia V. de. *Irresistible Empire: America's Advance through Twentieth Century Europe*. Cambridge, MA. 2005.

Hickethier K. *Geschichte des deutschen Fernsehens*. Stuttgart and Weimar 1998.

Kaelble H. "Europäische Besonderheiten des Massenkonsums, 1950–1990." In *Europäische Konsumgeschichte. Zur Gesellschafts- und Kulturgeschichte des Konsums (18. bis 20. Jahrhundert)*, ed. H. Siegrist, H. Kaelble, and J. Kocka. Frankfurt a. M. 1997, 169–203.

Kaelble H. "The Historical Rise of a European Public Sphere?" *Journal of European Integration History* 8, no. 2 (2002): 9–22. (French: "Un espace public européen? La perspective historique." In *Gouvernance et identités en Europe*, ed. R. Frank. Brussels, Bruylant, and Paris 2004, 159–173; German: in H. Kaelble, *Wege zur Demokratie: Von der Französischen Revolution zur Europäischen Union*. Stuttgart and Munich 2001, chap. 9.)

Klein A. et al., eds. *Bürgerschaft, Öffentlichkeit und Demokratie in Europa*. Opladen 2003.

Marssolek J. "Radio in Deutschland 1923–1960: Zur Sozialgeschichte eines Mediums." *Geschichte und Gesellschaft* 27 (2001): 207–239.

Meyer J.H. "Europäische Öffentlichkeit aus historischer Perspektive." In *Europäische Öffentlichkeit*, ed. C. Franzius and U.K. Preuss. Baden-Baden 2004.

Niedermüller P. "Kultur, Transfer und Politik im ostmitteleuropäischen Sozialismus." In *Transnationale Öffentlichkeit und Identitäten im 20. Jahrhundert*, ed. H. Kaelble, M. Kirsch, and A. Schmidt-Gernig. Frankfurt a. M. 2002, 263–302.

Peters B. et al. "National and Transnational Public Spheres: The Case of the EU." In *Transformations of the State*, ed. S. Leibfried and M. Zürn. Cambridge 2005, 139–160.

Requate J. "Öffentlichkeit und Medien als Gegenstände historischer Analyse." *Geschichte und Gesellschaft* 25 (1999): 5–32.

Requate J. and M. Schulze Wessel, eds. *Europäische Öffentlichkeit: Transnationale Kommunikation seit dem 18. Jahrhundert*. Frankfurt a. M. 2002.

Risse T. "Auf dem Weg zu einer europäischen Kommunikationsgemeinschaft: Theoretische Überlegungen und empirische Evidenz." In *Europäische Öffentlichkeit*, ed. C. Franzius and U.K. Preuss. Baden-Baden 2004, 139–154.

Sassoon D. *The Culture of the Europeans. From 1800 to the Present*. London 2006.

Schanze H. "Integrale Mediengeschichte." In *Handbuch der Mediengeschichte*, ed. H. Schanze. Stuttgart 2001.

Schildt A. "Das Jahrhundert der Massenmedien: Ansichten einer zukünftigen Geschichte der Öffentlichkeit." *Geschichte und Gesellschaft* 27 (2001): 177–206.

Schulz A. "Der Aufstieg der 'vierten Gewalt': Medien, Politik und Öffentlichkeit im Zeitalter der Massenkornrnunikation." *Historische Zeitschrift* 270 (2000): 65–97.

Sorlin P. *European Cinemas, European Societies, 1939–1990*. London 1994, 81–110.

Steeg M. van den. "Bedingungen für die Entstehung europäischer Öffentlichkeit in der EU." In *Bürgerschaft, Öffentlichkeit und Demokratie in Europa*, ed. A. Klein et al. Opladen 2003, 169–190.

Trenz H.J. *Zur Konstitution politischer Öffentlichkeit in der Europäischen Union: Zivilgesellschaftliche Subpolitik oder schaupolitische Inszenierung*. Baden-Baden 2002.

UNESCO. *Cultural Diversity, Conflict and Pluralism: World Cultural Report 2000*. Paris 2000a.

UNESCO. *International Flows of Selected Cultural Goods, 1980–98*. Paris 2000b.

Weisbrod B. "Medien als symbolische Form der Massengesellschaft: Die medialen Bedingungen von Öffentlichkeit im 20. Jahrhundert." *Historische Anthropologie* 9 (2001): 270–283.

Wessler H. "Europa als Kommunikationsnetzwerk: Theoretische Überlegungen zur Europäisierung der Öffentlichkeit." In *Europäische Union und mediale Öffentlichkeit*, ed. L.M. Hagen. Cologne 2004.

Wilke J. *Grundzüge der Medien- und Kommunikationsgeschichte von den Anfängen bis ins 20. Jahrhundert*. Cologne 2000.

Chapter 9

Social Movements, Conflicts, and Civil Society

The second group of societal actors seeking to influence government and state administrations comprised social movements and civil society. Like the media, they played a significant role in the second half of the twentieth century and became more international and European in nature.

Social movements, social conflicts, and civil societies are closely connected to each other but are not the same. As a rule, social movements are not viewed as set, long-term, centralized, and bureaucratic organizations, but instead as networks of various groups. Trade unions, churches, and parties can take part in social movements but are more permanently organized than social movements. Social movements are oriented around a common societal reform objective or stand in resistance to a policy, and their participants generally possess a common identity. They bank on temporary personal commitment, not on permanent membership, and primarily act publicly through gatherings, committees, demonstrations, rituals, and symbols. They address the government or political parties for the most part, acting locally, nationally, and often transnationally. Conversely, social movements are not just singular events, such as an individual mass demonstration or uprising, but usually survive longer. And finally, social movements are neither purely religious movements nor cultural networks such as fan clubs, museum associations, or postage stamp exchanges—they pursue political goals.

Civil society in contrast is understood as a sector of society beyond politics and economy, often referred to as the "third sector," that can be either national or transnational. This sector is not focused on the values of political power or economic gain but instead normally concentrates on solidarity, trust, and helping others as well as civility, nonviolence, and general interest. Civil society is autonomous from political power and from business. It is generally decentralized, consists of a variety of organizations, movements, and projects, and is closely affiliated with the public. Civil society can also be exclusive and exclude citizens, however; it does not just protect democracies but can also be utilized in dictatorships and stand for intolerance, violence, and civil war.

This perception of civil society is controversial, and whether it always supports the values of trust, solidarity, civility, and nonviolence is questioned. There is no consensus as to whether civil society is actually a sector, or whether it is only a principle that politicians or entrepreneurs can also follow for a period of time. It is also controversial whether this concept can be applied to non-Western societies, i.e., whether it can be applied to the eastern part of Europe as well. There is great advantage, however, in that it exists in all of the important European languages and with certain modifications can also be applied to the transnational European level. This transnational side of civil society will be covered here.

Something different in turn is also meant by "social conflicts." Social conflicts are manifest public disputes that take place between groups, not between individuals, and that revolve around social topics. Social conflicts come in a broad variety of forms ranging from manifestos, petitions, gatherings, and demonstrations to strikes, armed internal conflicts, and revolutions. Social conflicts do not always originate from social movements. Civil societies can be mediums of social conflict as well, and social conflicts can also, of course, be transnational.

State of Research

As of yet there is no European overview of these topics, not even among the manuals on social history mentioned at the beginning of this book. The only exception is the compendium by Göran Therborn, which contains a chapter on civil society and collective action (Therborn 1995). There are European summaries covering individual aspects of these topics. Overviews, as well as short chapters in a number of social history handbooks, have been published recently on the history of trade unions, a traditional topic in the field of social history (Ebbinghaus and Visser

1997; Guedj et al. 1997; Bussière and Dumoulin 1998; Saly et al. 1998; Eley 2002; see also the introduction in this book). In her book on the history of women, Gisela Bock covered the European women's movement (Bock 2000). There are European overviews and sketches of the student movement by Ingrid Gilcher-Holtey and Etienne François, as well as by Carole Fink, Philipp Gassert, and Detlef Junker (François 1997; Fink et al. 1998; Gilcher-Holtey 2001). Almost all of these overviews are limited to Western Europe, however. Comprehensive overviews are lacking for Eastern Europe or Europe as a whole. There is not a single comparative presentation of the dissident movements within the Soviet sphere of influence.

The Postwar Period

The immediate postwar era was an ambivalent period for social movements and civil societies. On the one hand, civil societies and social movements were threatened, as the individual was often isolated in a fight of everyone against everyone, and the family became the last retreat within social life. In substantial parts of Europe, life was limited to the search for housing and food, foraging, illegal black markets, and theft, along with the painstaking battle against illnesses that could quickly become life-threatening. Apathy toward life in general was widespread. Many Europeans pulled back from civil societal organizations; solidarity in action rarely took place. Civil society faced the threat of collapse, particularly in bombed-out cities, and of slipping into the solidarity offered by the criminal black market or gangs. A paralyzing postwar apathy weighed heavily on undamaged and unoccupied cities as well, however. From his hometown of Cognac in Southwest France, Jean Monnet reported "the misery, the exhaustion among the population after the initial exuberance of liberation, filled me with heartfelt anxiety … The task of survival absorbed all means, all energy" (Monnet 1980: 285f.).

On the other hand, the postwar period was often also a fresh start for social movements in civil society. Three were particularly in vogue: the trade union movements, churches, and the transnational European Movement. Never had so many laborers been organized in unions throughout almost all of Europe, West as well as East (before Sovietization), as in the years after the Second World War. This extraordinary boom was owed in part to the moral prestige the unions enjoyed after the collapse of the right-wing dictatorships and occupying regimes, and in part to the Europeans' higher expectations for a better standard of living and for more political involvement, which resulted from the bitter need caused by war. However, there was also widespread skepticism toward the capitalist market economy that emerged from the devastating Great Depression of the 1930s, not least because of the close ties many businesses had had to the right-wing dictatorships. This revival of trade unions was the beginning of a long period of strength for labor unions in some European countries, such as Great Britain, Germany, Sweden, the Netherlands, and Belgium. In other countries, and above all in France and Italy, this unique peak was quickly followed by a drop in trade union involvement (cf. Figure 9.1). At the same time in many European countries in the late 1940s, strikes took place as never before or after. More workdays were lost to striking in France, Belgium, the Netherlands, Finland, and Denmark in these years than in the entire second half of the century. Strikes were extraordinarily intense in Italy, Austria, and Switzerland as well.

It was not just trade unions but also other areas of civil society that experienced a boom. Churches recorded increases in members and in people attending services. They profited from their reputation for integrity with regard to the dictatorships (whether or not this reputation was justified), but also from the expectation of church assistance in times of need, to which many Europeans succumbed due to the war.

The European Movement likewise experienced a high point during this period, with close to a hundred thousand members. It profited from its role in the European opposition to the National Socialist occupation of Europe and from the distance preserved between a large part of the European Movement and the right-wing dictatorships. It was an early example of a transnational social movement, but it had already lost appeal by the 1950s due to the Cold War and the founding of the "small" EEC.

The 1950s and 1960s: The Heyday of the Trade Union

The Height of the Union

The trade union's influence and membership base reached its peak in Europe between the 1950s and 1970s, the golden quarter century for European unions. The number of members continued to increase in a large part of Western Europe—in Scandinavia, Great Britain, the Federal Republic of Germany, the Netherlands, and Belgium—reaching unprecedented levels that would never be attained again in most European countries. In France and Italy a different development set in. Unions split along ideological lines due to the Cold War. Membership numbers fell in the 1950s. But in the 1960s membership numbers shot up again in Italy, and in France the decline was at least stemmed (cf. Figure 9.1). Unions additionally had a strong public presence thanks to extensive coverage in the press, large-scale demonstrations on 1 May, festivals, and the threat of strikes or actual striking, which was mostly followed by successful wage settlements. The strike was the predominant, most conspicuous social conflict—all other conflicts trailed far behind it. In some countries trade unions even established entire economic empires, for example the housing associations and retail cooperatives in Germany. At the European level the European unions founded the ETUC (European Trade Union Confederation) in 1973, though it remained nothing more than a coordination office.

This heyday of the trade unions occurred for a series of reasons. In the second half of the twentieth century, union political power grew more than ever before, thanks to their influence on the social democratic governments in Great Britain, Scandinavia, and France, and to employers' now generally recognizing them as social partners. In some countries, such as France, West Germany and Belgium, political power for the unions also grew through new corporate codetermination. Economic prosperity helped the unions as well. The long economic revival put them in an advantageous negotiating position that afforded them great success in negotiating wage increases and reducing working hours. They meanwhile retained the solid social foundation of the industrial workforce, which was more numerous during this time than ever before or after (see Chapter 2 on labor). The distance they maintained from National Socialism and fascism as well as from the occupying regimes after the Second World War likewise made them attractive. The unions also simultaneously profited from the general skepticism of capitalism that spread throughout Europe after the experience of the Great Depression of the 1930s.

The first signs of a trend toward a European transnational civil society, which always emerged alongside the national civil society, also appeared during this era. There were still mental barriers to this during the 1950s and 1960s, though. The experience of two world wars stood between European nations that continued to distrust each other long after the end of the war. The Cold War divided Europe, which not only prevented transnational civil societies between East and West but also dug deep trenches between communist and other political milieus within Western Europe. Finally, the extremes between the Catholic, Protestant, and secular milieus positioned each of their respective civil societies as a counterpoint to the other milieus.

Despite this, the initial and still weak transnational European civil societies came into being during this era, and in fact did so in two differ-

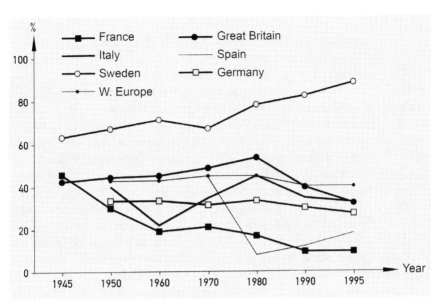

Figure 9.1 Trade Unions in Western Europe, 1945–1995
(Members by percent of those employed)
Source: B. Ebbinghaus and J. Visser, *Trade Unions in Western Europe* (Basingstoke 2000), 63
(Calculated later: Average for all of Western Europe)

ent directions. On the one hand, the transnational European civil society was expanding. Organizations such as Amnesty International, founded in 1961, and European international sports associations, the Union of European Football Associations best known among them, strengthened the older transnational civil societies—both those that had developed since the interwar period, including the international Rotary and Lions Clubs, and older ones like the International Red Cross, which had been in existence since 1861. This transnational civil society fundamentally continued to address the national governments, though during the Cold War these were primarily the Western European governments.

On the other hand, the European Coal and Steel Community and the EEC, industrial and agricultural interest groups, the COPA, the European farmers' association, and UNICE, the European industrial association, came into being. Admittedly, these interest groups were not yet numerous and were additionally limited to the member states of the EEC, in which no more than a third of the European population lived. They were pure umbrella organizations lacking their own members and significantly dependent on the extent to which EEC institutions heard them, in particular the European Commission and its social and economic committees.

The New Social Movements
from the Late 1960s through the 1980s

In the late 1960s, social movements that had not existed a decade before, or that had only led a shadowy existence, moved to the focus of public attention: the student movement and regional movement appeared alongside the trade unions. In the 1970s and 1980s, they were joined by the environmental, feminist, peace, and dissident movements in the eastern part of Europe as well as other social movements. They were certainly not all completely new. Regional movements, peace movements, and women's movements had been in existence in the nineteenth century (van der Linden 2003). Their methods of protest differed, however, from the traditional methods of manifestos and demonstrations or trade union strikes. As their groups tended to be small in number, they attracted attention by staging provocative events, often using the new medium of television. The objectives of these social movements were also new.

These new social movements had common causes. They aimed to alter values and change day-to-day life norms by more rapidly realizing liberalized social relations and greater sociability, shifting the goals of education, changing attitudes to property and violence, and increasing tolerance of minorities. Another cause was the rapid modernization of Europe during the 1950s and 1960s—extensive urbanization, educational expansion, and emergence of the mass consumption society. And a third contributor to the emergence of the new social movements was the modification of international relationships, the collapse of colonial empires, the altered East-West relationships, the changing image of communism after Stalin's death, and the long period of peace in Europe.

The Student Movement

The student movement was one of two early "new" social movements during the second half of the twentieth century. Since this time it has become a virtual legend and therefore an important object of historical research. It was an international movement, and though not centrally organized, it was firmly united across national borders. It was most strongly developed in France, Italy, and West Germany but also was active in other European democracies and furthermore in the Western European dictatorship of Greece and in communist Eastern Europe—Poland, Czechoslovakia, and Yugoslavia. It was not a purely European but rather a worldwide movement. The student movement initially, and most forcefully, developed in the US, but it then proceeded in Latin America, Turkey, Africa, India, Pakistan, and Japan as well. In addition to demonstrations, new forms of protest evolved, primarily "happenings"—visual, staged, provocative, and public violations of rules that generated attention for the movement's political goals. These new forms of protest were closely bound to the new medium of television.

The student movement reached its peak with massive demonstrations in France—the spectacular May 1968 in Paris—and in the western part of Berlin, but ended shortly thereafter. The movement was mostly limited to the intellectual and student milieu and thus did not become a broader youth movement. The motivation for the student movement in Western Europe was the US's Vietnam War; in Eastern Europe it was the USSR's post-Stalin repressions and its invasion of Prague. In the West, the students' objectives included the end of the Vietnam War, a liberalization of politics and education, more involvement in decisions, more freedom in sociability, and more liberal contact between the sexes. In Eastern Europe the goal was primarily liberalization of the communist rule. There were also country-specific objectives, for example addressing the NS past in the former Federal Republic of Germany.

The causes of the student movement are controversial to some extent. The rapid modernization of Europe during the 1950s and 1960s, with the vast experiential differences it created between the war generation and the 1960s student generation that had grown up amidst economic prosperity, is an undisputable reason. Completely different attitudes emerged between these two generations, not just about the war but also with regard to political decisions, individual freedoms, educational goals, and sexuality. The easing of tension between the West and East is also among the undisputed causes. By contrast, an entire range of other motivations is controversial. Only part of the research considers intellectual forerunners—who had prepared the student movement since the early 1960s and were predominantly European intellectuals or American intellectuals of European origin—as a central cause. Likewise, only part of the research considers the U.S. student and civil rights movements as a key basis or recognizes the Americanization of Western Europe as an element in the European student movement. Lastly, whether changes to European values in the second half of the 1960s were a cause of the student movement or whether the opposite is true, i.e., it was the student movement that precipitated this value change, is also debated (see Chapter 4 on values).

It is not only the assessment of the student movement that is particularly controversial, but also its effect. It is clear that the movement was not immediately successful in Eastern Europe and that it was unable to implement a lasting liberalization in the late 1960s and 1970s. It is, however, debatable whether continuities existed between 1968 and 1989. The effects are still subject to heated discussion in Western Europe. For some, who view the European student movement as successful, or even too successful, changes that have received mixed assessments generally count among its achievements: the fundamental change in values and education; the end of political taboos—in particular the end of the silence regarding the NS period in Germany; and the triggering of later social movements. Also counted among its achievements are contributions to political turning points, such as the changes in government in 1969 and 1981 respectively in West Germany and France, and the distance created from the USSR's party lines in Italy by the PCI. Student movement activists' ascent to the standing of leading intellectuals, and in some European countries even to positions of power in the 1990s, is also included—Lionel Jospin, Guy Verhofstadt, Joschka Fischer, and Gerhard Schröder were examples of this. Others view the student movement as a failure because no sweeping successes can be demonstrated when measured against its objectives and because it was also far too short in duration for this to occur. Internal divisions, among them the split regarding the use of violence, are quoted as the main reason for its short-lived existence (François 1997; Fink et al. 1998; Gilcher-Holtey 2001; van der Linden 2003).

Regional Movements

The second early, "new" form of social movement was the regional movements that were revived throughout Europe in the second half of the 1960s and have at times been loosely connected with the student movement. These regional movements were in no way new, but they had generally been in decline in Europe since the Second World War.

The renaissance of the European regional movements in the late 1960s was particularly intense in Western Europe, in the French regions of Alsace, Brittany, Occitania, and Corsica; the British regions of Wales and Scotland; the Flemish and Walloon regions of Belgium; the Spanish regions of Catalonia, Basque country, and Galicia after the collapse of the Franco dictatorship; and in the Italian South Tyrol. Although no movements were allowed in Eastern Europe, robust regional identities developed, in particular in Polish and Ukrainian Galicia, in Czech Moravia, in Polish and Czech Silesia, in Romanian Transylvania, and in the multilayered regionalisms and nationalisms in Yugoslavia and the USSR. In European countries like West Germany, Switzerland, Austria, Scandinavia, Ireland, or Portugal, regional movements were less common and weaker, partially intercepted by federalist constitutions. Yet even in these countries the growing identification with regional cooking, architecture, and lifestyles, as well as regional dialects, is not to be underestimated. A center for the regional movements was as uncommon as with the student movements, and the movements were by nature decentralized, adopting only rituals and symbolic policies from one another. They can, nonetheless, be viewed as a European movement in two senses: they shared forms of protest and common goals, and they saw an opportunity to better attain their goals in European integration and thus founded the Congress of Local and Regional Authorities in 1975.

The regional movements were closely connected to disillusionment about centralized planning and intervention within society as well as to the search for decentralized methods of government that were more closely situated to regional problems. They also had to do with the weakening of trade unions. In the 1990s the regional movements sank back into decline everywhere government decentralization programs were implemented, including in France, Italy, and Great Britain. However, they did not disappear entirely.

The regional movements' political impact was considerably more significant after the 1960s than in previous eras. Starting in the 1970s, countries that were politically highly centralized, like France, Great Britain, Italy, and Spain, gave their regions more authority in decision-making and more money than ever before, even though not one of these countries had a federal constitution. Influential political elites and careers developed as a result in a number of regions. At the European level, the European Union furthered the recognition of these regions with the establishment of an EU committee for "local authorities," although this did not grant real decision-making powers (Gerdes 1985, 1994; Wehling 1987; Schmale 1998; Applegate 1999; Ther and Sundhaussen 2003).

Environmental Movements

The environmental movements that began to emerge in the 1970s were also not completely new, for the same people and milieus who were often active in them had also been active in the student or regional movements. They did, however, mark a decisive point. They came into being in the wake of certain eye-opening publications on the environmental damage caused by the modern economy, including the *Limits of Growth* by D. L. Meadows, commissioned by the Club of Rome (Meadows 1972). The environmental movements' European geography looked somewhat different from that of the other social movements covered thus far. They were particularly strong in West Germany, Great Britain, Scandinavia, and Italy. Unlike the student movement, they were supported not just by young adults but by all age groups; also, they were not as clearly associated with political ideologies. Like the student movements, the environmental movements achieved mass mobilization through large demonstrations and also utilized more recent techniques like events and stagings by small groups. Purposeful conflicts with state authorities were counted among their means, as were traditional instruments of democracy: memorandums, manifestos, reports, petitions, and parliamentary initiatives. There were large national differences among the environmental movements, and the topics they centered on were not the same in every country. Their impact hinged significantly on their respective degrees of political influence, which in some countries came about more in local or regional politics and in other countries could be seen more in national policy. At the same time, influential international organizations like Greenpeace and Robin Hood emerged and organized professional international public events.

One of the reasons for the emergence of the environmental movements was continuing industrialization—the enormous increase in production in agriculture and the transportation revolution—in Europe during the 1950s and 1960s. The resulting environmental damage did not remain confined to industrial regions but was visible and noticeable everywhere, in air pollution, water pollution, and the deterioration of food quality. A second reason was the prominent role played by scientists. A number of responsibly minded experts and intellectuals alerted the public to environmental damages. Environmental movements were also connected with the end of the euphoric views regarding growth and planning, the petering out of optimism for the future and future utopias, and growing skepticism regarding progress. Lastly, the environmental movements also profited from the European population's slowly changing understanding of democracy. Democracy did not mean merely giving elected politicians a show of confidence, but instead continuously and publicly controlling their decisions through the media and experts.

On the whole, environmental movements had substantial success. They were not only the motivation for legislation at the national and European levels, but above all changed attitudes among the public, the political class, and business leaders so that environmental protection became a generally recognized high priority. An entire economic sector of environmental products came into being. What is more, environmental protection was not an important topic in Western Europe alone but was also an early focal point of dissident movements in Eastern Europe.

The Women's Movement

The women's movement was also not new but had a history dating back to the middle of the nineteenth century. It reemerged in the 1970s as a part of the new social movements. The new feminist movement differed significantly from the traditional women's movement. It no longer had to fight for access to education and careers, admission to the public sphere, women's suffrage, or the right to found associations. The goal of the new feminist movement was much more about the implementation of full equality for women in politics and society. It strove for other roles for women and men in the home and in public, and for more autonomy regarding abortion, divorce, and sexuality. Lastly, it was concerned with the reevaluation of gender hierarchies and values. The movement's representatives therefore called not just for better opportunities for women, but also for other attitudes and values. Furthermore, the movement adopted new forms of protest from other social movements; in addition to the traditional instruments of demonstrations, public speeches, and petitions, it used new means like spectacularly staged media events.

The feminist movement was "purposely eccentric" (Bock 2000: 321). Stronger than the traditional women's movement, it also wanted to work its way into society. Self-awareness brought about through seminars, summer university programs, films, literature, ladies' journals, and self-help was used to alter women's consciousness and attitudes and to develop new ways of life. Women's studies accompanied and strengthened these processes. Self-awareness was taken more seriously and was more effective in the women's movement than in the other new social movements. Furthermore, the new feminist movement was more decentralized than its traditional form; it consisted of numerous local networks, initiatives, and editorial and exhibition teams. Central governance and planning through national or even European organizations did not develop. The new feminist movement was just as local as international and spanned all age groups—not only young adults, as was the case in the student movement.

The geography of the women's movement likewise differed somewhat from the traditional feminist movement of the pre- and interwar periods in its European geography. Great Britain, France, Italy, and West Germany did indeed remain the important locations. Communist rule prevented the East Central European women's movement from playing any role. To what degree the new feminist movement oriented itself to the example of the American feminist movement has been examined little thus far.

The traditional women's movement also differed from the feminist movement in its international focus. Europeans and Americans had largely supported the international women's movement organization, the International Council of Women (ICW), which had been founded in 1888 and was shaped by the European and Western sense of superiority over non-Western civilizations, as well as a sense of dominance over the European periphery. In contrast to this, the ICW of the 1970s was more globally composed and acted more strongly on the assumption of a pluralistic worldview. In any case, the movement's demands found a far more effective platform: the UNO, which from the 1970s on organized regular World Conferences on Women in Mexico (1975), Copenhagen (1980), Nairobi (1985), and Beijing (1995). At the European level, meanwhile, women's organizations slackened, as no successor organization emerged after the originally predominantly European ICW went global. The European Commission did indeed push for equal status for women in the job market, and the European Court of Justice in Luxembourg passed important rulings regarding equality, but these acts occurred without a powerful European women's organization pressing for them. Although the European Union was well liked by the new women's movement, it lacked a broad focus on societal and cultural transformation, and its engagement remained limited to the equality of women within the job market.

The new feminist movement was nonetheless more successful than its traditional predecessor, so long as success is not measured by the demands made by the feminist wings of the women's movement. After the 1970s, educational opportunities for women improved, and more doors opened for access to careers in politics, education, scholarship, culture, public administration, and law as well as science, though to a lesser degree. Furthermore, the roles of mother and father also gradually changed. The demands of the women's movement were certainly not yet fully met by the end of the century, but much was shifting.

The Peace Movement

An additional new social movement, the peace movement, emerged in the early 1980s and likewise built on a longer European tradition. It primarily revolved around NATO's so-called Double-Track Decision, which envisioned massive armament and deployment of nuclear weapons in Europe as the answer to the Soviet nuclear weapons program. The peace movement was also more pragmatic than shaped by ideological concepts. Its foundation was composed not of students alone but of all age groups. Experts such as social, political, and natural scientists played a significant role here as well. The peace movement created its own symbols, working with the traditional means of reports, memorandums, and demonstrations with hundreds of thousands of participants in the Netherlands, Belgium, and West Germany in the early 1980s, but also staging political events. The peace movement was internationally oriented; like the environmental movement, it revolved around an international topic and its supporters were closely interwoven at the international level. It was most strongly represented in Northern and Western Europe—in Great Britain, Scandinavia, the Netherlands, and West Germany—yet also gained a foothold under extremely difficult conditions in the eastern part of Europe. It is difficult to judge whether it was successful because the movement's subject, the NATO Double-Track Decision, was dropped upon the collapse of the USSR. It is likewise difficult to say to what extent the European political class accepted the movement's fundamental goals, as international peace-keeping radically changed and completely different threats emerged.

The Dissident Movement

The dissident movements in the eastern part of Europe cannot be separated from the social movements in Western Europe. They raised similar issues: human rights, peace, and the environment. They also originated in the 1970s. They were not, however, publicly allowed in communist countries and either operated underground or in the best-case scenario established a limited and often only local counter public sphere. Access to Western culture was thus crucial to the dissidents (see Chapter 8 on media). Due to the communist regimes' special conditions these movements developed forms of protest other than those developed by the new social movements in Western Europe. Manifestos, books, articles, underground texts, and private meetings were the most important forms of protest, far removed from the new Western methods of eccentric events and happenings.

The dissident movements were supported by the same social milieus as other new social movements—intellectuals, artists, scientists, religious milieus, and students. They were not mass movements, but rather networks of friends (see the section on intellectuals in Chapter 5). Only fifteen hundred people signed the famous Czech "Charter 77." Poland was the sole Eastern European country where a dissident movement supported by all age groups built a bridge to the working class. Dissidents were involved in strikes through the committee for the defense of workers, the KOR, which was founded in 1976.

The dissident movements were closely tied to the social movements in Western Europe. Intellectual debates about Europe, which increased in the European public sphere from the 1980s on, were initiated by East Central European intellectuals like Milan Kundera, György Konrád, and Bronisław Geremek. The term *civil society*, which is common in Europe's political vocabulary today, was also introduced in the 1980s by Eastern European intellectuals. The dissent movements in Eastern Europe operated under completely different conditions from those in the West, however, and thus developed completely different forms of protest, symbols, and goals, and to a certain extent another vocabulary as well. "Antipolitics," a key term coined by György Konrád, reflects such differences.

Social movements in Western Europe did not adopt the term. Dissident movements were particularly strong in three countries: Poland, Czechoslovakia, and Hungary. In the GDR, in contrast, they remained weaker because many potential dissidents migrated to the Federal Republic of Germany and furthermore because the idea of the anti-fascist GDR retained power after the experience of the NS regime. Dissident movements did not emerge in the GDR until the final years before the collapse of the Soviet empire (Jaworski 1988; Schulze Wessel 1988; Beyme 1994; Fehr 1996; Lutz 1999; Kocka 2000; Niedermüller 2002).

The decisive factor for the dissident movements was communist dictatorships' incompatibility with the European understanding of individual freedoms. This dissonance was reinforced by the inconsistency between the freedoms the communist constitutions presented on paper and the political realities, and the contradictions were intensified by the communist governments' sigining of the Helsinki Accords. The dissident movements also resulted from the communist governments' failures with regard to central issues like environmental protection, peacekeeping, and economic investments.

The extent of the dissident movements' success is controversial: they are often viewed as narrow, self-referential intellectual circles that had no interest in urgent economic problems and therefore also lacked mass effect. For this reason they were rarely able to gain a foothold in politics even after the collapse of the Soviet empire. The mass movements directly before the collapse of the Soviet Union were supported by other milieus that appeared more in everyday life against the communist regimes. Nevertheless, it was thanks to dissident movements that the other, noncommunist, unofficially Eastern Europe remained known in Western Europe, and that other bridges were built beyond the official diplomatic and economic relationships. One of European politics' basic principles, giving political freedom a voice within the European public sphere, was kept alive through them. The Western European intellectuals were generally not as active in politics as the dissidents. Furthermore, a number of dissidents like Václav Havel and Bronisław Geremek played a major role in East Central Europe's politics and academia after 1989–90.

Trade Unions and Social Conflict

The trade unions developed in a completely different manner. They entered a long crisis in Europe beginning in the 1970s and 1980s and lasting into the present. Membership numbers sank in many countries, not dramatically and not always at the same point in time, but in a clearly recognizable manner in France, Great Britain, Italy, West Germany, the

Netherlands, Belgium, Norway, Switzerland, and Austria. It was only in the Scandinavian countries, with the exception of Norway, that the number of union members continued to increase and showed no sign of decline. In the 1990s, as will be discussed later, this trend changed in only a few countries: in Belgium, the Netherlands, and Norway the number of union members began to increase again (Ebbinghaus and Visser 2000; Funk 2003: 20; see also Figure 9.1).

Social conflicts also changed noticeably. Compared to the wave of strikes in the late 1960s and 1970s that culminated in high numbers of lost workdays, strikes in the 1980s were carried out differently. They no longer lasted as long, and the number of workdays lost to strikes noticeably dropped and remained low in the 1990s and at the beginning of the twenty-first century (Kaelble 1994; Lesch 2003: 31ff.; Robert et al. 2005).

The unions also lost public attention and importance in comparison with the new social movements. Union presses had to absorb massive losses in many countries, and unions had little choice but to adopt new public relations methods, seek professional advice from publicity experts, and adjust to the new medium of television. Huge union demonstrations decreased in most Western European countries. The observance of 1 May changed. Festivals that were open to many replaced the public marches. Class struggle–related ideologies and vocabularies tailed off, and throughout Europe public opinion became more skeptical of unions. The communist unions in France and Italy had less influence. The dwindling of union power is highlighted by two entirely different and highly symbolic events. The first was the failed attempt at a communist takeover in Portugal after the end of the Salazar dictatorship and during the Carnation Revolution, which had effects far beyond Portugal. The second was the purposeful and successful weakening of unions in Great Britain during the Thatcher administration, particularly union leader Arthur Scargill's defeat in the spectacular mining strike of 1984 (Eley 2002; Robert et al. 2005).

The slow but continuous debilitation of unions and the decline in strikes were grounded in several factors. Economic difficulties after the first oil shock in 1973 led to struggles against first inflation and then unemployment. Less able to succeed in these new situations, the unions went on the defensive and were less attractive as a result. Furthermore, the industrial societies in Western Europe were past their peak by the 1970s. Industrial employment declined, and the service-oriented sector became more important (see Chapter 2). The proletarian industrial worker milieu, which had been the unions' most important base, was also eroded (see Chapter 5). Those employed in the growing service sector were, for the most part, not easily won over by the unions because their opportunities for promotion were often better, their social position was frequently more advantageous and the boundaries separating them with lower social classes typically stronger, the companies were usually smaller, and female employment without a lifelong perspective occurred more often. Moreover, the number of male skilled workers in industry also decreased. Instead, there were ever more women, as well as immigrants, who were difficult for the unions to access. Unions were also less present in the new mass consumption society (see Chapter 3), in the vacation and tourism cultures, and in the new forms of media. They represented employee interests but seldom concerned themselves with the new and more important consumer interests.

Willingness to commit to any organization—be it a church, nation-state, professional association, or even a union—generally waned. Union activists also changed as a result of this individualization process. The lifelong activist, who spent his entire life and all of his free time in service to the labor union and who was a link between members and the union, became rarer. He was partially replaced by the new activist, who juggled family life and career with the duties of a professional functionary and union dues. And finally, the political climate also changed to the disadvantage of the unions. Neoliberal arguments that unions often viewed as slowing economic impetus won ground in times of economic problems (Mouriaux 1986; Rosanvallon 1988; Kaelble 1994; Ebbinghaus and Visser 1997, 2000; Streeck 1998; Eley 2002; van der Linden 2003; Robert et al. 2005).

Transnational European Civil Society

The transnational European civil society expanded between the late 1960s and 1980s. The previously mentioned interest groups, and as of 1973 the European Trade Union Confederation as well, expanded both spatially and numerically in the new member states. European integration was consolidated in this manner, often without being perceived by the public. The new social movements, which did not always remain loosely connected networks but frequently developed into stable transnational organizations like Amnesty International or Greenpeace, also contributed to the expansion of the transnational European society. Also forming were transnational European organizations, European city and town associations, and the already mentioned European regional organizations, European university president conferences and cultural organizations, and international sports associations. The initiative for this no longer came solely from governments, but more frequently from civil society itself. European civil society's connection to the European Commission and

European Parliament was weak, however, as the European Community was still mostly concentrating on the creation of a European economic market (Kohler-Koch 1992; Kaelble 2003; Weßels 2003a, 2003b).

There were several reasons for this expansion of civil society. Distrust between European nations had decreased and knowledge of others improved due to town twinning, student exchanges, rapidly increasing tourist and business travel, and cooperation between European elites and experts. The new transnational communication and transport technologies—telephone, fax, and high-speed trains and airplanes—as well as shopping carts with more European contents and consumption, eased and encouraged communication among Europeans. Meanwhile, the sharp lines separating the various Christian religious milieus grew less distinct.

The 1990s

The chronological distance from the 1990s is still too short for anyone to designate this period as a new era with certainty. It does, however, differ from the period before 1989–90 in many respects. First, the dynamic by which new movements time and again replaced the old in the public's eye, ended in the 1990s. The student movement in the late 1960s was followed in the 1970s by the new women's movement and the environmental movement, and in the 1980s by the peace and dissident movements—but in the 1990s no new movement followed. Considering that regional movements experienced a renaissance—particularly in the eastern part of Europe—the 1990s were certainly not a movement-free period. Overall, however, they were more a time of consolidation for the new social movements.

Second, the new social movements were now institutionalized. Opposition movements quite often became organizations close to the government; minority demonstrations and manifestos became proposals for aid programs; young politically and socially ostracized movement members became feminist or environmental representatives or notables for an established civil society; inexperienced new social movements became highly professional networks. New social movements rarely emerged, as their real causes had evaporated: highly centralized countries like France and Great Britain had become more decentralized; the educational opportunities for women had clearly improved and career opportunities were somewhat better; the third world was more diverse; environmental damages no longer seemed to be increasing; and with the end of the East-West conflict, peace in Europe was not directly threatened, and the regimes dissidents had turned against had collapsed. The new dangers in the 1990s and at the beginning of the twenty-first century were terrorism, new epidemics, and new forms of social exclusion. Unemployment among university graduates was no less explosive. However, these threats were poorly suited to be goals for social movements. New methods that were effective for the public were developed by small active groups that cannot be labeled as social movements: the creation of popular websites or the professional execution of events was what now attracted the public's attention.

Third, a naturally appearing connection between social movements and their placement on the political spectrum changed: the student, regional, women's, environmental, and peace movements generally considered themselves politically left until the 1990s and viewed parties in the left camp as their most important partners or target groups. This changed in the 1990s. Social movements now also emerged from the right-wing radical scene and among Christian as well as Muslim fundamentalists. They adopted quite a bit from the new social movements, but also utilized new means of communication like the Internet and often developed into tight milieus, closed off from the outside. In addition, civil societal organizations for ethnic minorities and non-European minorities played an increasingly significant role. This did, in part, result in some intense conflicts such as the ethnic revolts by young people in British and French suburbs, and in Yugoslavia it even resulted in civil war. This "ethnicized" form of civil society had little to do with the political milieus that had been closely connected to the new social movements between the late 1960s and 1980s.

Finally, the civil society that was geared toward the European Union also expanded during this time, as the European Union spread to include most Western European states that were neutral at the time as well as Central and Eastern European countries. This was also a result of the European Union having considerably added to its competencies. At the end of the twentieth century, the European Union was not just a project to create an economic entity but had gained new expertise in the areas of domestic security, immigration, and social policy, as well as cultural, foreign, and international security policy. For this reason, numerous interest groups, networks, liaison offices, and political service providers were founded at the European level. There were approximately as many lobbying groups registered with the European Union in Brussels at the end of the twentieth century as there were national lobbying groups in Germany. Between 1995 and 2000 alone, the number of intermediary groups with offices in Brussels increased from about 2,200 to nearly 3,500. It was not only the lobbying groups, but also other civil societal organizations that became more diversified and simultaneously more professional during this era (Kaelble 2003; Weßels 2003a, 2003b).

Divergences

Until 1989–90, Western and Eastern Europe differed fundamentally regarding the specific nature of civil societies and the goals of social movements and conflicts. Civil societies in Eastern Europe overwhelmingly lacked autonomy from the respective governments and communist unity parties, were controlled from above, were not as decentralized as in the democratic part of Western Europe, and were also not tied to a public sphere that was independent of the government. The values they represented often differed from those of the civil societies in Western Europe. Only the civil societies centered on religion and dissidents resembled the Western civil societies, with the crucial difference, however, that they did not possess uncontrolled access to the public.

The social movements were also different. There were indeed student protests in both the eastern and the western parts of Europe during the late 1960s and early 1970s. But the student protests in Eastern Europe focused on opposing the Soviet intervention in Czechoslovakia in 1968, not the United States' Vietnam War, everyday cultural and educational norms, or the NS past of the elites, as was the case in the Western student movement. Furthermore, there was only limited, if not often prominent integration between the civil societies in Western and Eastern Europe.

Other decisive and lasting divergences emerged between the North and South of Europe. In Scandinavia, the Netherlands, Germany, and the eastern part of Europe, the vast majority of citizens were members in civil societal organizations. In Latin Europe—France, Spain, Italy, and Portugal—in contrast, only a minority of the population were committed in this way, presumably because sociability was more developed both in public spaces like cafés, street, and squares, and in the private familial context. Whether the stronger northern commitment can in fact be explained by the long tradition of municipal guilds or by the voluntary Protestant tradition of associations must be further studied (Therborn 1995: 306ff.). This North-South difference should also not be overestimated. As shown, it is not found again among social movements.

The European North-South differences within social conflicts and union movements were, in comparison, examined much more frequently and were also classified into typologies. Three basic types of industrial relations are distinguished. In the *conflict-oriented* model in Southern Europe, industrial relations were regulated relatively little. Conflict played a central role. Unions and employers were poorly organized, as involvement in civil societal associations was generally poor. The extremes that developed during the Cold War between the communist and noncommunist unions weakened the employees' side further, and older differences between secular and church-related unions were revived again. Strike funds rarely existed. Rules regarding the mediation of work conflicts were seldom developed by the conflicting parties or by courts. Strikes served to mobilize supporters, constantly retesting the power held by the conflicting parties and above all indicating the balance of power. Due to the lack of appropriate regulations, the state frequently had to intervene as a neutral third party in the social conflicts, which were therefore often politicized. Labor disputes were common, but they rarely lasted long as strikers received little support from strike funds.

The *corporate* model of social conflict in Northern Europe stood in complete contrast to this. Open conflicts, strikes, or other forms of walkouts were rare. Consensus was key. The partners in conflict were better organized than in the conflict-oriented model, especially in light of the greater civil societal involvement in Northern Europe. Consolidated trade unions were predominant. Conflict resolution was highly regulated: the social partners themselves developed the rules pertaining to conflict, partly with involvement from the courts. Before the onset of a strike, set rounds of negotiation, mediation, and strike votes generated strong public interest. The state participated little in the negotiations because management and the trade unions were each invested with individual responsibility for the common good and because the autonomy of the bargaining parties was regarded as very important. For a long time wage agreements were negotiated at the industry level and not at the plant level. Labor law entertained many collective elements. Labor conflicts were rare, but when they did occur they could take a long time if the strike funds were amply filled. This type of social conflict could be found in Scandinavia, Germany, Austria, and Switzerland (Shorter and Tilly 1975; Crouch 1993; Ebbinghaus and Visser 1997, 2000; Pasture 1997; Eley 2002; van der Linden 2003; Robert et al. 2005; Saly et al. 2008: 218–234).

The *pluralistic* model of social conflict was rare in Europe and typically found only in Great Britain and Ireland. It was based on membership-strong, but still fragmented, unions and above all on strong union representatives within the companies, known as shop or union stewards. The regulations for conflict were less elaborate and institutionalized than in the corporate model, but more developed than in the conflict-oriented model. Consensus was less important. An orientation toward the common economic good was rarely expected of the management and trade unions. Power alternated between the unions and employers depending on the ruling government majorities, even though the government tended to stay out of the conflicts and significantly intervened only during the Thatcher era. Strikes were common but did decrease. Wage agreements were mostly negotiated at the company level. Labor law was geared toward individual contract law.

To be sure, such a typology cannot encompass all the differences among social conflicts. Not every European country can be clearly assigned to a model—some oscillate among the various models. This typology does, however, serve to indicate the basic divergences.

Overall, the intra-European differences among social movements, social conflicts, and civil societies did not recognizably diminish during the second half of the twentieth century. There were indeed serious changes in civil societal involvement, the degree of unionized organization, the intensity of social movements, and the frequency of social conflicts and strikes as well as other conflicts, but the differences were no less clear in Europe in 2000 than they had been in 1950.

European Trends

Despite these deep intra-European differences, the history of social movements and civil society since 1945 is more than just a history of national differences and East-West contrasts. In fact, a European history of social movements and civil societies is worth writing primarily because of three common European elements that emerged in those decades: the many and distinct parallels between national developments and the numerous transfers between the individual European countries; the increasing transnationality of social movements, chiefly since the late 1960s; and the formation of a common civil society at the European level.

The increasing transnationality within social movements after 1945 was entirely new. After the Second World War, unions were still largely national organizations, and despite some international rhetoric there was little networking across borders. It was with the new social movements that developed from the late 1960s on that transnational trends gradually began to grow more common—in the student movement, the regional and women's movements, and even more so among the environmental, peace, human rights, and anti-globalization movements. The new social movements not only increasingly pursued transnational issues, but also organized transnational demonstrations and established more and more transnational organizations. Organizations like Greenpeace, an important environmental organization, Amnesty International, the core of the human rights movements, and later "attac," a central anti-globalization organization, became completely transnational.

Finally, the previously mentioned emergence of a civil society at the European level was an additional new common European development. This followed an overall process of transnationalization, which led to European, as well as occidental or global, civil societies. It primarily came into being through European integration and was then completely oriented toward influencing EU policy.

European Hallmarks

The particularly European characteristic of civil societies and social movements was that they were not oriented to a national, but to a supranational European decision-making body. At the same time they remained largely autonomous and to some extent tied to an emerging transnational public sphere at the European level. As previously hinted, this transnational civil society became increasingly important as the EC and EU expanded throughout almost all of Western Europe and the EU's competencies extended to new policy areas beyond the establishment of a transnational economic market.

The European civil society looked different from the national civil societies, however. It was strongly influenced by the historical development of the European Union, which began around 1950 as a project to create an international economic market. Agricultural and industrial interest groups carried an unusual amount of weight, as European integration until the 1980s primarily revolved around establishing a European market for agricultural and industrial products. This asymmetry within the European civil society diminished starting in the 1970s as other interest groups also developed and the remaining civil society became more closely connected with European institutions. Yet the industrial and agricultural associations' influence remained abnormally strong into the following century, as can be seen in the exceptionally high agricultural subsidies, among other things, in the European budget.

European civil society also had a different relationship with the public than the national civil societies. It resorted less to the instruments used to publicly mobilize citizens: demonstrations, rallies, strikes, dramatic public events, ad campaigns, and television appearances. Quieter than the national civil societies, it was more likely to influence European policy with reports, petitions, memorandums, surveys, press conferences, talks, phone calls, emails, and meetings with experts. This quieter civil society was often—erroneously—viewed as a weaker civil society. This particularity of the European civil society was largely owed to the way European institutions functioned. The European Council, one of the European Union's two centers of power, was almost completely inaccessible to European civil society and ultimately could only be influenced through the national civil societies. The European Parliament was far weaker than the national parliaments and thus a less attractive audience for the European civil society. The European civil society mainly targeted the European Commission, a bureaucracy that was more swayed by quiet, unspectacular methods than by the sensational mobilization of European citizens. Meanwhile, close cooperation between the executive administration and civil society rarely materialized, as the European Union decided quite a bit but generally left implementation to the national administrations.

The rarity of public mobilization of European citizens also had to do with the fact that European civil society usually took shape under the umbrella of national organizations, without direct membership or direct contact with its members. It therefore had no local roots but generally worked together with spokespersons, activists, functionaries, political service providers, or professional lobbyists. For this reason it was seldom able to move its members to spectacular public actions.

Lastly, European civil society practiced a different form of autonomy than the national civil societies. The European Commission has shown significant interest in a developed, cooperative European civil society and has sometimes helped with its development, particularly since the 1980s ushered in a continuous drop in participation in European elections and the almost notoriously close and uncertain results of numerous European referenda. This benevolent creation of a civil society by the European Commission could, every now and then, also pose a threat to the autonomy of the European civil society.

References

Applegate C. "A Europe of Regions: Reflections on the Historiography of Subnational Places in Modern Times." *American Historical Review* 104 (1999): 1157–1182.

Beyme K.V. *Systemwechsel in Osteuropa*. Frankfurt a. M. 1994.

Bock G. *Frauen in der europäischen Geschichte*. Munich 2000.

Bussiére E. and M. Dumoulin, ed. *Milieux économiques et intégration européenne en Europe occidentale au XXe siècle*. Arras 1998.

Crouch C. *Industrial Relations and European State Traditions*. Oxford 1993.

Ebbinghaus B. and J. Visser. "Der Wandel der Arbeitsbeziehungen im westeuropäischen Vergleich." In *Die westeuropäischen Gesellschaften im Vergleich*, ed. S. Hradil and S. Immerfall. Opladen 1997, 376–475.

Ebbinghaus B. and J. Visser, eds. *The Societies of Europe: Trade Unions in Western Europe since 1945*. London 2000.

Eley G. *Forging Democracy: The History of the Left in Europe, 1850–2000*. Oxford 2002.

Fehr H. *Unabhängige Öffentlichkeit und soziale Bewegungen: Fallstudien über Bürgerbewegungen in Polen und der DDR.* Opladen 1996.

Fink C., P. Gassert, and D. Junker. *1968: The World Transformed.* Cambridge 1998.

François E. "Annaherungsversuche an ein aussergewöhnliches Jahr." In *1968 – ein europäisches Jahr,* ed. E. François, M. Middel, E. Terray, and D. Wierling. Leipzig 1997, 11–17.

Funk L. "Der neue Strukturwandel: Herausforderung und Chance für die Gewerkschaften." *Aus Politik und Zeitgeschichte B* 47–48 (2003): 14–22.

Gerdes D. *Regionalismus als soziale Bewegung: Westeuropa, Frankreich, Korsika. Vom Vergleich zur Kontextanalyse.* Frankfurt a. M. 1985.

Gerdes D. "Regionalismus und Regionalisierung in Frankreich: Ansatzpunkte einer vergleichenden Regionalismus/Nationalismusforschung." *Geschichte und Gesellschaft* 20 (1994): 385–401.

Gilcher-Holtey I. *Die 68er Bewegung: Deutschland, Westeuropa, USA.* Munich 2001.

Guedj F. and S. Sirot, eds. *Histoire sociale de l'Europe: Industrialisation et société en Europe occidentale 1880–1970.* Paris 1997.

Jaworski R. "Die aktuelle Mitteleuropadiskussion in historischer Perspektive." *Historische Zeitschrift* 247 (1988): 529–550.

Kaelble H. "Eine europäische Geschichte des Streiks?" In *Von der Arbeiterbewegung zum modernen Sozialstaat: Festschrift für Gerhard A. Ritter zum 65. Geburtstag,* ed. J. Kocka, H. J. Puhle, and K. Tenfelde. Munich 1994, 44–70.

Kaelble H. "Eine europäische Zivilgesellschaft?" *Jahrbuch des Wissenschaftszentrums.* Berlin 2003, 267–284.

Kocka J. "Zivilgesellschaft als historisches Problem und Versprechen." In *Europäische Zivilgesellschaft und Ost und West,* ed. M. Hildermeier, J. Kocka, and C. Conrad. Frankfurt a. M. 2000, 13–40.

Kocka, J. *Civil Society and Dictatorship in Modern German History.* Lebanon, NH, 2010.

Kohler-Koch G. "Interessen und Integration: Die Rolle der organisierten Interessen im westeuropäischen Integrationsprozess." *Die Integration Europas, Politische Vierteljahresschrift* 23, ed. M. Kreile. 1992.

Lesch H. "Der Arbeitskampf als Instrument tarifpolitscher Konfliktbewältigung." *Politik und Zeitgeschichte B* 47–48 (2003): 30–38.

Linden, van der M. *Transnational Labour History: Explorations.* Ashgate 2003.

Lutz A. *Dissidenten und Bürgerbewegung: Ein Vergleich zwischen DDR und Tschechoslowakei.* Frankfurt a. M. 1999.

Meadows, D.H. and D.L. Meadows et al. *The Limits to Growth.* New York 1972.

Monnet J. *Erinnerungen eines Europäers.* Munich 1980.

Mouriaux P. *Les syndicats face à la crise.* Paris 1986.

Niedermüller P. "Kultur, Transfer und Politik im ostmitteleuropäischen Sozialismus." In *Transnationale Öffentlichkeit und Identitäten im 20. Jahrhundert,* ed. H. Kaelble, M. Kirsch, and A. Schmidt-Gernig. Frankfurt a. M. 2002, 159–175.

Pasture P. "La classe ouvrière, le mouvement ouvrier et la construction des états providence dans l'Europe du Nord-Ouest." In *Histoire sociale de l'Europe: Industrialisation et société en Europe occidentale (1880–1970),* ed. F. Guedj and S. Sirot. Paris 1997, 213–228.

Robert J.-L., P. Pasture, and M. Pigenet, eds. *L'apogée des syndicalismes en Europe occidentale.* Paris 2005.

Rosanvallon P. *La question syndicale.* Paris 1988.

Saly P., M. Margairaz, M. Pigenet, and R.-L. Robert. *Industrialisation et sociétés: Europe occidentale 1880–1970.* Paris 1998.

Schmale W. *Historische Komparatistik und Kulturtransfer: Europageschichtliche Perspektiven für die Landesgeschichte. Eine Einführung unter besonderer Berücksichtigung der Sächsischen Landesgeschichte.* Bochum 1998.

Schulze Wessel M. "Die Mitte liegt westwärts: Mitteleuropa in der tschechischen Diskussion." *Bohemia* 29 (1988): 325–344.

Shorter E. and C. Tilly. *Strikes in France, Nineteen Thirty to Nineteen Sixty-Eight.* Cambridge 1975.

Streeck W. "Gewerkschaften zwischen Nationalstaat und Europäischer Union." *WSI-Mitteilungen* 51 (1998): 1–14.

Ther P. and H. Sundhaussen, eds. *Regionale Bewegungen und Regionalismen in europäischen Zwischenräumen seit der Mitte des 19. Jahrhunderts.* Marburg 2003.

Therborn G. *European Modernity and Beyond: The Trajectory of European Societies 1945–2000.* London 1995. (German: *Die Gesellschaften Europas 1945–2000: Ein soziologischer Vergleich.* Frankfurt a. M. 2000.)

Wehling H.-G., ed. *Regionen und Regionalismus in Westeuropa.* Stuttgart 1987.

Weßels B. "Contestation Potential of Interest Groups in the EU: Emergence, Structure, and Political Alliances." In *Dimension of Contestation in the European Union,* ed. G. Marks and M. Sternbergen. Cambridge 2003a, 195–215.

Weßels B. "Probleme der Demokratie in der EU." In *Entwicklung und Perspektiven der Demokratie in Ost und West, WZB-discussions papers P 2003-003,* ed. D. Klingemann et al. Berlin 2003b, 29–39.

Chapter 10

THE WELFARE STATE

The history of the welfare state has received more attention from a comparative approach than any other topic within the most recent social history. Using an intra-European or Atlantic comparison, a number of important books by sociologists and historians track the welfare state's development since the Second World War. These books generally approach the differences between national welfare states within Western Europe or within the West. There are three aspects that are, for the most part, not covered enough: the welfare state in Europe *as a whole*; the *transnational* side of the welfare state; and the welfare state *beyond* the narrow fields of public social security, i.e., housing policy, educational opportunities, the health care system, and the relationship between the state and social partners (Alber 1982; Flora 1986; Esping-Anderson 1990; Ritter 1991; Baldwin 1994; Hennock 2001; Rieger and Leibfried 2003; Lindert 2004; Tomka 2004; Schmidt 2005).

Terms

The term "welfare state" (état-providence, Wohlfahrtsstaat) in the modern sense is a recent concept. It was in the 1960s and 1970s that it gradually began to prevail as a neutral, scientific phrase. In the second half of the 1960s a dictionary stated that the phrase "welfare state" had "a polemic content," implying criticism that the government "bowed too easily to pressure from interest groups, professional groups, economic concentrations of power and granted the corresponding privileges (subsidies)" (Bertelsmann Lexikon 1966: 1171). The scholarly term welfare state is understood to mean general government intervention with four goals: the protection of a minimum standard of material and immaterial opportunities in life, in particular a minimum wage, basic living accommodations, health care, education, and protection of the family; equal treatment of all citizens by the welfare state; a right to welfare state services that are enforceable by courts and do not remain arbitrary governmental acts of mercy; and finally, compensation for the negative results of the market economy but not the elimination of the market economy.

Whether one can speak only of welfare states in democracies, where the conflicts around the welfare state's goals are publicly dealt with and decided, or whether the social security in the communist countries of Eastern Europe until 1989–91 should also be described as such, is controversial.

The phrase "social state" (*Sozialstaat*) is different from the internationally used term "welfare state." It is a specifically German term that is difficult to translate into other languages. It refers to the government services securing a basic standard of living and, to a large extent, legal regulations and protections such as labor laws protecting workers from unlawful dismissal, promoting job security, and protecting employees' right to a say in dismissal and hiring; legal provisions for employee participation in company decision making; regulations on wage disputes; and housing laws protecting tenants from unlawful eviction and regulating rent increases. Of course the *Sozialstaat* should not be overestimated. Other European countries also assigned importance to state welfare services and legal safeguards, the difference being that they were referred to in less catchy terms such as "social policy" or "législation sociale."

The Transformation of the Welfare State

The European welfare state went through not one, but two substantial transformations during the second half of the twentieth century. First, the modern European welfare state came into being, which marked a substantial deviation from the social policy of the pre- and interwar periods. Born of high hopes for the future and a sense of euphoria regarding planning, it developed against the background of extraordinarily high rates of economic growth. Then, as of the 1970s, criticism of the welfare state increased, triggered by increasing economic difficulties as well as the mental change from euphoria to skepticism about the future. The welfare state was nonetheless further developed and was not necessarily scaled down.

The Path to the Modern Welfare State

Postwar Period

The postwar period heavily influenced the development of the welfare state, as gaps due to the social strains caused by war were clearly visible at the time in the different welfare states. Meanwhile, social security in part of Western Europe, as well as in communist Eastern Europe, was being fundamentally reformed and reconstructed.

During this period, Europe's welfare states were riddled with gaps. Compared to present-day contributions, social security spending was modest. The various state social insurance systems were also far from covering the entire population. It was clear that the state welfare insurances grew out of worker's insurances. The many workers self-employed in trade, agriculture, the transport industry, and the craft sector were generally not protected by state insurance. In fact, barely half of Western Europeans were eligible for state worker's compensation insurance and state health insurance. Only in Sweden, Denmark, and England were the entire populations insured against the risk of illness. The pension insurance system was also lacking for substantial sections of the population in France, the western zones in Germany, and Italy. Only Great Britain and the Scandinavian countries approached full insurance coverage during this period. In most European countries, pensions were not yet dynamic and lagged far behind wage developments. Pensions were often still thought of as subsidies for the family that an elderly person lived with, not as a financial foundation for independent households for the elderly. Bitter poverty in old age was indeed prevented in most European countries, but at the same time becoming a retiree meant a drastic decline in one's standard of living. The gaps in unemployment insurance were particularly grave. There was not a single European country in which more than a fraction of the gainfully employed were protected against a loss of income in the case of unemployment. Overall, by our present understanding, the provision of state welfare services was frequently incomplete.

Furthermore, public social security was still a voluntary state-subsidized insurance in a number of countries. Nonstate social security through trade associations, municipal poverty management, foundations, and churches continued to carry great weight. The best-known international model for purely governmental social security during the interwar period was most likely still Germany, with relatively high social welfare expenditures, compulsory public insurance, a large self-governed insurance bureaucracy, and mixed financing through client and employer dues as well as state subsidies.

The welfare states at the time were extremely strained in those countries that had been affected by the Second World War. Public social security was often overburdened by the massive number of health problems caused by the war; by retirees and subsidies for the numerous war widows and orphans; by unemployment, which did indeed remain lower than during the Great Depression but regardless increased considerably in a number of war-ravaged countries; by the flood of refugees, displaced persons, and those bombed out and evacuated; by war damage to schools, hospitals, and other public facilities; and by the fight against stark famine and homelessness. A family sociologist in 1947 described a mother's bitterness about help from social services offices for her invalid son in Berlin: "All too often she was made promises and received nothing" (Thurnwald 1948: 235). The welfare states' heavy loads at the time are clearly revealed in the high percentage of social welfare expenditures in the state budgets. The percentage of spending for social security, housing, health care, and oftentimes education were rarely again as high as in the first years after the war in France, Great Britain, the Netherlands, Belgium, and the German western zones (Flora 1983: vol. 1, 355ff.).

The Beginning of Reforms during the Postwar Period

Despite the strain due to the consequences of war, in some countries the postwar period was at the same time also an important period of reform and historic course setting in the history of the welfare state. The most important country for reform at the time was the wealthiest and most developed country in Europe, Great Britain. It also therefore had extraordinary appeal, as it had not been occupied by the NS army during the Second World War but had successfully fought against the NS regime and as a result emerged from the war with a strong national identity. As a country of reform, Great Britain played a large role in the development of the welfare state in Europe after the Second World War.

Great Britain had already developed new principles of social policy during the Second World War in a parliamentary commission led by the liberal politician William H. Beveridge. This commission devised six new principles for the fundamental reform of the social state. There was to be, first, national social security for all citizens and no longer only for individual groups within the population; second, a guaranteed minimum income and not just case-by-case decisions; third, identical social welfare contributions for all and no sliding scale based on income, health risk, or age; fourth, identical benefits by the welfare state for all and no differentiation based on social group or income; fifth, child benefits for families with children up to the age of sixteen; and sixth, transparency within the social welfare system primarily via a large, central, unified insurance organization instead of numerous smaller, specialized social insurances. These principles of social security influenced the debate about social reform throughout Europe, as well as in the United States and East Asia. They were not implemented everywhere but were regardless an important criterion for reforms.

The British model gained influence not only through these new principles, but rather primarily also through reforms by the British government that were already being realized during the immediate postwar period. Standardized child benefits from the second child onward were introduced in 1945 with the Family Allowance Act. The year 1946 began with the development of the free British public health service and continued with the National Insurance Act and the establishment of a unified health insurance and pension system. The Education Act had already expanded access to secondary school in 1944. Social reforms in other European countries were measured against and oriented toward these reforms in Great Britain.

Sweden was a second country that was frequently discussed and regarded as a welfare state model. Having made preparations since the 1930s, Sweden also implemented important reforms immediately after the Second World War: a nationwide pension that was equal for everyone in 1946; in 1947, the trial launch of public health insurance with the same contributions for all; the adoption of universal child benefits, likewise implemented in 1947; and in 1950 the trial introduction of the comprehensive school (see Chapter 12).

Lesser known are the social reforms in France. As in Great Britain, they were not established by a single political party but rather supported by diverse governmental coalitions. The French welfare state reforms dealt only with the social security system, not with the educational system or housing. Nevertheless, social security was fundamentally changed with the establishment of the "sécurité sociale" in France. A unified organization encompassing health and disability insurance and a pension fund, a strong voice for clients, and joint financing by the state and above all by employers was implemented, and the nongovernmental, small, and often publicly subsidized social insurances, the *mutuels*, were significantly driven back. In principle the sécurité sociale covered all French people, even though a wide range of occupational groups, like civil servants and the self-employed, could initially retain their own insurance systems. The actual services provided by this new social security system were without a doubt limited at the beginning—it was not until the Fifth Republic that the services clearly improved. But the sécurité sociale marked an essential step taken on the way to the modern welfare state in France.

The immediate postwar period was similarly a time of reform in countries such as the Netherlands, Belgium, Ireland, and Finland. However, this was not the case in a section of Western Europe of approximately the same size, comprising West Germany, Switzerland, Austria, Italy, Norway, Denmark, Spain, and Portugal.

State social security in the Soviet-controlled territory in the eastern part of Europe was being converted in a completely different direction from that taken in the Western European reform countries. It complied with the social security principles in the Soviet Union, though with differences among the individual countries. This reorganization caused a deep upheaval in East Central Europe and the GDR in particular, as social security systems from the pre- and interwar periods were in many cases already in place there. During the interwar period the East Central European and Western European welfare states were closely related, but they developed differently after the postwar period (Tomka 2003, 2004a, 2004b).

The conversion of the state social security systems according to the Soviet model conformed to eight principles that differentiated the social states in Eastern and Western Europe until 1989–90. Uniform centralized social security systems were implemented that overrode all specialized insurances for individual occupational groups or social milieus and disbursed the same benefits. As a result, the state's role in social insurance carried more weight than it did in Western Europe. At the same time, however, the Soviet model introduced new forms of social inequality within social insurance: those self-employed in agriculture, manufacturing and services, as well as the so-called intelligentsia, and often the leadership personnel within the state apparatus were insured differently than laborers and white-collar employees. It also maintained better benefits to some extent. Another, particularly sharp difference arose between the gainfully employed and retirees. Retirement benefits were for the most part quite low. Furthermore, social security in the eastern part of Europe was an integral part of the government's economic and labor market policy. Whereas in Western Europe it was thought of as a corrective measure for the market economy, and therefore often possessed its own logic, in Eastern Europe it remained completely subject to the respective economic necessities. Retirees, disabled persons, and housewives, who were of no value for production, did not count for much in this system. Apart from this, social insurances and the welfare state services were very centered on workplaces, which were responsible for providing social services such as health care or nursery school.

Labor unions, like the FDGB in the GDR, functioned as the organizations responsible for social insurances for blue- and white-collar employees. Moreover, the cost-intensive subsidization of basic services, i.e., staple foods, local public transportation, and housing, were an essential element of social security. Additionally, there was no provision for unemployment within the social insurances, because compulsory employment meant that joblessness officially no longer existed. Unlike in Western Europe, there was also a lack of public critique and debate about state social security— its benefits, weaknesses, inequalities, and costs. An effective catalyst for keeping in touch with reality, thinking efficiently, and instituting reform was thus absent. Finally, the Soviet model also required, more than the Western European social state, a passive citizen who was managed by the state and had few individual decisions to make.

State social insurances in Eastern Europe were not fully identical, however. In the GDR, for example, dues were still based on income levels. The groups excluded from the public social security system were different from those in other Eastern bloc countries, and concepts from the Weimar Republic were taken up. But the social security principles were very similar throughout the Soviet sphere of influence.

Implementation of the Modern Welfare State up to the Mid 1970s

The 1950s to the 1970s were the welfare state's original golden age in Western Europe. It was established, enjoyed an excellent reputation, and was regarded as a model in North and Latin America as well as in East Asia during this time. The general optimism regarding the future, euphoria about planning, belief in universal material progress in Europe, and extraordinarily high expectations for the future were tied to the welfare state. It was thought that protecting citizens from all of life's risks and ensuring a worry-free life was possible through social welfare policy, seen to cut down social inequalities, implement new standards of living that were completely unknown at the time, achieve equal access to the educational system, end class struggle and the zero-sum game for economic growth, and distribute the increased income achieved through economic growth in a more equal manner than had been done previously. This optimism for the welfare state was closely connected with economic prosperity.

At this time, welfare state reforms were now being enforced in almost all European countries. It was not only in the pioneering countries of Great Britain, Sweden, France, Belgium, and the Netherlands that reforms were being continued and expanded. Most other Western European countries that had been averse to reform in the postwar period—West Germany, Italy, or Spain, for example—had decided in favor of fundamental reform since the 1950s and 1960s. These reforms included the steady expansion of those insured, improvement of insurance benefits not only for men but also for women, the coverage of increasingly more risks, and in part the breaking down of the divides between various client groups.

Despite divergences at the program level, the reforms in most countries followed similar basic principles of a new welfare state concept that had been developed during the postwar period: the guarantee of minimum requirements regarding income and housing, health care, and schooling; social security for the entire population; social security as an enforceable right, not only as charity; financing at least in part through taxes; a new concept of providing for the elderly as a basis for livelihood and not only as a subsidy for families with elderly people. The welfare state was also generally tied to a Keynesian optimism regarding the elimination of unemployment through governmental intervention. The welfare state in Western Europe was built upon a broad political consensus of social democratic, conservative, liberal, and communist parties as well as between labor unions and employers.

Between the 1950s and early 1970s, European governments decided for a historically exceptional increase in social security expenditures. Never before or since have expenditures on the welfare state grown so rapidly. According to calculations by the OECD, the Western European average increase in actual social expenditures in relation to the gross national product from 1960 to 1974 was close to 50 percent. In a few countries with particularly high expansion rates they even doubled, as in Hungary between 1960 and 1974 (see Table 10.1; Tomka 2004a: 133). Thus social expenditures grew significantly faster than the economy, which during this period of economic boom in Western Europe likewise boasted an unusually high rate of growth. The results of this dramatic growth are inconceivable today: in European countries with particularly high increases, like the Scandinavian countries, France, and the Netherlands, social expenditures multiplied twenty- to thirtyfold, in nominal terms. Even in the Western European countries with lower growth, like West Germany, Great Britain, Italy, Belgium, and Switzerland, the increase in social expenses was still close to tenfold (Flora 1983: vol. 1, 345ff.). By 1975 the welfare state had taken on a completely different character than around 1950, through not only the reforms but also this dramatic increase in social expenditures. Incidentally, the expenditures for education grew rapidly during this time as well (see Chapter 12).

Additionally, social security for the *entire* populations of the individual European countries was enforced significantly more during the period of economic boom. On the whole shortly after the Second World War, not much more than half of the population was safeguarded through the three

Table 10.1 Social Expenditures by Western and East Central European OECD States, 1960–2000
(Average shares in percent of gross domestic product)

Country	1960	1974	1989	1989 new calculation	1998
Belgium	11.5	18.0	23.2	16.3	16.0
Denmark	7.4	12.0	18.3	17.8	18.2
Germany	12.0	14.6	15.7	15.7	18.9
Finland	5.1	7.6	14.4	13.5	18.4
France	13.5	15.5	21.1	16.7	18.4
Greece	5.3	7.1	15.4	14.9	15.6
Great Britain	6.8	9.2	11.2	11.7	13.7
Ireland	5.5	11.4	14.2	14.2	9.8
Italy	9.8	13.7	17.6	17.6	17.0
Netherlands	—	20.7	24.7	24.7	13.0
Norway	7.6	13.3	15.4	15.4	15.0
Austria	12.9	15.5	19.7	18.0	18.6
Poland		—	—	17.9	17.3
Portugal	3.0	9.5	10.7	10.4	11.7
Sweden	8.0	14.3	19.4	19.4	19.3
Switzerland	5.7	10.6	13.6	13.4	11.9
Czech Republic	—	—	—	12.9	12.5
Hungary	3.2	7.5	—	11.5	14.5
European OECD— Country Average	9.5	13.2	16.8	16.0	16.8
Japan	3.8	6.2	10.9	10.9	14.6
U.S.	5.1	9.6	10.6	10.6	12.6

Sources: 1960–1974, 1974–1989: OECD, *Historical Statistics 1960–1995* (Paris 1997), 71; 1989–2000: OECD, *Historical Statistics 1970–1999* (Paris 2000), 67. "Social expenditures" is defined by OECD for 1960, 1974, and 1989 as all state social services for illness, pension, family, and welfare aid including business social services. In 1989 business social services were no longer included (OECD 1997: 79; OECD 2000: 74). The old and new calculations are listed for this reason for 1989. 1989–1998 for the 15 EU member states. For Hungary: Tomka 2004a: 133.

traditional insurance branches—disability, pension, and health insurance. By the end of the economic boom in 1975 this had changed to close to the entire population, thereby honoring the important principles of the Beveridge plan from the Second World War.

Poverty was considerably reduced during this era. The situation changed for the better with regard to all three dimensions by which poverty is measured: income, education, and life expectancy. Income differences noticeably diminished in Europe, among other things because the share of income among the lower earners substantially improved (see Chapter 6). Illiteracy was almost eliminated throughout Europe at this time, and educational differences lessened (see Chapter 12). Life expectancy increased rapidly. It can be argued as to whether the improvement in standard of living was primarily achieved through the welfare state or through better nutrition, hygiene, and medical progress, but the welfare state certainly contributed significantly.

Meanwhile, a broad sociopolitical consensus was forged among the left and conservative parties in Europe during this period. The important players in social reform came from almost all of the major political camps. A new milieu emerged, composed of social workers, doctors, social security experts, consultants specializing in social security, and social politicians, as well as employees within the social bureaucracy, social psychologists, and therapists. This milieu first found a common purpose through the welfare state, lived from it and for it, and viewed itself as an advocate of the clients financed by the welfare state—elderly, disabled, ill, and unemployed Europeans. This social security milieu implemented a new life plan that encompassed all of life early on and that generally fit well with the rules of the welfare state. It also stimulated a new concept of security that directed higher expectations at the state.

This modern welfare state stemmed from an entire series of upheavals. It was shaped by a loss of trust in the market, primarily due to the Great Depression that broke out in 1929. The largest economic crisis in modern economic history, it had catastrophic effects not only on the economy but also on democracy and peace within Europe. After this fundamental experience with crisis, Europeans saw state intervention as an important guarantor against another such crisis. Furthermore, in many populous European countries, the governments that had led their countries in the war against the NS regime had promised their citizens radical social reforms and more social security because of the tremendous loss of life during the war. These expectations had to be fulfilled.

Finally, the extraordinary prosperity and the exceptional growth in public revenue during the 1950s and 1960s offered a unique opportunity to increase social expenditures and fundamentally reform the social state. At the same time, transitional crises like the massive decline in agricultural work and the number of self-employed; the crisis among industry sectors like textiles, coal mining, and steel; and the large-scale flight of Europeans from the disintegrating colonial empires to Europe were also a part of this era. These crises were the genesis of sociopolitical constraints.

The Welfare State Crisis as of the Late 1970s

The welfare state's golden age lasted close to a quarter century, ending in the second half of the 1970s in a crisis that the European welfare state still has not conquered to this day. Three different crises came together simultaneously and mutually reinforced each other to create a singularly intractable situation.

First, the European welfare state entered into a financial crisis. For various reasons it reached the limit of its financial viability. The extraordinarily high increase in social expenditures could not be maintained in the long run. Slower economic growth after the oil shock of 1973 also reduced growth in tax revenue and forced governments to economize public budgets. The external economic pressure on the social state increased. The new industrial countries in East and Southeast Asia set up much less expensive social insurances and as a result also had lower production costs. Demographic problem—above all, the shift in age distribution, the sinking share of the gainfully employed who paid taxes and social security contributions, and the growing share of retirees—increasingly stressed the social security systems and drove them into the red. Lastly, many of the welfare state's goals were obviously pitched too high. The lowering of the retirement age, the pensions' alignment with the increases in wages, cost-intensive medical innovations, protection against unlawful dismissal, and the cushioning of the effects of unemployment in crisis regions often exceeded financial possibilities even in wealthy European countries. The welfare state's financial crisis was all the more massive and urgent as social expenses made up an increasingly large share of government expenditures. In West Germany the state social expenditures were just below 10 percent of the GNP in 1960; by 1989 they had risen to 17 percent (see Table 10.1). A financial crisis for the welfare state could thus quickly become a financial crisis for the entire government. Even European governments that had brooked no doubt about the importance of the welfare state's emergence now had to worry about its financial viability.

Second, the welfare state entered into a service-related crisis. Despite a bountiful expansion, it remained insufficient and full of gaps. Caring for elderly parents going through the physical deterioration of the fourth age and long-term care became a great burden for many families. In spite of the increase in pensions and the construction of numerous nursing homes, the welfare state could offer only limited help. City planning and housing policies in the welfare state did indeed allow for better-quality housing, yet they often yielded inadequate accommodations for life in the newly planned districts and inhospitable conditions in the suburbs. Ghettos emerged where the maintenance of services and personal security were not guaranteed. In most European countries the universities were hopelessly overcrowded despite the increase in educational budgets. Education was under serious threat, even as the job market for college graduates was diminishing.

Above all, however, a new poverty was springing up in spite of the welfare state. The social welfare state had successfully managed to alleviate poverty among industrial workers. But it was not in a position to thwart the new forms of poverty among single-parent families and families of the divorced, the unemployed, and immigrants. Inequality in the distribution of income rose as of the 1980s, whereby the lower-income population's share of the national income sank (see Chapter 6). The quality of education for the poorer segments of society deteriorated in particular. Life expectancy dropped for men and stagnated for women in the eastern part of Europe—a shocking indicator of this new poverty. And finally, the course of professional life changed in a way for which the welfare state was poorly prepared. The traditional, normal lifelong employment that had emerged in the late nineteenth and early twentieth centuries, upon which the welfare state was based, was no longer the general rule. Occupational résumés became heterogeneous due in part to the growing employment of the 1980s, in part to the rapid change in professions and the necessity of further education, in part to the breaks in familial life as a result of divorce and periods of poverty for single-parent families, and in part to the increase in immigration. For these groups the state social safety net had ominous gaps, whose extent is a matter of debate among social scientists.

Finally, and most striking, was the welfare state's political crisis. The welfare state had come under public criticism starting in the 1970s. That the criticism came from all political camps was key. This criticism was connected not only with the welfare state, but also with disillusionment in or even rejection of the faith in progress from the 1950s and 1960s. The credibility of progress, of which the welfare state was a symbol, was weakened in the eyes of many Europeans by the environmental boundaries to growth, the health risks from modern industrial and agricultural products, and the inhospitableness of the newly planned cities.

Three core arguments moved the public during this period of criticism of the social welfare state. The criticism first came from the neoliberal direction. These critics in particular accused the welfare state of making business investments and innovations much too expensive. They also claimed that it had allowed social security, as well as the rigid regulations regarding collective bargaining and labor law, mobility, and employee's work, to become unattractive. They maintained that the welfare state had thus led to significant economic damage and to growing unemployment, and that it threatened the European economy's global competitiveness, which depended particularly heavily on the world market. This critique called for loosening the regulatory framework and requiring the family, private accommodations, and the market to again take on more of social security's tasks—health insurance, education, and housing.

A second critique, aimed at the efficiency of the welfare state, was primarily directed against the power cartels of trade associations, unions, and the governmental bureaucracy that had constructed and politically ensured the welfare state. This political cartel, often referred to as "neo-corporatism," was seen as dangerous because it gave little opportunity for influence to the poorly organized clients, the new social movements, and often the experts. It cut the welfare state down to the interests of the three most important actors. This power cartel—according to critics—tended to freeze previously agreed upon compromises and to be oblivious to the new poverty, weaknesses within education, insufficient housing, and new forms of resumés. Greater political openness and ability for reform were now demanded.

Third and finally, anti-bureaucracy critics added their voices to the crowd. This criticism was directed at the highly centralized, strongly bureaucratized social security systems, the huge social insurances, massive housing associations, and large hospitals and universities. The social welfare state was accused not only of being too unwieldy, inefficient, and expensive, but also of patronizing citizens and planning their lives without involving them in the process. This school of thought demanded, and sometimes also developed, non-bureaucratic forms of social security, education, and housing through self-help organizations or small manageable networks.

These critiques were somewhat effective. They certainly did not lead to a return to the period before the emergence of the modern welfare state, but there were profound consequences in three respects. First, the decade-long reforms to strengthen the welfare state slowed down. In the late 1970s and 1980s the welfare state was seldom expanded through reform in the areas of social security, education, and housing. If reforms were carried out, they were more often aimed at a reduction of costs or greater efficiency at the same price.

The broad nonpartisan political consensus that had supported the welfare state reforms into the early 1970s broke further apart. The optimism for the welfare state that had once been characteristic of all political camps now changed into considerable criticism. In addition to this, sharp political conflicts emerged between new opponents and the traditional supporters of the welfare state. A few governments developed into sharp welfare state opponents, as for example was the case with the Thatcher government, while others did not want to undertake any radical dismantling. As a result, new intra-European differences that had been unknown during the welfare state's glory days came into being during this period.

Finally, the welfare state became less important in the public sphere: it was no longer seen as a burning issue among both right- and left-wing intellectuals. The environment, health hazards, new inequalities among women and minorities, educational quality, national identities, international relationships, and globalization drowned out the discussion about the welfare state. It became more of a technical, dull topic, like tax law or agricultural subsidies, that that was difficult for lay people to understand and now mobilized only experts. The charismatic hold that the European social model had once enjoyed dropped off in general. When the welfare state returned to public debate at the beginning of the twenty-first century, other issues were discussed. It was no longer a matter of social equality, universal social security, and the opening of the welfare state to minorities, but rather of job creation, better training, fighting poverty, and reducing costs.

The criticism also had astonishing boundaries, however. Surprisingly, the welfare state was not significantly scaled back anywhere. In any case, the percentage of state social security expenditures in the gross national product did not decrease on average in Western Europe. It did not even stagnate: according to OECD calculations it grew during the economic difficulty after the oil shock of 1973 as well; it was at 13 percent in 1974 and increased to 17 percent by 1998. Incidentally, Western Europe did not differ from the US or Japan in this regard. State social expenditures increased in these countries as well during this period, albeit at a lower level (cf. Table 10.1). These governmental expenses for social security certainly did not rise continuously as a whole. In Western Europe social security spending slightly stagnated or sank in relation to the gross national product during the inflation shock of the late 1970s, in the late 1980s during the neoliberal shift, and in the late 1990s as national budgets were being disciplined due to the coming euro. Yet the growth in state social expenditures during the each of the periods in between was stronger.

The differences between the individual European countries were also substantial. Surprisingly, the most significant drop in social security spending was not carried out in the countries whose governments most strongly polemicized against the welfare state—Great Britain during the Thatcher administration or the Netherlands during the Lubbers administration. Rather, it took place in Iceland during the 1970s and in Luxembourg, Ireland, and the Netherlands during the 1990s (OECD 2000: 67, 150ff.). Overall, spending for social security continued to rise despite extensive public critique from all political camps, as the necessities of social welfare were stronger than the political intentions of the governments. This can admittedly be deceiving, however: the services for clients were not necessarily better as a result. Quite to the contrary, the rise in expenses as of the 1970s was more an indicator of climbing unemployment, increasing health costs, growing poverty, an aging population, and a swelling number of retirees.

European Divergences, Convergences, and Hallmarks

In the period after 1945, the European welfare state was characterized by prominent intra-European convergences and, increasingly, divergences.

Divergences

Welfare states varied during the immediate postwar period as well as during the 1950s and 1960s. The differences that had already developed among the social welfare states during the pre- and interwar periods continued in many cases to exist after the Second World War. These included differences between the institutions and financing of the welfare states, in the conditions regarding public and private social security, in social welfare benefits and the share of participants who were covered through the state, and in the attitudes among elites and the public toward state social security. Some of these divergences accord with the differences between the wealthy center of Europe and the poorer European periphery. Poorer European countries, like Portugal and Greece, have not been able to manage the high Western European average for social spending in recent history. Such differences were no less pronounced in the 1990s, as the East Central and Eastern European social welfare states that could now be taken into account were far behind the Western European average with regard to social spending per person. These divergences even temporarily intensified during the transformation crisis after 1990 and the conversion of the social welfare state.

New divergences came about during the postwar period in Western Europe not only as a result of the Second World War, but also because the welfare state—as mentioned previously—underwent reform in part of Western Europe, while in a number of other countries state social security was changed very little. The reasons for the lack of reforms varied considerably from country to country. Germany and Austria, for instance, had long traditions of state social security and thus often went against inner trends toward reform, not considering reform necessary. Switzerland resisted comprehensive social security for a particularly long time because of its strong liberal tradition in comparison to the rest of Europe. Countries like Italy, Spain, and Portugal were not affluent enough to afford extensive state social insurances. These divergences ebbed to a large extent during the 1950s and 1960s.

The Cold War likewise led to new differences in social security. The dominant model in the western part of Europe fundamentally viewed the welfare state as a check on the market economy, expanded massively, and depended on an active citizenry. By comparison, the above-mentioned Soviet model that was pushed through in the eastern part of Europe completely subjected the welfare state to the demands of the planned economy and was based more on passive, managed citizens. These differences are now history.

Lastly, starting in the 1970s, new extremes formed among the European governments between the welfare state's defenders and opponents. These differences were no longer as sharp at the beginning of the twenty-first century as they had been in the 1980s and 1990s.

The sociologist Esping-Anderson distinguishes three types of welfare state in Europe: first, the *liberal Anglo-Saxon* type, in which the market has priority, the welfare state offers only minimal security and is often only governmentally subsidized, and its clients are often stigmatized through poverty tests. The second, or *corporatist continental European* type, offers social security for all citizens but is also often dependent on premiums and separated by social milieu, as well as oriented toward a traditional family ideal of the woman as housewife and mother. And the third, *socialist Scandinavian* type treats all citizens equally, safeguards the family and the employment of mothers, and dismantles the character of work as a commodity (Esping-Andersen 1990). The restriction to three types has been rightly criticized, not only because all of Western Continental Europe is crammed into a single type and moreover the differences among the three forms are blurred in reality, but furthermore because large parts of Europe go unnoted among these three forms of welfare state. For these reasons two additional types of welfare state have been proposed: a Southern European form, which follows the continental model but for economic reasons can offer only very limited social services, and the previously covered Eastern European type, which followed the Soviet model of social security.

Convergences

The European welfare states became similar in more ways than one as of the 1960s. The differences regarding social spending, which were originally quite significant, noticeably eased among Western European countries. The variation coefficient sank from 41 percent in 1974 to 37 percent in 1980 and further to 17 percent in 1995. The percentage of the population that was covered by national insurances likewise adjusted—the variation coefficient also dropped drastically in this regard. According to Bela Tomka's calculations, for the most important national insurances—health insurance and pension—it fell from 44 percent and 30 percent respectively in 1950 to 5 percent each in 1990 (Kaelble 2004: 38f.; Tomka 2004a: 135). The principles of financing national social security also came to resemble each other more. Voluntary insurances were pushed more into the background, and compulsory insurances increasingly prevailed. Governmental financing became more important, even when the insured and employers continued to contribute significantly to the costs. Governmental social benefits more often became enforceable rights. The new concept of a pension system under which the elderly could live on their own became accepted in a majority of European countries. Educational opportunities and the quality of housing also began to approximate each other in the various European countries (see Chapters 3 and 12).

The alignment of the welfare states in Europe had various causes. From the 1950s on, industrialization and the development of the service sector created a basic and similar need throughout Europe for the social security of industrial and service-oriented labor. Countries on the European periphery, like Finland, Ireland, and Portugal, had the economic opportunity to finance a welfare state. The establishment of democracy in Europe broadened the opportunities for transnational debate and transfers. The intense exchange of social welfare concepts was far more possible between democracies than between dictatorships or authoritarian regimes. In addition to this, national self-image changed. "Other countries" were less often viewed as strange or inferior, or as a different nation that one's own nation needed to distance itself from. Instead they were seen as neighboring countries that could be learned from. The Western European democracies became a sphere of communication of sociopolitical concepts.

European Hallmarks

The European particularities of welfare states also became more visible and openly discussed during this period. During the second half of the twentieth century, five characteristic features differentiated the European social model overall from the models in non-European industrial and emerging countries.

First, it was built upon a particularly long common European tradition of public intervention in the social security of its citizens, which had set in by early modern times. This particularly long historical development also led to stronger path dependence than was present in either of the other two large modern societies, the US and Japan, where decisive social reforms were first implemented in close connection with the Great Depression and the Second World War during the 1930s and 1940s. Of course public intervention from above was not the only aspect of this long European tradition: the civil-societal side of social security—the participation of clients—and discussion of alternative nongovernmental models were also parts. To view the European model solely as state intervention would be an unjustifiable simplification. However, path dependence should also not be overestimated. There was no final development process that led to the European welfare state.

Second, in most European countries in the second half of the twentieth century, the welfare state expanded more than it did in non-European industrialized countries. Social insurances for the four largest individual risks—poverty in old age, illness, the inability to work, and unemployment—became the European standard despite the diversity in social welfare regulations in the individual countries. In the US there continues to be a lack of general state health insurance. Furthermore, state social expenditures during the twentieth century were higher in Europe than elsewhere. In 1990, the Western and Central European average was roughly 16 percent of the gross national product. At 11 percent each, the US and Japan clearly spent less. Only Great Britain was at the same level as the US and Japan in 1990. This European particularity became noticeably less distinct in the 1990s, however, as social expenses in the US and Japan grew significantly, as opposed to the average in Europe (see Table 10.1). The gap between Europe and the less wealthy Asian or Latin American countries was even greater. Mexico's state social expenditures at the end of the twentieth century were 1 percent, and Korea's 3 percent, of the gross national product (OECD 2000: 67). Lastly, the inclusion of social fundamental rights in the European constitutions and laws also contributed in particular to the expansion of the welfare state in Europe.

Third, the European welfare state possessed a certain global attraction. Worldwide, any existing models for state social insurance were almost always European: German before the First World War, and British and Swedish after the Second World War. Admittedly, this global attraction to the European model fluctuated. Its peaks so far were during the interwar period and in the 1950s and 1960s, when the European social model had quite a bit of influence, especially in East Asia but also in North and Latin America.

Fourth, the European nation-state, which the Second World War had plunged into moral crisis through defeat and occupation, war crimes, and genocide, gained new legitimacy with the modern welfare state. A new national solidarity, which was achieved and secured through the national welfare state, was a deciding factor in the European nation-states' ability to surmount this deep crisis. The right of citizens to social welfare benefits came into being, as did new civic duties, above all in the form of payment of solidarity contributions to social insurances. A national solidarity between the workforce and the retired, between the healthy and ill, between the employed and unemployed was established in this manner. During the second half of the twentieth century, the welfare state stabilized the nation-states of Europe, which were viewed as discredited at the time, in a way that would have been difficult to imagine a half-century earlier. The Europeans' tie to the nation-state was changed in the process. It no longer consisted of a national loyalty that emerged when faced with an external enemy and was crowned by dying for one's nation, but instead was comprised of a bond with the state through material, mostly welfare state–related duties and rights.

The European welfare state's fifth distinctive feature, which is often overlooked, is its particularly well-developed transnational side. Without this dimension it would be incomprehensible that the international debate deals with a *European* rather than a Swedish or British model. This transnational side comprises several elements. It is made up of an intense international exchange of public social security concepts and policies between experts, politicians, administrators, intellectuals, and civil societal organizations. This European exchange first emerged in early modern times with an intense European debate about concepts in policy addressing poverty. It continued in the late nineteenth century with congresses, international collections of statistics, special research, and social reporting. Drawn into the maelstrom of strong rivalries between European nation-states, the exchange at that time served primarily to prevent and discredit the international influence of welfare state concepts. This changed again as the mental effects of both world wars began to fade.

The international social policies of European governments, which began to appear in bilateral treaties and in multilateral institutions, agreements, and charters at the beginning of the twentieth century, are an additional part of the transnational side of the European welfare state. They were initiated in particular in response to expanding labor migration from the European periphery to the industrialized, wealthy, and dynamic center of Europe. This labor migration necessitated an opening of national social states that had been closed to the outside and reserved solely for their own citizens. Before the First World War, it was regulated primarily through bilateral treaties, and afterward through multilateral institutions such as the International Labour Office in Geneva in particular. After the Second World War, the Council of Europe and its Social Charter of 1961 became regulatory players.

Finally, in the second half of the twentieth century a crucial element was added, which has yet to develop outside of Europe: the supranational public social security of the European Union. This was developed gradually, however. It was first in the 1990s that the EU gained importance as something more than just an instrument in the establishment of the Single European Market. The European Union evolved in three areas in particular. First, it pursued a policy for the social safeguarding of internationally mobile Europeans who studied, worked, and lived in other EU member states. As a result it pushed for all member-state citizens' equal access to all national welfare states. In the best-case scenario, migration within the European Union was to be as secure as migration within a nation-state. This is currently still far from the reality.

The European Union additionally pursued supranational additions to national social policies wherever national welfare states retained gaps in social welfare. This policy primarily consisted of sociopolitical guidelines, as well as basic social rights in European treaties such as the rights to mobility, employment, and education throughout the entire European Union, the equality of men and women, and the right to nondiscrimination of all kinds. The rights to collective organization and bargaining, to decent work, to the securing of minimum wage, housing, health, education, culture, and the protection of the family were also included. This complementary social policy could also take the form of expert reports, white and green books, and conferences that called attention to pressing sociopolitical problems. It is controversial whether this policy always remains complementary or whether it does indeed intervene in the national social states. In any case, a giant EU social bureaucracy has not yet emerged.

Third and finally, the harmonization of the enormous differences between the European social systems, which endangered the cohesion of the European economy and had potential to lead to conflicts between the member states, was also part and parcel of European social policy. This process was not just a matter of public social security systems, but also of industrial relations, job security and labor law, health care, housing, and education. This policy was carried out in part through regulations by the European Commission within the framework of its increasing competencies, but also in part through regularly occurring reportage, the "open method of coordination," expert commissions, and congresses. These methods made up a system alerting European policy makers to new, shared problems and to dangerous disparities between the national public social security systems. Overall the European Union's supranational social policy revolved around two primary objectives: the traditional goal of socially safeguarding the cohesion of the European economy and cushioning its costs, and the more recent goal of creating a stronger tie between the European citizen and the European Union.

References

Alber, J. *Vom Armenhaus zum Wohlfahrtsstaat. Analysen zur Entwicklung der Sozialversicherung in Westeuropa.* Frankfurt 1982.

Baldwin, P. *The Politics of social solidarity: Class bases of the European welfare state.* Cambridge 1994.

Bertelsmann Lexikon, Neuausgabe in 7 Bänden. Vol. 7. Gütersloh 1966.

Esping-Andersen G. *The Three Worlds of Welfare Capitalism.* Princeton 1990.

Flora P. *State, Economy and Society 1815–1975.* 2 vols. Frankfurt a. M. 1983.

Flora P. ed. *Growth to limits: The Western European welfare states since World War II,* 5 vols. Berlin 1986 ff.

Hennock, E.P. "History of the Welfare State." In *Encyclopedia of Social and Behavioral Sciences,* ed. N.J. Smelser and P.B. Baltes. Amsterdam 2001,vol. 8, 16439–16445.

Kaelble H. "Das europäische Sozialmodell—eine historische Perspektive." In *Das europäische Sozialmodell: Auf dem Weg zum transnationalen Sozialstaat,* ed. H. Kaelble and G. Schmid. Berlin 2004 (*WZB Jahrbuch 2004*), 31–50.

Lindert, J.P. *Growing Public: Social Spending and Economic Growth since the 18th Century.* Cambridge 2004.

OECD. *Historical Statistics 1960–1995.* Paris 1997.

OECD. *Historical Statistics 1970–1999.* Paris 2000.

Rieger E. and S. Leibfried. *Limits to Globalization: Welfare States and the World Economy.* Cambridge 2006.

Ritter, G.A. *Der Sozialstaat: Entstehung und Entwicklung im internationalen Vergleich.* Munich 2010.

Schmidt, M.G. *Sozialpolitik in Deutschland. Historische Entwicklung und internationaler Vergleich,* 3rd edition. Wiesbaden 2005.

Thurnwald H. *Gegenwartsprobleme der Berliner Familien: Eine soziologische Untersuchung an 498 Familien.* Berlin 1948.

Tomka B. "Western European Welfare States in the 20th Century: Convergences and Divergences in the Long-Run Perspective." *International Journal of Social Welfare* 12 (2003): 249–260.

Tomka B. *Welfare in East and West: Hungarian Social Security in an International Comparison, 1918–1990.* Berlin 2004a.

Tomka B. "Wohlfahrtsstaatliche Entwicklung in Ostmitteleuropa und das europäische Sozialmodell, 1945–1990." In *Das europäische Sozialmodell: Auf dem Weg zum transnationalen Sozialstaat,* ed. H. Kaelble and G. Schmid. Berlin 2004b (*WZB Jahrbuch 2004*), 107–140.

Chapter 11

URBAN EXPANSION, CITY LIFE, AND URBAN PLANNING

After the welfare state, the city and urban planning are a second major area of government influence on society.

State of Research

European research on urban history has experienced a noticeable revival in recent years, after quite a long period of silence on the topic. City growth and metropolises, public institutions and urban planning, urban ghettos and minorities, city visions and discourse regarding the city have become new and attractive topics for historians. A good overview of the history of European cities since 1945 was written by Guy Burgel (Burgel 2003). Beyond this, we have overviews on worldwide urban development (Mumford 1961; Bairoch 1988; Moricini-Ebrard 1994a, 1994b), on the history of cities in individual countries (Aghulon 1983; Reulecke 1984; Krabbe 1989; Walter 1994), on certain aspects of urban history such as the growth of European cities (Friedrichs 1985; Cheshire and Hay 1989; Kunzmann and Wegener 1991; Nitsch 2001), on urban planning in Europe (Hall 1988; Häußermann 1996; Albers 1997; Le Galès 2002), and on European metropolises (Sassen 1991; Zimmermann 1996).

The European City in Transition

Continuities

Urbanization was in no way a new experience for Europeans. The industrialized areas of Europe had been experiencing rapid city growth since around the middle of the nineteenth century. This development was in fact more dynamic for a number of European countries before the First World War than it was in the second half of the twentieth century.

Further, the relationship in size between the European cities remained almost unchanged in the second half of the twentieth century (Table 11.1). The largest urban agglomerations were essentially the same in the year 2000 as in 1950. The two single global cities, London and Paris, stood at the top of this hierarchy in 2000 as well as in 1950. Included in this top bracket in both 1950 and 2000 were several particularly large capital regions such as Madrid, Rome, Athens, Vienna, and Berlin, and several economic regions such as the Ruhr district, Milan, Naples, Barcelona, Birmingham, Manchester, Katowice, the Rhine Main area, Hamburg, Stuttgart, and Munich. Only two cities, Lisbon and Warsaw, entered this top group between 1950 and 2000. Two other cities, Copenhagen and Budapest, belonged among the twenty-two largest European agglomerations in 1950 but by 2000 were no longer included. When one examines the former USSR, one sees the same continuity. The two great metropolitan centers, Moscow and St. Petersburg, belonged in the top category in both 1950 and 2000. Only the Ukrainian urban agglomeration of Kiev entered this league. Things were different in Turkey. In 1950 no major Turkish city belonged in this group, but in 2000 the two Turkish metropolises of Istanbul and Ankara did.

Continuities existed in urban planning and public services as well. Urban planning, which enjoys a long history in Europe, had, in a modern sense, already emerged in the nineteenth and early twentieth centuries. The same was true of the local public transportation systems: subways, trams, buses, and commuter rails had long since been invented and were widely in use; they lost their preeminence in the second half of the twentieth century with the rise of the automobile, however. Public services such as sanitation, water supply, street maintenance, lighting, and paved roads were also underway in the nineteenth century. In the same vein, city law, the extent of cities' autonomy, and elections of city parliaments and mayors were no differently regulated in 2000 than they were in 1950. Neither had the morphology of the cities changed fundamentally: contrasts between urban ghettos, slums, and wealthy quarters still shaped the image of the city. The distribution of business districts, shopping districts,

Table 11.1 The Largest European Urban Agglomerations
(Over 2 million residents in 2000)

Agglomerations ranked by 2000 Europe	Population 2000	1975	1950	For comparison: Agglomerations ranked by 1950
1. Paris	9.6	8.9	5.4	1. London
2. London	7.6	8.2	8.7	2. Paris
3. Rhine-Ruhr North	6.5	6.5	5.3	3. Rhine-Ruhr North
4. Milan	4.3	5.5	3.6	4. Milan
5. Madrid	4.0	3.8	1.6	5. Berlin
6. Lisbon	3.9	1.2	0.8	6. Naples
7. Rhine-Main	3.7	3.2	2.3	7. Rhine-Main
8. Katowice	3.5	3.0	1.7	8. Manchester
9. Berlin	3.3	3.2	3.3	9. Birmingham
10. Rhine-Ruhr Central	3.2	2.6	2.0	10. Hamburg
11. Athens	3.1	2.7	1.8	11. Rhine-Ruhr Central
12. Naples	3.0	3.6	2.8	12. Athens
13. Barcelona	2.7	2.8	1.6	13. Vienna
14. Rome	2.7	3.0	1.6	14. Rhine-Ruhr S
15. Rhine-Ruhr South	2.7	2.3	1.8	15. Katowice
16. Hamburg	2.7	2.5	2.1	16. Madrid
17. Stuttgart	2.7	2.3	1.5	17. Rome
18. Warsaw	2.3	1.9	1.0	18. Budapest
19. Birmingham	2.3	2.4	2.3	19. Barcelona
20. Manchester	2.3	2.4	2.5	20. Stuttgart
21. Munich	2.3	2.0	1.3	21. Munich
22. Vienna	2.1	2.0	1.8	22. Copenhagen

USSR (Russia, Ukraine) and Turkey				
Moscow	8.4	7.6	5.3	
St. Petersburg	4.6	4.3	2.9	
Kiev	2.5	1.9	0.8	
Istanbul	8.9	3.6	1.1	
Ankara	3.2	1.7	0.5	

Source: UN, *World Urbanization Prospects: The 2001 Revision* (New York 2001), 131ff., 256ff. This table permits only rough conclusions, as the agglomerations are not fully comparable. The definition of agglomeration is not standardized by the UN. The UN relies on the respective national statistics bureaus. According to these technical and purely artificial definitions, Rhine-Ruhr South is the area spanning Cologne, Leverkusen, and Bohn; Rhine-Ruhr Central encompasses Düsseldorf, Remscheid, Mönchengladbach, Solingen, and Wuppertal; Rhine-Ruhr North indicates the Ruhr district itself, Rhine-Main Frankfurt, Offenbach, Darmstadt, and Wiesbaden.

and residential areas was also in principle the same in 2000 as in 1950, even though many new service centers sprang up and many industrial areas disappeared. The European city in the year 2000 thus resembled, in many aspects, the city of 1950.

City Growth and Urbanization

Nevertheless, the second half of the twentieth century represented a distinct break in the history of the urbanization of Europe. In 1950 Europe was still divided into generally urban and generally rural countries. According to the United Nations' estimates, the large majority of the population lived in city agglomerations in Great Britain, Belgium, the Netherlands, Sweden, and Germany. France, Italy, and Spain, as well as Norway, Estonia, and Lithuania, were still half urban, half rural societies at that time. In Finland, Ireland, and most of the Southern European, East Central, and Eastern European countries, in contrast, only a minority of the population lived in urban agglomerations or in cities at all (see Table 11.2). As a whole, Europe was still not a completely urbanized civilization. According to these estimates, less than half of Europeans lived in urban agglomerations in 1950 (see Table 11.2).

Over the course of the second half of the twentieth century, however, nearly all of Europe's rural countries developed into predominantly urban societies. Only a small number of countries remained largely rural, for example as Albania did, or like Yugoslavia and Romania became half urbanized. According to the UN, seven in ten Europeans lived in urban agglomerations in 2000 (see Table 11.2). With this transition, Europe became an urbanized civilization.

This process had its origins in a strong urban boom. Particularly between the 1950s and the 1970s, cities in Europe expanded rapidly. Many of Europe's larger cities virtually exploded. Taken as a whole, the period of time between the 1950s and the 1970s is the second greatest period of urbanization and physical urban expansion, after the earlier and more dynamic period of growth between the mid nineteenth century and the First World War. In contrast to the nineteenth century, cities expanded not only in industrialized areas of Europe, but throughout the continent.

There were four primary reasons for this most recent phase of urbanization in Europe to date. First, migration from the country into cities increased notably; this was accompanied by a rapid decrease in agricultural activity and a complete shift from agricultural to industrial and later to service-oriented employment. For a range of European countries, the rural-urban migration was never so pronounced as in the 1950s and 1960s. A second reason for this development was that natural population growth was still relatively high in all European countries, and in any case significantly higher than in 2000. Particularly in Southern Europe and Eastern Europe, this formed a foundation for urbanization. Third, the emigration overseas that had begun directly after the Second World War once again subsided. Subsequent waves of migration went in much higher numbers to European cities than in earlier periods, and far fewer migrants went to non-European cities. The migration was often transnational: immigrants moved away from agrarian regions of Portugal, Spain, Italy, Greece, and Yugoslavia to cities in France, Belgium, Austria, Switzerland, West Germany, and Great Britain (see Chapter 7 on migration). Added to this was new immigration from non-European societies into European cities, in particular from the southern and eastern Mediterranean regions as well as from former colonies in the Caribbean, India, Pakistan, and Africa. The fourth reason was that a historical obstacle to urbanization that had played an important role well into the nineteenth century—feeding the urban population—disappeared completely in the second half of the twentieth century owing to the unprecedented increase in European agricultural productivity.

This rapid urbanization slowed down in the 1980s and 1990s. Between 1950 and 1980, the portion of the total population that lived in urban agglomerations shot from just under one-half to around two-thirds. Between 1980 and 2000, in contrast, this portion increased by only a few percentage points. Of particular note is that urbanization stagnated in the 1990s in almost all regions of Europe (see Table 11.2). One of the central reasons for this is the drop in population growth. Migration from countryside to city lessened, either because most people had already migrated or because rural areas prospered economically. Furthermore, immigration from non-European countries was curtailed by most European governments beginning in the 1970s (see Chapter 7).

Urbanization in the second half of the twentieth century was certainly not the same everywhere. Cities on the European periphery grew especially dramatically. Southeast and Eastern European societies were practically catapulted into urban areas during the communist era. In Romania, Bulgaria, the former Yugoslavia, Slovakia, Slovenia, and Lithuania the degree of urbanization doubled between 1950 and 1980, according to estimates by the UN (see Table 11.2). Above all, the capital cities of these countries grew with great speed. The population of Bucharest climbed from 1.1 to 2 million, that of Sofia from 0.6 to 1.2 million, and that of Belgrade from 0.4 to an astonishing 1.7 million. The gap between the capital and the provincial towns was much more pronounced than in Western Europe. This growth was so extreme that after the political upheavals of 1989–90 it could only considerably decrease in some areas. The cities in the Soviet Union followed a similar course, which was a model for large parts of Eastern Europe. Between 1950 and 1990 the Moscow agglomeration grew from 2.9 to 4.9 million inhabitants. St. Petersburg grew from 2.9 to 4.9 million people. The growth of these cities also stagnated in the 1990s (Sundhaußen 1999: 143ff.; UN 2004: 256ff.).

Even in Western Europe, the rate of city growth was high in places. In several countries that were still considered peripheral in 1950, urbanization increased at a similarly rapid pace. The portion of Portugal's population that lived in urban agglomerations tripled. In Spain, Greece, Finland, and Norway, this portion rose by more than 20 percent. The same type of growth even occurred in France and Switzerland (see Table 11.2). The examination by P.C. Cheshire and D.G. Hay of Western European cities between 1971 and 1981 showed that prime examples of growth included, in particular, cities in the Mediterranean regions of Greece, Southern Italy, France, and Spain, as well as cities in Western France and in the French Alps (Cheshire and Hay 1989; Kunzmann and Wegener 1991: 28, Table 2). Large cities such as Paris, Madrid, Barcelona, Marseilles, Lyon, and Rome, and even Stuttgart, Munich, and Stockholm, doubled in size; Lisbon and Porto even quadrupled or quintupled between 1950 and 2000. Still more rapid than in these dynamic areas of Europe was the urbanization in Turkey. Ankara grew from 0.3 to 3.2 million between 1950 and 2000, and Istanbul grew from 1 million to 8.7 million—phenomenal growth by any European scale (UN 2004: 265ff.).

Meanwhile, urbanization in other areas of Western and Northern Europe was much less dynamic. Here, rates lay clearly below the Eastern and Southern European averages (see Table 11.2). The metropolitan areas of London, Copenhagen, Berlin, Hamburg, the Ruhr district, Amsterdam, Lille, Vienna, Milan, and Naples grew much more slowly or stagnated in contrast to the above-mentioned Portuguese, Spanish, French, Swedish, and South German metropolitan areas. In an entire range of cities in this part of Europe, the population even shrank after the 1970s, especially in English, German, Italian, and Belgian industrial and port cities (Cheshire and Hay 1989; UN 2004: 262ff.).

The Changing Economic Dynamic of the City

A fundamental economic change to the European city lay behind these developments. In the 1950s and 1960s, the most dynamic cities in Europe were either industrial cities such as the Ruhr district, Birmingham, Manchester, Katowice, and Milan, or port cities such as Rotterdam, Antwerp, and Marseilles. Paris, London, Brussels, Amsterdam, and Lisbon profited from their roles as colonial metropolises. All three aspects came together in the two global cities of Paris and London. Nevertheless, these dynamic processes subsided. The European colonial empires began to fall apart directly after the Second World War. Beginning in the 1960s, the European navigation and shipbuilding industry found itself in crisis. Once-glamorous port cities such as Hamburg, Bremen, Nantes, Bordeaux, Bristol, and Liverpool lost their importance. Starting in the 1970s, the industrial sector in Europe experienced a shift in the particular dynamics of production, partly because the sector's productivity rapidly increased and it could therefore work with fewer and fewer personnel, and partly because industry withdrew to low-wage countries. Furthermore, cutting-edge technology was no longer being developed in Europe, but rather in Japan and the United States. Many industrial cities that had still been experiencing a boom in development in the 1950s and 1960s now found themselves in crisis (see Chapter 2 on labor). Neglected industrial facilities, impoverished industrial cities, immigrant ghettos, and debt-ridden and helpless city governments supported by national or European subsidies were now also characteristic of the picture of a European industrial city.

Two new types of dynamic city economies emerged. On the one hand was the international tourist city. The most successful cities, at the forefront of global tourism—primarily Paris, London, Florence, and Rome, and secondarily Lisbon, Madrid, Barcelona, Pisa, Brussels, Amsterdam, Berlin, Prague, Budapest, and St. Petersburg—competed against each other by means of museums, operas, concert halls, exhibition projects, cultural events, historical city projects, and restaurants. Discos, concerts, techno-parades, and bar districts played an increasingly greater role for young people in particular, though. The second new type of city, on the other hand, was now the seat of global companies, banks, legal and architectural firms, and consulting and planning companies with international managers and employees; or it was the seat of global organizations with international personnel. Paris and London are particularly representative of this type of city.

The Fading Contrasts between City and Country

A third fundamental change in the second half of the twentieth century was closely linked to urbanization: the fading of the traditionally sharp distinctions between city and country that had existed since the Middle Ages, namely with regard to self-perception, economic activity, law, and lifestyle. It is true that this sharp social barrier had changed significantly

Table 11.2 Urbanization in Europe, 1950–2000
(Residents of cities as percentage of total population)

Country	1950	1960	1970	1980	1990	2000
Northern Europe	53	58	66	71	73	73
Denmark	68	74	80	84	85	85
Estonia	50	58	65	70	71	69
Finland	32	38	50	60	61	59

Great Britain	84	86	89	89	89	90
Ireland	41	46	52	55	57	59
Latvia	52	57	62	68	70	69
Lithuania	31	40	50	61	68	69
Norway	50	50	65	71	72	75
Sweden	66	73	81	83	83	83
Western Europe	63	73	77	79	81	83
Belgium	92	93	94	95	97	97
Germany	72	76	80	83	85	88
France	56	62	71	73	74	75
Netherlands	83	85	86	88	89	90
Switzerland	44	51	55	57	60	
Southern Europe	31	37	45	51	55	59
Albania	20	31	32	34	36	39
Greece	37	43	53	58	59	60
Italy	54	59	64	67	67	67
Croatia	22	30	40	50	54	58
Portugal	19	22	26	29	47	65
Slovenia	20	28	37	48	50	49
Spain	52	57	66	73	75	78
Yugoslavia	19	29	39	46	51	52
Eastern Europe	34	41	48	59	63	64
Bulgaria	26	39	52	61	67	68
Poland	39	48	52	58	61	62
Romania	26	34	42	49	54	55
Slovakia	30	34	41	52	57	57
Hungary	39	43	49	57	62	65
Czech Republic	41	46	52	75	75	75
Europe	45	51	58	64	66	69
Variations coefficient for Europe	57%	45%	29%	24%	18%	16%
U.S.	64	70	74	74	75	77
Russia	45	54	63	70	73	73
Japan	50	63	71	76	77	79
Turkey	21	30	38	44	59	65

Source: UN, *World Urbanization Prospects: The 2003 Revision* (New York 2004), 168ff. Definition of city: most urban agglomerations over 750,000 residents; in only a few countries all cities, for lack of further data. These UN statistics must be used with caution, as the UN does not standardize the definition of city, but rather relies on the respective national statistics bureaus. Still, I have not used a personal data set on European cities with populations over 20,000, as there are too many gaps for Eastern Europe for the 1990s. Variation coefficient for Western Europe: 58 percent 1930, 41 percent 1950, 23 percent 1980 (see H. Kaelble, "Europäische Vielfalt und der Weg zu einer europäischen Gesellschaft," in *Die westeuropäischen Gesellschaften im Vergleich*, ed. S. Hradil and S. Immerfall [Opladen 1997], 4); for cities with a population over 5,000: P. Bairoch, *Cities and Economic Development: From the Dawn of History to the Present* (Chicago 1988), Table 13.4.

over the centuries and by the nineteenth century was weakened by the far-reaching implementation of legal equality and the dismantling of limitations on migration from the country to the city. Still, a sharp rural-urban contrast in economies, social norms, and lifestyle remained in most European countries even in the middle of the twentieth century. Only in the second half of the twentieth century did the creation of the mass consumer society and the revolutions in transportation and communication substantially smooth out these contrasts. Amenities such as water supply and sewage systems, once strictly urban provisions, became available in the country. Life in the country increasingly resembled city life thanks to new forms of communication such as telephone, television, and Internet; new means of transportation, especially the automobile; new forms of commercialization such as shopping centers, department store catalogues, and Internet shopping; tourism; and new leisure enterprises in the country such as riding schools, golf courses, vacation schools, ski schools, and the city dweller's second home in the country. Consumption habits in cities and in the country became more similar. Most importantly, life in the country was no longer an agrarian life as a rule, but for the most part played itself out in occupations similar to those in the city.

The Social Segregation of City Districts and the Use of City Centers

The social differences between the respective city districts also changed in the second half of the twentieth century. In the middle of the century clear lines of separation still existed between social milieus—between the upper and lower middle-class districts, for instance, or between middle-class neighorhoods and working-class company accommodations. These social milieus were a European particularity that had emerged in the nineteenth century. Since the late nineteenth-century inner-city transportation revolution, which enabled the distribution of the various social milieus into various city sections, these milieus often lived in physically segregated districts, at least in the large cities. These milieus gradually declined from the 1960s on.

Instead, new social differences emerged, for example between a new upper class in the city centers the wealthy classes had abandoned only temporarily in the 1950s and 1960s, to which the wealthy young unmarrieds and wealthy pensioners returned starting in the 1970s, and a broad majority of city dwellers who enjoyed stable jobs and income and lived in much less luxurious residential districts. Other city districts, characterized by a new poverty, were inhabited by the unemployed, whose numbers had increased to an unusually high level since the 1970s and 1980s (see Chapter 2 on labor); by single-parent families, the consequence of the climbing divorce rate, but also of new and diverse family models and options (see Chapter 1 on family); by students, who had grown in number due to the education expansion and similarly helped to characterize entire quarters; by the clearly growing group of drug addicts; and lastly by immigrants, as Europe became one of the most important immigration destinations in the world after the 1960s and 1970s (see Chapter 7 on migration).

City Visions

European city visions and planning goals fundamentally changed in the second half of the twentieth century. The vision of modern European ur‐ ban planning played an important role in the first three decades after the Second World War. This vision had already emerged in the first half of the century in opposition to the nineteenth-century Victorian, Hausma‐ nian, and Wilhelminian cities with their historical facades and tenement houses; their unhealthy, hazardous living conditions; their mix of work, residence, administration, and business on the same block or street; their minimal planning; and even their sharp, and desired, national contrasts in architecture.

A common European vision now emerged of a city with functional geometric facades; less densely built blocks that could be filled with light and air; bright, airy, and healthful housing; a physical separation of indus‐ try, housing, administration, and business in different quarters of the city; functional architecture including fully geometric blocks as well as rural outer suburbs and garden cities. The advantages of the new possibilities in transportation and communication—the automobile and the telephone— were exploited. The new private spaces offered larger apartments with more privacy for all family members. Economies of scale brought about the urban mass society's great traffic arteries and especially its high-rise build‐ ings. Great European architects like Le Corbusier, no longer mere lone voices, achieved status in the public sphere as members of a new profes‐ sional group—urban planners. This vision developed gradually in the first half of the twentieth century; it was tested out in individual districts of the city, but could not yet prevail in the city of the nineteenth century. Only after the Second World War were these concepts turned into reality.

The massive realization of this Western European vision after the 1950s led to a common European, or at least Western European, counterreac‐ tion in the 1960s. The desolation of the commuter towns, the hostility of inner cities burdened by traffic, the radical demolition of city centers, the unimaginativeness of reconstruction efforts after the Second World War, and the monotony of functionalism came in for heavy criticism. The focus turned to urban redevelopment, which maintained well-developed human networks and renovated older buildings instead of replacing them. New spaces were created for pedestrian zones; the quality of the services in the new districts— schools, libraries, and traffic connections—was improved. Saving energy and protecting the environment became important concerns. City and neighborhood centers saw a general return to a small scale and multifunctionality, with greater proximity of residence, work, and shopping. Broad sections of traffic networks were stripped down, and a new architectural aesthetic with diverse styles and purposely illusionary facades arose.

In Eastern Europe, however, the postwar communist regimes aligned themselves with the Soviet vision of imposing city centers with impressively high public buildings visible from great distances, with spacious boulevards, expansive squares for political marches, and compact urban blocks. This architecture drew a striking contrast between the respective capital and other cities by concentrating mostly on the capital's center, making it a symbol of the strong centralized regime. This East-West opposition was limited to the city centers, however. The new districts and decentralized residential neighborhoods with high-rise buildings, schools, libraries, and businesses springing up in the eastern part of Europe looked quite similar to those in the western part of the continent.

City Planning

Given the new city visions and other city growth, European city planning changed over the course of the second half of the twentieth century as well. The initial decades after the Second World War became the golden age of European city planning, which grew out of an unusual optimism for planning and progress in a time of unusual economic prosperity and followed visions of a functional city. European city planning bureaus built entire commuter towns and suburbs.

Once city growth began to abate in the 1970s and skepticism with regard to progress began to grow, however, the spacious, spectacular urban planning fell from favor, and counter-visions reacting to functional urban architecture became influential. City planning in Europe largely reduced its focus to smaller projects, often in close collaboration with private developers. Environmental protection and quality of life were established as new priorities. The public participated in city planning to a greater extent and had its say through citizens' initiatives as well. European cities began to vie for preeminence in business locations, services, spectacular museum projects, cultural centers, world exhibitions, the Olympic Games and world championships, theater, cultural events, and even in new identity politics and politics of memory within the cities. Planning had indeed become largely routine and lost its glamorous novelty, but this in no way caused it to disappear. Instead, it remained an important development in European cities in the second half of the twentieth century.

Convergences and Characteristics of the European City

New Divergences

Along with the traditional local and national differences in urbanization, urban planning and municipal administration, and the use of public spaces, all of which were still visible and influential after the Second World War, three new divergences in particular emerged after 1945.

The most dramatic differences existed between cities that had suffered massive destruction in the Second World War and those that had survived undestroyed. The architectural styles of the 1950s and 1960s were dominant in the destroyed cities; older buildings were comparatively rare. Several destroyed city centers, for instance those in Rotterdam and Coventry, were completely replanned. In other destroyed cities, on the other hand, the old street configurations were kept intact and earlier styles were restored or even reconceived, as was the case in Budapest, Muenster, La Rochelle, and Warsaw. Great Britain even reacted to the destruction of the war with a new city planning law, the New Towns Act of 1946. Many other European countries did without city planning legislation.

A second divergence, which similarly emerged only after the Second World War, was the previously mentioned contrast between communist and Western European planning and development of city centers. Finally, observable differences concern modern architecture and urban planning. Several city centers, such as in Frankfurt or London, are characterized by modern high-rise buildings. Other cities, like Paris and Rome, kept their centers exactly as they had appeared until the nineteenth or early twentieth century and built their high-rise districts outside the city center, as with the Défense in Paris.

Convergences

The implementation of a unified international architecture is the most attention-attracting commonality among European cities. The functional style that prevailed from the 1950s to the 1970s was followed in the 1980s and 1990s by newer styles known by various names. City centers with administrative and business buildings, new neighborhoods with residential high-rises or single-family houses, and neighborhoods with vacation homes, now varied little. Until the middle of the century, national and even regional archictectures consciously distinguished themselves from one another, and as a general rule it could be immediately determined whether it was a French, Italian, Spanish, or English, Prussian, or South German city. After the Second World War, though, urban architecture largely lost these national features. In the 1960s, journalist Anthony Sampson found his attention caught "initially by the conformity. When I found myself in the suburbs of Hamburg, Brussels, or Bonn, the impression that I was not staying in England" was difficult to maintain (Sampson 1969: 270).

A second commonality was the final implementation of urbanization. The sharp contrasts between rural and urban countries that still characterized the continent in 1950 had greatly disappeared by 2000. Urbanization increased in all European countries. A third convergence appeared within the domain of urban planning. One the one hand, international exchange redoubled, especially through the intensive international integration of city planners and architects in professional organizations but also via the regular conferences that had been in place since the first half of the nineteenth century. A milestone was passed upon publication of the Athens Charter of 1933. By the second half of the twentieth century, at least in Western Europe, this international exchange was no longer hindered by the ideological barriers to the exchange of ideas that had been erected by European nationalism, fascism, and communism (Commission for the European Communities 1991, 1994).

Hallmarks of the European City

Five particularly European commonalities were prominent in the second half of the twentieth century.

The Appearance of the European City

Most European cities possessed a clearly identifiable ancient or medieval, or sometimes early modern, city core, generally the relic of a particular European city autonomy. This was still often recognizable, as it is today, in medieval or early modern buildings, churches, squares, town halls, towers, city walls, and fortifications, and sometimes also in Roman ruins. Even in places where all the ancient or old European buildings had been destroyed, the winding layout of passageways or the street names often served to identify the old city center.

Furthermore, large European city centers still boasted the imposing public edifices that had resulted from nineteenth-century urban renovations: the town hall, court, schools, the train station and its city district, libraries, monuments, squares and parks, and in larger cities the theater, opera, and museum. As a rule, these buildings were more concentrated in city centers than is the case in the US or in Asian cities. Similarly, the historic city center was ringed by broad, urban, tree-lined streets or boulevards lined with multi-story apartment buildings, often dating to the nineteenth century and usually built on the site of the torn-down medieval city wall. In contrast to US cities, European city districts were very seldom laid out as a grid of right-angled streets. Only a few European cities or city districts, such as La Roche-sur-Yon, Bari, Mannheim, or Berlin's Friedrichsstadt, reflected the eighteenth-century belief in improvement through geometric regularity, whereas US cities retained this structural principle into the nineteenth and twentieth centuries. Another characteristic feature of the European urban space was the regularity of many nineteenth- and twentieth-century European cities, be it the determination of the height and breadth of buildings or the conforming neighborhoods composed of countless small individual houses. In the outward appearance of the European city, one could generally recognize the well-planned avoidance of wild city growth, one of the most striking differences from the largest cities in Asia, Africa, and Latin America.

The industrial revolution in the nineteenth century was much less visible in the US, India, China, or the Arab world than it was in European cities, which reflect the unusually high level of industrial activity in Europe in the nineteenth and early twentieth centuries (see Chapter 2 on labor). The European density of cities—another legacy of the industrial era—stretched from the English midlands over to Southwest England, the North of France, the Netherlands, and Belgium, then branching into the central part of Germany, Southern Poland, the western and southern parts of Germany, Eastern France, and Northern Italy. Upon closer examination, the sharp social contrasts of the nineteenth and twentieth centuries, discussed above, were apparent in many European cities even after the twentieth century, when social milieus were still segregated by city section, or by front and back entrances to apartment buildings, levels, or streets. On the other hand, the European city center lacked a contrast that could be still be seen in many large Arab, African, India, and South Asian cities, and even in the Chinese city Shanghai: the contrast between the European section, which was built in the style of European cities, and that of the Arabic bazaar, the Indian city, or the Chinese city of Shanghai.

In addition, the consequences of the bombing and destruction from the First and especially the Second World War are evident in many European cities in a broad path that sweeps across Europe from Southern England through the North of France, the Netherlands, Germany, Northern Italy, Poland, and Hungary into the former Soviet Union.

Limited City Growth and Fewer Megacities

Limited city growth—or at least, more limited than in non-European societies—was another hallmark of the European city in the latter half of the twentieth century. In many non-European societies in the industrialized or developing world, urban expansion was even more dramatic than in Europe—in East Asia as much as in the Middle East, and in Africa as much as in Latin America. City growth in Europe remained lower than the worldwide increase: the number of city dwellers worldwide rose from three-quarters of a billion in 1950 to three billion in 2000, according to estimates by the UN; in Europe, however, this number only increased from a quarter billion to a half billion. Even in North America, this number increased more significantly (see Figure 11.1; UN 2004: 178ff.). This limited city growth in Europe had much to do with the unusually slow European population growth and the comparatively limited migration to the cities.

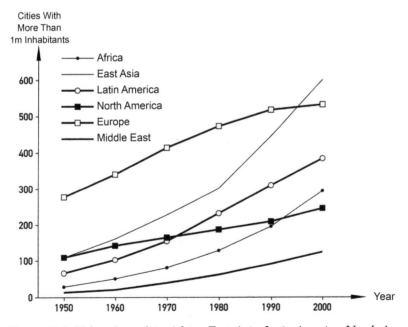

Figure 11.1 Urban Growth in Africa, East Asia, Latin America, North America, Europe, and the Middle East 1950–2000
Source: UN, *World Urbanization Prospects: The 2003 Revision* (New York 2004), 178ff.

A result of this process was the greater importance of the middle-sized city in Europe (see Figure 11.2). Only around one in five people lived in a city with a population over one million in Europe in 1950. In the US and Japan in 1950, however, over one-third of the population lived in cities with over one million inhabitants, and the tendency was increasing. In the Middle East, Latin America, Africa, and East Asia put together, continuously greater portions of the population took up residence in cities with over one million inhabitants (see Figure 11.2). The limited attractiveness of such cities in Europe led Europe to differ increasingly from global development in the second half of the twentieth century. In the middle of the twentieth century, five European and two Russian cities still belonged among the twenty largest cities in the world. By the end of the twentieth century, however, only one European city, Paris, and one Russian city, Moscow, could still be counted in this list. (UN 2004: 258ff.).

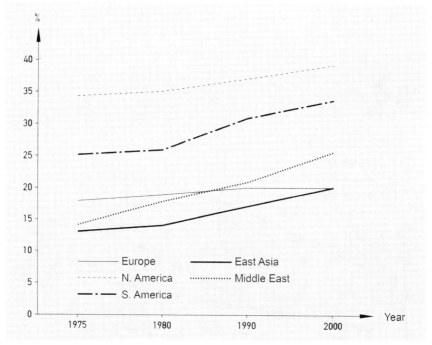

Figure 11.2 Degree of Metropolitan Growth in Europe, North America, South America, East Asia, and the Middle East, 1950–2000
(Population in cities over 1 million, as percentage of the whole population).

Source: Compiled according to G. Mertis, *Stadtentwicklung im globalen Vergleich* (2003), Website of the Berlin Institute for Population and Development (based on UN, *World Urbanization Prospects: The 1999 Revision* [New York 2001]).

Social Segregation by City Quarters

A third European peculiarity was the change in social segregation among city sections. Social segregation in the majority of European cities developed differently than in most non-European societies. In the middle of the twentieth century, the contrasts of the social milieus—between the bourgeois quarters, the middle-class quarters, and the working-class quarters—still heavily characterized most large European cities. These social milieus and their social segregation in cities declined over the course of the second half of the twentieth century. The new social segregations that emerged thereafter were particularly European. Wealthy inner-city residential neighborhoods maintained a stronger presence than in many non-European cities through institutions catering to wealthy clientele such as theater, concert halls, operas, museums, restaurants, cafes, boutiques, and department stores in the city centers. A relatively significant public sphere that was generally accessible stayed intact in these districts. Compared to wealthy quarters in the centers of North American cities, they were not as strictly controlled or fenced off, and they did not turn the general public away. Poor districts also sprang up in Europe, but they did not experience the uncontrolled growth that many South American, African, or Asian slums did. They tended to have enough basic public services and generally were located outside the city centers, unlike in the US.

Use of City Centers

A fourth peculiarity of European cities went hand in hand with city social segregation: the use of urban space in the nineteenth and early twentieth centuries differed from that in non-European societies. Naturally, the differences with respect to North American cities were not the same as those with respect to Arabic, Indian, East Asian, or Latin American cities.

The center of the city in particular was used in a typically European way. In the twentieth century, it was not solely a center of business and administration and occasionally the seat of government. In contrast to many non-European societies, it was also a place for the prestigious, elegant residences of the wealthy Europeans, and thus also for elegant streets, squares, and businesses. As previously mentioned, the center was also visibly a place for prestigious culture: operas, museums, concerts, theater, and processions. This presence and the political pressure of the wealthy in the city centers certainly contributed significantly to the fact that the city politics in Europe guaranteed a certain quality of life. In contrast to non-European cities, European cities in general in the twentieth century tried more energetically, more sensitively, and mostly successfully to avoid slums and ghettos in the city center; to suppress, control, and sanitize poor districts; and to maintain a minimum measure of public services, public security, quality of life, and European urbanity, even if the contrasts between rich and poor districts could not and should not have been made to disappear. For this type of city politics, incidentally, the slower growth of the European cities was a favorable condition.

Power of the City Administrations and Visions for the City

Finally, city administrations' influence on European cities' development was greater than in the US, Asia, Latin America, and Africa. During the second half of the twentieth century this was especially evident in urban planning, which was particularly influential in Europe. In the global debate on urban planning, most of the models originated in Europe. Europeans seldom borrowed urban planning models from other continents. Even when the urban planning euphoria had receded, Europe's municipal planning bureaus remained more influential than elsewhere.

European municipal offices' hold on power was rooted in both recent practice and older history. Since the end of the nineteenth and in the early twentieth century, it had been supported and strengthened by the newly formed professional group of city planners, which had positioned itself in the general public with considerable vision and impressive memoranda. The particularity of European urban planning cannot be understood without considering the success of this professional group. After the Second World War, meeting regularly in various international organizations or at international exhibits, it developed an international public expertise in city planning with a concentration in Western Europe. As a whole, therefore, European cities exhibited unmistakable hallmarks in the second half of the twentieth century. They refrained from simply merging into a new type of global city, despite the close economic and cultural ties Europe's metropolises maintained with non-European cities.

Notes

1. This is a simplification, as it incorporates differing definitions of city. In Italy, for example, villages and rural regions that identified with the nearest larger city were often counted as cities. In neighboring Switzerland, though, they would still have been understood as villages. Thus, the urbanization of Italy developed on account of a different understanding of city, not by virtue of a continued increase in population

density of urban settlements. The pure numbers of urbanization in Europe are therefore not fully comparable when taken individually. However, this does not change the division of Europe at the time into largely urban and largely rural societies.

References

Agulhon M. et al. "L'histoire de la France urbaine." In *La ville de l'âge industriel*, vol. 7. Paris 1983.
Albers G. *Zur Entwicklung der Stadplanung in Europa: Begegnungen, Einflüsse, Verflechtungen*. Braunschweig 1997.
Bairoch P. *Cities and Economic Development: From the Dawn of History to the Present*. Chicago 1988. (Original French edition: *De Jéricho à Mexico, Villes et économie dans l'histoire*. Paris 1985.)
Burgel G. "La ville contemporaine: De la seconde guerre mondiale à nos jours." In *Histoire de l'Europe urbaine*, ed. J.-L. Pinol, 2 vols. Paris 2003, 553–807.
Cheshire P.C. and D.G. Hay. *Urban Problems in Western Europe*. London 1989.
Commission of the European Communities. *Europe 2000: Outlook for the Development of the Community's Territory*. Luxembourg 1991.
Commission of the European Communities. *Europe 2000+: European Cooperation for Territorial Development*. Luxembourg 1994.
Friedrichs J., ed. *Stadtentwicklungen in West- und Osteuropa*. Berlin 1985.
Hall P. *Cities of Tomorrow: An Intellectual History of Urban Planning in the Twentieth Century*. Oxford 1988.
Häußermann H. "Von der Stadt im Sozialismus zur Stadt im Kapitalismus." In *Stadtentwicklung in Ostdeutschland*, ed. H. Häussermann and R. Neef. Opladen 1996.
Kaelble H. "Europäische Vielfalt und der Weg zu einer europäischen Gesellschaft." In *Die westeuropäischen Gesellschaften im Vergleich*, ed. S. Hradil and S. Immerfall. Opladen 1997, 27–68.
Krabbe R. *Die deutsche Stadt im 19. und 20. Jahrhundert*. Göttingen 1989.
Kunzmann K.R. and M. Wegener. *The Pattern of Urbanisation in Western Europe 1960–1990*. Dortmund 1991.
Le Galés P. *European Cities: Social Conflicts and Governance*. Oxford 2002.
Mumford L. *The City in History*. London 1961.
Nitsch V. *City Growth in Europe*. Berlin 2001.
Reulecke J. *Geschichte der Urbanisierung in Deutschland*. Frankfurt a. M. 1984.
Sampson A. *Die neuen Europäer*. Munich 1969.
Sassen S. *The Global City*. New York, London, and Tokyo 1991.
Sundhaussen H. "Bevölkerungsenwicklung und Sozialstruktur, in Südosteuropa." In *Gesellschaft, Politik, Wirtschaft, Kultur: Ein Handbuch*, ed. M. Hatschikjan and S. Troebst. Munich 1999.
UN. *World Urbanization Prospects: The 2003 Revision*. New York 2004.
Walter F. *La Suisse urbaine 1750–1950*. Geneva 1994.
Zimmermann C. *Die Zeit der Metropolen: Urbanisierung und Großstadtentwicklung*. Frankfurt a. M. 1996.

Chapter 12

EDUCATION

Alongside state social security and city planning, education at schools and universities in Europe was the third large area of societal governmental intervention in the second half of the twentieth century. To a large extent, education in Europe was organized and controlled by the state. Even as private schools and universities became more prevalent at the end of the twentieth century and at times gained prestige, the state remained the central supervisory and regulatory authority in general. This does not mean, however, that educational development in the second half of the twentieth century depended entirely on the government and can only be understood through an analysis of governmental decisions. Social processes, cultural attitudes, and economic circumstances were central factors in the changes in education in Europe.

Changes in education only ever affect society slowly, as the educational qualifications of youth and young adults are manifest in the whole of society only decades later. The effects of the transformation of European education in the late twentieth century will first appear among European society as a whole in the early decades of the twenty-first century. And the future of Europe in the coming three to four decades can be read in the history of education at the end of the twentieth century.

There has not yet been an overview of the social history of education in Europe since 1945. The essays by sociologist Walter Müller come closest to being an overview, though they do not cover the full half-century since the Second World War (Müller 1993, 1999; Müller and Wolbers 2003). The summary by the OECD covering the 1960s through the 1980s is very useful for educational debates and policy, but is again limited to Western Europe and a period of three decades (OECD 1994). Special overviews on the history of universities in Europe since 1945 are very helpful (Teichler 1990; Windolf 1990; Rüegg 2010). The number of national overviews available is not sufficient to provide a picture of Europe as a whole. A remedy might be to produce overviews like Antoine Prost's on the French history of education since 1945 and the last volume of the *Handbuch der deutschen Bildungsgeschichte* (Handbook of German Educational History) for other European countries and for Europe as a whole (Prost 1997, 2004; Berg et al. 1998).

The Expansion of Educational Opportunities and Their Causes

In the second half of the twentieth century, education expanded more rapidly than ever before, and at all levels.

Literacy

The first fundamental change in the second half of the twentieth century was the final elimination of illiteracy in Europe. The traditional illiteracy based on a lack of school attendance should not be relegated to the history books on nineteenth-century Europe. Illiteracy was still prevalent, even if quite unequally distributed, in Europe in 1950. It had indeed been eliminated in Central and Northern Europe in the nineteenth century, but Southern and Eastern Europe in particular were still far from its eradication. In 1950, 44 percent of the population in Portugal, 18 percent in Spain, 14 percent in Italy, 27 percent in Yugoslavia, 26 percent in Greece, 24 percent in Bulgaria, and 23 percent in Romania were illiterate. Generally speaking, illiteracy was found far more often among elderly adults and in the poorer regions of these countries. Thus in the poor Italian regions of Calabria and Basilicata, almost half of the population over the age of five could neither write nor read. Throughout Europe, the school system was insufficiently developed. Parents in rural and agricultural families often had little interest in education for their children. Large-scale landowners and urban employers of uneducated employees did not place much value on educating their employees. The state and church did not yet support the full eradication of illiteracy everywhere.

However, over the course of the second half of the twentieth century the classic illiteracy due to lack of schooling was broadly eliminated throughout Europe. In Italy and Spain the illiteracy rate in 1980 was only

4 percent, and in 1991 it was down to 5 percent in Greece, 7 percent in Yugoslavia, and 12 percent in Portugal. Yet in Turkey in 1990 it was still at 21 percent (UNESCO 1965: 42ff., 1991: 133f., 1995: 1ff., 1998: 1ff.; Flora 1983f.: vol. 1, 80). Various factors contributed to this decline in illiteracy: pressure from the global public, which increased upon UNESCO's publication of illiteracy rates; the influence of countries' respective intellectuals; the desire on the part of governments for lasting literacy, which existed in the modern democracies as well as communist regimes but had not, in contrast, been present in the European authoritarian and fascist regimes; the growing utilization of machines and new materials that made reading and writing necessary; and the migration of illiterates to wealthier parts of Europe, whereby the illiteracy rate significantly decreased, at least among the children of migrants.

Preschools

The increase in preschool attendance is often overlooked when reviewing the educational expansion. It was in the second half of the twentieth century that preschools first became an inherent part of life. Though they existed before 1950, only a minority had made use of them then. It has been a matter of debate whether schooling includes kindergarten. In Germany it was understood more as a function of charity institutions; in France, on the other hand, it has long been viewed as part of the education system. In any case, over the course of the second half of the twentieth century the trend to begin education before school age at a kindergarten or a separate preschool took hold throughout Europe. The age when schooling began changed little, yet education began de facto at an earlier age.

Around the mid 1960s barely one-half of children (three-year-olds) attended kindergarten in France, which was a pioneering country in this regard. By the mid 1970s this share was over 80 percent, while in West Germany it was still at 50 percent (INSEE 1987: 54; *Statistisches Jahrbuch der Bundesrepublik* 1978: 58, 1979: 396). At the end of the twentieth century, by contrast, the vast majority of four- to five-year-old children attended a preschool or kindergarten in most European countries. Nevertheless, there persisted significant differences that defy general explanation. In some wealthy countries like Switzerland and Finland only a minority of children attended preschools at the end of the twentieth century. Yet this was also true in poorer countries like Croatia, Serbia, the Baltic states, and Portugal, and recently in Poland as well, while in Turkey only the tiniest of minorities did. Yet these countries were ultimately exceptions (UNESCO 1995: 356ff.).

Preschool services and attendance became widespread for several reasons. A first, decisive reason was the increase in working mothers (see Chapter 2 on labor). Parallel to the growth in maternal employment, many European parents' ideas about raising children seemed to have changed. It now was not only a child's contact with his or her parents that was important; increased emphasis also was placed on developing social skills through encounters with other children the same age and with the outside world. Kindergartens also gained parents' trust as nursery school teachers became more professional and were trained in nursery school education. Finally, there were fewer and fewer alternatives to nursery school. The streets, squares, courtyards, and fields that had earlier been playing terrain for children became increasingly more dangerous, primarily due to traffic. The network of individuals raising the children in addition to parents—grandparents, unmarried aunts, older siblings, and neighbors—had been falling away for some time, either being also employed or living elsewhere due to growing geographical mobility; at the most they could take the children during school holidays. The family business, where children were nearby and could be supervised from a young age, likewise became more seldom. Alternatives to kindergarten did not disappear entirely, however. Primarily in countries with shorter spans between generations, grandparents continued to play an important role in everyday parenting if they lived locally. Wealthier social groups could furthermore afford household help, au pairs, or mature women with experience raising children, but these replaced kindergarten or day nannies less and less.

Secondary School

A third fundamental expansion within the European educational system is better known: the expansion of secondary schools. This expansion is not easy to grasp, however, as the definition of secondary school is not uniform throughout Europe.

By the late nineteenth century, secondary school students had become more numerous, and the discussions regarding this topic had become more intense. Yet secondary school attendance continued to remain a special right for a small part of the population, and graduation a privilege for a small minority. This still applied in the 1950s, when only 10 to 35 percent of a respective age group attended secondary school in most European countries. Only in a few countries like Great Britain, Sweden, Denmark, the Netherlands, and West Germany did a majority go to secondary school, at least according to UNESCO surveys. According to Peter Flora's calculations, this was not even the case for these Western European countries (UNESCO 1964: 109–111; Flora 1983: vol. 1, 553ff.).

In the 1960s and 1970s, secondary schools became normal state schools that students attended free of charge. By 2000, the overwhelming majority of students attended secondary school for at least a couple of years. Only a minority, usually from the lowest of the lower social levels and outsiders, still followed the previous school path and did not attend secondary school, in cases where there was still an alternative. Completing the lower levels of secondary school in particular became the rule rather than the exception in the second half of the twentieth century. By 1970, close to two-thirds of European young people attended secondary school. Only in a few countries like Albania, Czechoslovakia, Hungary, and Romania did secondary school attendance remain under 50 percent. These countries also joined the overall European trend in the late 1970s, however. Secondary school attendance in the USSR developed in line with the European average. Turkey, in contrast, fell short of the European pattern for quite some time. A majority of boys there first attended secondary school in the 1980s, and until the mid 1990s only a minority of girls did so (UNESCO 1972: 109ff.; UNESCO 1982: III-68ff.; UNESCO 1995: 3–65ff.). It is interesting, in comparison, that by the 1970s more girls than boys were attending secondary school in a number of completely different European countries—for example in Bulgaria, Hungary, Finland, Sweden, Great Britain, France, and Portugal.

The increase in students at the upper secondary school level, which led to graduation, changed the life course of many Europeans even more drastically. The number of students attending upper secondary school grew early on and rapidly in England and Wales, going from 25 percent in 1946 to 52 percent in 1975; in Finland, from 9 percent in 1945 to 45 percent in 1975; and in Ireland, from 8 percent in 1945 to 33 percent in 1975. France, West Germany, Belgium, and Norway were more on average, with increases from low percentages to approximately a fifth between the end of the war and the 1970s. The increases in the Netherlands, Italy, and Switzerland in comparison were below average, with only a sixth or ninth of the respective age groups attending secondary school (Flora 1983: vol. 1, 553ff.).

The reasons behind this extraordinary growth in the number of secondary school students had to do with both parents' and students' desire for education, as well as with the demand for qualified individuals in the job market; educational policy also played an important role. With the economic boom of the 1950s and 1960s, real income rose in Europe as never before. For many Europeans this meant that a secondary school education no longer entailed the dramatic loss of income it had required in the first half of the twentieth century. Farmers, craftsmen, tradesmen, and skilled workers, who had previously rarely sent their children to secondary school, could now increasingly provide their children with secondary school education, which in some cases had become more important for the parents' careers as well. The sinking birthrate further strengthened the demand for secondary school, as financing a longer period of education was considerably easier than it had been for the larger families of the first half of the century. Moreover, families began to invest in better educations for their daughters.

In the meantime, the demand for upper secondary school graduates increased. The rapid expansion of white-collar careers in industry, the expansion of the service sector and public administration, and the increased productivity in the agricultural, industry, and service sectors required more qualifications from the workforce. There was less and less demand for unskilled laborers who had only an elementary school education. Finally, public educational policy in most countries in Europe either purposefully developed, or at least accepted the expansion of, secondary school education. Public financing for the expansion of secondary schools—the investment in buildings and teachers' salaries—was certainly made easier by the economic boom. Yet investment in education in general continued to grow even during the economically difficult period that began in the 1970s.

Universities

The best known of the four expansions within the educational sector in the second half of the twentieth century is the increased number of university students. Like others, this expansion was not fully new, as the end of the nineteenth century had already seen an increase in students attending university. But this development affected only a small section of the population through to the mid twentieth century. In 1950 only approximately 4 percent of European young adults studied at universities, among them only a small group of women. It was first in the second half of the twentieth century that higher education was accorded a fundamentally different level of importance. By the end of the century more than two of every five young adults went to universities, and a course of studies had become an important stage of life for a substantial number of young Europeans. The European average percentage of university students among 20–24 year olds grew from only 4 percent in 1950 to 14 percent in 1970 and then further to 30 percent in 1990 and over 40 percent in 1995 (cf. Table 12.1). By the century's end, Europe's university students numbered 13 million, or 18 million including Russia and Turkey. This number

Table 12.1 University Attendance in Europe, 1910–1995
(Number of students as percentage of all 20–24-year-olds)

Country	1910	1950	1960	1970	1980	1990	1995
Albania			5	8	8	10	10
Belgium	1	3	9	18	26	40	54
Bulgaria	1	5	11	15	16	31	39
Federal Republic of Germany	1	4	6	14	26	34	44
Denmark	(1)	6	9	18	28	37	45
GDR		2	10	14	23	22	—
Finland	1	4	7	13	32	49	70
France	1	4	7	16	25	40	51
Greece	0	3	4	13	17	25	43
Great Britain	1	3	9	14	19	30	50
Ireland		4	9	14	18	29	39
Italy	1	4	7	17	27	31	41
Yugoslavia		4	9	16	28	16	18
Netherlands	1	8	13	20	29	40	49
Norway	1	3	7	16	26	42	59
Austria	4	5	8	12	22	35	47
Poland		6	9	11	18	22	25
Portugal	0	2	3	8	11	23	37
Romania	1	3	5	10	12	10	23
Sweden	1	4	9	21	31	32	46
Switzerland	2	4	6	8	18	26	33
Spain	1	2	4	9	23	37	49
Czechoslovakia		4	10	10	18	16	22
Hungary	2	3	7	10	14	14	24
Europe	1	4	8	14	22	30	42
Variation coefficient Europe	65	34	31	26	27	33	30
Western Europe	1	4	7	15	22	34	48
Variation coefficient Western Europe	66	36	33	27	26	21	20
USSR/Russia			11	25	52	52	43
Turkey			3	6	5	13	18
US	3	17	21	31	56	75	81
Japan			9	17	31	30	—

Source: 1910–1970: H. Kaelble, *Soziale Mobilität und Chancengleichheit im 19. und 20. Jahrhundert. Deutschland im internationalen Vergleich* (Göttingen 1983), p. 200; 1980–1990: UNESCO, *Statistical Yearbook 1995* (Paris 1995), p. 3 ff.; UNESCO, *Statistical Yearbook 1998* (Paris 1999), p. 3 ff.; GDR 1980 and 1988 (not 1990): *Statistisches Jahrbuch der DDR 1981,* p. 343, 1990, p. 58 (Universities and Trade Schools). Very small European countries were not recorded. USSR successor states and Yugoslavia's successor states were not listed, as no time series are available for them before 1995. They are however included in the European average and variation coefficient for 1995.

would have been unimaginably high for mid-century Europeans. Despite this rapid growth of university students, Europe continued to increasingly lag more clearly behind the US, whose educational system is difficult to compare. Other industrial societies, however, like Japan, had similar student numbers (cf. Table 12.1; UNESCO 1999: II-246ff.).

The first of several reasons for the development of universities was simply the growing demand from young adults, which increased primarily due to the economic boom of the 1950s and 1960s, as studies could be more easily financed through parents' growing income and governmental scholarships. Thus the student rate grew particularly rapidly, quadrupling throughout Europe. But even after the economic boom, incomes remained high enough that young adults could finance a university education in far greater numbers than in 1950. This trend was supported by the growing demand for a highly qualified workforce. The increasing need for academics in commerce, in public administration, which was growing quickly everywhere, in the sciences, and in the educational sector likewise stimulated university development. This trend lingered despite the cyclical crises within the individual academic labor markets.

And finally, the Europeanwide transnational public debate about the university system was an additional important stimulus for the expansion of higher education. The discussion was dominated by Sputnik shock and fear of Western decline in comparison with the rapidly climbing number of academics in communist Europe; the challenge of the economically and culturally more successful US, with its consistently higher student numbers; and the debate about equality of opportunity, which could only be implemented by opening up the universities and creating more slots for students. European governments' higher education policies also played a role in the increase in the number of university students, primarily through the temporarily better financing of the educational sector and the founding of new universities. We will return to this topic later.

Following these developments Europeans' lives changed radically. Unlike in the past, the majority of young Europeans remained in school at least until they were sixteen. Furthermore, almost half pursued at least some higher education and first left school as adults. By the end of the century, the period of education in the eastern part of Europe on average lasted 11–12 years—in Western Europe even 15–16 years, i.e., approximately twice as long as in 1950. Educational qualifications changed through a quiet and little-discussed, yet almost revolutionary and far-reaching development: in 1950 Europe was still a society of primary school graduates with a select academic class and widespread illiteracy in the south and east. By 2000, in contrast, Europe had become a society of university and trade school graduates, who among younger generations were as common as industrial workers had been a half-century earlier.

Change in Educational Opportunities

Access to the educational sector changed drastically in the second half of the twentieth century. It opened to groups that had still come up against considerable barriers in 1950, a few of which are discussed below.

Women

Women, as a group, were the most numerous beneficiaries of the expanded educational system. In 1950 women in Europe suffered considerable disadvantages compared to men regarding opportunities for access to secondary schools and universities. The demand for better access had long been debated among the European public. Legal barriers to women pursuing higher education had been abolished in most European countries before the First World War. Yet realizing equal rights to education in light of the entirely different norms and values held by parents, teachers, professors, and future employers on the job market, and in part also by the young women themselves, took more than half a century. In 1950 some progress had been made—on average close to one-fourth of students at European universities were women. Yet young European women were still far from equal opportunity in comparison to men.

By the end of the twentieth century, however, general equality in access to education had been largely implemented for women. As many young women as men attended secondary schools throughout almost all of Europe in the 1970s. This basic equality in access had been attained at the university level by the 1990s. Only in a few countries, such as the Czech Republic, Germany, the Netherlands, Switzerland, Austria, and Greece, was the percentage of women among students still lower than the percentage of men. Generally speaking, the opposite was true: the percentage of women was considerably higher than the percentage of men in both the eastern and western parts of Europe. On European average, 52 percent of all students were women (see Table 12.2). Despite this, women advanced only very slowly in certain technical and scientific subjects. And tellingly, equality in education access did not have a commensurate impact on equal access to academic careers (see Chapter 2 on labor).

This extensive opening of universities to women was a response to women's altered life plans, the job market, and education policy. Women's life plans had changed fundamentally—employment was no longer seen as a temporary phase before marriage or before having children or perhaps as a possible second life phase after raising the children, but instead as a lifelong pursuit. Academic careers, which generally required a longer period of life than did women's careers theretofore, and which usually did not fit with the traditional life plans among women, also opened up.

Table 12.2 Percentage of Women among European University Students, 1950–1995

Country	1950	1960	1970	1980	1990	1995
Albania	33	18	33	50	52	53
Belgium	16[a]	26	36	44	48	50
Denmark	24	35	36	49	52	54
Bulgaria	33	—	51	56	51	61
Federal Republic of Germany	16	23	27	41	41	45
GDR	23[b]	32	43	58	52[d]	—
Finland	37	46	48	48	52	53
France	34[a]	41[a]	45[a]	50[c]	53	55
Greece	24	26	32	41	49	48
Great Britain	22[a]	23	33	46[c]	48	50
Ireland	30	28	34	41	46	51
Italy	26[a]	27	38	43	50	53
Yugoslavia	33	29	39	45	52	53
Netherlands	21	26	28	40	44	47
Norway	16[a]	34	30	48	53	55
Austria	21[a]	23	29	42	46	48
Poland	36	41	47	56	56	57
Portugal	26[a]	30	46	48	56	57
Romania	33	33	43	43	47	53
Sweden	23[a]	36	42	52[c]	54	56
Switzerland	13[a]	17[a]	24	30	35	
Spain	14	24	27	44	51	53
Czech Republic	—	34	36	40	44	47
Hungary	24	33	43	50	50	52
Europe[e]	25	30	38	42	49	52
Variation coefficient Europe	29	24	19	17	14	7
Western Europe[e]	22	29	34	41	49	52
Variation coefficient Western Europe	31	26	21	15	11	7
Eastern Europe	34	33	42	50	50	54
USSR/Russia	53	43	49	—	54	56
Turkey	20	20	19	25	34	—
USA	30	37	41	51	54	56
Japan	11[a]	19[a]	28	33	40	44

a = Definition "University" identical with tertiary education
b = 1951
c = 1985–86
d = 1988
e = unweighted average

Source: H. Kaelble, *Social Mobility in the 19th and 20th Centuries: Europe and America in Comparative Perspective* (Leamington Spa 1985), 86f.; UNESCO, *Statistical Yearbook 1963* (Paris 1963), 219ff.; UNESCO, *Statistical Yearbook 1977* (Paris 1978), 324ff.; UNESCO, *Statistical Yearbook 1985* (Paris 1985): III-266ff. Also UNESCO, *Statistical Yearbook* (Paris 1993), 342ff.; (Paris 1994), 357ff.; (Paris 1999): II-213ff. Very small European countries were not recorded. The successor states of the USSR and the successor states of Yugoslavia were not listed, as no time series are available for them before 1995. The category "Eastern Europe" was retained in 1995 only for the purposes of comparison, even though the Cold War term has become devoid of meaning.

Furthermore, the demand for an academic workforce increased so sharply that men alone could no longer satisfy the need. Finally, the public debate about education for women, which was led by intellectuals, experts, journalists, the women's movement, and politicians, influenced educational policy as well as educational decisions by parents and young women.

Lower Classes

A second, and significantly limited, opening up of universities extended access to laborers, lower-level salaried employees, and small-scale farmers. This process is far less documented Europe-wide than the access to universities for young women. The numbers that are available are often difficult to compare internationally; thus general trends are only roughly apparent. In 1950, very few members of the lower social classes reached university. There had been a distinct opening of the universities since the nineteenth century, but it was primarily the middle class that profited from it. Estimates indicate that not more than a couple per thousand laborers' children—1 percent at the highest—became university students. But opportunities for children from underprivileged backgrounds gradually increased beginning in the 1950s. A general conjecture is that an average of approximately 2–3 percent of working-class children were able to become university students in the 1970s. At the end of the twentieth century the rough estimate was approximately 10 to 13 percent (estimated by Euro student report, quoted in Schnitzer 2003; Table 12.1).

Several factors contributed to this opening for the lower classes. The demand for a university education rose in the lower-class milieus during the economic boom, as working-class families were more able to afford considering study programs for their children. In many traditional working-class professions in mining, steel, and textiles, for example, the future of work carried out by the fathers became increasingly dim. Sons looked for a different, better-paid career. The strong bond to milieu and the rejection of nonproletarian choices in career diminished with the decline of the traditional working-class milieu. At the same time, the number of secondary schools and universities increased, and they were often geographically closer to working- and lower-class neighborhoods. The public debates about education and educational policies regarding access to universities for the lower classes certainly also contributed.

Immigrants

The growth of educational opportunities for immigrants is worse documented than other developments and is thus difficult to trace. University statistics did not separate the children of immigrants, who held a foreign passport, from foreign students, who came to the respective country only for their studies. Conversely, the children of immigrants, who held domestic passports, were generally not counted separately in university statistics. There are few analyses of educational opportunities for immigrant children, and most of these only examine a point in time and draw no comparative conclusions on change. There is no doubt that at the beginning of the twenty-first century, the educational opportunities for immigrant children are still worse than for average children among the local population. But inequality with regard to educational opportunity does seem somewhat reduced, even if this development to date is only fragmentary. It can be assumed that the illiteracy rate among second-generation immigrants has fallen because the countries of immigration had compulsory education.

Secondary school attendance for immigrant children also increased. According to the Amsterdam Institute for Migration and Ethnic Studies, for example, upper secondary-school attendance by children of Turkish immigrants, the largest immigrant group, grew in the Netherlands from 7 percent in 1991 to 15 percent in 1998, and university attendance increased from 1 percent in 1991 to 4 percent in 1998 (one-fifth of the percentage of Dutch students attending university). In West Germany the percentage of immigrant children without a school-leaving qualification fell from 31 percent to 17 percent between 1983 and 2003. The percentage of secondary school graduates (*Realschule*) rose from 19 to 32 percent, and the percentage of high school graduates with university entrance qualifications rose from 4 percent to 9 percent, close to a fourth of the percentage of non-immigrants (Geißler 2006: 244f.). The decisive factor in these somewhat better educational opportunities for immigrant children was likely not only school and university policies implemented by European governments, but also the changes to the immigrant milieus, parts of which have climbed to the secure, or even wealthy, middle and upper classes.

Considerable differences emerged between the European countries. One of the few comparative studies on the largest Mediterranean immigrant group, Turks, shows that their educational opportunities and access to university were twice as high in France as in Germany for a number of reasons: school in France began at an earlier age, the choice between general secondary school or university-track secondary school was made later, and the individual support at school was far better. It should be added, however, that the dropout rates were higher. The educational system in German-speaking countries, in contrast, offered better opportunities for vocational training, easier access to the job market, and less unemployment (Crul and Vermeulen 2003).

Changes to Educational Policy

The educational policy of European governments, which both stimulated and often slowed educational development and access, likewise changed significantly in the second half of the twentieth century. During the postwar period and the 1950s all signs pointed toward modernization. Far-reaching reforms were carried out in the West as well as in the communist parts of Europe. Western Europe, Great Britain and Sweden implemented reforms in particular. Great Britain's Education Act, which brought about a fundamental reform of the school system, was passed in 1944. The sharp divide between primary schools and the schooling tracks that led to secondary school was overridden, and a new school system was created. This new system consisted of obligatory and free elementary schools for everyone between the ages of 5 and 11, and thereafter likewise obligatory, but subdivided, secondary school for the ages between 11 and 15 or 16, and finally a non-compulsory education from age 16 on. Comprehensive schools—common classes for all students during the first nine school years—were introduced in Sweden in 1950, initially for a trial period of ten years. The other Scandinavian countries followed, starting in the 1950s.

There was intense discussion of the recommendations by the Langevin-Wallon Commission in France. The debate primarily revolved around the elimination of the line sharply dividing the secular, republican primary schools and the secondary schools, but also around schools' adopting a stronger focus on careers. Reforms were not carried out until the 1960s, however. Similar debates attended the reforms carried out in the German western zones, which were instigated by the US occupying power's recommendation to implement a system like that in the United States and to tear down the wall dividing elementary and secondary school. Schools were actually reformed in only a minority of the federal states during this time. The schools were also radically changed in Eastern Europe, mostly becoming state institutions. All students attended common classes in the first seven to ten school years, followed by either higher education or state vocational school. Lessons in Marxism and Leninism were obligatory, as were Russian language classes. Considerable differences originated during this period not only between Eastern and Western Europe but also within the West between reform countries and those that did not carry out reforms.

A second era of educational policy began in most countries in the 1960s and 1970s, though in some countries they had already started by the 1950s. This period was primarily governed by the euphoria of educational growth and the goal of equal opportunity. Cost-intensive reforms were carried out during the period of the economic boom from the 1950s to the early 1970s: an extension of school days, the previously mentioned massive expansion of secondary schools and universities, the construction of numerous new schools and universities, the establishment of full-day schools in large parts of Europe, and the expansion of the number of teachers in schools and universities. In 1970 the average Western European government's expenditure for education was 4.5 percent of the gross national product and growing. There were intense discussions about the rise in opportunities at secondary schools and universities. Appeals by Myrdal in Sweden, Bourdieu and Passeron in France, and Picht in Germany were read often. The paths between school branches were widened through a variety of instruments. Graduation from upper secondary school became more accessible, and new scholarship programs tried to open schools to rural and working-class areas. At the same time fierce conflicts raged over this modernization, but also over participation at the universities. In many countries the universities were completely reorganized.

During the late 1970s and 1980s, education moved more to the political sidelines. Educational policy entered a period of crisis similar to that of the social welfare state, exhausted by the reduced economic growth, inflation, and the public financial crisis, but also due to the growing unemployment in the academic job markets. The primary goals of educational policy became the financial control and efficiency monitoring of the educational sector. Stopping, or at least curbing, educational expansion was the hidden or blatant goal of a number of governments in Western as well as Eastern Europe. State spending on education initially continued to grow but later stagnated or even decreased proportionately: in 1980 educational expenditures were still at 5.3 percent of the gross national product, but by 1990 they were 5.0 percent.

Three new developments became discernible as of the 1990s. First, education increasingly moved to the center of public interest. It was recognized more as an economic factor by the public and in politics and met new interest because of this. Educational quality and the cost-efficient organization of universities following the model of corporate enterprises were now the important topics within public debate and much less, by contrast, the topic of equal opportunity. The educational sector grew particularly fast in a few Eastern European countries, as a backlog of educational needs surfaced after the collapse of the Soviet Union. And lastly, educational investments now noticeably increased again, from 5 percent in 1990 to 6 percent in 1995 in Western Europe. Educational investments in Eastern Europe were just barely lower in 1995 at 5.5 percent—which, however, is a far lower contribution in absolute terms, as the gross national product was much less. A few wealthy countries in Western Europe including Germany, Luxembourg, and Belgium admittedly veered away from this pattern, spending less than 5 percent of their gross national product on education. Russia likewise remained far below the European average in 1995 at 3.5 percent. And at 2.2 percent, Turkey was even farther below the European level of investments in education (UNESCO 1999).

Divergences and Convergences

The extent of differences in educational systems within Europe in the second half of the twentieth century is controversial.

Steadfast Differences

It is claimed on the one hand that the basic principles of national educational policies were not in alignment. Each European country responded differently to similar financial and political demands on its educational system because each country was building upon special educational traditions and operated and made decisions within a specific political culture. The French system of "grandes écoles" with its "concours," preparatory schools, the privileged access its graduates had to the job market, and the lifelong networks between those graduates was just as unique as the English private school system, the "public schools," and the strict hierarchies among the British universities with Oxford, Cambridge, and the London School of Economics at the top. These were again quite different from the German "mass" universities, or "degree factories," with their changing hierarchies among a field's university departments. Three differences in the educational sector stood out in particular.

First was the divergent development between communist Eastern Europe and Western Europe. During the postwar period and in the 1950s, most communist governments increased the number of places available in universities relatively quickly in order to simultaneously meet a large backlog of demand for politically acceptable, highly qualified students and implement equal opportunity at the universities. The number of university students grew faster than the Western European average. The number of students in a majority of communist countries was thus higher than the European average in 1960 (cf. Table 12.1). In contrast, the number of students in Western European countries seldom increased so quickly, as secondary school and study programs were too expensive for many households during the postwar period and most governments had neither the political will nor the financial resources to speed up university expansion.

At the same time, directly after the communist takeover in the eastern part of Europe, educational opportunities for working-class children were heavily promoted, although often at the expense of children from other social milieus. According to the statistics from these countries, which often have not yet been verified, one-fourth to one-third of the university students during the postwar period came from the working-class milieu. Educational opportunities for children from underprivileged backgrounds remained far behind this in Western Europe—to varying extents, however, as will be covered shortly. Less known, finally, is that the communist countries also opened universities to women to a far greater extent than Western European countries during this time. Close to one-third of university students in Eastern Europe were female, in comparison to one-fifth of students in Western Europe (cf. Table 12.2). At the time, communism seemed to mean more university places and better educational opportunities for the lower classes and women.

This changed after the 1960s. Student numbers began to grow faster in most Western European countries for the previously discussed economic and political reasons. In most communist countries, in contrast, university expansion was curbed, especially in Czechoslovakia, Hungary, Romania, and the GDR. In 1989–90 just barely every fifth young adult in the European communist countries outside of the USSR attended university. This rift between East and West became particularly wide during the 1980s and does not seem to have closed immediately after the political upheaval of 1989–90 (cf. Table 12.1). As a result, educational opportunities for underprivileged children in Western Europe also substantially increased with the rapid expansion of university education in the 1980s and 1990s. The proportion of lower-class students was reversed between the western and eastern sections of Europe.

Educational opportunities for women also reversed for the same reason. The percentage of young women studying at universities was far higher in Western Europe, and the share of women among university students evened out (cf. Table 12.2), particularly because the number of university places expanded far more drastically (cf. Table 12.1). The university sector in communist Europe, for the most part narrowly constrained, allowed a dangerous gap in human resources to emerge and also reinforced the population's impression of paralyzed and limited opportunities.

A second difference concerned the prosperity that underpinned the rise in available slots for university students in Western and Eastern Europe alike. In less wealthy countries on the European periphery like Portugal, Greece, and Romania, the percentage of students among their age cohort remained far behind the European average. Educational opportunities in these countries were the lowest in all of Europe, though still higher than in Turkey. Meanwhile, in particularly wealthy European countries such as Norway, Denmark, Finland, and France, the percentage of students climbed particularly fast. The highest percentage of students among young adults was in these countries (see Table 12.1).

Yet the contrasts in political systems and economic prosperity fail to explain all the differences, especially those within Western Europe. The customs and traditions in the individual European countries played a big role. This is the only way to understand how in 1990 a wealthy country in the West like Switzerland could have a far lower rate of university students than a clearly poorer country such as Spain.

Educational opportunities for the lower classes were implemented in Western Europe in completely different phases. Great Britain and Scandinavia had already opened to underprivileged students during the interwar period. Approximately one-fourth to one-fifth of students in these countries in 1970 came from working-class environments. A second, later phase took place during the 1950s and 1960s in a series of continental countries like Italy, Belgium, and Denmark, where the percentages of underprivileged children increased to almost the same level as in Great Britain and Scandinavia by the 1970s. Around the same time, a more modest phase in France, West Germany, Austria, Switzerland, and the Netherlands increased the share of working-class students, which nonetheless remained significantly lower than in other European countries and until the 1970s amounted to no more than 10 to 15 percent. Even in 2005 Germany still brought up the rear with regard to educational opportunity for the working class.

The opening up of the universities should not be overstated, even among the European pioneering countries. If the perspective is changed to examine how many children from the working class attended university, as opposed to how many students came from working-class backgrounds, these changes look considerably more humble. As a rule in 1970 no more than 2 to 3 percent of all working-class children studied at colleges—only in Sweden was this percentage somewhat higher (Kaelble 1985: 80f.).

Finally, educational opportunities for women also developed to quite different extents. Western Europe in the 1990s was very clearly divided into a Western Europe with favorable educational opportunities for women—to which the North, France, Belgium, and the Iberian Peninsula belonged—and a Western Europe with limited educational opportunity for women, including Germany, the Netherlands, Switzerland, Austria, Italy, and Greece. In 2005 Germany was at the bottom of the league in this regard as well (HIS 2005: 26, 62).

These significant differences, or even new divergences, occurred because important factors for a massive convergence among European education were missing in the second half of the twentieth century. There was neither a uniform European educational market nor a common European educational policy that could have enforced a convergence of European educational programs. Both a European and an international educational public sphere exerted pressure on the national governments, but in the second half of the twentieth century they were never influential enough to noticeably reduce the many national characteristics (cf. Teichler 1990; McLean 1998).

Converging Educational Patterns

On the other hand, trends toward the reduction of inner-European contrasts could be observed. Differences between the individual European countries in the extent of school and university attendance decreased in the second half of the twentieth century. The elimination of illiteracy in Southern and Eastern Europe, and with it a reduction in deep disparity, was an early development blunting intra-European national differences. Furthermore, the intra-European divergences in school and university attendance subsided at all levels. The decline in differences was unmistakable throughout Europe, albeit interrupted by a limited renewed intensification primarily during the 1980s and during the upheaval of 1989–91 (cf. also the Correlation Coefficient in Table 12.1). Even the educational opportunities for women evened out over the course of the second half of the twentieth century, which was the case throughout Europe in general as well as in Western Europe (cf. Table 12.2). Unquestionably, there persisted indications of "national particularities surviving" (Teichler 2000) in 2000. But differences did decrease in general.

Transfers

Over the course of the second half of the twentieth century, transfers between European countries increased to an unprecedented degree. Student and teacher exchanges between European countries intensified significantly. In 1980 close to 120,000 European foreign students were studying at European universities, and by 1995 the number was close to 350,000. If Russia is included, there were actually already 375,000 European foreign students (calculated according to UNESCO 1985: III-440; UNESCO 1999: II-486ff.). In addition to Great Britain, France, Germany, Spain, and Italy, particularly important international places of study included smaller countries as well, like Belgium, Switzerland, and Austria.

Several reasons can be named for this. The boost in student exchange reflected the political lessons that European politics drew from the catastrophe of the Second World War, and the European Commission concluded that student exchanges were of fundamental importance to European integration and the emergence of a European identity. Extensive scholarship systems were established for stays abroad, of which the Erasmus/Socrates program is the largest and most successful to date. Student exchanges certainly also increased because students wanted to improve their foreign language ability and collect bonus points for their careers. And growing European prosperity made stays abroad financially possible in the first place.

Intra-European educational transfers were not just limited to the migration of people, but rather also applied to educational concepts. The comparison of educational systems increasingly served to inform educators and students about alternatives and the possibility of incorporating other educational concepts into one's own educational program.

European Debates

Similar debates about education—tightly entwined with one another—arose in most European countries despite the unmistakable differences and peculiarities among the national educational reforms. International expert networks were reinforced; international organizations like the OECD, UNESCO, and later the EU took a hand in these international debates and nudged them along. As previously mentioned, these common European and Atlantic debates about education policy in the 1950s and 1960s revolved around the shock of the West lagging behind and around the introduction of the natural sciences in class. The close connection between education and economic growth was discussed, and the necessity of a rapid educational expansion and stronger educational planning was recognized. In the 1960s and 1970s, the inequality of educational opportunities, particularly the disadvantage suffered by women and the lower classes, was at the center of the debate. In the 1980s topics included the quality of education, teaching, and teachers' role in the integration of immigrants, the handicapped, and the socially excluded. Since the 1990s, the focus has been lifelong learning, difficult job markets, the public or private financing of education, and the rediscovery of education and research as a factor in economic growth. Each country had its own educational topics in addition, but a substantial part of the European rapprochements consisted of these common themes within the educational policy debates.

The European Union

The European Union played a limited but important role in the harmonization of trends between European educational systems. The Erasmus/Socrates program started in the EU in the 1980s, though still poorly funded, remains the largest foreign studies program in the EU to date. The European Union also established a financially comprehensive program with various subprograms for European research funding, which strengthened European contacts between researchers and thereby led to many transfers of knowledge. At the beginning of the twenty-first century this program has a budget of 17 billion euros; as such it is larger than many national funding programs and will mostly likely grow faster than they do as well. Furthermore, with individual proposals such as a common European evaluation of doctoral theses at universities, reciprocal recognition, and most recently the standardization of university degrees (BA and MA), the EU facilitated studying in European countries outside of one's own. And finally, through its general promotion of intra-EU mobility regarding practical issues like bank transfers or insurance in EU countries, it made staying abroad in other member states considerably easier for European students and teachers.

Similar Reasons

It was crucial to European rapprochement that educational development in Europe was influenced by similar factors: the rise in private demand for education due to the increase in income and changed attitudes regarding education, particularly on the part of women; the rise in demand for qualified individuals in the changing industrial and service sectors; lifelong education; the common educational policy debates; and the new appreciation for foreign study among Europeans.

To be sure, these similarities did not amount to a homogeneous educational market, similar educational policy, and identical investments in education by young adults and parents in Europe. Nor would this necessarily have been desirable, as European diversity often allows more innovation than a fully standardized Europe.

European Hallmarks

Despite clear convergences in education in Europe, fewer European particularities are discernible in comparison with non-European societies than is the case within other social history topics.

Three European particularities should not be overlooked, however. Education was more strongly organized by the state than in the US or in Japan—which had major repercussions. Educational development was particularly subject to cycles within state budgetary resources. It was able to steadily expand during the economic boom, but suffered greatly in the 1970s and 1980s due to economic difficulties and neoliberal budget restrictions. At the same time, the European "mass" university, with its impersonal education and deteriorating quality, was also a consequence of Europe's systematically underfinanced public universities.

A second European peculiarity was the inconsistent Europeanization of education. On the one hand, students in Europe increasingly Europeanized during the second half of the twentieth century. The number of foreign European students rose significantly during this time. In the 1990s close to a third of a million young Europeans studied at universities in a European country not their own. Yet there was practically no European job market for professors. In most European countries professors were recruited almost solely within their own country or language area. The academic job market was far less internationalized than in the US. Educational programs thus Europeanized very little.

The third characteristic was that Europe gained increasing importance as the world's second-largest educator, after the US. In 1980 close to 260,000 and in 1995 close to 410,000 non-European foreign students studied at European universities (outside of Russia). In the US in 1980 there were 312,000 students and in 1995 close to 450,000 non-American students studying at American universities. In Japan there were close to 6,500 non-Japanese students in 1980 and about 54,000 by 1995 (UNESCO 1993: 333f.; UNESCO 1999: II- 486–488). The gap between Europe and the US was clearly closing. Upon return to their homelands these students brought not only knowledge with them, but as a rule also European ideas and lifestyles. This was only one element of Europe's role as a cultural hub at the end of the twentieth century. Europe was furthermore the world's largest exporter of books and magazines and most important center for language translation. And as a tourist destination Europe was unparalleled, being by far the largest global cultural tourism magnet in the world.

References

Berg, C. et al., ed. *Handbuch der deutschen Bildungsgeschichte*, vol. 6, Section 1: "Bundesrepublik Deutschland"; Section 2: "DDR und neue Bundesländer." Göttingen 1998.

Crul M. and H. Vermeulen. "The Second Generation in Europe." *International Migration Review* 37 (2003): 965–968.

Flora P. *State, Economy and Society in Western Europe, 1815–1970.* 2 vols. Frankfurt a. M. 1983ff.

Geißler R. *Die Sozialstruktur Deutschlands.* Wiesbaden 2006.

HIS. *Eurostudent 2005: Social and Economic Conditions of Student Life in Europe.* Hanover 2005.

INSEE. *Données sociales 1987.* Paris 1987.

Kaelble H. *Social Mobility in the 19th and 20th Centuries: Europe and America in Comparative Perspective.* Leamington Spa 1985.

McLean M. *Educational Transitions Compared.* London 1995.

McLean M. "Education." In *Western Europe, Economic and Social Change Since 1945,* ed. M. S. Schulze. Harlow 1998, 191–211.

Müller W. "Bildungsexpansion und Bildungsungleichheit." In *Einstellungen und Lebensbedingungen in Europa,* ed. W. Glatzer. Frankfurt a. M. 1993, 225–268.

Müller W. "Wandel in der Bildungslandschaft Europas." In *Deutschland im Wandel. Sozialstrukturelle Analysen,* ed. W. Glatzer et al. Opladen 1999, 337–356.

Müller W. and M. Wolbers. "Educational Attainment in the European Union: Recent Trends in Qualification Patterns." In *Transitions from Education to Work in Europe: The Integration of Youth into EU Labour Markets,* ed. W. Müller and M. Gangl. Oxford 2003, 23–62.

OECD. *Education 1960–1990: The OECD Perspective.* Paris 1994.

Prost A. *Education, société et politiques: une histoire de l'enseignement de 1945 à nos jours.* Paris 1997.

Prost A. *Histoire de l'enseignement et de l'éducation,* vol. 4: *Depuis 1930.* Paris 2004.

Rüegg W., ed. *Geschichte der Universität in Europa,* vol. 4: *Vom Zweiten Weltkrieg bis zum Ende des zwanzigsten Jahrhunderts.* Munich 2010.

Schnitzer K. *Die soziale Dimension im europäischen Hochschulraum. Der Euro Student Report als Monitorsystem.* HIS. Kurzinformation. Hanover 2003.

Statistisches Jahrbuch der Bundesrepulik 1978–1979.

Teichler U. *Europäische Hochschulsysteme: Die Beharrlichkeit vielfältiger Modelle.* Frankfurt a. M. 1990.

Windolf, P. *Die Expansion der Universitäten 1870–1985.* Stuttgart 1990.

UNESCO. *Statistical Yearbook 1963–1998.*

Chapter 13

SUMMARY

This book has addressed three primary concerns: the extent of change within European societies, the divergences and convergences between European societies, and hallmarks distinguishing Europe from non-European societies. What conclusions can be drawn from this passage through a half century of social history?

Social Change

All European societies experienced profound change after 1945, often in the form of several social changes occurring one after another. What in 1970 was viewed as modern and final may already have been outdated or obsolete in 2000. Yet the second half of the twentieth century was not, in sum, a period of rapid upheavals. There is no evidence of an enormous acceleration of social change or societal visions, as was often alleged in public debates. Indeed, the nineteenth century often changed more rapidly.

Postwar Period

The immediate postwar period was rife with contradictions that are difficult to comprehend today. On the one hand, the Second World War and the destruction it wrought loomed large over much of Europe. The supply of food, fuel, and housing often collapsed. Black-market crime emerged. Gangs formed. Parents' and youths' family roles changed. Social networks often dissolved. Jobs had been lost. Integrating soldiers, refugees, and evacuees was difficult. Compounding the already existing extremes between social milieus, new inequalities emerged between refugees and native populations; starving cities and farms; deportees, prisoner of war, and those who had remained at home. Life in the destroyed cities was laborious, numerous challenges impeded study in schools and universities, and the welfare state was overburdened. The last large exodus from an impoverished Europe took place, primarily to the Americas. All this transpired against the backdrop of colonial wars and the tensions of the Cold War that would soon lead to the social and cultural East-West division of Europe.

On the other hand, the course set in the postwar period would shape Europe for decades thereafter. New, unusual family forms came into being during this time that anticipated the 1970s and 1980s. The Americanization of European societies began. Trade unions gained power and churches became more attractive. Many newspapers, publishers, broadcasters, and other new media outlets were founded. Fundamental reforms of the social welfare state and educational system were carried out in some parts of Europe. Democracy began to advance throughout virtually all of Western Europe.

A Period of Economic Prosperity

During the 1950s and 1960s, Europe—i.e., primarily Western Europe—experienced the exact opposite of the postwar period: the heyday of the *wirtschaftswunder*, a unique economic period of growth, an extraordinarily advantageous job market, and an unparalleled increase in private income and state revenue. Europeans returned to the traditional family, but employment for mothers and education for girls increased at the same time. Career opportunities were exceptionally favorable during this last peak of European industrial society. Mass consumer society prevailed during this period, and with it the automobile and television. Values changed: there was more permissiveness in the family, more satisfaction at work, and more secularization. The class tensions between the middle class, lower middle class, and rural and working classes began to lose importance.

Labor migration to industrialized European countries soared as never before. The immigrants came mostly from the European periphery, and also from non-European countries. Europeans who fled from the colonies or from communist states were also generally able to earn a livelihood. Inequality in income and wealth clearly decreased. Opportunities for social promotion improved slightly. European trade unions experienced their heyday, and traditional city planning also had its golden period. The modern social welfare state was established. Educational expansion was significantly accelerated. The many years of economic prosperity fueled the expectation that it would continue into the future as well. It was later clear that this era was an exception, and that the mistakes made during this period—including inhumane urban development, a welfare state oriented toward traditional families and professional lives, and "mass" universities (degree factories), as well as the societal and cultural division of Europe into East and West that solidified during this period—would continue to have repercussions for quite some time.

The 1970s and 1980s: After the Prosperity

A new era began with the oil crisis and changed values of the late 1960s. It was a time of difficulty but also of new options. The economy grew more slowly. Dangerous inflation developed in the 1970s. Unemployment continued to grow in the 1980s until it was eventually higher than in Japan and the US. Eastern Europe struggled primarily with national debt, gaps in investment, supply shortages, and weak productivity.

A variety of family models that formed during this time supplemented the traditional model of the nuclear family headed by an employed husband and housewife. Individualization and secularization continued. From this time onward, professional life no longer proceeded so straightforwardly as previously; it was interrupted by unemployment as well as by continuing education and career changes. The service-oriented society took hold in Europe as well, at least in the western part, accompanied by crises in the textile, iron, and coal industries. Optimism for the future gave way to fears of ecocide, energy shortage, epidemics, and a new war in Europe. At the same time, individualization continued to intensify and social inequality increased again. A new poverty emerged, in particular among immigrants, single-parent families, and the unemployed. Trade unions fell into crisis; new social movements in Western Europe and dissident movements in Eastern Europe formed simultaneously. A new public critique of the welfare state viewed it as stifling economic initiative, too expensive, or too bureaucratic. City planning and education also came under fire, and trust in public institutions decreased.

After 1989–90

The upheaval of 1989–90 was not a turning point in all respects. Whereas societies in Eastern Europe were fundamentally transformed, which was itself perceived as an upheaval, the basic structures of family, work, consumption, social inequality, and state intervention changed little in Western Europe. Trust in public institutions increased somewhat throughout Europe, however. Secularization did not continue; rather, churches played a more important role in the private sphere and civil society. After the collapse of communism, the East-West immigration that had been prevented until then was reintroduced. Immigrants from outside Europe increasingly chose Southern and Eastern European countries as a new goal. Immigration became a general European experience, no longer limited to industrialized countries. Social inequality increased again. Job security and employment moved to the fore in increasingly livelier debates about social security and educational reforms. The European Union also changed: it was no longer limited to building up the economic market, but engaged more and more in social and cultural fields. As a result, the topic of European politics entered the European public sphere.

Divergences, Convergences, Integration

Divergences

The foremost divergence after the Second World War was the Cold War division of Europe. Contrasts in political systems, deeply embedded in European societies and cultures, resulted in deep cleavages between Eastern and Western Europe in family life, work, social milieus and social inequality, immigration, cities, education, and social security. Differences in the area of consumption and consumer policy even became a central cause of the collapse of socialist countries. These societal and cultural East-West differences did not simply disappear after 1989–90. Rather, new East-West differences formed during the transformational period of the 1990s as Eastern Europe's economic underdevelopment, a legacy of poor investments before 1989–90, now became visible for the first time. Dramatic deindustrialization—which had taken place much earlier, more slowly, and above all with a high level of social protection in the West—now proceeded in a brutal manner in Eastern Europe, with adverse social consequences. The reorganization of state social security caused significant upheaval, which could be observed in the stagnation, or even decline, in life expectancy. The new challenges provoked a transformation crisis for the family as well: the divorce rate fell, but birthrates did as well. The often claimed East-West differences in family values, work, and social coexistence cannot be proven, however.

A second, older social difference was the contrast between the wealthy, industrial, and dynamic center of Europe and the poorer, agricultural, and less developed European periphery, primarily in the South and East but also in the far West and North of Europe. This contrast had gradually developed during the industrialization of the nineteenth century and was still sharp in the 1950s and 1960s. Only in the core of Europe, in countries like Great Britain, Belgium, France, Germany, Switzerland, Austria, and Northern Italy, did a broad industrial sector and a modern rural economy give rise to a powerful middle class and a broad working class. In these regions, modern mass consumption, significant immigration from the European periphery, modern media and welfare states, spacious city planning, modern health care systems, the elimination of illiteracy, and an expanding educational sector came into being. These divergences also slowly decreased over the course of the second half of the twentieth century. Today formerly peripheral countries like Finland and Ireland, as well as Italy as a whole, no longer differ from the wealthy parts of Europe. Countries like Spain, Portugal, Greece, Slovenia, Estonia, and Latvia have caught up. It is only the Eastern and Southern European periphery—in particular Bulgaria, Romania, Ukraine, Moldova, and the Balkans—that are still far behind. How they will develop still remains to be seen.

A third divergence goes back to the Second World War, which struck European countries in very different ways. Enormous rifts were torn open during and directly after the Second World War between countries hit by the war, including Poland, the Soviet Union, the war instigator Germany, France, the Benelux states, Italy, and Great Britain, and those lands that had been spared the war, like Spain, Switzerland, and Sweden, to name just the most extreme cases. War-ravaged countries faced the challenges of coping with the war dead and wounded, the destruction caused by bombardment, and the collapse of public service and the economy. Furthermore, the European governments drew different conclusions from the war. In some countries like Great Britain or France, profound social, health, and educational reforms were enforced. Other countries, for example Germany and Italy, carried out few such reforms for some time to come. As distance from the European wars increased over the course of time, these differences decreased as well, however.

A fourth and often examined divergence took the form of differences between entire groups of countries. A solid geography of these differences did not emerge, though. The geographical boundaries varied for each social topic: family, the trade union and new social movements, consumption, labor, public social security.

Convergences and Interconnection

The diversity of differences between European regions and countries is indubitably of great importance up to the present. To this day, Europeans' perceptions of Europe have much to do with such social differences. Some intellectuals even go so far as to view this internal diversity as Europe's most unusual feature. Despite this, Europe's social history has also been significantly shaped by similarities.

To begin with, three of the four divergences discussed above had a limited lifespan. The differences that resulted from both world wars faded with time. The devastation of war was slowly eliminated in those countries that had been affected; the traumatic experiences of war slowly receded into the background. The reforms that were implemented during the postwar period did not remain limited to a few countries—other lands also undertook reforms. Furthermore, the past few decades have muted the divergences that had gradually set in since the nineteenth century between Europe's industrialized center and agricultural periphery. Finally, the deep differences between the East and West also decreased. As mentioned, new East-West divergences did indeed once again emerge due to the upheaval of 1989–90. But these deep social rifts between Western and Eastern Europe gradually diminished later.

Separate, long-term development paths also shaped Europe, however. In Great Britain, France, Spain, Poland, Scandinavia, Switzerland, and Germany, these individual and nationally different developments have been highlighted with particular frequency. But reliance on these separate development paths has also diminished over the last few decades, for a number of reasons.

A first reason was Europe's political merging. For the first time in almost all of Europe—including Spain, Portugal, and Greece since the 1970s and East Central Europe since 1989—the same political basic principles of democracy and human rights, a market economy, and furthermore a novel, lasting, secure peace prevailed. Democracy and peacekeeping led to an increased willingness to learn from other European countries, which was now a matter of exchange between political systems that in principle were identical. A well-meaning, nonthreatening competition for the best political solutions developed. This also explains how, even though institutions did not necessarily conform to each other in many areas of society, the results within society were indeed similar. Just one example: schools and universities remained different, yet the differences in educational qualifications and opportunities clearly decreased, from kindergarten through to universities.

Second, the European Union and its precursors pursued a policy of standardization that generally applied to goods, services, employment, and business up through the 1980s and, since the 1990s, has also included numerous areas of social and cultural policy. In doing so, the European Union followed two different philosophies: on the one hand, a functioning common European market should be ensured through the standardization; on the other, a philosophy of competition should enable differences to smooth themselves out. A number of these convergences were global processes that were particularly effective between Western European countries, and later between European countries in general.

Finally, social transfers were essential to the rapprochement of European states, for both the integration and exchanges between national societies and the experience of the "other." Goods, knowledge, and values were generally not simply imitated through these everyday transfers, but adopted and, in the process, altered. They nevertheless toned down national differences. There were certainly also new partitions during the second half of the twentieth century, in particular between Eastern and Western Europe before 1989. But overall an increase in interconnection prevailed. This interconnection developed through international marriages as well as through the exchange of family policy concepts, in the growth of jobs in international companies, and not least through mobility—in completely different careers and social classes, of managers and scientists or intellectuals, among the liberal professions as well as salaried employees, skilled workers as well as unskilled laborers, and even among retirees. The assimilation of the welfare state, health care, city planning, and educational concepts also intensified through exchange among experts, politicians, and clients. Education in other European countries, and with it the experience of other European countries for the young people who were still developing, likewise dramatically increased.

The growing international exchange of consumer goods was particularly formative for everyday life in society. Mass consumption on the whole was more Europeanized than it was shaped by the US or Asia, as the vast majority of consumer goods were imported from other European countries. Travel also counted among the internationalized consumer goods, which multiplied between European societies—though travel statistics for the most part do not differentiate between tourist and business travel. These trips were undertaken not only by Northern Europeans to the South of Europe, but also to an increasing degree by Southern Europeans to the North. Only a small minority of young Europeans in 1990 had not visited another country, i.e., another European country.

Finally, cultural interconnection also consolidated. In any case the crucial cultural prerequisite for this, knowledge of a foreign language, increased considerably. According to the Eurobarometer, only a minority of older Europeans possessed a solid understanding of a foreign language at the end of the twentieth century, while a large majority of European youth and young adults could make themselves understood in a foreign language. However, the degree of foreign language knowledge varied significantly from country to country.

European Hallmarks

Specific particularities among European societies in comparison to non-European countries are apparent. In addition to quite long-term European hallmarks, which cannot be examined here (cf. for these Eisenstadt 2003; Mitterauer 2003; Joas and Wiegandt 2005), intermediate-term peculiarities in the second half of the twentieth century are particularly easy to spot in several areas (cf. also Kaelble 2005; also introduction to this volume).

The first worth mentioning here is the family. In comparison to families in non-European countries, the European family was significantly isolated from the outside world. It was organized as an intimate unit, with independent households established by young married couples, an older age at the time of marriage for both spouses, and low birthrates. Three-generation households were rarer. A new diversity among family models could be observed as of the 1970s, however, accordingly blunting the differences between European and non-European families.

A second European hallmark was in the structure and organization of work. The workforce structure had already developed in a particular way in the nineteenth century: it was only in Europe that the industrial sector became the largest employment sector, thus making the number of those employed in industry particularly high. A special attitude toward work also formed subsequently in Europe after 1945. On the one hand, work and a career were valued as the center of life and as a realization of the individual personality. But on the other hand, an especially sharp divide between work and free time came about. After the 1950s, daily and weekly work hours in particular dropped more than in non-European societies, including the US and Japan. Shorter working hours and free evenings and weekends were viewed as the basic essentials of social progress. Yearly vacation time was longer than anywhere else, and the vacation culture was more pronounced. The span of working years was likewise shorter in Europe than outside of Europe, as Europeans often entered the workforce later and, given the highly developed social state, were also able to leave earlier. Unlike in North American and Asian industrialized countries, a substantial share of women did not enter the workforce at all in much of Europe. This special European arrangement of a higher work motivation and sharper divide from free time is not more than a half century old, however.

A third European peculiarity can be identified in the area of values and religion. Europeans developed a particular attitude toward religion and the church over centuries. Religion seems to have no longer been an important European particularity for quite some time, however, appearing instead to have been increasingly marginalized through secularization, even as intra-religious tensions decreased due to ecumenical Christian compromise. At the same time, the distinguishing feaures of Christian churches were not exclusively European, as they were also important for the Americas and for the Christian parts of Africa and South Asia. It certainly became clear over the last few decades of the twentieth century that secularization was not a worldwide process, but clearly a European and in part East Asian one. In any case, it was definitely not a North or Latin American, South Asian, or African characteristic. At the same time, the public was strongly aware of certain religious tensions, for example the conflicts between Catholic Croatians and Orthodox Serbs, and between Muslim minorities and Christian or secular majorities.

A fourth and initially surprising difference from non-European societies crops up in the way violence is dealt with. In recent history it has increasingly been regulated differently compared to lands outside of Europe: private violence, beatings as a means of discipline, and private possession of firearms have been prevented as much as possible and subordinated to the state monopoly on the use of force. As a result, criminality in cities has been kept lower than in most, if certainly not all, cities outside of Europe. Moreover, state use of violence toward its own citizens has been significantly reduced, in particular through the elimination of the death penalty. And finally, Europeans have become sharply skeptical of war. The negative experience of the devastating consequences of two world wars, which were far more cataclysmic in Europe than in the Americas, Africa, South or South East Asia, as well as the positive experience of success with stable peacekeeping through negotiation, agreements, reconciliation, and the mutual control of once-enemy nation-states, led to a particularly European opinion regarding the legitimacy of war.

The different social classes were a fifth European hallmark that, quite contrary to religion and violence, had disappeared from public discussion after having been a subject of public interest in the nineteenth and early twentieth centuries. No longer a focus of public attention but still important for recent history was the special European mix of social milieus that developed since the late eighteenth century. Five social classes in heightened tension with one another have particularly shaped European society. The aristocracy was grounded in its claim to primacy, its sharp division from other social classes, its norms, and its ties to monarchy as well as to churches within the Ancien Régime. The middle class, in contrast to the aristocracy, developed new values with regard to education, labor, family, civil society, and public duties. It likewise elevated its claim to political dominance and separated itself from lower classes, even if by other means. The European peasant class, which was completely focused on the family economy, was poorly educated for the most part, with handed-down knowledge. Peasants were closely interconnected with one another and consequently closed off from the outside, which fed a conflictual relationship with both the aristocracy and the middle class. The European petty bourgeoisie, or lower middle class, was primarily focused on the family economy, with its own set of values and individual class culture. And finally, the European working class, which often presented a counter-model to the middle-class way of life, built its own support networks for personal life crises, developed an individual class consciousness, and often also closed itself off from the outside and the higher social classes. Although these five contrasting milieus particularly shaped Europe during the late nineteenth and early twentieth centuries, their individual distinctions have been increasingly fading since the 1970s.

Sixth, Europe rapidly developed from an emigration into immigration continent. In no other region of the world has such a radical change played out in a mere ten to twenty years.

A seventh European characteristic developed primarily after the Second World War around the welfare state in the broadest sense of the term: not only did it secure social security with regard to personal crises and old age, but it also intervened in the development of cities and ensured living and educational standards. Whereas in other societies it was more often the family, individuals, local civil society, the market, or patrons and charitable organizations that provided assistance, the welfare state in Europe took on this role to a particularly large extent. Nowhere else did the government so comprehensively establish a public social security system, plan cities and housing, and control the educational system. Another aspect of this European particularity was admittedly also that it was continuously criticized, and other, market- or family-based forms of social security were called for. This European particularity, built on a century-old tradition of public intervention in Europe, had its heyday from the 1950s to 1970s. This European hallmark remains in both Eastern and Western Europe, despite frequent vociferous criticism. It was chiefly after the Second World War that the welfare state became the core component of the European system, serving at times as a model in Latin and North America as well as in East Asia, Japan, and Korea.

Finally, the orientation toward the transnational developed differently in Europe than in other societies in the world—whereby differences varied greatly depending on which society a comparison was drawn with. Transnationality held particular importance in polycentric Europe, where different centers of power competed. A lasting unified European empire never formed, although it was attempted several times. As a result, the experience of the "other" was far more intense than in empires like China. The incessant comparison, as well as the conflict and war with the other, was constitutive for Europe. Furthermore, the European civilization was particularly open to the outside, appropriating many basic ideas, concepts, lifestyles, people, and goods from other civilizations: from numerals to the setting of time; from the Jewish to the Muslim peoples; from the leading religion, Christianity, through to the important European symbol of Europa on the bull; from the horse to the potato. And lastly, Europe's decisive influence on world history—due to colonial and informal empires lasting nearly a century or more, as well as the extraordinary amount of emigration—counts among its transnational hallmarks. This particular relationship to transnationality may be receding in recent history, as Europe's influence on world history is plummeting even as a relatively stable common European decision-making center, the European Union, is forming. Yet this special European path influences both intra-European and non-European transnationality to this day.

These are by far not all of the European hallmarks—economic, cultural, and political values and institutions can be added. They often spread out far beyond Europe to become universalized, losing their character as European characteristics in the process. The values of the Enlightenment, human rights and democracy, European scholarship and art, and Christianity, as well as European economic, industrial, and business principles, count among these in particular.

References

Eisenstadt, S.N. *Comparative Civilizations and Multiple Modernities*. 2 vols. Leiden 2003.

Joas, H. and K. Wiegandt, eds. *Die kulturellen Werte Europas*. Frankfurt a. M. 2005.

Kaelble, H. "Boom und gesellschaftlicher Wandel, 1948–1973: Frankreich und die Bundesrepublik Deutschland im Vergleich." In *Der Boom 1948–1973: Gesellschaftliche und wirtschaftliche Folgen in der Bundesrepublik Deutschland und in Europa*, ed. H. Kaelble. Opladen 1991, 219–247.

Kaelble, H. *Europäer über Europa: Die Entstehung des modernen europäischen Selbstverständnisses im 19. und 20. Jahrhundert*. Frankfurt a. M. 2001.

Kaelble, H. *Wege zur Demokratie: Von der Französischen Revolution zur Europäischen Union*. Stuttgart and Munich 2001. (French and Spanish versions 2005.)

Kaelble, H. "Vers une histoire sociale et culturelle de l'Europe pendant les années de l'"après-prospérité'." *Vintième Siècle*, no. 84 (October–December 2004): 169–179.

Kaelble, H. "Eine europäische Gesellschaft?" In *Europawissenschaft*, ed. G.F. Schuppert, I. Pernice and U. Haltern. Baden Baden 2005, 299–330.

Mitterauer, M. *Warum Europa? Mittelalterliche Grundlagen eines Sonderwegs*. Munich 2003.

INDEX